HUMAN RIGHTS OBLIGATIONS
OF BUSINESS

In recent years, the UN Human Rights Council has approved the 'Respect, Protect and Remedy' Framework and endorsed the Guiding Principles on Business and Human Rights. These developments have been welcomed widely, but do they adequately address the challenges concerning the human rights obligations of business?

This multi-author volume engages critically with these important developments. The chapters revolve around four key issues: the process and methodology adopted; the source and justification of corporate human rights obligations; the nature and extent of such obligations; and the implementation and enforcement thereof. In addition to highlighting several shortcomings of the Framework and the Guiding Principles, the contributing authors also outline a vision for the twenty-first century in which companies have obligations to society that go beyond the responsibility to respect human rights.

SURYA DEVA is an associate professor at the School of Law, City University of Hong Kong. His primary research interests include business and human rights, constitutional law, globalisation and sustainable development.

DAVID BILCHITZ is a professor in the Faculty of Law at the University of Johannesburg. He is also Director of the South African Institute for Advanced Constitutional, Public, Human Rights and International Law (SAIFAC).

HUMAN RIGHTS OBLIGATIONS OF BUSINESS

Beyond the Corporate Responsibility to Respect?

Edited by

SURYA DEVA

and

DAVID BILCHITZ

CAMBRIDGE
UNIVERSITY PRESS

CAMBRIDGE
UNIVERSITY PRESS

University Printing House, Cambridge CB2 8BS, United Kingdom

Cambridge University Press is part of the University of Cambridge.

It furthers the University's mission by disseminating knowledge in the pursuit of education, learning and research at the highest international levels of excellence.

www.cambridge.org
Information on this title: www.cambridge.org/9781107596177

© Cambridge University Press 2013

First published 2013
First paperback edition 2015

A catalogue record for this publication is available from the British Library

ISBN 978-1-107-03687-1 Hardback
ISBN 978-1-107-59617-7 Paperback

Cambridge University Press has no responsibility for the persistence or accuracy of URLs for external or third-party internet websites referred to in this publication, and does not guarantee that any content on such websites is, or will remain, accurate or appropriate.

CONTENTS

v

CONTRIBUTORS

AIKATERINI ARGYROU is a researcher at Utrecht University and Nyenrode Business University in the Netherlands. She is involved in various research projects on CSR, including 'CSR in Indonesia', 'Company Leadership and Sustainability' and 'Social Entrepreneurship as a New Economic Structure that Supports Sustainable Development'. She holds an LLM in International Business Law and Globalisation from Utrecht University and a Bachelor's degree in Law from the University of Athens. She is a qualified corporate lawyer and member of the Athens Bar Association. She has practised corporate law, corporate/commercial transactions and mergers and acquisitions. Since 2011, she has been involved in various research projects on CSR at The Hague Institute for the Internationalisation of Law (HiiL) (research trainee), The Hague Utilities for Global Organisations programme (HUGO Initiative) and the Economic and Commercial Affairs Office of the Greek Embassy in The Hague.

DANIEL AUGENSTEIN is an assistant professor at Tilburg University in the Netherlands. Prior to joining Tilburg, he held appointments at the School of Law of the University of Edinburgh (UK) and at the Free University of Bolzano (Italy). 'Business and human rights' has been one of Daniel's core research interests for a number of years. His research in this area focuses on the relationship between global business operations and international human rights protection in the context of the UN 'Protect, Respect and Remedy' Framework, with particular reference to the European Union. Daniel has contributed business and human rights work to major international political and academic fora, including the European Parliament, the European Commission, the Council of Europe, the UN Treaty Bodies, national governments, national human rights institutions and various NGOs.

DAVID BILCHITZ is a professor in the Faculty of Law at the University of Johannesburg and Director of the South African Institute for Advanced Constitutional, Public, Human Rights and International

Law (SAIFAC). He is currently Secretary General (Acting) of the International Association of Constitutional Law. In 2012 he received a rating as an internationally acclaimed researcher by the National Research Foundation of South Africa. He has a BA (Hons) LLB *cum laude* from the University of Witwatersrand (South Africa) and an M. Phil. and Ph.D. from the University of Cambridge. His monograph *Poverty and Fundamental Rights* was published in 2007 and a co-edited volume on South African Constitutional Law in 2012. One of his specialities is the field of business and human rights, and he has related publications in the *South African Law Journal, SUR International Journal on Human Rights* and *Theoria*. He has also supervised reports in this field commissioned by the International Commission of Jurists and the SRSG's mandate. He has made submissions for reform in this area to the South African Parliament and the King Commission on Corporate Governance. He is also on the editorial advisory board of the NGO *Lawyers for Better Business* and sits on the editorial board of several journals.

KARIN BUHMANN is an associate professor at Roskilde University, Denmark. She holds a Ph.D. from the Department of Law at Aarhus University (Denmark) and degrees in law from the University of Copenhagen and the Raoul Wallenberg Institute of Human Rights and Humanitarian Law at Lund University, Sweden. Her current research interests are in the legal and regulatory aspects of Corporate Social Responsibility (CSR) and business responsibilities for human rights. Karin's research approaches these topics from the perspective of public regulation at international and national levels, and draws on theories of new forms of law, global administrative law, reflexive law and discourse analysis to conceptualise and analyse the emerging public regulation of CSR and its implications. Karin has published widely on these topics in international and Nordic journals and in international edited volumes. Karin is a member of the Danish National Contact Point under the OECD's Guidelines for Multinational Enterprises, appointed for the 2012–15 term by the Minister for Growth and Commerce upon recommendation by Danish civil society organisations. She is involved in several international research networks on international human rights law, business and human rights and CSR/business ethics.

SURYA DEVA is an associate professor at the School of Law of City University of Hong Kong. He has taught previously at the Faculty of Law,

University of Delhi and at the National Law Institute University, Bhopal, India. Surya's primary research interests lie in Corporate Social Responsibility (CSR), Indo-Chinese constitutional law, international human rights, globalisation and sustainable development. He has published numerous chapters in edited books and journal articles in these areas and also prepared two major reports on 'Access to Justice: Human Rights Abuses Involving Corporations' (concerning India and China) for the International Commission of Jurists (ICJ), Geneva. Surya's recent and forthcoming books include *Confronting Capital Punishment in Asia: Human Rights, Politics, Public Opinion and Practices* (co-edited with Roger Hood) (2013), and *Regulating Corporate Human Rights Violations: Humanizing Business* (2012). He is also the Faculty Editor of the *City University of Hong Kong Law Review*.

NICOLA JÄGERS is a professor of International Human Rights Law at the Law School of Tilburg University in the Netherlands. Over the past ten years Nicola has worked on the transformations that have occurred in international (human rights) law relating to changes in the relationships between states and markets and changes in the regulatory roles and capacities of NGOs and transnational business corporations. In 2002 Nicola published one of the earliest books on the issue of corporate responsibility for human rights violations: *Corporate Human Rights Obligations: In Search of Accountability*. Ever since, the consequences of the two dominant faces of globalisation – the expansion of trade beyond borders and the universalising effects of the human rights movement – have remained Nicola's core research interest resulting in participation in various research projects, and multiple publications on the issue. More recently, Nicola has begun to consider the ways in which regulatory approaches might be useful for the enforcement, socialisation and protection of human rights. In 2012 Nicola was appointed as a Commissioner at the National Human Rights Institute of the Netherlands. She is also a member of the Dutch government's Advisory Committee on International Law, a member of the Executive Board of the *Netherlands Quarterly of Human Rights* and a board member of the Dutch School of Human Rights Research.

DAVID KINLEY holds the Chair in Human Rights Law at the University of Sydney. He is also an Academic Panel member of Doughty Street Chambers in London, a member of the Australian Council for Human Rights, and was a founding member of Australian Lawyers for Human Rights. His particular expertise is in human rights and the global economy, focusing on the respective roles and responsibilities of corporations and states. His most recent publications include *Civilising Globalisation: Human Rights and the Global Economy* (2009), and he edited *Corporations and Human Rights* (2009) and *The WTO and Human Rights: Interdisciplinary Perspectives* (2009). Two other (jointly) edited collections will be published in 2013: *Principled Engagement: Promoting Human Rights in Pariah States*, and *Human Rights: Old Problems and New Possibilities*. He is currently working on two new books – one focusing on intersections between global finance and human rights entitled *An Awkward Intimacy: Why Human Rights and Finance must Learn to Love Each Other* – and a textbook on *The International Covenant on Economic, Social and Cultural Rights*.

TINEKE LAMBOOY is an associate professor at Utrecht University (School of Law) and Nyenrode Business University (Centre for Sustainability) in the Netherlands. Her research focuses on Corporate Social Responsibility (CSR) and corporate law, annual reporting, transparency of multinationals' policies and activities, due diligence and human rights, and remedies. At Nyenrode, she conducts multidisciplinary research projects aimed at enhancing sustainability standards for private actors. Her Ph.D. study 'Corporate Social Responsibility: Legal and Semi-legal Frameworks that Support CSR' (Leiden University, the Netherlands) was published in 2010. In 2011 she acted as an expert in a Dutch Parliament hearing about Shell's application of the Ruggie Framework in Nigeria. From 2010–12 she was an advisor to the Hague Utilities for Global Organisations programme (HUGO Initiative). Since 2007 Tineke has been a board member of the NGO 'Stand Up for Your Rights', which aims to promote the recognition of a right to a clean and healthy environment. Tineke is a member of a research team, awarded a competitive grant by the Norwegian Research Council, on 'Sustainable Companies: How to Make Companies Contribute Effectively to Mitigate Climate Change?' She is also Editor of the *International Company and Comparative Law Journal* and Special Editor for the annual CSR issue of *European Company Law*.

CARLOS LÓPEZ is Senior Legal Advisor at the International Commission of Jurists (ICJ). He joined the ICJ in January 2008 to lead the programme on International Economic Relations/Business and Human Rights. Carlos was on the staff of the Office of the High Commissioner for Human Rights for six years in various capacities and posts, which included work on the rule of law and democracy, economic and social rights and the right to development. Before that he worked for the ICJ (1998–99), the Graduate Institute of International Studies in Geneva (2000) and for several international human rights organisations as well as national human rights NGOs in his country, Peru. In 2009 he acted as lead legal advisor to the UN Fact-finding Mission into the Gaza Conflict (the 'Goldstone Report'). He holds a Ph.D. and Masters in public international law (Graduate Institute of International Studies, Geneva University) and a Diploma in sociology studies. He obtained his law degree at the Catholic University of Peru.

RICHARD MEERAN has been a partner at Leigh Day & Co., London since 1991. He has pioneered claims against UK multinationals, including Cape plc for 7,500 South African asbestos miners and Thor Chemicals for South African workers poisoned by mercury. He obtained two landmark jurisdiction victories in the House of Lords, *Connelly* v. *RTZ Corporation plc* [1997] 3 WLR 373 and *Lubbe* v. *Cape plc* [2000] 1 WLR 1545. He represented 31 Peruvian torture victims in a case against Monterrico Metals plc, which was settled (without admission of liability) in July 2011. The obtaining of a worldwide freezing injunction for the claimants broke new ground (*Tabra* v. *Monterrico Metals plc* [2009] EWHC 2475; [2010] EWHC 3228). He is currently acting for former South African gold miners with silicosis in proceedings against Anglo American South African Ltd in South Africa and England. He was the UK Liberty/Justice Human Rights Lawyer of the Year (2002).

BONITA MEYERSFELD is the Director of the Centre for Applied Legal Studies and an associate professor of law at the School of Law, University of Witwatersrand, Johannesburg (NRF Y1 rating). She is an editor of the *South African Journal on Human Rights* and the founding member and chair of the board of Lawyers against Abuse. Bonita teaches international law, business and human rights and international criminal law. Prior to working in South Africa, Bonita worked as a legal advisor in the House of Lords in the United Kingdom and was the gender consultant to the International Centre for Transitional Justice in New York. Bonita obtained her LLB from University of Witwatersrand Law School and her LLM and JSD from Yale Law School. She is the author of *Domestic Violence and International Law* (2010). Bonita has worked in the area of business and human rights for several years, focusing on gender, financial institutions, institutional investment and law reform. In 2011 she worked with several institutions, including private law firms and international organisations, to set up two round-table discussions on the role of financial institutions in the protection of human rights in Africa. Bonita is also a founding member of the informal Business, Human Rights and Gender Global Reference Group, which seeks to influence the UN's work on business and human rights in respect of gender.

SABINE MICHALOWSKI is a professor of law at the University of Essex, UK. Her research interests include business and human rights and the socio-economic dimensions of transitional justice. She is the author of *Unconstitutional Regimes and the Validity of Sovereign Debt: A Legal Perspective* (2007); 'No Complicity Liability for Funding Gross Human Rights Violations?' (2012) 30:2 *Berkeley Journal of International Law* 451; 'Jus cogens, Transitional Justice and Other Trends of the Debate on Odious Debts: A Response to the World Bank Discussion Paper on Odious Debts' (2010) 48:1 *Columbia Journal of Transnational Law* 61 (co-authored with Juan Pablo Bohoslavsky); and 'Sovereign Debt and Social Rights – Legal Reflections on a Difficult Relationship' (2008) 8 *Human Rights Law Review* 35. She has recently edited a book on *Corporate Accountability in the Context of Transitional Justice* (2013).

JUSTINE NOLAN is the Deputy Director of the Australian Human Rights Centre and a senior lecturer in law at the University of New South Wales, Australia. Her research is focused on human rights and corporate accountability. She has worked closely with a broad range of representatives from NGOs, government, companies and the United Nations in consulting on business and human rights issues. Prior to her appointment at UNSW in 2004, she was the Director of the Business and Human Rights Program at the Lawyers Committee for Human Rights (now Human Rights First) in the United States. Justine is a member of the Australian Department of Foreign Affairs and Trade Human Rights Grants Scheme Expert Panel and of New South Wales Legal Aid's Human Rights Panel. She is an editor of the *Human Rights Defender*. Her recent publications include *The International Law of Human Rights* (co-authored with A. McBeth and S. Rice) (2011).

ANITA RAMASASTRY is the UW Law Foundation Professor at the University of Washington School of Law in Seattle, where she directs the Sustainable International Development Graduate Program. Her research focuses on business and human rights, anti-corruption and the role of economic actors in weak governance zones. She teaches courses on commercial law, international law and law and development. From 2009–11 she served as a senior advisor with the International Trade Administration of the US Department of Commerce while on leave from the University of Washington. In 2008 she was a Fulbright Scholar at the Irish Centre for Human Rights at the National University of Ireland in Galway.

MARY VARNER received an LLM in International Business Law and Globalisation from Utrecht University, the Netherlands in August 2011. She also holds a Juris Doctor from Washington University in St Louis, USA with a focus on transnational law, and is an *alumna* of the Summer Institute for Global Justice. Her academic interests are focused on Corporate Social Responsibility (CSR) from a corporate perspective. In 2011–12 she worked on a project for the NGO 'Stand Up for Your Rights' on recognising the right to a clean and healthy environment for children.

FLORIAN WETTSTEIN is Professor and Chair of business ethics and Director of the Institute for Business Ethics at the University of St Gallen in Switzerland. His research focuses on business and human rights, corporate responsibility, the political role and responsibility of multinational corporations, and on business/economic ethics in general. He has published widely on topics at the intersection of business ethics and human rights and is the author of *Multinational Corporations and Global Justice: Human Rights Obligations of a Quasi-Governmental Institution* (2009). Previously, Florian taught in the Department of Ethics and Business Law at the University of St Thomas (Minneapolis/ St Paul, USA) and in the Business and Society Program at York University in Toronto, Canada. He is a past fellow of MIT's Program on Human Rights and Justice.

FOREWORD: BEYOND THE GUIDING PRINCIPLES

When, on 20 April 2005, the United Nations Commission on Human Rights adopted a resolution requesting that the UN Secretary-General appoint a Special Representative on the Issue of Human Rights and Transnational Corporations and Other Business Enterprises (SRSG),[1] the field was a deeply divided one. After a wide consultation of all relevant stakeholders including in particular the business community, the UN Sub-Commission for the Promotion and Protection of Human Rights – made up of independent experts appointed by the Commission on Human Rights to provide expert advice in support of its work – had approved in August 2003 a set of Norms on the Human Rights Responsibilities of Transnational Corporations and Other Business Enterprises (Norms).[2] The draft Norms presented themselves as a restatement of the human rights obligations imposed on companies under international law. They were based on the idea that 'even though States have the primary responsibility to promote, secure the fulfillment of, respect, ensure respect of and protect human rights, transnational corporations and other business enterprises, as organs of society, are also

---

[1] Commission on Human Rights, 'Human Rights and Transnational Corporations and Other Business Enterprises', Res. 2005/69 adopted on 20 April 2005 by a recorded vote of forty-nine votes to three, with one abstention (Ch. XVII, E/CN.4/2005/L.10/Add.17).

[2] Norms on the Human Rights Responsibilities of Transnational Corporations and Other Business Enterprises (Norms), UN doc. E/CN.4/Sub.2/2003/12/Rev.2 (2003). For the Commentary on the Norms, which the Preamble of the Norms states is 'a useful interpretation and elaboration of the standards contained in the Norms', see UN Doc. E/CN.4/Sub.2/2003/38/Rev.2 (2003). On the drafting process of these Norms and a comparison with previous attempts of a similar nature, see D. Weissbrodt and M. Kruger, 'Norms on the Responsibilities of Transnational Corporations and Other Business Enterprises with Regard to Human Rights' (2003) 97 *American Journal of International Law* 901; D. Weissbrodt and M. Kruger, 'Human Rights Responsibilities of Businesses as Non-State Actors' in P. Alston (ed.), *Non-State Actors and Human Rights* (Oxford University Press, 2005), 315.

responsible for promoting and securing the human rights set forth in the Universal Declaration of Human Rights', and therefore 'transnational corporations and other business enterprises, their officers and persons working for them are also obligated to respect generally recognized responsibilities and norms contained in United Nations treaties and other international instruments'.[3]

However, as documented in a report prepared in 2004–05 by the Office of the High Commissioner for Human Rights, the Norms were deeply contentious.[4] Some stakeholders challenged the very idea that international human rights law was relevant to corporations: they asserted that international law could not impose direct obligations on companies, who are not subjects of international law. Others questioned the choice of the experts of the Sub-Commission on Human Rights to base the Norms they were proposing on a range of instruments that were not necessarily ratified by the countries in which the corporations operate, thus in fact imposing on business actors obligations that went beyond the duty to comply with the legal framework applicable to their activities. Moreover, it was said, the Norms were inapplicable, due to the ambiguities of the standards guiding certain key questions, such as the definition of the situations which corporations had a duty to influence. Principle I of the Norms referred in this regard to the notion of 'sphere of influence' to provide such a definition,[5] but that was considered exceedingly vague and the source of legal insecurity for both the victims of human rights abuses of corporations and for these corporations themselves.

Not only were the Norms highly contentious due to the prescriptions they contained, they also were seen as objectively competing with the flagship initiative of the United Nations in promoting corporate social responsibility, the Global Compact. The Global Compact was first proposed by the United Nations Secretary-General Kofi Annan at the 1999 Davos World Economic Forum. It was conceived as a voluntary process,

---

[3] Norms, n. 2, Preamble, 3rd and 4th Recitals.
[4] Commission on Human Rights, 'Report of the United Nations High Commissioner on Human Rights on the Responsibilities of Transnational Corporations and Related Business Enterprises with Regard to Human Rights' (15 February 2005), UN doc. E/CN.4/2005/91.
[5] 'Within their respective spheres of activity and influence, transnational corporations and other business enterprises have the obligation to promote, secure the fulfillment of, respect, ensure respect of and protect human rights recognized in international as well as national law, including the rights and interests of indigenous peoples and other vulnerable groups.' Norms, n. 2, para. 1.

meant to reward good corporate practices by publicising them, and to promote mutual learning among businesses. The companies joining the process pledge to support a set of values in the areas of human rights, labour and the environment, to which anti-corruption was added in 2004. They report annually on initiatives that contribute to the fulfilment of these values in their business practices, through a 'Communication on Progress'. By 2011, more than 2,000 participating companies had been 'de-listed' from the Compact website for failure to comply with the reporting requirement.[6]

Six years later, in June 2011, the Human Rights Council – which had by then succeeded the Commission on Human Rights – adopted a set of Guiding Principles on Business and Human Rights (Guiding Principles) that are now seen as the most authoritative statement of the human rights duties or responsibilities of states and corporations adopted at the UN level.[7] These Guiding Principles go beyond the plethora of voluntary initiatives, often sector-specific, that existed hitherto. They have been widely endorsed by business organisations and in inter-govermental settings, including, notably, by the Organisation for Economic Co-operation and Development (OECD) when it revised its Guidelines on Multinational Enterprises in 2011.[8] They have also been invoked, albeit at times grudgingly, by civil society. And they are now subject to a follow-up mechanism within the United Nations system, through the Working Group on Business and Human Rights and an annual forum to be held on this issue.[9]

This is not a meagre achievement. It required from Professor John Ruggie, appointed the SRSG in July 2005, considerable talent in building bridges across various constituencies, and in seeking to build consensus across governments. His former affiliation to the Global Compact process, of which he was the main architect, undoubtedly made his task easier, reducing the perception of a competition between the two

---

[6] 'Number of Expelled Companies Reaches 2,000 as Global Compact Strengthens Disclosure Framework', Press Release of the Global Compact Office (20 January 2011), www.unglobalcompact.org/news/95-01-20-2011 (last accessed 17 April 2013).

[7] Human Rights Council, 'Human Rights and Transnational Corporations and Other Business Enterprises', A/HRC/Res./17/4 (16 June 2011).

[8] The new version of the OECD Guidelines on Multinational Enterprises includes a Chapter IV on human rights, that is based on the 'Protect, Respect and Remedy' Framework.

[9] The Working Group on the Issue of Human Rights and Transnational Corporations and Other Business Enterprises was established by Resolution 17/4 of the Human Rights Council, at the same time that the Council endorsed the Guiding Principles.

processes – one focused on human rights compliance and developed under the supervision of an inter-governmental body (i.e. the Human Rights Council), and another addressing broader areas of corporate social responsibility, led by the private sector and facilitated by the United Nations Secretariat but without any direct role for governments.

But the achievement owes less to where John Ruggie came from than to his tactical sense: when, in early 2008, he presented an initial framework (the 'Protect, Respect and Remedy' Framework), the skeleton proposed was so lean that hardly any stakeholder could see a reason to challenge it, though some did express the concern that the Framework lacked ambition. However, when, in 2011, the flesh was put on the bones, the trap had closed on the governments and the business community: since they had accepted the Framework three years earlier, how could they refuse its implications, which the final report of John Ruggie was now setting out in the form of the Guiding Principles? In addition, as Karin Buhmann rightly notes in her contribution, the SRSG sought to build a consensus by using language that sought to appeal to the business community – referring, for example, to 'responsibilities' rather than to 'duties' – and emphasising the business case for good corporate behaviour. This too was a tactic, and it paid off. However, as Surya Deva notes, substantive choices may hide behind terminological matters. For instance, mentioning 'impacts' rather than 'violations' reveals a shift from a legal to a managerial conception of the responsibility of business that human rights lawyers may see as a step backwards.

This important volume takes stock of this achievement. It asks what made it possible, providing a uniquely well-informed insight into the decision-making processes within the United Nations. But it also asks whether the price for consensus was too high: as Surya Deva and David Bilchitz aptly put it in their introduction, if John Ruggie was inspired by an idea of 'principled pragmatism', has pragmatism – the need to achieve concensus across a wide range of often conflicting interests – led to a sacrifice of principles? If consensus was achieved, is it 'consensus without content'? Far from sharing the enthusiasm of most governments and of the business community, most of the contributions collected here adopt a rather sceptical stance.

This diversity of views is entirely understandable. The Guiding Principles are not a blueprint, and they are not the final word. They are a step in a process that is still unfolding. They contain certain formulations that will require more elaboration in the future. The concept of 'due diligence', discussed in the chapter by Sabine Michalowski, is

illustrative in this regard. The SRSG wanted to avoid the pitfalls associated with the notion of 'sphere of influence' and sought to refrain from
imposing on corporations certain responsibilities – to protect, promote
and fulfil human rights – that would overlap with the duties of the state.
But he did realise, at the same time, that defining for corporations
responsibilities of a purely 'negative' nature was insufficient: would
not corporations be tempted to adopt a 'hands-off' approach even
in situations they were in a position to influence, if their only responsibility was to abstain from being involved in abuses?

The concept of 'due diligence', which was included as part of the
definition of the requirement that business enterprises respect human
rights – the second component of the Framework – was seen as a way out
of this apparent dilemma. The Guiding Principles provide that corporations should 'act with due diligence to avoid infringing on the rights of
others and to address adverse impacts with which they are involved'.[10]
Principles 15 and 17 further describe the notion, and the OECD
Guidelines on Multinational Enterprises, as revised in 2011, replicate
this. These instruments define the human rights due diligence responsibility of corporations as having three key components: to identify
impacts; to prevent and mitigate impacts thus identified; and to account
for impacts and establish grievance mechanisms. But, as the Guiding
Principles themselves acknowledge, it is a notion that must be interpreted according to context, and that will vary, for instance, 'with the size
of the business enterprise, the risk of severe human rights impacts, and
the nature and context of its operations'.[11]

We should avoid confusing ambiguities with gaps. The relative vagueness of 'due diligence' may in fact be seen as an opportunity, as the
various business sectors, civil society groups and courts will gradually
both clarify the expectations it conveys and build the notion – not top-
down and by decree, but bottom-up and incrementally. Thus, in 2012,
non-governmental organisations commissioned a study on the various
meanings of due diligence in different contexts, and on what states could
do to encourage companies to be proactive in this regard.[12] In 2013, the

---

[10] Human Rights Council, 'Guiding Principles on Business and Human Rights: Implementing
the United Nations "Respect, Protect and Remedy" Framework', A/HRC/17/31 (21 March
2011), para. 6 ('Guiding Principles').

[11] *Ibid.*, Principle 15(b).

[12] O. De Schutter, A. Ramasastry, M. B. Taylor and R. C. Thompson, *Human Rights Due
Diligence: The Role of States* (International Corporate Accountability Roundtable, the

High Court in Kampala found a German coffee-producing company liable for compensation to people evicted from their lands in order for the coffee plantation to be established: although the evictions took place prior to the arrival of the investor, the court stated that the company concerned should have acted with due diligence and actively sought information about the conditions under which the land was being made available to them.[13] Due diligence shall continue to live on. It is a welcome fact that the Guiding Principles, far from foreclosing the discussion on its significance and relevance in different contexts, encourages this conversation.

That is not to say, of course, that the Guiding Principles are beyond reproach. There is one area in particular where they do seem to set the bar below the current state of international human rights law: that concerns the extraterritorial human rights obligations of states, including, in particular, the duty of states to control the corporations they are in a position to influence, even outside the national territory. Augenstein and Kinley offer a comprehensive discussion of this issue. The Guiding Principles provide that 'States should set out clearly the expectation that all business enterprises domiciled in their territory and/or jurisdiction respect human rights throughout their operations'.[14] This includes operations abroad. As the Commentary to the Guiding Principles affirms: 'There are strong policy reasons for home States to set out clearly the expectation that businesses respect human rights abroad, especially where the State itself is involved in or supports those businesses.'[15]

However, the United Nations treaty bodies have gone beyond that cautious, almost subliminal reference to the extraterritorial obligations of states. They have repeatedly expressed the view that states should take steps to prevent human rights contraventions abroad by business enterprises that are incorporated under their laws, or have their main seat or main place of business under their jurisdiction. The Committee on Economic, Social and Cultural Rights in particular affirms that states parties should 'prevent third parties from violating the right [protected under the International Covenant on Economic, Social and Cultural

European Coalition for Corporate Justice, the Canadian Network on Corporate Accountability, 2012).

[13] See FIAN, 'Ugandan Court Orders Compensation be Paid to Evictees of the Kaweri-Coffee-Plantation', Press Release (11 April 2013), www.fian.org/news/article/detail/ugandan-court-orders-compensation-be-paid-to-evictees-of-the-kaweri-coffee-planta tion/ (last accessed 17 April 2013).

[14] Guiding Principles, n. 10, Principle 2.   [15] *Ibid.*

Rights] in other countries, if they are able to influence these third parties by way of legal or political means, in accordance with the Charter of the United Nations and applicable international law'.[16] Specifically in regard to corporations, this Committee has further stated that: 'States Parties should also take steps to prevent human rights contraventions abroad by corporations that have their main seat under their jurisdiction, without infringing the sovereignty or diminishing the obligations of host states under the Covenant.'[17] Similar views have been expressed by other human rights treaty bodies. The Committee on the Elimination of Racial Discrimination (CERD) considers that states parties should also protect human rights by preventing their own citizens and companies, or national entities, from violating rights in other countries.[18] Under the International Covenant on Civil and Political Rights, the Human Rights Committee noted in 2012 in a concluding observation relating to Germany:

> The State party is encouraged to set out clearly the expectation that all business enterprises domiciled in its territory and/or its jurisdiction respect human rights standards in accordance with the Covenant throughout their operations. It is also encouraged to take appropriate measures to strengthen the remedies provided to protect people who have been victims of activities of such business enterprises operating abroad.[19]

It is noteworthy that these statements, while they confirm the views of the human rights treaty bodies that these bodies had expressed in the past, were reiterated after the endorsement of the Guiding Principles by the Human Rights Council. The Guiding Principles are not a restatement of international law: they are a tool, meant to provide practical guidance both to states and to companies, in order to ensure that all the

---

[16] Committee on Economic, Social and Cultural Rights, 'General Comment No. 14 (2000), The Right to the Highest Attainable Standard of Health (Art. 12 of the International Covenant on Economic, Social and Cultural Rights)', E/C.12/2000/4 (2000), para. 39; Committee on Economic, Social and Cultural Rights, 'General Comment No. 15 (2002), The Right to Water (Arts. 11 and 12 of the International Covenant on Economic, Social and Cultural Rights)', E/C.12/2002/11 (26 November 2002), para. 31.

[17] Committee on Economic, Social and Cultural Rights, 'Statement on the Obligations of States Parties Regarding the Corporate Sector and Economic, Social and Cultural Rights', E/C.12/2011/1 (20 May 2011), para. 5.

[18] See CERD, 'Concluding Observations for Canada', CERD/C/CAN/CO/18, para. 17; CERD, 'Concluding Observations for the United States', CERD/C/USA/CO/6, para. 30.

[19] Human Rights Committee, 'Concluding Observations on the Sixth Periodic Report of Germany', CCPR/C/DEU/CO/6, para. 16.

instruments at the disposal of both shall be used to improve compliance with human rights in the activities of business. Nor are the Guiding Principles intended to freeze the development of international law: they allow, and to a certain extent encourage, the further clarification by human rights bodies of the implications of the duties of states and, indirectly, of corporations. I am convinced that the gradual strengthening of the extraterritorial duties of states in the area of human rights, including their duties to regulate the activities of corporations whose conduct they can influence, constitutes the next frontier in this regard: the endorsement by a range of experts and organisations of the Maastricht Principles on the Extraterritorial Obligations of States in the Area of Economic, Social and Cultural rights is a first and important step in this regard.[20]

This book makes a highly valuable, and timely, contribution to this discussion. The authors identify the choices that were made in the Guiding Principles. They do not only highlight certain insufficiencies; they also identify ways forward. I have no doubt that it shall remain for many years an essential reference for all those who work on corporate responsibility and human rights. And it is my hope that it shall influence the next steps on the long road towards humanising globalisation.

*Olivier De Schutter**

---

[20] The text of the Maastricht Principles is reproduced with a commentary in (2012) 34 *Human Rights Quarterly* 1084–1171 (commentary authored by O. De Schutter, A. Eide, A. Khalfan, M. Orellana, M. Salomon and I. Seiderman). See also M. Langford, W. Vandehole, M. Scheinin and W. an Genugten (eds.), *Global Justice, State Duties: The Extraterritorial Scope of Economic, Social and Cultural Rights in International Law* (Cambridge University Press, 2013). As regards the duty of the state to regulate corporations, see in particular the chapter by Smita Narula.

* United Nations Special Rapporteur on the Right to Food; Professor at the University of Louvain; Visiting Professor at Columbia University.

PREFACE

This book stems from an international conference that took place in Johannesburg in late January 2012. The conference was organised by the two editors under the auspices of the South African Institute for Advanced Constitutional, Public, Human Rights and International Law (SAIFAC), a Centre of the University of Johannesburg, and the School of Law of City University of Hong Kong with the financial support of the Konrad Adenauer Stiftung. The conference – which attracted several leading scholars, practitioners and civil society representatives working in the area of business and human rights in different parts of the world – sought to engage critically with the 'Protect, Respect and Remedy' Framework (Framework) and the Guiding Principles on Business and Human Rights (GPs). This edited collection contains some of the most thought-provoking and original papers that were presented at the said conference. It represents one of the first scholarly works that offer a systematic critique of the Framework as well as the GPs. In many areas, it also suggests future directions that should be pursued in this important, cutting-edge area of scholarship in relation to the human rights responsibilities of business.

The conference was held at Constitution Hill, the historic site in South Africa where both Gandhi and Mandela – two of the foremost defenders of the ethos underlying human rights – were imprisoned. The site, where the new Constitutional Court of South Africa was built, also represents the triumph of the values for which they fought and the importance of institutions being set up to protect the human rights of all in society. The challenges faced by human rights defenders often change over time: whereas the focus of the struggles led by Gandhi and Mandela was on fighting colonisation and apartheid, one of the key challenges today is to harness the economic power of corporations in the quest to realise human rights and to revisit the ways in which their responsibilities are conceived. Just as a historic transformation occurred in South Africa, so too do we hope that the international community will see the importance of developing a more robust framework for regulating the activities of business in relation to human rights.

This book hopes to make an important intellectual and conceptual contribution to what the relationship between business and human rights should look like. A project of the magnitude of the conference and resulting book could not be accomplished without the support of many people. In bringing the conference together, we would like to thank the Konrad Adenauer Stiftung for their valuable support – financial and otherwise. Dolores Joseph provided superb assistance in co-ordinating the conference and Vusi Ncube also helped ensure its smooth running from a logistical point of view.

In putting the book together, the editors would like to thank the entire team at Cambridge University Press in rendering professional and efficient service. Kim Hughes, the Senior Commissioning Editor, deserves special mention and gratitude for being very supportive of this project throughout the process. We are also grateful to the anonymous reviewers who provided timely and valuable suggestions to us. Last but not least, all the contributing authors – who worked during weekends and Christmas/ New Year holidays to meet our demands – deserve our sincere thanks for their co-operation and patience. We could not have accomplished this project without the unflinching commitment of each contributor to strive towards the goal of making companies accountable for human rights violations.

We are also grateful to Professor Olivier De Schutter for agreeing to write a foreword for this book, despite his extremely busy schedule. During the editing process, Anita Jay, Ngwako Raboshakga, Warren Bowles and Michael Dafel provided us with valuable help in verifying sources and revising the footnote style. We thank them all.

Surya Deva would like to thank the City University of Hong Kong Law School for providing the vital financial resources to hire a research assistant in finalising the manuscript. Surya is also grateful to Swati, Vyom and Varun for offering all the support, care and love one could hope for during the entire project, and generally. Without the best wishes of parents and other family members, I could not have come this far. Each one of them deserves special thanks for believing in me and letting me do what I wanted to do.

David Bilchitz would like to extend thanks to the Faculty of Law, University of Johannesburg for their support of the conference and the book project. I also deeply appreciate the support of all the staff at SAIFAC, which provided the institutional setting for the conference. On a personal level, I would like to thank Jeffrey Davis for being my wonderful life partner, a true companion who has deeply enriched my life on multiple levels since our first meeting almost four years ago. My parents – Reuven and Cynthia Bilchitz – have always provided me with the background and unstinting support that has enabled me to flourish academically and in many other ways. My gratitude to them knows no bounds. In recent years, Lennie and Lara – my brother and his wife – have had a child, Gavriel, who is a wonderful new addition to the family. I hope that when Gavriel grows up, he will inherit a fairer world, where business plays its role in contributing towards the realisation of human rights and some of the ideas canvassed in this book become a concrete reality.

The human rights obligations of business: a critical framework for the future

DAVID BILCHITZ AND SURYA DEVA

Business and human rights: four key questions

In the last decade or so, significant developments have taken place at the international level in articulating the human rights responsibilities of business and devising a regulatory framework which can provide effective remedies to victims of corporate human rights violations. One development that stands out is the work done by Professor John Ruggie, who was appointed in July 2005 as the Special Representative of the Secretary-General on the Issue of Human Rights and Transnational Corporations and Other Business Enterprises (SRSG). After submitting two reports to the United Nations Human Rights Council (HRC), in 2006 and 2007, the SRSG proposed the 'Protect, Respect and Remedy' Framework (Framework) in the 2008 report to provide 'a common conceptual and policy framework, a foundation on which thinking and action can build'.[1] After the Framework was accepted by the HRC and his mandate renewed for another three years, the SRSG focused upon 'operationalising' the Framework. This work culminated in the Guiding Principles on Business and Human Rights (GPs), which were submitted to the HRC in March 2011[2] and endorsed on 16 June 2011.[3]

---

[1] Human Rights Council, 'Protect, Respect and Remedy: A Framework for Business and Human Rights', A/HRC/8/5 (7 April 2008), para. 8 (SRSG, '2008 Framework').
[2] Human Rights Council, 'Guiding Principles on Business and Human Rights: Implementing the United Nations "Protect, Respect and Remedy" Framework', A/HRC/17/31 (21 March 2011) (SRSG, 'Guiding Principles').
[3] Human Rights Council, 'New Guiding Principles on Business and Human Rights Endorsed by the UN Human Rights Council' (16 June 2011), www.ohchr.org/en/ NewsEvents/Pages/DisplayNews.aspx?NewsID=11164&LangID=E (last accessed 14 January 2013).

The GPs have generally received a positive reception by the international community and have become a sort of common reference point in the area of business and human rights. States, national human rights institutions, multi-stakeholder initiatives, companies, non-governmental organisations (NGOs) and academics have invoked them in diverse ways.[4] However, do the Framework and the GPs adequately address the challenges that arise in considering the relationship between business and human rights? Barring a few exceptions,[5] both these documents have not received a detailed or systematic critical evaluation. This book seeks to fill this gap.

It does so by subjecting the Framework and the GPs to rigorous scrutiny against four key questions that arise in the area of business and human rights.[6] The first question relates to the process undertaken and the method-ology adopted by the SRSG that led to the final products: the Framework and the GPs. What did the SRSG do differently to achieve the unanimous endorsement of the GPs by the HRC, a feat that no previous UN-led initiative could accomplish? What is the nature and extent of the 'consensus' that the GPs are said to represent? Were the deeply divisive and contested issues surrounding business and human rights intentionally bypassed to sustain the project of building the consensus? Did the goal of achieving a consensus and securing the support of the business community override the goal of developing a robust regulatory framework of corporate accountability for human rights violations? In other words, did 'principled pragmatism' undermine the cause of subjecting business to the mandate of international human rights law?

The second key question concerns the normative grounding of the Framework and the GPs. This question has two components: what is the source of bindingness of corporate obligations; and why ought businesses to have human rights obligations? In relation to the first component, we are concerned with the question of whether these obligations are merely

---

[4] See Business and Human Rights Resource Centre, 'Implementation and Uses of Guiding Principles', www.business-humanrights.org/Documents/UNGuidingPrinciples (last accessed 24 January 2013).

[5] See R. Mares (ed.), *The UN Guiding Principles on Business and Human Rights: Foundations and Implementation* (Leiden: Martinus Nijhoff, 2012). A few journal articles have also critiqued the Framework and GPs. See, for example, P. Simons, 'International Law's Invisible Hand and the Future of Corporate Accountability for Violations of Human Rights' (2012) 3:1 *Journal of Human Rights and the Environment* 5.

[6] These four questions are an extension of the three-fold challenges (the *why*, *what* and *how*) in obligating companies to observe human rights norms, developed elsewhere by one of the editors. S. Deva, *Regulating Corporate Human Rights Violations: Humanizing Business* (London/New York: Routledge, 2012).

voluntary and should be rooted in 'social expectations'. Moreover, can human rights norms be 'binding' other than in a legal sense? The second component requires us to develop a reasoned account of why corporations ought to have obligations for the realisation of human rights. This is a question of political philosophy and requires engagement with the moral bases for corporations to be bound by particular obligations.

The third question relates to the actual content of the obligations that corporations have in relation to human rights. In other words, what is (or ought to be) the extent of corporate human rights obligations? This is a complex area to navigate and raises several sub-questions. What is the justifiable division of responsibility between the state and corporations? Do corporations merely have the responsibility to respect human rights or do they also have positive obligations to protect and fulfil human rights? What are the responsibilities of corporations for the actions of third parties – from state agencies to subsidiaries and suppliers – with whom they are connected? The issue of complicity, especially for companies operating in conflict zones or where repressive and authoritarian regimes are in power, poses a number of conundrums which require systematic attention.

The fourth and final question concerns how to make companies accountable for human rights violations. How could the obstacles that victims experience in access to justice be overcome? Is it adequate to rely primarily on states or the 'courts of public opinion' to hold corporations accountable for violations of human rights? What forms of alternative remedies are likely to provide effective relief for victims of human rights abuses? More importantly, do the measures proposed by the GPs empower victims adequately to take on the mighty multinational corporations (MNCs)? How does one deal with companies that fail to live up to the 'due diligence' recommendations outlined in the GPs?

We organise the discussion in this introductory chapter as well as the parts of the book around these four questions. In the second section of this chapter, we consider briefly the historical backdrop of the UN's engagement with the issue of business and human rights. This should help readers to contextualise the SRSG's mandate. The third section then offers a critical introduction to the key features of the Framework and the GPs. The fourth section provides a brief outline of the chapters in this volume and their authors' views about the adequacy of the responses of the Framework and the GPs to the four questions identified above. Finally, we conclude by briefly considering some of the outstanding issues and a possible way forward for developing further the human rights obligations of business.

The book does not claim that the Framework and the GPs are devoid of any merit. Nevertheless, we believe that critical insights will be vital to further the cause of putting in place a robust framework regarding the human rights obligations of companies. While a book of this length cannot possibly cover all aspects of the Framework and the GPs, it covers a range of issues in a systematic way. We do hope that more such critical inquiries will follow. These critical engagements should help, amongst others, the UN Working Group on Business and Human Rights 'to explore options and make recommendations ... for enhancing access to effective remedies available to those whose human rights are affected by corporate activities'.[7]

A few signposts are necessary regarding the terminology used in this book. Although the debate at times was personified by John Ruggie, we have generally used the term 'SRSG' to indicate that the recommendations emerged from a UN mandate and to ensure that any critiques should not be taken in an ad hominem manner. Also, the contributors to this volume have not generally maintained as sharp a distinction between 'responsibility' and 'duty/obligation' as was done by the SRSG. And we use the terms 'corporation' and 'company' interchangeably to refer to all forms of business entities that have human rights obligations.

The UN's engagement with business and human rights: a historical context

It might be useful to review at the outset the history and context[8] in which the SRSG was invited to break the stalemate in the UN's quest to establish a regulatory framework concerning the human rights responsibilities of business.[9] The UN's direct engagement with MNCs[10] and the

---

[7] Human Rights Council, 'Human Rights and Transnational Corporations and Other Business Enterprises', A/HRC/17/L.17/Rev.1 (15 July 2011), para. 6(e).

[8] This section draws on S. Deva, '"Protect, Respect and Remedy", but Why, What and How?: A Critique of the SRSG's Framework for Business and Human Rights', paper presented at a conference on 'Corporate Social Responsibility, Business Responsibilities for Human Rights and International Law', held in Copenhagen on 6–7 November 2008.

[9] Even the SRSG considered 'the history that preceded its creation' an important variable: see Commission on Human Rights, 'Interim Report of the Special Representative of the Secretary-General on the Issue of Human Rights and Transnational Corporations and Other Business Enterprises', E/CN.4/2006/97 (22 February 2006), para. 3 (SRSG, '2006 Interim Report').

[10] Transnational corporations (TNCs) is the UN's preferred terminology. But we use the term 'MNCs' here for the sake of consistency in this book.

impact of their activities on society (which was the initial focus of the UN in this area) can, broadly, be divided into three phases. Apart from the timespan, the three phases differ from each other in terms of the focus of engagement, the key participating actors, and the driving force for such an engagement.

The first phase: MNCs' rights versus responsibilities

The first phase can be traced back to the early 1970s when the UN's Economic and Social Council requested the Secretary-General to constitute a Group of Eminent Persons to study the impact of MNCs on the development process (especially in developing countries) and international relations.[11] The Group recommended that the UN establish a Commission on MNCs, which, amongst other things, should formulate a code of conduct for them.[12] The quest to establish an agreeable code under the aegis of the Commission continued for more than a decade, but the Draft Code of 1990 could not be adopted due to various disagreements between developed and developing countries.[13] It is arguable that the first phase ended in the early 1990s with the suspension of negotiations on the Code and the renaming of the Commission on MNCs as the Commission on International Investment and Transnational Corporations.[14]

During the first phase, the proposed code sought to deal with *both* responsibilities (linked to MNCs' activities) and rights (linked to MNCs' treatment by host states). For obvious reasons, whereas developing countries were more interested in solidifying their right to regulate MNCs and outlining the responsibilities of MNCs, developed countries were keener to secure a level playing field for their MNCs operating in emerging markets. Consistent with the then prevailing view of international law, states were the principal actors which pushed for such a code and negotiated its content.

Writing in 2007, the SRSG asserted that '[h]uman rights did not feature' in the code formulation initiative of this phase.[15] This assertion

---

[11] P. Muchlinski, *Multinational Enterprises and the Law* (Oxford: Blackwell Publishing, 1999), 593.
[12] *Ibid.*   [13] *Ibid.*, 593–97.
[14] Economic and Social Council, 'Integration of the Commission on Transnational Corporations into the Institutional Machinery of the United Nations Conference on Trade and Development', Resolution 1994/1 (14 July 1994).
[15] J. Ruggie, 'Business and Human Rights: The Evolving International Agenda' (2007) 101 *American Journal of International Law* 819.

does not seem to be correct, because paragraph 14 of the Draft Code of 1990 had stated that MNCs *'shall respect human rights* and fundamental rights and fundamental freedoms in the countries in which they operate'.[16] The SRSG was probably misled by the fact that the Draft Code, unlike the similar instruments drafted in the next two phases, did not focus exclusively on the human rights responsibilities of MNCs. But this does not mean that human rights issues were not on the discussion table during the first phase.

The second phase: between voluntarism and binding obligations

The second phase of the UN's engagement with MNCs' activities began at the end of the twentieth century when the UN became concerned with the impact of globalisation as well as of MNCs on the realisation of human rights. Taking leads from the paper submitted by Mr El-Hadji Guisse on the impact of MNCs on the realisation of economic, social and cultural rights,[17] in August 1998 the Sub-Commission on the Promotion and Protection of Human Rights decided to establish a five-member Working Group on the Working Methods and Activities of Transnational Corporations.[18]

While the Working Group was still mapping its future course, on 31 January 1999, at the World Economic Forum in Davos, the then UN Secretary-General, Kofi Annan, proposed the Global Compact originally consisting of nine principles in the areas of human rights, labour, and the environment.[19] This was a clear attempt on the part of the UN to re-engage with non-state actors and push for a 'public-private' partnership to make globalisation more inclusive and equitable.[20] The Global Compact, which was officially launched in 2000 and became popular with corporations, received significant criticism from human rights

---

[16] 'Draft Code on Transnational Corporations' in UNCTC, *Transnational Corporations, Services and the Uruguay Round* (1990), Annex IV, p. 231 at 234, para. 14 (emphasis added). See also paras. 25, 37 and 41–43.

[17] Sub-Commission on Human Rights, 'Working Document on the Impact of the Activities of Transnational Corporations on the Realisation of Economic, Social and Cultural Rights', E/CN.4/Sub.2/1998/6 (10 June 1998).

[18] D. Weissbrodt and M. Kruger, 'Norms of the Responsibilities of Transnational Corporations and Other Business Enterprises with Regard to Human Rights' (2003) 97 *American Journal of International Law* 901, at 903–04.

[19] The tenth principle (anti-corruption) was added to the Global Compact in 2004.

[20] S. Deva, 'Global Compact: A Critique of UN's "Public-Private" Partnership for Promoting Corporate Citizenship' (2006) 34 *Syracuse Journal of International Law and Commerce* 107.

advocates for being too vague and providing nothing more than voluntary moral guidance to companies.[21]

Against the backdrop of these criticisms, the Working Group drafted detailed substantive provisions as to the human rights responsibilities of MNCs and other business enterprises and also incorporated provisions for the implementation of these responsibilities.[22] In mid-2003, it presented to the Sub-Commission the final draft of the Norms on the Responsibilities of Transnational Corporations and Other Business Enterprises with Regard to Human Rights (UN Norms).[23] The UN Norms unsurprisingly attracted criticism from several leading MNCs and business organisations. Although the Sub-Commission approved the UN Norms,[24] the Commission on Human Rights in its 2004 session resolved, much to the satisfaction of the business community, that the UN Norms have 'no legal standing'.[25] The Commission then, in its 2005 session, requested the UN Secretary-General to appoint a Special Representative on the issue of human rights and transnational corporations.[26] This resolution effectively drew the curtain on the second phase in that it did not even refer to the UN Norms.[27]

In comparison with the first phase, the primary focus of the second phase – which lasted for a much shorter period than the first phase – was on cataloguing the human rights responsibilities of MNCs and other business enterprises. The omission of MNCs' rights from the drafting debate during this period could be explained by the proliferation of bilateral investment treaties since the 1990s,[28] and the establishment of

---

[21] J. Nolan, 'The United Nations' Compact with Business: Hindering or Helping the Protection of Human rights?' (2005) 24 *University of Queensland Law Journal* 445; Deva, 'A Critique of UN's "Public-Private" Partnership', n. 20.

[22] See Weissbrodt and Kruger, n. 18, 903–07.

[23] Sub-Commission on the Promotion and Protection of Human Rights, 'Norms on the Responsibilities of Transnational Corporations and Other Business Enterprises with Regard to Human Rights', UN Doc. E/CN.4/Sub.2/2003/12/Rev.2 (13 August 2003) (UN Norms).

[24] Sub-Commission on the Promotion and Protection of Human Rights, Resolution 2003/16 (13 August 2003), E/CN.4/Sub.2/2003/L.11, 52–55.

[25] Commission on Human Rights, Agenda Item 16, E/CN.4/2004/L.73/Rev.1 (16 April 2004), para. (c).

[26] Commission on Human Rights, 'Promotion and Protection of Human Rights', E/CN.4/2005/L.87 (15 April 2005).

[27] See D. Kinley and R. Chambers, 'The UN Human Rights Norms for Corporations: The Private Implications of Public International Law' (2006) 6 *Human Rights Law Review* 447, at 459–60.

[28] See D. Bishop, J. Crawford and M. Reisman, *Foreign Investment Disputes: Cases, Materials and Commentary* (The Hague: Kluwer Law International, 2005), 1–10.

the World Trade Organisation in 1995. These two developments allowed MNCs to demand, in various forums, directly or through their home states, fair and equal treatment from host states. It did not, therefore, remain equally critical to catalogue the rights of MNCs. Another notable difference between the first two phases was that, unlike in the first phase, MNCs, business organisations and NGOs played an active role in the second phase in mobilising opinion for or against the UN Norms. This provided good evidence of the emerging importance of non-state actors in moulding the contours of international law.

The third phase: principled pragmatism or business in the driving seat?

The third phase began in July 2005 with the appointment of John Ruggie as the SRSG and is ongoing, with the constitution of the Working Group tasked with the responsibility to disseminate and implement the GPs still underway. During the six years of his mandate, the SRSG conducted wide-ranging consultations, participated in meetings with diverse organisations, gave numerous speeches, prepared several reports, proposed the Framework and drafted the GPs.

While it will not be possible to review all the SRSG reports here, we highlight how this phase differed from the previous two phases. Firstly, extensive consultation with a wide range of stakeholders (perhaps with the exception of victims of human rights abuses) was a defining feature of this phase. In fact, this phase illustrated how non-state actors such as MNCs, NGOs and individual scholars could play an even more vital role than states in developing international law norms from the 'bottom up'.[29]

Secondly, this 'bottom-up' approach of international law-making allowed MNCs and business organisations to play an unprecedented role in defining the contours of rules that were to apply to them. The business sector not only enjoyed proximity to the SRSG,[30] but its voices

---

[29] See S. Deva, 'Multinationals, Human Rights and International Law: How to Deal with the Elephant in the Room?', Keynote Address at the 'GLOTHRO Workshop on the Direct Human Rights Obligations of Companies in International Law', held in Bled, Slovenia, on 17–19 January 2013.

[30] For example, out of the fifteen-member Leadership Group constituted in September 2008 to advise the SRSG, six members came from the corporate world, while there was no representative from prominent human rights NGOs such as Amnesty International and Human Rights Watch. 'Global Leadership Group to Advise on Business and Human Rights', www.

also seemingly had more influence on the text of the Framework and the GPs as compared to the voices of NGOs. Human rights in the context of business thus hardly remained as 'trumps',[31] because the business sector was able to negotiate narrow and non-binding human rights standards applicable to itself.

Thirdly, the SRSG's work was underpinned by the notion of 'principled pragmatism', that is, 'an unflinching commitment to the principle of strengthening the promotion and protection of human rights as it relates to business, coupled with a pragmatic attachment to what works best in creating change where it matters most – in the daily lives of people'.[32] Although this notion rightly received criticism from human rights scholars and NGOs,[33] it also allowed the SRSG to achieve consensus and secure unanimous support at the UN level. At the same time, this approach enabled the SRSG to bypass smartly, as we show below, many contentious issues in the area of business and human rights.

The appointment of Ruggie as the SRSG was perhaps a recognition of the reality that in the third phase of the UN's engagement with MNCs, business would play a dominant role in setting the human rights agenda affecting itself. It is not without significance that Ruggie was 'the principal drafter of the UN Global Compact'.[34] One should not, therefore, be too surprised if his past publicly-stated views were reflected in how he discharged his mandate as the SRSG. For example, writing in 2002 in defence of the voluntary character of his brain-child (i.e. the Global Compact), Ruggie had observed that the 'probability of the General Assembly's adopting a meaningful code anytime soon approximates zero. . . . any UN attempt to impose a code of conduct not only would

reports-and-materials.org/Leadership-group-22-Sep-2008.pdf (last accessed 26 January 2013).

[31] R. Dworkin, *Taking Rights Seriously*, 2nd Indian repr. (New Delhi: Universal Law Publishing, 1999), xi. See also F. J. Garcia, 'The Global Market and Human Rights: Trading Away the Human Rights Principle' (1999) 25 *Brooklyn Journal of International Law* 51, 75; J. Donnelly, *Universal Human Rights: In Theory and Practice* (Ithaca: Cornell University Press, 1989), 9–10.

[32] SRSG, '2006 Interim Report', n. 9, para. 81.

[33] See, for example, D. Weissbrodt, 'International Standard-Setting on the Human Rights Responsibilities of Business' (2008) 26 *Berkeley Journal of International Law* 373; Misereor & Global Policy Forum Europe, 'Problematic Pragmatism: The Ruggie Report 2008: Background, Analysis and Perspectives' (June 2008); FIDH, 'Comments to the Interim Report of the Special Representative of the Secretary-General on the Issue of Human Rights and Transnational Corporations and Other Business Enterprises, 22 February 2006' (442/2, 15 March 2006).

[34] Weissbrodt, 'International Standard-Setting', n. 33, 383.

be opposed by the business community, but also would drive progressive business leaders, who are willing to engage with the Compact, into a more uniform anti-code coalition'.[35] In short, the approach adopted by the SRSG in the third phase has undone the contribution that the UN Norms sought to make in marking a clear departure from merely voluntary regulation and the over-reliance on the states' role in regulating MNCs.

Key features of the Framework and the GPs

This section outlines some of the key elements that defined the work and output of the SRSG's mandate, in particular the Framework and the GPs. We engage with these key features in a critical manner, seeking to show both a number of shortcomings and omissions in the work of the SRSG.

Process: consensus without content?

One distinguishing feature of the SRSG's mandate was the process adopted by him. The first important element of this process was the adoption of an explicitly consultative approach. The SRSG perhaps learned a lesson from the failure of the UN Norms, which had been criticised for failing to engage with a wide range of stakeholders. The wide-ranging consultations conducted by the SRSG undoubtedly enhanced the legitimacy of the mandate to set norms and outline expectations that society has from both states and companies. Even if not all stakeholders had the same kind of impact on the text of the Framework and the GPs, they at least had a sense of participation in what was unfolding. A black spot in relation to this legitimacy, however, was the SRSG's reluctance to engage in any direct consultation with victims of corporate human rights abuses. Despite many calls by civil society for him to meet victims, the SRSG took a strategic decision at the outset to keep a distance from the victims of corporate human rights abuses. This allowed him to avoid the process becoming an adversarial battle between NGOs and MNCs.

Consultations were not carried out merely to acquire legitimacy. They were also employed to build consensus – the second key aspect of the process. The SRSG did not try to impose on companies human rights

---

[35] J. Ruggie, 'Trade, Sustainability and Global Governance: Keynote Address' (2002) 27 *Columbia Journal of Environmental Law* 297, at 303.

obligations akin to the 'command and control' model of norm setting. Corporate leaders were, rather, lured through a range of engagements into accepting the idea of businesses having a responsibility to respect human rights. Against the background of decades of intense frictions and multiple failures at the UN level to adopt an instrument that catalogued corporate human rights responsibilities, achieving consensus on anything in the domain of business and human rights became a goal in itself. One strategy that helped the SRSG in accomplishing this goal was to stay away from controversial issues, whether for states (e.g. acknowledgement of a positive obligation on states to regulate MNCs extraterritorially) or companies (e.g. formulation of legally binding human rights obligations).

The third and final aspect of the process was a push for alignment. Concerted efforts were made by the SRSG and his team to ensure that all other regulatory initiatives in the field of business and human rights – whether soft or hard, national or international, uni- or multi-stakeholder – embraced the conceptual tools advanced by the Framework and the GPs. The SRSG was quite successful in selling, for example, due diligence as a strategy to discharge the responsibility to respect human rights and also, perhaps, avoid complicity. Everyone from states to companies, NGOs and academics started speaking the language of due diligence, without fully appreciating that due diligence in commercial contexts might be very different from due diligence in the field of human rights.[36] While the push for such an alignment was conducive to meeting the SRSG's publicly stated goal of the Framework and the GPs becoming 'an authoritative focal point', this also meant that no other initiatives sought to go beyond these documents and address their shortcomings. The approach adopted so far by the Working Group on Business and Human Rights illustrates this, as it does not seemingly wish to break the cage of the GPs, even in those cases where doing so might be desirable to strengthen human rights protection.[37]

---

[36] See S. Deva, 'Guiding Principles on Business and Human Rights: Implications for Companies' (2012) 9:2 *European Company Law* 101, at 106–07.

[37] It is though fair to note that the Working Group has moved beyond the SRSG's approach and the GPs in certain ways or areas. For instance, the Working Group has shown a willingness to conduct country visits. It has also decided to prepare a thematic report on how indigenous peoples are adversely affected by business-related activities disproportionately. See Human Rights Council, 'Report of the Working Group on the Issue of Human Rights and Transnational Corporations and Other Business Enterprises', A/HRC/23/32 (14 March 2013), paras. 59–62 and 65.

Principled pragmatism: a flawed methodology?

As mentioned above, 'principled pragmatism' was the core methodology applied by the SRSG in all of his work. The interrelation of 'principle' and 'pragmatism' is not entirely clear. For example, when is principle sacrificed on the altar of pragmatism and when does it guide compromises that need to be made with real-life constraints? The human rights discourse is not entirely divorced from pragmatism. The progressive realisation of human rights under the International Covenant on Economic, Social and Cultural Rights (ICESCR) is a case in point,[38] because it is pragmatic to concede that the full realisation of socio-economic rights immediately requires a certain level of resources and capacity that some states might not have. This might lead us to develop stronger obligations (a minimum core) to focus on particular urgent needs in the shorter term, whilst allowing fully adequate levels of socio-economic provision to be realised in the longer term.

However, this pragmatism under the ICESCR is different in nature: it is visible only at the stage of realising human rights. When it comes to setting aspirational norms, human rights ought to be principled. The SRSG, however, sought to introduce pragmatism at every level of his work. By introducing pragmatism at the stage of setting human rights norms applicable to business, he has (in)advertently set the threshold of corporate human rights obligations at a very low level. We think that an *alternative* reading of principled pragmatism would have required him to develop strong human rights standards for the business sector appropriate in an era of state privatisation, and then outline a road map for the progressive escalation of corporate obligations.

Source of corporate responsibility: social expectations?

The SRSG, in his first report, in a rather breathtaking manner distanced himself from the UN Norms, and denied that companies have any binding human rights obligations under international human rights law beyond what would constitute international crimes. Nevertheless, he later recommended companies to ascertain their human rights responsibilities with reference to the International Bill of Rights and the ILO's Declaration on Fundamental Principles and Rights at Work. The SRSG sought to resolve this apparent contradiction by invoking the 'social expectations' rationale. The amorphousness inherent in the

---

[38] International Covenant on Economic, Social and Cultural Rights, 993 UNTS 3, Art. 2.

notion of 'social expectations' enabled him to present – without much empirical support – the responsibility to respect human rights as a 'global standard of expected conduct'.[39]

Grounding the human rights responsibilities of corporations in social expectations is problematic for a number of reasons, elaborated upon in several contributions to this volume. If such expectations simply involve voluntary adherence, then the SRSG failed to recognise limitations of soft-voluntary regulation as well as the 'business case' for human rights that led to the push for imposing legally binding human rights obligations on corporations. Voluntarism is also problematic in this context because human rights do not give rise to optional responsibilities.[40] If social expectations involve some binding component, what is that element? The SRSG at times seems to suggest that this ultimately lies in the self-interest of corporations, a 'social license to operate',[41] without which they would not be able to conduct their businesses effectively. But we assert that compliance with human rights norms should be a non-negotiable precondition for doing business, rather than becoming a matter of expediency, only being relevant when it might impact (adversely or positively) the bottom line of companies.

Pillars: an adequate response to the challenges?

Both the Framework and the GPs are based on what the SRSG terms as the three pillars: the state duty to protect human rights, the corporate responsibility to respect human rights, and the access to remedies.[42] We consider briefly whether each of these pillars offers an adequate response to the challenges.

The first pillar of the Framework and the GPs brings back the focus on the role of states in safeguarding individuals from human rights violations by non-state actors. The 'protect' obligation of states involves ensuring that corporations do not commit human rights abuses. This requires states to take 'appropriate steps to prevent, investigate, punish and redress such abuse through effective policies, legislation, regulations and adjudication'.[43] By retaining the state as the predominant institution

---

[39] SRSG, 'Guiding Principles', n. 2, Commentary on Principle 11.
[40] D. Bilchitz, 'Corporate Law and the Constitution' (2008) 125 *South African Law Journal* 760–61.
[41] SRSG, '2008 Framework', n. 1, para. 54.
[42] *Ibid.*, para. 9; SRSG, 'Guiding Principles', n. 2, General Principles.
[43] SRSG, 'Guiding Principles', n. 2, Principle 1.

for the regulation of MNCs and denying that companies have any direct human rights obligations under international law, the SRSG embraced the traditional approach of international law towards non-state actors. States undoubtedly have a critical role in ensuring that companies do not violate human rights. Yet, there are significant limitations to this indirect approach. States, on occasion, are unable and/or unwilling to discharge their well-established duty to protect individuals against human rights abuses by private actors operating in or from their territory. The SRSG was aware of this limitation, but still insisted on relying primarily upon states to enforce human rights obligations against companies. In the absence of any international mechanism, victims can be left without any effective remedy where states are unable or unwilling to perform their duty.

Does the obligation of states to protect individuals extend outside their respective territories? The GPs answer the question in a diplomatic manner: states are neither required nor prohibited under international human rights law to regulate the extraterritorial activities of companies domiciled within their territory and/or jurisdiction.[44] This stance is far from satisfactory because 'home' states of MNCs must be required to act where 'host' states lack the capacity or willingness – whether on account of conflicts, weak governance or authoritarian regimes – to regulate effectively corporate actors operating within their territorial boundaries.[45] As Augenstein and Kinley demonstrate in Chapter 11, it is also arguably inconsistent with international human rights jurisprudence in this area.

On the positive side, the GPs rightly remind states to take multiple regulatory and policy measures to create an environment that encourages companies to respect human rights. States, for example, should ensure that corporate law does 'not constrain but enable business respect for human rights',[46] that they 'maintain adequate domestic policy space to meet their human rights obligations when pursuing business-related policy objectives with other States or business enterprises',[47] and that multilateral institutions dealing with business-related issues do not restrain their ability to protect human rights.[48] While this might sound

---

[44] *Ibid.*, Commentary on Principle 2.

[45] See S. Deva, 'Acting Extraterritorially to Tame Multinational Corporations for Human Rights Violations: Who Should "Bell the Cat"?' (2004) 5 *Melbourne Journal of International Law* 37.

[46] SRSG, 'Guiding Principles', n. 2, Principle 3(b).   [47] *Ibid.*, Principle 9.

[48] *Ibid.*, Principle 10.

paradoxical, the GPs recommend states to be proactive in ensuring that companies operating in conflict-affected areas do not become involved with human rights abuses.[49]

Since the SRSG conceived of companies as 'specialized organs, performing specialized functions',[50] he differentiated their human rights obligations from that of states. Indeed, the SRSG even distinguishes the language employed in relation to corporations: companies do not have any binding obligations; rather, they merely have *responsibilities*. The responsibility of corporations is articulated as being merely to 'respect' human rights, which the SRSG defines as avoiding an infringement of such rights. The focus is thus upon a negative responsibility not to infringe rights rather than on any positive responsibility to assist in the realisation of human rights. Whilst, at times, positive actions may be necessary to 'address adverse human rights impacts', the focus of any such action is linked to the avoidance of harm. This approach has reduced expectations of business and has undoubtedly played a role in business support for the SRSG's work. Yet, we are of the view that it unreasonably restricts the scope of corporate human rights responsibilities.

In order to discharge their responsibility to respect human rights, companies are required to take a range of measures. They should adopt a 'policy commitment to meet their responsibility to respect human rights', conduct a due diligence enquiry 'to identify, prevent, mitigate and account for how they address their impacts on human rights', and have in place processes 'to enable the remediation of any adverse human rights impacts they cause or to which they contribute'.[51] A key element of the SRSG's proposals in this regard is the due diligence process: the GPs outline in detail a range of measures that a company should take to manage risks associated with human rights violations.[52] Continuous due diligence should be exercised by the company not only in relation to its own activities, but also regarding activities 'which may be directly linked to its operations, products or services by its business relationships'.[53] The term 'business relationships' includes the supply chain, but it is very unclear if it is intended to encompass subsidiaries too. This seemingly intentional ambiguity concerning the responsibility of a parent company for the conduct of its subsidiaries is consistent with the general approach adopted by the SRSG to bypass contentious issues.

---

[49] *Ibid.*, Principle 7.   [50] SRSG, '2006 Interim Report', n. 9, para. 66.
[51] SRSG, 'Guiding Principles', n. 2, Principle 15.   [52] *Ibid.*, Principles 17–21.
[53] *Ibid.*, Principle 17(a).

Under certain circumstances, corporations may be held responsible for being 'complicit' in the actions of third parties.[54] The SRSG closely links conducting due diligence measures to the avoidance of complicity, an issue that has stimulated two contributions in this volume.

The third pillar of the Framework and Part III of the GPs relate to access to diverse remedies for victims of corporate human rights abuses. Whereas states must take appropriate judicial, administrative, legislative or other steps to ensure access to an effective remedy,[55] companies should establish or participate in effective grievance mechanisms for individuals and communities who may be adversely affected by their operations.[56] The GPs acknowledge various legal, procedural and practical barriers to accessing judicial remedies against companies to seek redress for human rights violations.[57] The SRSG also outlines in detail the 'effectiveness criteria' for non-judicial mechanisms.[58]

Several points of critique can also be made in relation to this pillar. Although access to a remedy is considered to be an independent human right under international human rights instruments, the GPs essentially construe this pillar as flowing from both the state duty to protect human rights and the corporate responsibility to respect human rights. It also appears that the GPs give preference to non-judicial mechanisms over judicial remedies. To illustrate, whereas the SRSG devoted significant attention to outlining the 'effectiveness criteria' for non-judicial grievance mechanisms, hardly any attempt was made to canvass some policy options for states to reduce well-known barriers to judicial remedies. Finally, what if companies do not put in place operational-level grievance mechanisms, or the established mechanisms fail to meet the effectiveness criteria? The GPs do not really indicate the role that states and market forces could play in encouraging companies to take this recommendation seriously.

Too many bypassed questions?

We have so far reviewed what the SRSG has proposed. Yet, it is also instructive to consider what he omitted to propose. In seeking to achieve consensus, the SRSG seemingly followed an 'unstated' principle throughout his mandate, that is, to bypass contentious issues or not

---

[54] *Ibid.*, Commentary on Principle 17 and Principle 23 (including Commentary).
[55] *Ibid.*, Principle 25.   [56] *Ibid.*, Principle 29.   [57] *Ibid.*, Commentary on Principle 26.
[58] *Ibid.*, Principle 31 (including Commentary).

take any clear stand on them. It is, for instance, not easy to ascertain and catalogue the exact human rights obligations of companies. So, the SRSG avoided this complex task by referring companies to the International Bill of Rights, despite knowing full well that deducing responsibilities of companies with reference to these state-centric instruments would not be straightforward. Similarly, should a parent company be liable for human rights violations carried out by its subsidiaries and/or be allowed to plead *forum non conveniens* to frustrate victims' quest for justice? While the GPs identified these as legal barriers that victims experience in holding companies accountable for human rights abuses,[59] no serious attempt was made to outline the kinds of steps that states could (and should) take to reduce these barriers.

The fact that companies can cause irreparable harm to the environment is well documented – from the Bhopal gas disaster to the BP oil spill in the Gulf of Mexico.[60] Even the SRSG in his reports acknowledged that companies can adversely affect the environment, that states face challenges in regulating companies in this regard, and that certain environmental initiatives/standards envisage responsibilities for business.[61] Nevertheless, the GPs neither explicitly prescribe any *direct* environmental responsibilities of companies nor refer to any environmental convention or declaration. Similarly, women, children and indigenous people are treated no better by the SRSG. Despite being specifically requested by the HRC to 'integrate a gender perspective throughout his work and to give special attention to persons belonging to vulnerable groups, in particular children',[62] the GPs do not include international instruments concerning the special interests of these groups in the 'minimum' list of internationally recognised human rights.

---

[59] *Ibid.*, Commentary on Principle 26.

[60] Amnesty International, *Clouds of Injustice: Bhopal Disaster 20 Years On* (London: Amnesty International, 2004); National Commission on the BP Deepwater Horizon Oil Spill and Offshore Drilling (US), *Deep Water: The Gulf Oil Disaster and the Future of Offshore Drilling* (2011).

[61] SRSG, '2006 Interim Report', n. 9, paras. 15 and 29; SRSG, '2008 Framework', n. 1, paras. 12, 30, 34–35 and 61; Human Rights Council, 'Business and Human Rights: Further Steps toward the Operationalization of the "Protect, Respect and Remedy" Framework', A/HRC/14/27 (9 April 2010), paras. 24, 29, 35, 40, 46, 69 and 91.

[62] Human Rights Council, 'Mandate of the Special Representative of the Secretary-General on the Issue of Human Rights and Transnational Corporations and Other Business Enterprises', Resolution 8/7 (18 June 2008), para. 4(d).

The Framework and the GPs: a critical evaluation vis-à-vis the four questions

We have so far outlined some key features of the Framework/GPs as well as several key lines of criticism. The authors in this volume focus on particular aspects of the SRSG's work. Some authors are of the view that the SRSG's work represents progress in particular areas that need further clarification and development in future. Others try and demonstrate that the SRSG mandate has taken the wrong course for business and human rights and that some of its core conceptual elements are mistaken. There are some similarities between the concerns of authors: most of them are worried about the 'narrow', 'imprecise' and 'non-binding' character of corporate human rights responsibilities canvassed in the Framework and the GPs or about the effective enforcement of such responsibilities. In this section, we seek to situate the different positions taken by authors in this volume in relation to the four key questions identified above. Clearly, there is an overlap between the four questions, and the answers provided by authors to one particular question can have an impact on others or may relate to more than one of the questions. The structure is not meant to be watertight but simply to assist in locating each author's chapter in relation to a dominant focus of engagement.

Process and methodology

Why did the SRSG succeed in securing unanimous support for the Framework as well as the GPs, while his predecessors failed on this front? Chapter 2 by Karin Buhmann tries to answer this question by employing systems theory-based reflexive law and discourse theory. She argues that the SRSG was successful in securing the support of companies because he strategically used the language that appealed to the business community. By framing corporate human rights responsibilities in terms of 'social expectations' and linking non-compliance with them to the 'courts of public opinion', the SRSG highlighted economic risks to business that may result from their disregard of human rights. Due diligence again proved popular with companies because they could relate to this familiar process as a means to discharge their responsibility to respect human rights.

In Chapter 3, Carlos López provides another perpective on the process adopted by the SRSG. He examines whether the GPs represent a definitive shift towards corporate social responsibility by conceiving the human rights responsibilities of business in 'voluntary' terms. This process, he contends, resulted in steering the debate away from putting in place legally binding international human rights norms applicable to companies. López also questions the grounding of the corporate responsibility to respect as a 'social norm'. For instance, when social expectations by their very nature are bound to evolve and change over time, how could the GPs claim to be comprehensive and authoritative? Moreover, he questions the sidelining of victims from the consultation process and points out that the consensual acceptance of the GPs cannot hide the view of many actors that stronger rules are needed to tame MNCs. López wonders whether 'the "Ruggie process" appears to have ended where it started, with the fundamental question of whether business corporations are bound by international human rights law, and if so, which rights are they bound to respect' remaining unanswered.

While Buhmann sees virtues in engaging the business community in the language that they understand, Surya Deva contends in Chapter 4 that the GPs dilute the human rights responsibilities of business by a deliberate use of carefully chosen terms (e.g. 'responsibility' rather than 'duty'; 'impact' rather than 'violation') and concepts (e.g. social expectations and due diligence). Deva also exposes the fragility and hollowness of the oft-quoted claim that the GPs represent a 'consensus' on the issue of business and human rights. He demonstrates – by comparing the text of the draft GPs and the final GPs – that the *core* of the Ruggie project was not open for change. In other words, extensive consultations did not mean much. Deva, in short, tries to show how the GPs have not taken the human rights discourse seriously.

Source and justifications of corporate obligations

While dealing with the source and justifications of corporate human rights obligations, David Bilchitz, in Chapter 5, identifies two notions of normativity: 'binding normativity' relates to the bindingness of legal rules and principles, while 'moral normativity' concerns the moral justification for an entity to have obligations. He contests the SRSG's rejection of law as a source of binding normativity for corporate human rights obligations. Bilchitz makes a positive and negative argument. The positive argument is that binding obligations for corporations can be derived from international human rights law by necessary implication. The negative argument seeks to show why 'social expectations' are an inadequate source of binding normativity. The root of the problem, according to Bilchitz, lies in the failure of the SRSG to engage adequately with the moral normative foundations of human rights. Engaging with these philosophical questions would result in the conclusion that corporations are not only bound by existing human rights law but also that their obligations extend beyond the realm of the responsibility to respect. By considering the obligations of both the state and individuals in relation to human rights, Bilchitz argues that corporations should have to shoulder the burden of positive responsibilities to help fulfil rights and, in particular, to address some of the most pressing global challenges arising from severe poverty around the globe. He suggests, importantly, that obligations for human rights realisation should not be conceived of competitively but rather as a collaborative endeavour amongst a range of social actors.

In Chapter 6, Justine Nolan focuses on the question of binding normativity and, in particular, the role of 'soft law' in helping to regulate business activity in relation to human rights. For Nolan, the Framework and the GPs are a form of 'soft law'. She provides a historical backdrop to explain why the SRSG opted for such an approach given the failure to achieve any significant agreement on more binding initiatives at the international level. Nolan argues that 'soft law' initiatives are valuable and are not simply voluntary in nature: some codes of conduct in this field are so widely accepted that they are in essence 'binding' on corporations operating in these areas. Key criteria to consider in the effectiveness of soft law relate to whether these initiatives are 'consistent, comprehensive and implemented'. Nolan contends that, unfortunately, many features of the SRSG's work are 'too soft': the source of corporate responsibility is inchoate and the language adopted in the GPs is weak and non-authoritative. Echoing a similar point made by Deva, she writes that these soft law guidelines 'prize dialogue and consensus over ambition'. One way of strengthening the SRSG's work is to require states to ensure that the due diligence component of the corporate responsibility to respect becomes legally binding.

Recognising the need to render soft law more binding, in Chapter 7 Anita Ramasastry considers the road not taken by the SRSG: could a binding treaty comprehensively outlining corporate human rights obligations be developed? Against the backdrop of the history relating to this issue, the author first outlines the reasons the SRSG gave for refusing to follow a treaty route. Although recognising that he was probably correct in the shorter term, Ramasastry does not believe that the international community should forego all hopes of a binding treaty (or treaties) on these issues in the longer term. In considering how such a treaty might evolve, she draws on a comparison with the adoption of the United Nations Convention Against Corruption (UNCAC), which came into force on 14 December 2005. Thirty years of international discussions culminated in this development, and only after strong state practice and regulation had emerged. The author notes that, in a similar way, binding rules for corporations are beginning to be recognised in a diverse range of fields such as in relation to illegal logging and conflict minerals. Ramasastry argues that the emerging practice in the business and human rights field might suggest that it is better to develop a series of concrete treaties in particular areas rather than one comprehensive human rights instrument that will of necessity attempt to cover perhaps too many diverse social issues.

Nature and extent of corporate obligations

Multiple issues arise in relation to the nature and extent of corporate obligations. In Chapter 8, Bonita Meyersfeld explores an under-investigated issue, that is, the gendered analysis of the Framework and the GPs. She begins by making a case for the business and human rights debate to include an analysis of gender. Meyersfeld rightly anticipates a legitimate question in this regard: why should the experience of women receive special consideration and not also the experiences of children, the disabled and indigenous groups? Her response is that the gender lens should be invoked for all human rights norms because the 'manifestation of a seemingly generic human rights violation may be different for women depending on the communal, social or state policies that define women's experiences in society'. Meyersfeld goes on to explore the scope and content of a gendered analysis of the business and human rights discourse, especially in relation to the state duty to protect human rights and the corporate responsibility to respect human rights (including the due diligence processes).

The next two chapters in this volume – Chapter 9 by Sabine Michalowski and Florian Wettstein's Chapter 10 – confront the issue of corporate complicity. Michalowski addresses the relationship between the responsibility to conduct due diligence investigations and the responsibility to avoid being complicit with third parties in human rights abuses. She addresses two main questions: firstly, whether due diligence can function as a tool to avoid complicity; and secondly, the role of due diligence where a corporation is faced with complicity charges. In relation to the first issue, common sense suggests that complicity can be avoided by conducting an adequate due diligence process. However, the problem, as Michalowski points out, is that the notion of complicity is not limited to what would attract legal liability but also includes social and non-legal understandings of this notion such as beneficial and silent complicity. Given the lack of clear definitions for these forms of complicity, the scope and ambit of a due diligence responsibility are thus somewhat undefined. The inclusion of non-legal notions of complicity by the SRSG, Michalowski argues, has both positive and negative effects: companies are required by the GPs to be more vigilant in relation to a wider range of possible areas in which they can be complicit; on the other hand, a violation of such wide due diligence responsibilities will often not have enforceable consequences. On the second issue, Michalowski demonstrates that the SRSG does not envisage that a properly conducted due diligence enquiry will function as a *complete* defence against complicity charges. She argues that this approach could have the perverse effect of discouraging companies from being too proactive in exercising their due diligence responsibilities so they can avoid finding out about areas of possible complicity. Ultimately, Michalowski favours an approach whereby a properly exercised due diligence process can exclude legal liability for complicity.

Wettstein too concerns himself with a facet of the SRSG's wide approach to complicity and, in particular, with the non-legal notion of 'silent complicity'. As his chapter notes, the SRSG includes the avoidance of silent complicity within the ambit of the corporate responsibility to respect rights. Wettstein then analyses the notion of silent complicity which, he argues, presupposes a duty to speak out against human rights abuses. Such a duty arises when four conditions are met: the corporation must have some leverage over the perpetrator, must not be jeopardised to an unreasonable degree if it speaks out, must have a morally significant connection to the human rights abuse, and must have some social or political status in order for its actions to carry weight. However, if corporations have such a responsibility to avoid silent complicity, then this means that they have clear positive obligations to take active steps to distance themselves from abuses. Yet, the SRSG claims that corporations primarily only have negative responsibilities to avoid harming rights that flow from the 'corporate responsibility to respect'. Wettstein thus demonstrates that there is an inconsistency at the heart of the SRSG's Framework: either the SRSG must give up the notion that corporations only have negative responsibilities or he must eliminate the notion of silent complicity from his Framework. Like Bilchitz, Wettstein sees this inconsistency as arising from the failure of the SRSG to engage with the deeper normative questions regarding the ambit and scope of corporate human rights obligations.

Implementation and enforcement

The last four chapters in this volume explore different possible approaches to the implementation and enforcement of human rights obligations in relation to companies. Chapter 11, by Augenstein and Kinley, responds to a hotly contested aspect of the GPs, namely, whether states have an extraterritorial obligation to regulate overseas operations of companies domiciled within their territory and/or jurisdiction. After pointing out that economic globalisation poses significant challenges to the Westphalian paradigm of human rights protection that allocates human rights obligations within and between sovereign states, the authors posit that, under the Framework's first pillar, 'states have both direct (vertical) obligations as regards their own actions and indirect obligations to ensure the horizontal protection of the human rights of individuals within their jurisdiction against corporate violations'. Augenstein and Kinley contend that the question of whether states are *permitted* to take measures to better promote and protect human rights in relation to extraterritorial corporate abuse (the 'permissive question') is quite different from the question of whether states are *obliged* to do so as a matter of international human rights law (the 'prescriptive question'). The GPs, they argue, marginalise the 'prescriptive question' in favour of the 'permissive question'. By relying on extensive human rights case law, Augenstein and Kinley demonstrate that what is decisive for the determination of extraterritorial human rights obligations to protect against corporate violations is not the state's exercise of *de jure* authority, but its assertion of *de facto* power over the individual rights holder.

Nicola Jägers is impressed with the power of certain 'soft' initiatives to have an effect on the activities of business in relation to human rights. Her Chapter 12 begins by praising the SRSG for recognising the power of transnational private regulation in this area. The mandatory/voluntary dichotomy, she argues, is no longer that important as corporations respond to a range of pressures from diverse stakeholders, including from consumers, investors, employees, and the wider societies in which they operate. Increasingly, corporations choose to join transnational private regulatory regimes that have a variety of benefits for them. Yet, to be effective, Jägers argues, the availability of transparent information concerning the activities and impact of corporations is vital because it enables stakeholders to put pressure on them to join such initiatives and to hold them to their commitments. She stresses the need for information to be made available that can be independently verified such that it does not simply become a marketing tool for corporations. She argues that the right to independent information flows from international law and that this should be the basis for future developments in this area.

Lambooy, Argyrou and Varner are concerned specifically with the usefulness of the GPs in determining how corporations should approach the provision of remedies to victims of human rights violations. Their Chapter 13 adopts a more empirical approach than other contributions in this volume. After outlining various criteria developed by the SRSG for effective remedies, the authors examine three case studies of oil spills where corporations have negatively impacted upon human rights and the environment. An analysis of these case studies against the effectiveness criteria identified in the GPs leads the authors to reach conclusions about what needs to be done to improve access to effective remedies. They find that the remedies offered in these cases mostly fall short in relation to the criteria of accessibility (to the victims) and transparency (by the corporations). The focus of remedies still lies largely in judicial proceedings: these are often difficult for victims to access and the authors recommend wider use of alternative, non-judicial remedies. The case studies suggest how such alternatives should be structured and demonstrate the need for governmental oversight over any private sector remedies that are offered.

Richard Meeran, in Chapter 14, examines an alternative route – tort action – to render companies accountable for human rights violations. Drawing on his unparalleled experience of litigation against MNCs, he argues that tort law offers a viable option to enforce human rights against companies. More importantly, Meeran shows how the principles developed by the United Kingdom courts could help in overcoming substantive (piercing of the corporate veil), procedural (the doctrine of *forum non conveniens*) and practical (costs and incentives for claimants' lawyers) obstacles to access to justice. While he applauds the judicial innovations in this area (e.g. the evolution of a parent company's direct duty of care), Meeran criticises the United Kingdom government for supporting the GPs but at the same time enacting the Legal Aid, Sentencing and Punishment of Offenders Act 2012, which will have a detrimental effect on victims' quest to seek justice against MNCs.

The future of business and human rights: moving beyond the *responsibility* to *respect*?

The various perspectives provided in this book highlight the fact that the Framework and the GPs, whilst valuable, contain many ambiguities, inconsistencies and areas which have not been developed sufficiently. The Working Group, which has succeeded the SRSG's mandate, should not, in our view, focus its activities solely on disseminating and implementating the GPs, but also on building on the norms contained therein and seeking to address some of their fundamental problems. In our view, and considering the views expressed in this book, the next phase of the business and human rights debate needs to focus on a number of issues.

Firstly, in relation to process, we think that the SRSG did not give adequate expression to the concerns and perspectives of the human rights community. Nor does the text of the final products – the Framework and the GPs – reflect its concerns. In going forward, the focus should be on adopting positions that are best from the perspective of realising human rights and not just those that are likely to win the support of business.

Secondly, there is a need to try developing a more binding character for the human rights obligations of corporations. Such obligations, of course, could be expressly recognised in a treaty which, given current political realities, could be developed only in the distant future. In the interim, such binding obligations can be read in through a purposive interpretation of international human rights instruments, the implementation of international human rights norms under domestic law, and declarations of commitment to the International Bill of Rights by corporations in their voluntary codes. States have a critical role to play in developing their constitutional and legislative frameworks to recognise such binding obligations. Courts can also help firm up some of these obligations. The development of state and regional regulation over time can have an important impact on the evolution of international binding norms in the longer term.

Thirdly, the human rights obligations of companies should be firmly grounded in a sound normative base (e.g. the philosophical underpinnings of human rights) rather than social expectations or the self-serving 'business case' for human rights.

Fourthly, there is a need to extend corporate obligations beyond a responsibility to respect. While a few authors have shown how the notion of complicity may link to an obligation to protect, others have contended that there is also a responsibility upon corporations to contribute positively towards the realisation of human rights. Further work is needed to define the ambit and scope as well as the limits of such obligations to 'protect' and 'fulfil' human rights.

Finally, ways to overcome legal (both substantive and procedural) and practical barriers experienced by victims in their attempts to make companies accountable for human rights violations must be considered. It should not be forgotten that non-judicial grievance mechanisms will become more effective if supported by robust judicial mechanisms.

The SRSG's work, in our view, should not be discounted: it has produced a number of useful reports which have dealt with a wide range of issues connected with business and human rights. The Framework and the GPs should not, however, be the last word on the subject. The chapters in this volume will hopefully stimulate debate and discussion about the trajectory that should be followed in taking the business and human rights debate 'beyond' the conceptual contours set by the SRSG. We need to envision a future in which the global market-place understands the normative commitments underpinning the international order and the role of the business sector is harnessed to meet the challenges of human rights realisation in the twenty-first century.

PART I

Process and methodology

2

Navigating from 'train wreck' to being 'welcomed': negotiation strategies and argumentative patterns in the development of the UN Framework

KARIN BUHMANN

The creation of the Special Representative post came about as a result of a train wreck in Geneva. It was an outgrowth of an effort by the Sub-Commission for Human Rights to draft what was intended ultimately as a legal code, called the Norms, regulating the human rights impact of multi-national corporations ... This endeavour produced a train wreck because much of the business community was vehemently opposed to it, as were many governments.[1]

Introduction

During his 2005–2008 mandate as the Special Representative of the Secretary-General (SRSG), John Ruggie developed the 'Protect, Respect and Remedy' Framework (Framework), which was 'unanimously welcomed' by the UN Human Rights Council (HRC) in 2008.[2] This stands in stark contrast to the reception of the Norms on the Responsibilities of Transnational Corporations and Other Business Enterprises with Regard to Human Rights (UN Norms)[3] that had been developed between 1998 and 2003 by a Sub-Commission under the UN

---

[1] SRSG, 'Remarks: Delivered at a Forum on Corporate Social Responsibility, Co-Sponsored by the Fair Labor Association and the German Network of Business Ethics, Bamberg, Germany' (14 June 2006) (SRSG, '2006 Remarks').

[2] Human Rights Council, 'Resolution 8/7: Mandate of the Special Representative of the Secretary-General on the Issue of Human Rights and Transnational Corporations and Other Business Enterprises' (18 June 2008).

[3] Sub-Commission on the Promotion and Protection of Human Rights, 'Norms on the Responsibilities of Transnational Corporations and Other Business Enterprises with Regard to Human Rights', E/CN.4/Sub.2/2003/12/Rev.2 (26 August 2003) (UN Norms).

Human Rights Commission (Commission). The Commission's debate in 2004 led to a resolution, noting that the UN Norms 'as a draft proposal' had no legal standing.[4] Subsequently, the debate became heated to the extent that the SRSG characterised the UN Norms project metaphorically as a 'train wreck in Geneva'.[5] The SRSG process stands apart from the UN Norms process by more factors than the SRSG's formal appointment by the UN Secretary-General. In particular, the SRSG process involved business organisations to a more extensive degree than is conventional in international (human rights) law-making, and in the capacity as prospective duty-holders. While inherently related to the core of the project on the human rights responsibilities of business, which implies that companies should have duties regarding human rights, this differs from other human rights law-making because non-state actors are normally addressed and involved in international law-making as rights-holders.[6]

Under international law, multinational corporations (MNCs) are neither duty-holders nor entitled to participate in law-making. Yet, in his 1964 study on the changing character of international law, Wolfgang Friedman argued for their inclusion in international law-making.[7] In 1983, Jonathan Charney contended that because MNCs represent major independent powers of influence, failure to include them in negotiations under the UN or other inter-governmental auspices to produce norms for MNCs' behaviour would result in rules that do not accurately reflect the realities of MNC interest and power.[8] The absence of MNCs' participation would lead to resistance to implementation and non-compliance with rules.[9] At the present time of climate and other sustainability concerns requiring global solutions affecting not only governments but also the private sector, understanding how to develop norms with broad support is crucial.

---

[4] Commission on Human Rights, 'Resolution 2004/11', E/CN.4/2004/L.73/Rev.1 (20 April 2004).

[5] SRSG, '2006 Remarks', n. 1.

[6] See K. Buhmann, 'The Development of the UN Framework: A Pragmatic Process towards a Pragmatic Output' in R. Mares (ed.), *The UN Guiding Principles on Business and Human Rights: Foundations and Implementations* (Boston: Martinus Nijhoff, 2012), 85.

[7] W. Friedmann, *The Changing Structure of International Law* (London: Stevens & Sons, 1964), 71 and 85.

[8] J. I. Charney, 'Transnational Corporations and Developing Public International Law' (1983) 32 *Duke Law Journal* 748, at 756.

[9] *Ibid.*

The Framework attains a character of international law-in-the-making with the UN Guiding Principles on Business and Human Rights (GPs) based on it. The difference in the making of the Framework and that of the UN Norms as well as some other previous efforts under the UN to formulate norms for business in relation to human rights makes the 2005–2008 SRSG process an obvious candidate for analysis to seek to identify what caused such difference.

Adopting a socio-legal perspective, combining reflexive law with discourse theory, this chapter considers the argumentative structures and strategies of the SRSG, business representatives and civil society during the 2005–2008 mandate in order to understand how these elements contributed to an output whose fate has been radically different to that of its predecessor.

Due to space constraints, this chapter is limited to the SRSG's 2005–2008 mandate. This mandate formed much of the basis for argumentative patterns and related dynamics during the 2008–2011 mandate that led to the GPs.

Theoretical framework and methodology: reflexive law and discourse analysis

Fundamentally concerned with effective regulation through self-regulation, systems theory-based reflexive law considers society as a composition of social sub-systems, notably the political system (which comprises not only formal and informal policy-makers, but also executives and other implementing agencies), the economic system (companies) and the legal system (courts and other legal institutions).[10] According to systems theory, sub-systems communicate through 'binary codes' (language) based on their key interests. The political system code relates to power/no power and related binaries, and by extension to the implementation/non-implementation of public policy goals. The economic system code relates to profit/no profit and related binaries, and the legal system code to coercive/non-coercive and related binaries.[11] Through autopoiesis that builds on systems theory, a system

---

[10] See N. Luhmann, 'Limits of Steering' (1996) 14 *Theory, Culture and Society* 41; and 'The Coding of the Legal System' in G. Teubner and A. Febbrajo (eds.), *State, Law and Economy as Autopoietic Systems: Regulation and Autonomy in a New Perspective* (Milan: Guiffre, 1992), 146.

[11] P. Edwards (ed. in chief), 'The Encyclopedia of Philosophy' (New York: Macmillan Publishing, 1972) (entry 'System, formal, and models of formal systems'); N. A. Andersen, 'Supervisionsstaten og den politiske virksomhed' in F. Christian (ed.), *Virksomhedens*

changes or recreates itself based on a process of responding to perturbation caused by the environment. This may lead to self-regulation. In other words, the political system does not change the legal system but may provide perturbation which, as a result of the legal system's internal reaction, may lead to change. The SRSG process may be considered to function as a reflexive law forum.[12] The SRSG himself did not represent one social sub-system, but acted on behalf of the Commission/HRC, a body charged with monitoring international human rights law and promoting the realisation of human rights as matters of policy and law.

A sub-system may draw on ('mimic') another sub-system's codes to affect changes within the recipient system. For example, changes within the economic system related to perturbation caused by the use of economic system's language making reference to that system's profit-generating interest should lead to self-regulation or acceptance rather than resistance to external demands. This realisation may lead to collaboration rather than antagonism.

Discourse analysis is a method for studying processes related to the establishment of societal constructs, for example policies, norms, and normative concepts such as corporate social responsibility (CSR). Originating in linguistics and elaborated in political science, discourse analysis in legal studies is a relatively novel but not untested method in legal scholarship, particularly within international law-related studies.[13]

By analysing statements as discursive usage of system-specific language to induce perturbation with recipients, the subsequent analysis in this chapter illustrates how such communication worked as a dynamic in the SRSG process towards the construction and reception of the UN Framework.

Politisering (Frederiksberg: Samfundslitteratur, 2004), 231 at 236. To put the distinction into perspective, the system of medicine encodes, or constructs, the world into what is healthy and what is unhealthy, that of science into what is true or false, and that of accountancy into debits and credits. G. Teubner, R. Nobles and D. Schiff, 'The Autonomy of Law: An Introduction to Legal Autopoiesis' in J. Penner, D. Schiff and R. Nobles (eds.), *Jurisprudence* (New York: Oxford University Press, 2005), 897.

[12] See K. Buhmann, 'Regulating Corporate Social and Human Rights Responsibilities at the UN Plane: Institutionalising New Forms of Law and Law-making Approaches?' (2009) 78 *Nordic Journal of International Law* 1, at 46–48.

[13] See, for example, R. Holdgaard, *Legal Reasoning and Legal Discourses: External Relations Law of the European Community* (The Hague: Kluwer Law International, 2008); D. Kennedy, 'The Sources of International Law' (1987) 2 *American University Journal of Law and Policy* 1.

From the UN Norms to the SRSG mandate

Conflicting stances were at play around and after the presentation of the UN Norms in 2003. From the Commission's discussion of the UN Norms in 2003 to its resolution on the SRSG mandate in April 2005, the debate was marked by contention and antagonism between governments, and between civil society and business organisations. In line with much debate at UN human rights bodies, statements made in the language of the legal system dominated. Legal system language was especially prominent in arguments from organisations and states opposed to the idea of institutionalising human rights responsibilities for business. International business organisations and the International Confederation of Free Trade Unions (ICFTU) argued against the UN developing standards of conduct on human rights for business.[14] These organisations employed legal and political systems language to address international law-makers and policy-makers. By referring to international law doctrines and policy objectives on democracy, the organisations addressed recipients in the systems-specific language of the audiences, using arguments apt to cause irritation within the recipient systems. Some governments' usage of political system language, especially on business contributions to international development, also had the potential to cause 'irritation' among states and civil society by relating to their policy objectives on international development and social and economic rights.[15]

In April 2005, the Commission adopted a resolution requesting the Secretary-General to appoint a Special Representative on the issue of human rights and business enterprises.[16] The mandate included identification and clarification of standards of corporate responsibility and accountability for business enterprises with regard to human rights; elaboration of the role of states in effectively regulating and adjudicating the role of business enterprises with regard to human rights; and clarification of the implications for business enterprises of concepts such as 'complicity' and 'sphere of influence'.[17]

The resolution referenced a 2005 report on business and human rights prepared by the Office of the High Commissioner for Human Rights (OHCHR), which had been drafted on the basis of a consultative process

---

[14] Buhmann, 'The Development of the UN Framework', n. 6, at 96–101. [15] *Ibid.*
[16] Commission on Human Rights, 'Human Rights and Transnational Corporations and Other Business Enterprises', E/CN.4/2005/L.87 (15 April 2005).
[17] *Ibid.*, para. 1.

involving business representatives as well as representatives of other
non-state actors. Wording employed in the Preamble of the mandate
resolution indicates that the Commission made an explicit effort to
include and address concerns that had led to the mixed reception of
the UN Norms. The resolution requested the mandate-holder 'to consult
on an ongoing basis with all stakeholders'.[18] It listed not only states and
inter-governmental organisations but also 'transnational corporations
and other business enterprises, and civil society, including employers'
organizations, workers' organizations, indigenous and other affected
communities and non-governmental organizations'[19] among the parties
to be consulted. The instructions indicate that inclusion of a wide group
of stakeholders was intended to facilitate a widely accepted outcome.
Referring to 'channelling the benefits of business towards'[20] the promotion of respect for human rights, the impact of business on human rights
is worded in an affirmative manner rather than with emphasis on
adverse impact. Opening the resolution on a positive (rather than a
business-critical) note sent an inclusive message of recognition to
those who represented business interests.

From the establishment of the mandate to the 2006 interim report

The first year of the SRSG's 2005–2008 mandate culminated with the
presentation of the interim report in 2006. The report basically ended
further discussion of the UN Norms during the mandate. As the fate of
the UN Norms in relation to the SRSG's work was unknown (and
unexpected) to many actors, several statements made during the first
year continued to refer to the UN Norms.

A statement from Amnesty International upon the Commission's
adoption of the mandate resolution noted that '[t]he UN Norms are
the most comprehensive statement of standards relevant to companies in
relation to human rights'.[21] References to 'standards', holding companies 'accountable' and identification of 'mechanisms to ensure these
standards are adhered to'[22] exemplify extensive legal system-orientated

---

[18] *Ibid.*, para. 3.   [19] *Ibid.*   [20] *Ibid.*, Preamble.
[21] Amnesty International, '2005 UN Commission on Human Rights: Amnesty
International Welcomes New UN Mechanism on Business and Human Rights', IOR
41/044/2005 (21 April 2005), www.amnesty.org/en/library/info/IOR41/044/2005 (last
accessed 6 January 2013) (Amnesty International, 'Public Statement 2005').
[22] *Ibid.*

language, probably both mirroring tradition and style in the interaction of human rights non-governmental organisations (NGOs) with the UN human rights system, and the (habitual) style of communication with a legal environment.

In a June 2005 statement, the International Commission of Jurists (ICJ) proposed applying 'due diligence' in the human rights and business context in relation to states' duties.[23] As an organisation comprising lawyers and judges, the ICJ's audience would include public as well as private and company lawyers. The ICJ supported the idea of making clear to companies that they should not disregard their impact on human rights. Due diligence processes are common in corporate law activities of law firms in relation to mergers and acquisitions. However, in that context due diligence is related to financial and not human rights obligations. Due diligence was not employed in the text of the UN Norms, but was mentioned twice in the appended Commentary with reference to companies.[24] Due diligence has also been applied in human rights case law and literature in relation to states' duty to protect against violations by individuals.[25] It was adopted by the SRSG and his team as well as some stakeholders, who supplied statements and comments in the SRSG process. However, as noted below, the SRSG shifted focus from states to companies, supporting the legal system practice with economic system arguments (such as risk management). The notion gained a prominent role as part of the 'corporate responsibility to respect' human rights, which was formally introduced as part of the Framework in the SRSG's 2008 report.

A speech in 2005 by the ICJ's Secretary-General referred extensively to economic system interest of companies, arguing a case for the development in international law of standards on human rights for companies.[26]

---

[23] International Commission of Jurists, 'Corporate Accountability, International Human Rights Law and the United Nations' (9 June 2005).

[24] UN Norms, n. 3, paras. A(b) and C(d).

[25] The Inter-American Court of Human Rights and the Maastricht Principles on Violations of Economic, Social and Cultural Rights, amongst others, have applied the notion of state due diligence in the human rights context, referring to the state's lack of care to prevent human rights violations by non-state actors. See also J. A. Zerk, *Multinationals and Corporate Social Responsibility: Limitations and Opportunities in International Law* (Cambridge University Press, 2006), 84 and 86.

[26] N. Howen, 'Business, Human Rights and Accountability: Delivered at the "Business and Human Rights" Conference Organised by the Danish Section of the ICJ, Copenhagen' (21 September 2005), www.ihrb.org/pdf/Business_Human_Rights_and_Accountability. pdf (last accessed 6 January 2013).

Invoking economic system considerations, he argued that 'there is an advantage in legal rules for many corporations', especially socially responsible companies.[27] Voluntary standards were viewed as distorting competition because 'companies lose out to competitors who make no investment in compliance with human rights'.[28]

A September 2005 letter from Amnesty International to the newly appointed SRSG applied a combination of political and legal system language with some usage of economic system language. Amnesty International made a case for 'a UN set of universally recognized normative standards applicable to business'.[29] Connecting to legal system and public policy goals, Amnesty argued that 'the activities of business can provide an enabling environment for the enjoyment of human rights', but that this requires that business be 'effectively regulated'.[30] Economic system references linked the specific activities of business with their potential negative impact on public policy and legal objectives of states, including 'serious negative impact on the protection of human rights'.[31] The letter differed from many other statements that were made during the SRSG process by non-business stakeholders, by including a considerable amount of economic system references and by relating economic interests and activities of companies to public policy and legal duties of states as well as the UN. Several points mentioned in the letter, including the reference to states unwilling or unable to protect human rights, were later addressed by the SRSG in his reports of 2006, 2007 and 2008. Amnesty International's letter and argumentative strategy seemed to make an imprint on priorities of the SRSG.

A few months after the inception of the mandate, the SRSG set out his understanding of the institutional framework for the issues to be addressed under the mandate. Much like in the approach and analyses adopted in his other capacities as an academic and advisor to the UN Global Compact, the SRSG described the institutional framework as a discrepancy or conflict between the immediate post-World War II era and the early twenty-first century world.[32] The main argument was that international law had developed to provide increased protection of MNCs' rights, with much weaker protection of human rights that

---

[27] *Ibid.*   [28] *Ibid.*
[29] Amnesty International, 'Letter to Professor John Ruggie', AI Ref UN 260–2005 (16 September 2005).
[30] *Ibid.*   [31] *Ibid.*
[32] SRSG, 'Opening Remarks: Delivered at the Wilton Park Conference on Business and Human Rights' (10–12 October 2005).

might be adversely impacted by company activities. Having initially focused on firms' economic interests, the SRSG shifted to legal system-related observations on accountability as a counterweight to economic and legal rights of companies, and to political system considerations, by adding that companies' leverage might serve towards public policy objectives on human rights. The SRSG countered the argument that formalising business responsibilities for human rights would allow states to dishonour their international obligations. He drew on legal system references (i.e. 'if governments everywhere did what they are supposed to') to remind states as well as other stakeholders that slack state delivery of their obligations contributes to the 'urgency' of formalised business responsibilities for human rights.[33]

In a speech in December 2005, the SRSG laid out the focus on 'weak governance zones' that was to become a main thread of his work.[34] The statement addressed the economic risks that companies may encounter if they disregard human rights ('as companies are discovering at their peril') and connected to legal system observations ('operations in weak governance zones do not occur in "law free zones"').[35] The speech combined divergent interests in a statement that implicitly referred to economic, political and legal system considerations at once ('the alternatives would be bad for business and human rights alike').[36] The speech built on this to call on 'the business and human rights communities' to work on shared interests rather than differences.[37]

Overall, doctrinal legal system language and arguments dominated stakeholder statements during the first year of the mandate prior to the SRSG's presentation of his first report. While business persisted in referring to doctrine on international obligations being state obligations, NGOs made connections between national and international law and different aspects of (national) law that protects individuals. As exemplified by the statements of the ICJ and Amnesty International, economic system arguments on the benefits that companies might derive from formalised human rights responsibilities for business were making their way into arguments. The SRSG during this time employed legal system language both to draw attention to the discrepancy between companies'

---

[33] Ibid.
[34] SRSG, 'Remarks: Delivered at the Business and Human Rights Seminar, Old Billingsgate, London' (8 December 2005), www.reports-and-materials.org/Ruggie-remarks-to-Business-Human-Rights-Seminar-8-Dec-2005.doc (last accessed 6 January 2013).
[35] Ibid.   [36] Ibid.   [37] Ibid.

rights under international trade law and their impact on societies, and to states' obligations to implement and enforce their international obligations in national law. Although the SRSG employed international legal system doctrinal arguments, contrary to several business statements, he did so with a clear message that human rights matter to both states and business. He employed economic and political system language to strengthen that argument by drawing up implications, for companies and states alike, of neglecting human rights.

The 2006 interim report

The SRSG's interim report was published seven months into the mandate.[38] While mainly invoking political and legal system language, the report also contained some economic system language, referring to the profit-based economic system made up of private corporations.

Setting out the societal framework for the mandate, Part I of the interim report addressed globalisation, overall patterns of corporate human rights abuses and their correlates, and the characteristic strengths and weaknesses of existing responses. Like some of the SRSG's speeches, the report noted a number of recent developments that have enabled the economic system to influence human rights of individuals, and several legal system developments that have reinforced the rights of business (especially in relation to trade).[39] Using a combination of legal and economic system language, it alluded to an increase of 'the rights of transnational firms – their ability to operate and expand globally . . . as a result of trade agreements, bilateral investment treaties, and domestic liberalization'.[40] Making an economic system reference, the interim report advanced an argument that 'good practices' may be turned into a 'competitive advantage' for companies by referring to companies that actively engage to avoid human rights problems.[41]

The report suggested that economic system features may cause human rights to be violated, unless the basics of the economic system's objective of making profits and its institutional manifestations were controlled. It made reference to governance as a strategy for 'devising instruments of

---

[38] Commission on Human Rights, 'Interim Report of the Special Representative of the Secretary-General on the Issue of Human Rights and Transnational Corporations and Other Business Enterprises', E/CN.4/2006/97 (22 February 2006), para. 12 (SRSG, '2006 Interim Report').

[39] *Ibid.*, para. 12.   [40] *Ibid.*, para. 23.   [41] *Ibid.*, para. 15.

corporate and public governance to contain and reduce' human rights abuse by business.[42]

Proposed options to deal with the challenges were presented as 'policy responses'. Legal terminology such as *lex ferenda* or 'legal policy' was not used, or expressed in plain terms as 'policy preferences about what the law should become'.[43] The insistence by the SRSG on his work being policy-oriented rather than any type of legal standard-setting – as the UN Norms had been perceived by some to be – was maintained throughout the mandate (including the 2008 report, formally labelled a 'policy framework'). This insistence was upheld despite references to the (non-)'doctrinal' debate, 'evidence based [findings]' and providing 'conceptual clarification',[44] all of which suggest legal system elements. Legal doctrine arguments were particularly clear in the interim report's section on the UN Norms. The SRSG noted that the UN Norms had contained 'useful elements' but lacked precision and conceptual clarity.[45] He observed, for example: '[t]wo aspects are particularly problematic in the context of this mandate. One concerns the legal authority advanced for the Norms, and the other the principle by which they propose to allocate human rights responsibilities between states and firms'.[46] This led him to discard the UN Norms altogether for the purposes of his future work.

With a marked shift from the policy-oriented observations in Part I of the interim report to specific international law reasoning in Part II, the report drew on legal theory and method to establish the current legal status of human rights obligations of states and companies. It made the point that 'instruments that do have international legal force . . . impose obligations on states' and that 'all existing instruments specifically aimed at holding corporations to international human rights standards' are voluntary.[47] It did, however, recognise that companies may be held liable 'for committing, or for complicity in, the most heinous human rights violations amounting to international crimes'.[48]

Several paragraphs of the interim report indicated that responsibilities of business with regard to human rights are not just a matter of law in the strict sense, or of politics, but also of social norms and moral considerations. Alluding to how companies may self-regulate in response to expectations of their environment, the report described 'individual company policies and voluntary initiatives' as

---

[42] *Ibid.*, para. 23. [43] *Ibid.*, para. 65. [44] *Ibid.*, paras. 7 and 59. [45] *Ibid.*, para. 57.
[46] *Ibid.*, para. 59. [47] *Ibid.*, para. 61. [48] *Ibid.*

'a reflection of how social expectations influence' their conduct.[49] While no direct reference was made to reflexive law, this exemplifies how the interim report employed a line of thinking indicative of related observations or ideas, present in the thinking that spurred the development of the reflexive law theory, on how companies may react to externalities.

The final paragraph set out the essence of what the SRSG referred to as 'principled pragmatism' in terms of method and expected outcome.[50] This 'principled pragmatism' was elaborated by the SRSG in a letter issued shortly after the interim report as considering '*whatever* measures work best in creating change where it matters most'.[51] That approach may also account for the relative absence of legal terminology in relation to the legal policy aspects of the SRSG's work. By avoiding reference to the mandate and its outcome in terms of legal policy, the SRSG worked around certain objections and consequences such as those which met the UN Norms.

By the time the interim report was discussed by the HRC in September 2006, it had already generated considerable response among stakeholders, mainly due to its rejection of the UN Norms.[52] In his response to this critique, the SRSG reiterated that the issue of standards was controversial. Employing legal system language, he opened his response by stating that international human rights standards had been adopted by states for states.[53] Moving into politics of law yet still formally sticking to the 'policy' approach, the SRSG elaborated by explaining that the main issue was which of these standards, if any, should be transposed to become human rights standards for corporations.[54]

---

[49] *Ibid.*, para. 74.   [50] *Ibid.*, para. 81.

[51] SRSG, 'Letter to Olivier De Schutter and Antoine Bernard, FIDH' (20 March 2006) (emphasis added).

[52] See, for example, K. Nowrot, 'The 2006 Interim Report of the UN Special Representative on Human Rights and Transnational Corporations: Breakthrough or Further Polarization?' Policy Papers on Transnational Economic Law, Transnational Economic Law Research Center, Halle (March 2006), http://telc.jura.uni-halle.de/sites/default/files/telc/PolicyPaper20.pdf (last accessed 6 January 2013); Earthrights International, 'Ominous Outlook for the UN Norms' (22 March 2006), www.earthrights.org/legal/ominous-outlook-un-norms (last accessed 27 December 2012); Oxford Analytica, 'International: Human Rights/Business Report Divides' (14 March 2006); Ethical Corporation, 'Business, Human Rights and the UN: John Ruggie – The Story So Far' (10 March 2006).

[53] Business and Human Rights Resource Centre, 'Excerpts from United Nations Press Releases: Discussion of Interim Report by John Ruggie, Special Representative of the UN Secretary-General for Business and Human Rights, at the United Nations Human Rights Council' (25–26 September 2006).

[54] *Ibid.*

Comparison between the statements of the SRSG and stakeholders and the interim report suggests that two types of arguments were particularly effective in influencing the SRSG's findings in the report. The first type comprises legal arguments, referring to conventional international law doctrine on states' human rights obligations. This type of *'lex lata'* argument was mainly made by business organisations and their representatives. The impact of this argument appears to have been stronger than the second type, which was mainly made by the civil society groups and comprised *lex ferenda* arguments in favour of introducing standards of responsibilities for business from a general political perspective or a legal-political perspective on how the law should evolve. In terms of the weight with which the UN Norms might have carried over into the SRSG mandate, critique of the UN Norms coached in legal-doctrine arguments focusing on weaknesses from a legal perspective of precision and conceptual clarity won the case for the future of the UN Norms, to the detriment of softer arguments on the Norms' value as a basis for an inventory of human rights standards for business.

In terms of the discursive struggle to define the extent and substance of business responsibilities for human rights, these findings are interesting both regarding observations on what types of actors were successful in arguing their case, and in terms of the type of arguments that turned out to be influential in the context. In relation to the UN Norms, arguments based on conventional legal and international law doctrine on states' obligations prevailed. As those arguments had been made mainly by business organisations, the economic system had successfully promoted its interests through legal system language.

Although the SRSG claimed to approach his mandate from a non-doctrinal perspective, doctrinal legal arguments were in fact very influential for the interim report. This is not by itself surprising in a highly legal context such as that of international law-making, including processes of 'law-in-the-making' such as the making of international soft law. Yet, the fact that the doctrinal arguments were successful somewhat contradicts the SRSG's allegedly 'non-doctrinal' approach. As we shall see, legal doctrines continued to influence the SRSG's arguments, but with increased integration of newer international law doctrines, especially on the state duty to protect and the recognition of states' obligations in relation to horizontal human rights violations.

Also arguing on doctrinal lines, NGOs had some influence in highlighting needs of victims of corporate human rights violations. The SRSG's consideration of local communities and victims of corporate human rights abuses increased during the mandate, and was especially evident in the 2008 report with its third pillar on access to remedy.[55]

Economic system arguments on the risks to business that may result from its disregard of human rights had some impact. Such arguments, made by NGOs, including those that specialised in socially responsible investment (SRI), were limited during this phase, yet their impact was seen in the interim report's reference to litigation risks. This suggests that a combination of arguments relating to economic system concerns of business and the combined economic and legal risk aspects (the economic losses in a wide sense that may result from litigation) fed into a general argumentative strategy to prepare stakeholders to accept the idea that businesses have human rights responsibilities. Arguments on company interests in respecting human rights in terms of risk management became more prevalent during the second and third years of the mandate.

From the interim report to the 2007 report

During the second year of the mandate, the SRSG and his team conducted a mapping exercise of state obligations for corporate acts under the UN human rights treaty system and made a report on state responsibilities to regulate and adjudicate corporate activities, focusing on the core human rights treaties.[56] The SRSG and his team also compiled a report on business recognition of human rights, looking at global patterns and regional and sectoral variations.[57] In May 2006, the SRSG sent a questionnaire to the UN member states asking for information on the

[55] The 2008 report, for example, notes that the principle of access to remedy is 'an essential component of the framework . . . because even the most concerted efforts cannot prevent all abuse, while access to judicial redress is often problematic, and non-judicial means are limited in number, scope and effectiveness'. Human Rights Council, 'Protect, Respect and Remedy: A Framework for Business and Human Rights: Report of the Special Representative of the Secretary-General on the Issue of Human Rights and Transnational Corporations and Other Business Enterprises', A/HRC/8/5 (7 April 2008), para. 9 (SRSG, '2008 Report').

[56] Human Rights Council, 'Business and Human Rights: Mapping International Standards of Responsibility and Accountability for Corporate Acts', A/HRC/4/35 (19 February 2007), para. 17 (SRSG, '2007 Report').

[57] M. Wright and A. Lehr, 'Business Recognition of Human Rights: Global Patterns, Regional and Sectoral Variations' (12 December 2006), Corporate Social Responsibility Initiative, Working Paper No. 31 (December 2006), www.hks.harvard. edu/m-rcbg/CSRI/publications/workingpaper_31_wright_lehr.pdf (last accessed 19 June 2013).

governments' policies in relation to business and human rights. Only a small number of states responded to the questionnaire.[58]

During the second year, the SRSG conducted thematic consultations on human rights impact assessment and on human rights and the financial sector. Regional consultations held in Johannesburg, Bangkok and Bogota addressed corporate-related human rights challenges posed by businesses operating in areas of conflict or otherwise weak-governance zones, human rights issues in supply chains, and how companies can establish and maintain a social licence to operate with regard to local communities, in particular indigenous peoples. Workshop participants included NGOs and trade unions, business, governments, international organisations and academics, mainly from the region where each workshop took place. Workshops with legal experts discussed corporate responsibility for human rights under international law, and extraterritorial legislation as a tool to improve the accountability of MNCs for human rights violations.

A statement submitted in May 2006 by a large group of NGOs argued in favour of achieving corporate accountability for human rights through the adoption of global standards.[59] It was mainly argued in legal system language based on international law. Business responsibilities were referred to as derived from states' obligations under international law. The statement referred specifically to 'responsibilities' of business and to the 'obligation [of states] to protect', translating into states' 'duty to ensure that businesses act' in accordance with each state's international obligations.[60] The Framework refers precisely to the 'state duty to protect' and to business 'responsibilities'. It appears that this part of the statement and input from legal experts contributed to the particular construction of the Framework and its terminological distinction between the role of states and that of companies in relation to human rights. The Framework paid attention to the horizontality theory of newer international human rights law and the way in which human rights law differs in this respect from general international law and international trade law.

Business statements to the SRSG following the interim report were limited. Referring to voluntary transnational schemes (the Kimberley

---

[58] SRSG, '2007 Report', n. 56, para. 17.
[59] 'Joint NGO Letter in Response to Interim Report' (18 May 2006), www.fidh.org/IMG/pdf/Joint_NGO_Response_to_Interim_Report.pdf (last accessed 6 January 2013).
[60] *Ibid.*

Process and the Voluntary Principles on Security and Human Rights), a March 2006 statement from the International Council on Mining and Metals (ICMM) encouraged the SRSG to recognise benefits that mining may provide to 'the poorest countries in the world', partly as a result of foreign investment.[61] Referring to company economic system interests (including long-term protection of investments), the statement acknowledged that the mining industry is able to contribute to social concerns without a need for formalised regulation. It was suggested that investment and, by implication, the activities of the mining sector, would benefit host countries by promoting economic growth and development. Referring to the public policy objectives of social and economic development rather than the interests of companies or the mining industry, the statement built an argument that industry investment in states in which they meet CSR challenges should be supported by law and policy, as the alternative would mean 'reinforcing the exclusion of the poorest countries from the global economic mainstream'.[62] Reminding its audience that 'basic welfare provision, after all, is a core task for the state'[63] and that debates over companies' responsibilities would not arise if 'governments ensured rights were upheld',[64] it drew on legal system language to reinforce the mining industry's argument against mandatory regulation on business responsibilities.

In a statement at a meeting organised by the Fair Labor Association and the German Network of Business Ethics,[65] the SRSG outlined some key directions in his future work, particularly the role of states in relation to business and human rights. Taking a point of departure from company practices and reasons for non-compliance, the SRSG combined application of economic and legal system observations to argue that more emphasis should be given to the part that governments play. Somewhat echoing points made by the ICMM as well as his own views on governance gaps on several occasions, the SRSG built an argument that the problems in the business sector are basically due to governments' failure.[66] The SRSG met companies on their arguments on states not fulfilling their own obligations, but did not use this to release companies from human rights responsibilities. The SRSG further

---

[61] International Council on Mining and Metals, 'Clarity and Consensus on Legitimate Human Rights Responsibilities for Companies could Accelerate Progress: Submission to UN Secretary-General's Special Representative on Human Rights and Business' (March 2006), www.icmm.com/document/217 (last accessed 6 January 2013), 2.
[62] *Ibid.*, 3.   [63] *Ibid.*, 7.   [64] *Ibid.*   [65] SRSG, '2006 Remarks', n. 1.   [66] *Ibid.*

combined economic and legal system considerations into a recommendation to strengthen emphasis on social responsibility as a requirement in government procurement policies.[67] By introducing these aspects of the ways in which governments and legislators may draw on the mechanisms of the economic system to induce socially responsible practices in companies, the SRSG opened a new track in his argumentative strategy. The economic system and its mechanisms as drivers of social responsibility and business self-regulation from the public as well as the private perspective were to complement other parts of the SRSG's argumentative strategy as the mandate term proceeded.

Two submissions from a socially responsible investment group, Interfaith Centre on Corporate Responsibility, explicitly deployed economic system considerations to underscore its argument in favour of standards for business conduct. One submission emphasised that human rights are important for limiting reputation damage, work stoppage and litigation risks for businesses, and thus made a direct reference to the 'business case'.[68] Applying a strategy like the one adopted by the SRSG, an earlier statement explicitly incorporated litigation risks and other 'risks to shareholders associated with corporate violations of human rights'.[69]

A second ICMM submission (October 2006) reverted to government obligations and public policy interest, indicating that many of the mining industry's human rights challenges were due to governments' inaction.[70] The statement rolled the issue of business impact on human rights back to the discussion of states' obligations under international law, employing legal system language to raise the point.

A study on the role of business in weak-governance zones – which the International Organisation of Employers (IOE) had undertaken with the International Chamber of Commerce (ICC) and Business and Industry Advisory Committee (BIAC) at the invitation of the SRSG – was

---

[67] Ibid., esp. at 5.

[68] Interfaith Center on Corporate Responsibility, 'Letter to John Ruggie' (10 October 2006), www.iccr.org/news/press_releases/pdf%20files/ruggieltr10-10-06.pdf (last accessed 6 January 2013).

[69] Interfaith Center on Corporate Responsibility, 'Letter to John Ruggie' (6 February 2006), www.iccr.org/news/press_releases/pdf%20files/ruggieletter020706.pdf (last accessed 6 January 2013).

[70] International Council on Mining and Metals, 'Second Submission to UN Secretary-General's Special Representative on Human Rights and Business: Mining and Human Rights: How the UN SRSG can Help Spread Good Practice and Tackle Critical Issues' (October 2006), www.icmm.com/document/216 (last accessed 6 January 2013), 2–3.

published in December 2006.[71] The eight-page document is an indication of the internal reflection and self-regulation that may result among business (or other) actors when invited to interact with public institutions with potentially regulatory powers. The IOE and ICC had taken a very strong stance against the UN Norms and the general idea of business responsibilities for human rights.[72] Contrary to that position, the December 2006 study viewed international law as a 'fall-back' position for companies operating in weak-governance zones where national law is not in place or enforced. The study stated that companies should 'respect the principles of relevant international instruments where national law is absent', adding that no company should take advantage of governance gaps in such areas.[73] Further, the study referred to the practice of due diligence, employing the legal system term in an economic system context of companies operating in conflict zones and elsewhere. This recommendation moved the due diligence concept, which had been employed by the ICJ previously, into the business sphere as part of a set of considerations that a carefully managed company will undertake to avoid risks of a law-related character to its economic nature.[74]

Just prior to the publication of the 2007 report, the SRSG increased emphasis on state obligations to regulate and adjudicate, with a particular focus on export credit agencies and international financial institutions. A multi-stakeholder consultation targeted at the financial sector was undertaken in co-operation with the OHCHR in Geneva in February 2007.[75] While the consultation report indicated considerable disagreement on many issues, there was a consensus that financial institutions have some degree of responsibility in relation to human rights. The report underscores that a shift in attention and argumentative strategy was taking place, focusing both on the state duty to protect (strengthened emphasis on public funding agencies which provide financial means for companies that may be involved in human rights violations) and risks

---

[71] International Organisation of Employers (IOE), International Chamber of Commerce (ICC) and Business and Industry Advisory Committee (BIAC), 'Business and Human Rights: The Role of Business in Weak Governance Zones: Business Proposals for Effective Ways of Addressing Dilemma Situations in Weak Governance Zones' (December 2006), para. 15.

[72] Buhmann, 'The Development of the UN Framework', n. 6.

[73] IOE, ICC, BIAC, 'Business and Human Rights', n. 71, paras. 15–16.

[74] *Ibid.*, para. 19.

[75] Human Rights Council, 'Report of the United Nations High Commissioner on Human Rights on the Sectoral Consultation entitled "Human Rights and the Financial Sector"', A/HRC/4/99 (16 February 2007).

posed to economic system actors by human rights violations in which they are involved directly (as producers, buyers, etc.) or indirectly (as funders). The shift towards economic risks to companies became evident in a speech delivered by the SRSG at a meeting hosted by a large law firm in London.[76] The SRSG stressed the risks that legal liability for human rights abuse may cause to companies and, expanding the line of argument from his previous stance of emphasising obligations for human rights as obligations for nation states, noted that '[n]othing prevents states from imposing international responsibilities directly on companies'.[77] By phrasing in such plain words the formal capacity of states to regulate companies' human rights responsibilities under international law, the statement brought additional clout to the argument that companies need to consider human rights and to the SRSG's encouragement to companies to do so without waiting for governments to introduce binding regulations. The SRSG made a point that was to reappear in some of his later statements, referring to 'the courts of public opinion'[78] as complementary to courts of law. Alluding to states' powers to regulate, if political will is present, and to the power of media and the market system to hold companies to account in reputational and economic terms, the SRSG connected economic and legal systems elements to underscore the self-interest of companies in observing international human rights law, although they are not formally bound by such standards.

The 2007 report

The SRSG's second report, published in February 2007,[79] contained a detailed presentation and discussion of issues at the core of international law relating to business responsibilities for human rights – from the state duty to protect to corporate responsibility and accountability for international crimes and other human rights violations under international law, and alternative or non-hard regulatory modalities, both in terms of soft law mechanisms and self-regulation.

---

[76] SRSG, 'Prepared Remarks at Clifford Chance', London (19 February 2007), www.reports-and-materials.org/Ruggie-remarks-Clifford-Chance-19-Feb-2007.pdf (last accessed 6 January 2013).
[77] SRSG, '2007 Report', n. 58, para. 36. [78] *Ibid.*, para. 84.
[79] SRSG, '2007 Report', n. 58.

The 2007 report discussed most issues using legal system language. Following the style and observations that were made in Part II of the interim report, the 2007 report confronted many of the international law and other law-related topics of contention that were propounded by various stakeholders in debates surrounding the UN Norms and/or other debates on business social responsibilities. Based on international law doctrines, scholarship and studies by the SRSG's team, the 2007 report took issue with arguments proposed by both sides of the previous 'doctrinal' debate. In addressing at the outset both the state duty to protect and the corporate responsibility in terms of a legal-scholarship-informed analysis of responsibility and accountability for international crimes, the report countered the continued relevance of the business side's arguments on (sole) state obligations as well as the civil society side's arguments that dealing with the business and human rights problem can only be solved through the setting of global binding standards. The report articulated an understanding of business and human rights that is based on the idea that states do have obligations relevant to business conduct and that new standards which affect legal and social expectations of companies are emerging. This created common ground for both (or all) sides and also acknowledged the benefits and weaknesses of inter-governmental soft law and of corporate self-regulation. Having considered that both approaches warrant merit but also suffer from weaknesses, the 2007 report was able to move on to its conclusion, which reverted in higher degree to the sort of political science and economic system language that prevailed in the interim report. The first and final parts of the report – typically those parts which are browsed by quick readers who want to get the gist of the text – perhaps also appeal particularly to readers outside the legal community, such as politicians and government actors as the makers of possible future hard or soft (inter-)governmental law on the matter, as well as the business sector.

In the final substantive part preceding the conclusion of the report, the SRSG brought up what he refers to as 'social expectations' of business.[80] Social norms and expectations also were to become an issue to be addressed in the 2008 report. Social expectations are a key feature of reflexive law in terms of informing sources of normative expectations between social sub-systems to induce self-regulation within a sub-system. Against the backdrop of the previous parts of the report, this

---

[80] *Ibid.*, para. 63.

penultimate part develops an argument that social expectations on corporate behaviour are connected to policies and practices that firms adopt voluntarily. In many cases, international law on human rights and labour rights informs social expectations of business and, by implication, provides normative guidance to business organisations as to the conduct expected by society.

Through legal system language, business may gain from greater legal clarity on the standards and expectations to which companies are held to account for human rights abuses. Bringing 'the courts of public opinion' into the argument, the report adds a twist on accountability in acknowledging, and making plain, that companies may face political or economic system reactions even if legal institutions are not in place. In such a scenario, non-legal stakeholders effectively function as 'courts' and corporations find themselves in a situation of legal and societal uncertainty. Connecting to the 'governance gap' noted previously by the SRSG, the argument was built that the absence of clear legal standards reflecting social expectations creates uncertainty for companies and leads to 'predictability gaps'. Thus, the report was able to conclude that specific standards of conduct would be of benefit to companies, thus building ground for the economic system-worded points in the conclusion, including a case for corporate self-regulation as a measure for firms to avoid being caught in an emerging regime of national and international liability, simultaneously meeting some concerns and arguments propounded by civil society.

It appears that comments made by the International Federation of Human Rights (FIDH)[81] and in the SRSG's workshops with legal experts, and perhaps related arguments made by other actors but rendered only in non-attribution form, influenced the report by updating the SRSG in terms of contemporary international law (horizontality) theory. This suggests that when addressing core institutional legal issues of duties and rights, an argument drawing on legal system language to refute outdated positions was effective in having an impact on the SRSG's own arguments. These legal arguments are of a somewhat technical nature that would be appreciated by lawyers, including the SRSG team and corporate lawyers. When linked to economic observations on free trade rights etc., the combined strength of the argument would appeal to

---

[81] FIDH, 'Position Paper: Comments to the Interim Report of the Special Representative of the Secretary-General on the Issue of Human Rights and Transnational Corporations and Other Business Enterprises' (22 February 2006).

business managers and others concerned with economic system interests, just like some of the SRSG's statements did.

Drafted mainly in technical legal language, the 2007 report differs from
the interim report. Given that the report is addressed to the HRC, the usage
of legal system language is a logical reflection of the formal audience. From
this perspective, it is also not surprising that the five substantive parts were
not only drafted in this type of language, but also addressed the complexities
and possible legal avenues from the perspective of international law and
legal theory. The use of legal system language and observations does,
however, indicate juridification of a topic which the SRSG had previously
described as political. The objectives may have been to de-politicise the
debate by fixing it in legal doctrine and solid legal analysis and to provide a
point of departure for operational recommendations based on findings and
facts of a (solid) legal nature that would not be questioned the way political
suggestions and arguments are. Compared to the interim report, responses
to the 2007 report were not as critical. The message to states and other
stakeholders is that 'the state duty to protect against nonstate abuses is part
of the international human rights regime's very foundation. The duty
requires states to play a key role in regulating and adjudicating abuse by
business enterprises or risk breaching their international obligations.'[82]

From the 2007 report to the 2008 report

During the mandate years, the SRSG conducted a series of multi-
stakeholder consultations addressing the role of home states in relation
to business and human rights in conflict zones, multi-stakeholder initiatives,[83] the role of states in relation to business and human rights,
accountability mechanisms for resolving complaints and disputes, and
the corporate responsibility to respect human rights. In June 2007, the
SRSG met with UN human rights treaty bodies to share his findings and
learn about the practice and experience under the treaties.[84] In August

---

[82] SRSG, '2007 Report', n. 58, para. 18.
[83] Multi-stakeholder initiatives are understood by the SRSG generally to refer to initiatives
whose stakeholders combine at least the private sector and civil society. See P. Brown,
'Principles that Make for Effective Governance of Multi-Stakeholder Initiatives', UN
SRSF/CCC Expert Workshop on Improving Human Rights Performance of Business
through Multi-Stakeholder Initiatives (6–7 November 2007); and implicitly SRSG, '2007
Report', n. 56.
[84] SRSG, 'Meeting between the SRSG on Human Rights and Business and Treaty Bodies,
19/06/07: Background Paper, Meeting with UN Special Procedures: Geneva' (19 June
2007).

2007, the SRSG team undertook a study with the International Finance Corporation (IFC), examining the relationship between investor rights and the human rights obligations of home states.[85]

In addition to the overall issues addressed at the consultations, the SRSG made use of these consultations and other meetings to introduce and test reception of elements that were to be presented in the final report. The consultations provided an opportunity for the SRSG to softly break ideas that might go into the report and to obtain reactions and responses as well as a kind of acceptance from stakeholders across the range in terms of actors as well as regions. Overall, statements during the final year were somewhat limited. The statements which were made during meetings organised by the SRSG were rendered in a 'non-attributional' style, which makes them unsuited for direct reference in the current context.

The 2008 report

'Protect, Respect and Remedy: A Framework for Business and Human Rights' was published on 7 April 2008 as the final report of the SRSG's first mandate.[86] A special companion report clarified the concepts of 'sphere of influence' and 'complicity'.[87] The main report introduced the three-pillared framework, which 'rests on differentiated but complementary responsibilities'.[88] It comprises three core principles: the state duty to protect against human rights abuses by third parties, including business; the corporate responsibility to respect human rights; and the need for more effective access to remedy. The three principles are argued to 'form a complementary whole in that each supports the others in achieving sustainable progress'.[89]

---

[85] International Finance Corporation, 'IFC and UN Cooperate on Study of Investment Contracts and Human Rights'. Press Release, Washington, DC (7 August 2007); International Finance Corporation and Office of the High Commissioner for Human Rights, Special Procedures of the Human Rights Council, 'Stabilization Clauses and Human Rights: A Research Project conducted for IFC and the United Nations Special Representative to the Secretary-General on Business and Human Rights', Washington, DC (11 March 2008).

[86] SRSG, '2008 Report', n. 55.

[87] Human Rights Council, 'Clarifying the Concepts of "Sphere of Influence" and "Complicity": Report of the Special Representative of the Secretary-General on the Issue of Human Rights and Transnational Corporations and Other Business Enterprises', A/HRC/8/16 (15 May 2008).

[88] SRSG, '2008 Report', n. 55, para. 9.   [89] *Ibid.*, Summary and para. 9.

The report founded the first of the three pillars – the state duty to protect – in a classical international law view of states as duty-bearers for international obligations. Having established the state duty not only in line with the state-centred international law doctrine as a matter of principle, but also invoking what had been argued prior to and during the mandate term by organisations and governments opposed to the institutionalisation of business responsibilities for human rights, the SRSG provided a point of departure by elaborating implications for governments as well as companies flowing from that doctrinal point. Thus, the three-pillared framework widened its focus towards implications for business by including human rights law doctrine on the state's duty to protect against violations at the horizontal level. The report adopted the less radical theory of horizontal human rights obligations,[90] according to which states have an obligation to protect individuals and communities against human rights violations by non-state actors. Through reference to state agencies at some distance from core state bodies but tasked with business-related responsibilities (such as Export Credit Agencies), the report emphasised that the duty to protect is not limited to core legislative, judicial and executive bodies. The implications were drawn up to explicitly indicate that state duties under international human rights law in practice require action on the part of states to prevent human rights violations by companies, and that this may mean for a state an increase in the obligations that companies need to honour in order to comply with national law. By elaborating state duties (international law doctrine) to encompass the duty to *protect* (the international human rights law doctrine on horizontal obligations), the SRSG made it clear that human rights matter to companies also as a result of activities that states are required to undertake in order to translate their international obligations into national law.

Employing due diligence as a requirement for the private sector, it was argued in the report that '[o]n policy grounds alone, a strong case can be made that [Export Credit Agencies], representing not only commercial interests but also the broader public interest, should require clients to perform adequate due diligence on their potential human rights impacts'.[91] This would allow such types of state agencies to react when serious human rights concerns call for greater care or monitoring.

---

[90] J. H. Knox, 'Horizontal Human Rights Law' (2008) 102 *American Journal of International Law* 1.
[91] SRSG, '2008 Report', n. 55, para. 40.

The second pillar, the corporate responsibility to respect human rights, was defined essentially as avoiding the infringements of the rights of others and addressing adverse impacts that may occur. This entails acting with 'due diligence', notably having in place 'a process whereby companies not only ensure compliance with national laws but also manage the risk of human rights harm with a view to avoiding it'.[92]

Alluding to the Preamble of the Universal Declaration of Human Rights, the report acknowledged that companies may be considered as 'organs of society'.[93] Nevertheless, it was argued that they are specialised economic organs, not democratic public interest institutions. As such, 'their responsibilities cannot and should not simply mirror the duties of states'.[94]

According to the SRSG, the responsibility to respect goes beyond complying with national laws to avoiding infringement of the rights of others. On this issue, the 2008 report left the terrain of legal doctrine and established legal institutions. Venturing into the field of 'social expectations' and 'courts of public opinion' and developing the point in relation to risk and general reputation management, the SRSG constructed an argument on social expectations as normative sources, which would appeal to companies by invoking economic implications. Often, social expectations are not in accordance with a conventional doctrinal approach, nor would the 'judgments' of the courts of public opinion in terms of consumer or investor decisions necessarily stand in a court of law. Yet, both are facts of modern social and economic life, and both may be as important to a company as a fine issued by a court of law.

Having established the economic benefits to companies of taking responsibility for their impact on human rights, the SRSG proposed a due diligence process to enable companies to become aware of, prevent and address adverse human rights impacts. 'For the substantive content of the due diligence process, companies should look, at a minimum, to the International Bill of Human Rights and the core conventions of the ILO [International Labour Organization], because the principles they embody comprise the benchmarks against which other social actors judge the human rights impacts of companies'.[95] Core elements of human rights due diligence comprise a human rights policy, undertaking a human rights impact assessment, integrating human rights throughout a company, and tracking and reporting performance.[96]

---

[92] *Ibid.*, para. 25.   [93] *Ibid.*, para. 53.   [94] *Ibid.*   [95] *Ibid.*, para. 58.
[96] *Ibid.*, paras. 59–63.

The third pillar, access to remedy, is both a part of and complementary to the state duty to protect as well as the corporate responsibility to respect. Without adequate remedy, the duty to protect could be rendered weak or even meaningless. As part of the corporate responsibility to respect, grievance mechanisms help identify, mitigate and possibly resolve grievances before they escalate and greater harm is done.

Following the presentation, the HRC on 18 June 2008 adopted a resolution,[97] which 'welcome[d]' the three-pronged framework presented in the report. The HRC's decision marked the first time a UN human rights body with a political composition (as opposed to the expert composition of treaty bodies and the former Sub-Commission) agreed to an affirmative approach to a proposal for promoting human rights responsibilities of business.

Discussion of observations

Recall that reflexive law generates change through perturbation resonating with the system-specific interests of a particular audience. This chapter's analysis of the SRSG process suggests that arguments addressing audiences through their system-specific code were the most influential. Initially, legal system arguments dominated statements from business as well as civil society, with some elements of political system arguments. Business referred to legal system doctrine and traditional international law *lex lata*, whereas civil society argued in terms of legal policy and *lex ferenda* to hold companies to account for abuse of human rights and to address public policy concerns. Civil society employed limited economic system language to argue that economic considerations cause human rights abuse by companies. Business arguments tended to be quite specific and addressed duties of states under international law in direct and doctrinal terms, whereas civil society arguments were less specific, more programmatic and suggested possible actions related to a change of the law rather than application of currently valid law.

The SRSG employed economic and legal system language from the outset, particularly on imbalances between international trade opportunities and business responsibilities for human rights. Later, his argumentative style shifted from emphasis on imbalances in the international trade and human rights regimes to a direct emphasis on liability and legal

---

[97] Human Rights Council, 'Resolution 8/7', n. 2 (18 June 2008).

compliance obligations that might eventuate for companies, due to obligations under national law as a result of the state duty to protect.

From the inception of the mandate, the SRSG's argumentative structure both referred to state duties and to economic or related risks to companies that may result from their engaging in actions that cause human rights abuse. As the SRSG's arguments grew increasingly legal and doctrinal towards the final part of the mandate, they also increasingly integrated newer international human rights law doctrine, emphasising states' duty to protect against horizontal human rights violations. Simultaneously, the SRSG's deployment of economic system language, especially in statements addressing audiences comprising business representatives, shifted emphasis from issues of a general character (such as global trade opportunities) to issues of specific relevance to any business (such as risk management).

Business arguments remained structured around legal system language, with an emphasis on state obligations for human rights, but during the second half of the mandate – particularly after the publication of the IOE/ICC/BIAC report – shifted from rejection towards increased recognition of international law as a relevant normative source for company action.

While NGOs remained focused on legal system language and *lex ferenda*, towards the end of the mandate term some civil society arguments became more specific and more operational and therefore more suited to immediate application by the SRSG, including by direct incorporation into his recommendations. This applies, for example, to statements relating to victims and redress which made their way into the 2008 report, with a full section on remedies (supported by input from the SRSG team). Some civil society statements indicate that civil society adopted (perhaps even internalised) SRSG arguments and employed these in subsequent statements.

Conclusion

Although unusual for international human rights law-making, the SRSG process involved economic non-state actors as prospective duty-bearers. This chapter's analysis indicates that the outcome resulted not only from business participation (as envisaged by Friedman and Charney, as noted above), but also from a discursive strategy that evolved during the process. This does not mean that international law-making to curtail adverse business impact on society should be subjected to the whims of business. What it does

suggest is that engaging with and appealing to the interests of key stakeholders offer a way towards the effective adoption of international policy
and law on issues that require a multi-stakeholder approach for their
solution.

Four main findings emerge from the analysis of the SRSG process and
the usage of system-specific language. Firstly, the SRSG's arguments on
economic system effects of business related human rights abuse appear
to have led company representatives to accept the idea of business
responsibilities for human rights as a fact of social expectations in a
globalised marketplace, instead of as an outgrowth of international law
that would shift state obligations to companies. This may have been
combined with or supported by the reflexive law approach of inviting
business organisations that opposed the idea to help define guidance.

Secondly, the SRSG's approach shifted from a limited deployment of
legal system language towards an extensive usage of legal system language, but deeply connected with the economic impact of legal system
observations and considerations. This is particularly clear in relation to
arguments on economic risks that human rights abuse may cause to
companies.

Thirdly, the analysis shows that the SRSG was successful in constructing the idea of business responsibilities for human rights based on the
full spectrum of human rights (namely, the International Bill of Rights
and the eight ILO core conventions), and in generating broad support
among stakeholders. He was also successful in generating acceptance of a
course of initially soft measures to guide companies towards internal-
ising respect for human rights standards into their practices, rather than
the often protracted process of formulating a declaration or convention.
In both cases, the SRSG's approach was to address audiences of business
organisations, civil society and (inter-)governmental organisations in
their system-specific languages in ways that also highlighted impact on
their system-specific interests that might follow by considering interests-
guiding actions of other sub-systems.

Fourthly, in addition to the impact of strategically used system-
specific language, the influence that stakeholders' statements had on
SRSG reports indicates that concretely formulated recommendations
from business or NGOs were more strongly reflected in SRSG reports
than more open or abstract recommendations.

The SRSG's inclusive process of consulting broadly, and his ability to
communicate with various stakeholders in ways that specifically
addressed interests at core to their social sub-system, led to a process

of developing the Framework, which had sufficiently broad support to be 'unanimously welcomed' by the HRC in 2008. The analysis in this chapter suggests that avoidance of lobbying such as that which helped kill the UN Norms was achieved through the argumentative strategy of addressing stakeholders in ways that created perturbation resonating with their interests, causing them to accept UN-based guidance on business responsibilities for human rights, including related state obligations and ensuing compliance requirements. Such acceptance was further promoted because the inclusive process allowed non-state actors, who are not directly represented at the HRC to contribute expertise, question assumptions and make proposals.

3

The 'Ruggie process': from legal obligations to corporate social responsibility?

CARLOS LÓPEZ[*]

Introduction

In June 2011, the United Nations (UN) Human Rights Council (HRC) 'endorsed' the Guiding Principles on Business and Human Rights (GPs).[1] The GPs were proposed by Professor John Ruggie, the Special Representative of the Secretary-General on the Issue of Human Rights and Transnational Corporations and Other Business Enterprises (SRSG). This event was the culmination of a process that began in 2005, when the HRC established the SRSG's post and the UN Secretary-General appointed Ruggie as the SRSG.

The GPs were warmly greeted by business representatives, but less so by non-governmental organisations (NGOs) and other civil society groups represented in the HRC – a sizeable number of these organisations expressed misgivings or openly opposed adoption of the GPs.[2] Member states of the HRC, a body of forty-seven states periodically elected for terms of two years, had mixed reactions. Nearly all Western governments expressed unqualified support for the document, but many others from the global South expressed misgivings publicly or

---

[*] This chapter has been written in the author's personal capacity and does not necessarily reflect the views of the ICJ. The author acknowledges the assistance and useful comments of D. Ansbro, L. Misol and T. Feeney, but remains solely responsible for the content.

[1] Human Rights Council, 'Guiding Principles on Business and Human Rights: Implementing the United Nations' "Protect, Respect and Remedy" Framework', A/HRC/17/31 (21 March 2011) (SRSG, 'Guiding Principles').

[2] See statements at Business & Human Rights Resource Centre, 'Statements to Human Rights Council by NGOs and Business Organisations', www.business-humanrights.org/SpecialRepPortal/Home/ReportstoUNHumanRightsCouncil/2011#85938 (last accessed 11 December 2012).

privately.[3] However, ultimately, none felt that they were in a position to oppose and vote against the resolution endorsing the GPs. This reaction was markedly different to the reception given in 2008 to the first, and arguably the main, product in the process – the 'Protect, Respect and Remedy' Framework (Framework). The adoption of the Framework, also known as the 'Ruggie Framework', had virtually unanimous support from states, businesses and civil society organisations.[4] During the debate in the HRC in 2011, a few human rights organisations expressed clear support for the proposed GPs.

Both the Framework and the GPs are presented not as a set of international law rules, but as a series of practical recommendations that elaborate on the implications of existing international obligations. They build on three pillars that are premised on the following legal and theoretical assumptions: states have obligations under international human rights law, but business corporations only have 'responsibilities'. Under the Framework, the responsibilities of companies are not based on any international legal obligation or on any other international standard, but on social expectations. This chapter looks at the broad process, but focuses fundamentally on the second pillar of the Framework, the corporate responsibility to respect all rights. Arguably, this issue is at the core of the original and ongoing controversy about human rights and business.

Due to the way the business responsibilities are articulated in the Framework and the GPs, some scholars do not hesitate to classify them flatly under the category of 'corporate social responsibility' (CSR) – understood as a set of social rules and principles compliance with which is optional for businesses – in order either to criticise their shortcomings or praise their potential.[5] Others have taken the opposite

---

[3] For details, see Chapter 4. See also statements, for instance those of Nigeria on behalf of the African group and Pakistan on behalf of the Organisation of the Islamic Conference. Business and Human Rights Resource Centre, 'Statements by Governments at Human Rights Council Session', www.business-humanrights.org/SpecialRepPortal/Home/ReportstoUNHumanRightsCouncil/2011#85938 (last accessed 11 December 2012).

[4] Human Rights Council, 'Protect, Respect and Remedy: A Framework for Business and Human Rights: Report of the Special Representative of the Secretary-General on the Issue of Human Rights and Transnational Corporations and Other Business Enterprises', A/HRC/8/5 (7 April 2008) (SRSG, '2008 Report'). At the adoption stage in the Human Rights Council, only South Africa expressed its discontent, but did not call for a vote.

[5] See, for instance, N. D. White, 'The Montreux Process and the Draft Convention: Developing a Responsibility Regime for PMSCs?' (unpublished paper, Nottingham University 2011, on file with the author) and M. Czarnecka, 'CSR Becomes Entrenched' [2011] *Lexpert* 53.

view and have emphasised that the Framework and the GPs are not 'mere CSR', but the expression of a policy consensus within the international community about the responsibilities of business.[6] Navanethem Pillay, the current High Commissioner for Human Rights, wrote in 2008 that the statement 'transnational corporations and other business enterprises have a responsibility to respect human rights' is 'an innovative position' and 'both sets a new and clear benchmark and represents an important milestone in the evolving understanding of human rights in our societies'.[7] A third, intermediate position recognises that the Framework has value in that it articulates certain core human rights principles in relation to businesses and that the GPs offer a number of concrete steps to be taken by governments and companies in order to meet their respective responsibilities, but they are not on their own the 'global standards'.[8]

However, both the Framework and the GPs fall short by not fully reflecting the state of international law in many respects. Further, the GPs in particular are often portrayed as the ultimate product, labelled as comprehensive and authoritative, and their promoters claim that all other initiatives should be 'aligned' with them. The supposed comprehensiveness and authority of the GPs leaves nearly no room for improvement or further development of additional standards and norms, a position contrary to the evolving nature of international law and standards.

Apart from the use of the phrase, the 'corporate responsibility to respect' all human rights, the SRSG coined the methodological concept of 'corporate human rights due diligence', described as an ongoing process to help companies avoid infringing human rights or becoming complicit with others who infringe such rights. Although the term 'due

---

[6] Remarks by ITUC delegate at Expert Meeting organised by the Committee on the Rights of the Child and International Commission of Jurists, Geneva, 21 September 2011, conducted under Chatham House rules.

[7] N. Pillay, 'The Corporate Responsibility to Respect: A Human Rights Milestone', www. ohchr.org/Documents/Press/HC_contribution_on_Business_and_HR.pdf (last accessed 11 December 2012).

[8] Human Rights Watch (HRW), 'Joint Civil Society Statement to the 17th Session of the Human Rights Council by Human Rights Watch and Others' (30 May 2011), www.hrw. org/news/2011/05/30/joint-civil-society-statement-17th-session-human-rights-council (HRW, 'Joint Civil Society Statement'). See also HRW, 'UN Human Rights Council: Weak Stance on Business Standards – Global Rules Needed, Not Just Guidance' (16 June 2011), www.hrw.org/news/2011/06/16/un-human-rights-council-weak-stance-business-standards (last accessed 7 January 2013).

diligence' evokes a legal standard, within the GPs it is fundamentally a concept that encapsulates a series of good practices without necessary or clear legal implications. Thus, just as with the 'corporate responsibility to respect', a company's failure to carry out human rights due diligence, as defined in the GPs, does not entail any legal responsibility.

The nature of the innovations presented by the Framework and the GPs has long been the subject of debate, which is likely to continue in the foreseeable future. One of the typical questions posed is whether they represent a real and definitive shift to CSR, whereby corporate human rights responsibilities are ultimately a voluntary undertaking, thus steering the debate away from the search for clear international legal standards applicable to companies. This chapter will first analyse the concept of the 'corporate responsibility to respect' as a 'social norm', and then move to consider the nature of the consensus around it within the UN to show that the general acceptance of the GPs cannot hide the views of many actors that stronger rules are needed. The final section of the chapter will revisit the need to tackle the resilient question of whether international norms on human rights can apply to transnational corporations.

The 'corporate responsibility to respect': the contours of a 'social norm'

The SRSG was appointed in 2005 with the explicit mandate, *inter alia*, '[t]o identify and clarify standards of corporate responsibility and accountability for transnational corporations and other business enterprises with regard to human rights'.[9] This mandate can only be fully understood when read against the background of the debate around the UN Norms produced by the UN Sub-Commission on Human Rights and rejected by its parent body, the then Commission on Human Rights.[10] The Sub-Commission, a subsidiary body of the then Commission and formed by some twenty independent experts from five regional groups,

---

[9] Commission on Human Rights, 'Human Rights and Transnational Corporations and Other Business Enterprises: Human Rights Council Resolution 2005/69', E/CN.4/2005/ L.10/Add.17 (20 April 2005), para. 1(a).

[10] Commission on Human Rights, Sub-Commission on the Promotion and Protection of Human Rights, 'Norms on the Responsibilities of Transnational Corporations and Other Business Enterprises with Regard to Human Rights', E/CN.4/Sub.2/2003/12/ Rev.2 (26 August 2003) (UN Norms). See also the Commentary to the Norms in the same document.

had been working on the project since 1997 through a special working group, which carried out public meetings and consultations.

In 2003, the Commission not only declined to endorse the UN Norms, but also declared that they had 'no legal status'.[11] Employer associations and some trade unions had also strongly objected to the project; many governments had opposed it and NGOs were divided, although a majority was supportive. The prevailing state of play before the SRSG's appointment has usually, and perhaps conveniently, been described as 'divisive' and 'deadlocked'.[12] A report of the Office of the UN High Commissioner for Human Rights, mandated to describe the status of existing initiatives after broad consultation, more accurately revealed 'a wide range of opinions amongst stakeholders on the value and content of the draft', with 'employer groups, many States and some businesses' critical of the draft while 'non-governmental organizations and some States and businesses as well as individual stakeholders' were supportive.[13] Despite the divided opinions, the High Commissioner's report concluded that 'the draft Norms, having the status of a draft proposal, could be subject to review and consideration by the Commission'.[14] However, no further review and consideration was to take place.

In his first interim report of 2006, the SRSG, rather than reviewing the UN Norms, adopted a radical criticism of them.[15] In the end, he decided to put them aside and start everything anew. In doing so, he highlighted the Norms' 'excesses' and internal inconsistencies.[16] Crucially, he challenged a fundamental basis of the Norms: that they represented a restatement of existing international law, contained mainly in treaties originally drafted with states in mind, as applying directly to business actors. The SRSG's view was that the Norms could not be a restatement of international

---

[11] Human Rights Commission Decision 2004/116, 60th session, para. (c), confirmed by ECOSOC Decision 2004/279, E/CN.4/2004/127.

[12] See Chapter 2.

[13] Commission on Human Rights, 'Report of the United Nations High Commissioner on Human Rights on the Responsibilities of Transnational Corporations and Related Business Enterprises with Regard to Human Rights: Report of the Sub-Commission on the Promotion and Protection of Human Rights', E/CN.4/2005/91 (15 February 2005), para. 19.

[14] Ibid., para. 22.

[15] Commission on Human Rights, 'Interim Report of the Special Representative of the Secretary-General on the Issue of Human Rights and Transnational Corporations and Other Business Enterprises', E/CN.4/2006/97 (22 February 2006) (SRSG, '2006 Interim Report').

[16] Ibid., para. 59.

law and at the same time pretend to be legally binding on companies, because international law, with a few possible exceptions, did not bind corporations.[17] The conclusion was clear and final – the UN Norms cannot be legally binding, because there is no human rights instrument that imposes binding obligations on business corporations. By putting aside the Norms and their legal ambitions, the 2006 interim report also seemed to be directed at burying the proposition that companies can be bound by international law. This finding, however, was supported by a very brief analysis of the current state of international law. Three legal workshops focusing on these issues were conducted in 2006 and 2007, but their final objective was never entirely clear since the interim report had already reached a conclusion on the matter. *Post facto* discussions among some of the leading experts in this field would not undo the main far-reaching conclusions of the 2006 report and the SRSG did not elect to subsequently reconsider his stance.

During the rest of 2006 and 2007, human rights organisations and advocates reacted by seeking an acceptable way to advance international standards in the wake of the SRSG's dismissal of the UN Norms. In October 2007, after the second report was published, human rights advocates, who had long called for inter-governmental standards on business and human rights, publicly asked the SRSG to devote the rest of his mandate to building international and government support for 'the eventual negotiation and adoption of a UN declaration or similar instrument outlining standards on business and human rights'.[18] The letter, which was signed by more than 200 organisations and individuals, contained some elaboration on the essential elements that a future UN declaration should include: states' obligations, businesses' responsibilities, and the issue of remedies. These organisations also asked that in the whole process the views and needs of the victims be actively sought and taken into account.[19]

---

[17] *Ibid.*, paras. 60–61.

[18] ESCR-Net, 'Joint Open Letter to UN Special Representative on Business and Human Rights – 2007' (10 October 2007), www.escr-net.org/docs/i/548976 (last accessed 11 December 2012). This letter was preceded by a letter from the International Commission of Jurists (ICJ) to the Secretary-General (April 2006) stating the view that 'moving towards the development of international soft law is a first and necessary step in a progressive development of international standards', and that we should work towards 'an inter-governmental soft law statement or what I have called an international public policy statement' (on file with the author).

[19] ESCR-Net, 'Joint Open Letter', *ibid.*

The SRSG's June 2008 report to the HRC contained a three-pronged conceptual and policy framework summed up as follows:

> ... the State duty to protect against human rights abuses by third parties, including business; the corporate responsibility to respect human rights; and the need for more effective access to remedies. Each principle is an essential component of the framework: the State duty to protect because it lies at the very core of the international human rights regime; the corporate responsibility to respect because it is the basic expectation society has of business; and access to remedy, because even the most concerted efforts cannot prevent all abuse, while access to judicial redress is often problematic, and non-judicial means are limited in number, scope and effectiveness. The three principles form a complementary whole in that each supports the others in achieving sustainable progress.[20]

The three pillars of the Framework are presented as mutually supportive and reinforcing, so that one cannot stand without the others. Thus, arguably, states, in exercise of their duty to protect, would ensure through regulation or otherwise that businesses respect human rights as defined in the second pillar. The scope of 'corporate responsibility to respect' was further elaborated as follows: '[i]n addition to compliance with national laws, the baseline responsibility of companies is to respect human rights ... Whereas governments define the scope of legal compliance, the broader scope of the responsibility to respect is defined by social expectations – as part of what sometimes is called a company's social licence to operate.'[21]

The Framework also proposed an operational method for companies to discharge their responsibility to respect rights by *showing* or *proving* that they do so: the concept of human rights due diligence.

Because the Framework's formulation of the 'corporate responsibility to respect' was worded in general terms, it left significant room for interpretation and possible developments. Arguably, this is one of the reasons why it gathered broad support, including from leading human rights NGOs. Commenting on the Framework, the Wall Street law firm Weil, Gotshal and Manges LLP stated: '[u]nfortunately, in outlining the role of corporations with respect to human rights, the Report uses language that ... is undefined, imprecise and subject to varied interpretations'.[22] However, the law firm had been 'assured by the

---

[20] SRSG, '2008 Report', n. 4, para. 9.   [21] *Ibid.*, para. 54.

[22] Weil, Gotshal and Manges LLP, 'Corporate Social Responsibility for Human Rights: Comments on the UN Special Representative's Report Entitled "Protect, Respect and Remedy: A Framework for Business and Human Rights": Memorandum' (22 May 2008),

Special Representative himself that the distinction between duties/obligations on the one hand, and responsibilities based on expectations on the other, is generally accepted UN terminology; and that his use of the term "responsibility" in the Report refers to moral obligations and social expectations – *not* binding law'.[23] Whether or not the distinction of duties or obligations on the one hand and responsibilities on the other is an accepted UN terminology is questionable. There is evidence to suggest that the opposite may be more accurate: in UN parlance, the term 'responsibilities' is usually taken as equivalent or derivative of duties and obligations.[24] In any event, the SRSG took businesses' concerns seriously and accordingly, in his 2009 report, he set out to clarify and develop the concept of 'corporate responsibility' in detail.

One of the salient features of the 2009 report is the suggestion that the 'social' responsibility to respect has a normative value.[25] Companies have to respect human rights, because that is what society expects from them and not because they have such an obligation under international law. At the same time, the report does not appeal to any source, ethical or moral system or religion-based ethics, as the normative underpinning of those social norms that give rise to corporate responsibilities. The argument that the Universal Declaration of Human Rights could provide the normative foundation for the concept of 'corporate responsibility', because it already recognises the role of every 'organ of society' in upholding human rights, was dismissed. The rationale on which the concept of 'corporate responsibility to respect' is based appears to be as follows: businesses should respect human rights because it is necessary for them as a condition to obtain their social licence to operate. In other words, it is necessary for them in order to be able to do business. The social licence to operate, it was said, 'is based in prevailing social norms'.[26] But, again, the origin and character of those social norms were never clarified. They were taken as a given fact. Moreover, the

---

www.reports-and-materials.org/Weil-Gotshal-legal-commentary-on-Ruggie-report-22-May-2008.pdf (last accessed 11 December 2012).

[23] *Ibid.* (emphasis in the original).

[24] See, for instance, International Law Commission (ILC), 'Draft Articles on Responsibility of States for Internationally Wrongful Acts', in Report of the International Law Commission on the Work of its Fifty-third Session, UN GAOR 56th Sess., Supp. No. 10, at 43, A/56/10 (2001).

[25] Human Rights Council, 'Business and Human Rights: Towards Operationalizing the "Protect, Respect and Remedy" Framework', A/HRC/11/13 (22 April 2009), paras. 46–49 (SRSG, '2009 Report').

[26] *Ibid.*, para. 46.

report recognises that social norms 'may vary by region and industry', but the 'corporate responsibility to respect', as a social norm, has acquired universal value.[27] It is difficult to find a consistent and solid theoretical and/or normative argument in this report's elaboration on the 'corporate responsibility to respect' and its character as a social norm.[28] From this point of view, the SRSG's project is as questionable as its predecessor, the UN Norms.

Without further guidance on the normative systems and the source of authority for the 'social norms' that are the foundation of corporate responsibilities, the 2009 report leaves companies and stakeholders alike in the dark regarding both the concrete content of the rights companies are called on to respect and the principled approach to a process or method with which to identify those rights. The proposed process of due diligence that companies should put in practice may eventually lead them to identify the rights that are most relevant for them, but without participation of external stakeholders in the process, this is ultimately left to the companies' discretion. The Framework and the GPs do not contain a catalogue of rights or bill of rights that should be respected at all times. Rather, they leave the identification of those rights to prevailing social norms in the region or industry, albeit against the backdrop of the International Bill of Rights. This situation has prompted some actors to start initiatives aimed at providing more concrete definitions of rights and rules that companies should commit to respect through internal policies and compliance mechanisms.[29] There have also been efforts to

---

[27] *Ibid.*

[28] For a more extensive analysis and critique of the normative basis of the 'corporate responsibility to respect', see Chapter 5. See also R. McCorquodale, 'Corporate Social Responsibility and International Human Rights Law' (2009) 87 *Journal of Business Ethics* 385. McCorquodale has asked, 'which society is the relevant society for determining the expectation?'.

[29] Initiatives such as the International Code of Conduct for Private Security Providers or the Children's Rights and Business Principles could be understood as attempts to identify the rights that companies should respect, providing improved clarity as to the content of rules and increasing the potential for compliance. Some CSR experts concur with the need to create more concrete tools (some sort of 'IKEA manuals') to help companies better understand their responsibilities. See Human Rights Council 20th Regular Session, Parallel Event, Sponsored by the ICJ, 'High Level Discussion on Advancing Human Rights and Business in the Human Rights Council: Summary Note of Event, 21 June 2012, *Palais des Nations*' (21 June 2012), Remarks by Ms. Rachel Groux-Nurnberg, www.icj.org/high-level-discussion-on-advancing-human-rights-and-business-in-the-human-rights-council/ (last accessed 7 January 2013).

provide further guidance to companies by attaching lists of 'relevant' documents and instruments to the recently updated OECD Guidelines on Multinational Enterprises.[30] However, these lists contain a wide range of international human rights instruments alongside documents or tools prepared by private organisations that are clearly not of the same rank or value. It is unclear how these lists of instruments will actually improve companies' position in identifying and understanding the content of human rights they are called to respect.

Taking social expectations as the basis of the corporate 'social' responsibility to respect would logically imply the acceptance that such expectations about companies' behaviour are bound to evolve over time as society evolves. The universal recognition that a social norm expecting companies to respect rights exists is an expression of such an evolution – that recognition would not have been possible in other times and circumstances. However, these logical assumptions seem difficult to reconcile with the claims that the GPs are comprehensive and authoritative. In fact, countries that traditionally sponsored the mandate of the SRSG within the HRC refused during negotiations to accept the possibility of review and update of the GPs according to need. Accepting that social expectations are the basis of the responsibility to 'respect' means that societies could potentially expect companies, or at least some of them, to bear other responsibilities beyond the need to respect (avoid harming) rights. This could include the promotion of and contribution to the realisation of rights. What is socially acceptable is essentially an evolving concept. What is socially unacceptable today in one place may be acceptable tomorrow or in other places. It can be said that limiting the formulation of corporate responsibilities to 'respect' rights does not necessarily hold in many parts of the world, where businesses are also expected to contribute positively to the realisation of rights.[31]

In this context, certain strategies to require all new international initiatives in the field of business and human rights to be 'aligned' to the language and concepts contained in the Framework and the GPs may have the, perhaps unintended, effect of freezing progress in international

---

[30] OECD, 'OECD Guidelines for Multinational Enterprises: Recommendations for Responsible Business Conduct in a Global Context' (25 May 2011), www.oecd.org/dataoecd/43/29/48004323.pdf (last accessed 10 December 2012).

[31] See Chapter 5.

standards. Against this trend, in considering a new resolution in September 2012 about the role of the UN in promoting the business and human rights agenda, the HRC – the same body that had adopted the GPs in 2011 – refrained from using language that would call for all new sets of standards to be 'aligned' with the GPs.[32] The HRC in fact preferred to use the word 'guided' instead of 'aligned' when referring to other practices, tools and initiatives in the area of business and human rights. This choice of words reveals that the HRC is prepared to consider options that may go beyond the GPs.

In the Framework, the term 'responsibility' is used to define the position of business enterprises vis-à-vis human rights: companies have the responsibility to respect human rights. 'Responsibility' is preferred over terms such as 'duties' or 'obligations', even though the latter two terms can also be based on moral or social rules rather than on law. On the other hand, the term 'responsibility' is clearly different from 'commitment' or similar words which require a voluntary act (in the sense that the company needs to make a commitment). One practical example of such a distinction can be found in the Children's Rights and Business Principles, elaborated jointly by United Nations Children's Fund (UNICEF), Save the Children and the Global Compact.[33] The Principles purport to 'set out corporate actions', rather than define general norms or principles to be found in the Convention on the Rights of the Child and other relevant ILO Conventions. However, the actual text of these Principles has a clear normative intent: it sets out the kind of conduct businesses should observe. The document makes clear at the outset the difference between 'corporate responsibility to respect' and 'corporate commitment to support' the rights of the child.[34] Although one may understand the origin of such a distinction, in practical terms the difference does not go beyond semantics. In both cases, any given enterprise may choose to comply or not, without the fear of sanctions.

---

[32] See Human Rights Council, 'Contribution of the United Nations System as a Whole to the Advancement of the Business and Human Rights Agenda and the Dissemination and Implementation of the Guiding Principles on Business and Human Rights: Report of the Secretary-General', A/HRC/21/21 (2 July 2012), Preamble, para. 6.

[33] UNICEF, Global Compact and Save the Children, 'Children's Rights and Business Principles', www.unicef.org/csr/css/PRINCIPLES_23_02_12_FINAL_FOR_PRINTER. pdf (last accessed 11 December 2012).

[34] *Ibid.*, at 5.

Consensus and participation

The process undertaken by the SRSG – the 'Ruggie process' – involved a series of meetings and invitations to submit written submissions, generally called 'consultations'. The SRSG embarked on this consultative exercise from the very beginning of his mandate, a trend that intensified in his second mandate and significantly contributed to adding a strong sense of legitimacy to the final outcomes. The resolutions adopted by the HRC highlighted in particular the consultation process as 'comprehensive' and open to broad participation by all groups with an interest in the debate.[35] Some meetings had a regional character, whilst others were international; some were thematic, whilst others were more general. The SRSG also spent time visiting capitals and meeting diplomats, business representatives and academics as well as selected NGOs. The string of meetings and trips extended over six years and was made possible by an unprecedented level – within the UN human rights system – of financial support from individual Western states, which also enabled the SRSG to have a large team of advisors.

The process generated high expectations among a relatively large universe comprised of diverse types of NGOs, trade unions, businesses and governments (primarily from the Northern hemisphere). The consultations resulted in a significant number of online written submissions. But taking this level of participation as a sort of agreement with or endorsement of the final outcomes would be wrong. It should be noted though that such an assumption is not exclusive to the 'Ruggie process'; in fact, it is also common to most processes that engage in open consultations. In practice, none of these processes are truly consensus-building. The final outcomes in the form of printed documents are written by an individual or a group then presented in her/its name, and are never intended to be the result of a negotiation and agreement process. In this model, many people may be 'consulted', but the final document is owned by the individual author. Although the Framework and the GPs were 'unanimously' adopted by the HRC, they are not the expression of a negotiated agreement among states and/or other stakeholders.

Despite the significant number of consultations and submissions, the 'Ruggie process' consistently failed to engage a very important set of

---

[35] See, for instance, Human Rights Council, 'Resolution 8/7: Mandate of the Special Representative of the Secretary-General on the Issue of Human Rights and Transnational Corporations and Other Business Enterprises' (18 June 2008), para. 3.

stakeholders, that is, the individuals and communities who claimed to be directly affected by corporate actions and/or omissions. As noted above, since 2007 NGOs had explicitly requested the SRSG to engage those individuals and communities by paying onsite visits, listening to their grievances and especially by drawing lessons from specific situations in order to create a robust basis for his conclusions. Over the years, some also suggested that the SRSG mandate should be able to act as an accountability mechanism by providing a basic level of justice to alleged victims by receiving communications on specific instances of abuse.[36] An explicit mandate that would require the SRSG to pay country visits and look into specific instances of abuse was never accepted. During informal interactions on the edges of the HRC, it was argued that such country visits were in fact occurring or could occur without an explicit mandate, that individuals and groups who claimed to be victims of abuse by companies were met on a regular basis and would continue to be invited to consultations, and that thus there was no need for changes in this approach. With regard to accountability for specific instances of abuse, it was argued that the nature of the exercise was to develop standards and provide guidance. Dealing with specific instances of abuse or complaints would derail the process and alienate businesses, who would then see it as another opportunity for criticism of them.

The conspicuous absence of these important 'stakeholders' in the process clearly had a significant impact on the overall levels of participation. A number of scholars and groups also resented the fact that their voices and contributions were sidelined. By contrast, the SRSG undoubtedly succeeded in involving the business community in the process. With strong voices and resources, the business community was clearly in no need of stewardship while participating in a process in which it had a huge stake, and arguably it did more than participate. Throughout the process, the participation of the business sector and its acceptance of the outcomes were clearly more important than the participation and acceptance of the affected communities. After all, the reasoning seems to go, it is the business community not the affected communities which needs to accept the human rights norms.

The HRC adopted the Framework and the GPs in 2008 and 2011 respectively, without the need for a vote. In the practice of the HRC, resolutions are adopted by consensus when no state (out of the 47 members of the HRC) calls for a vote and/or votes against. However,

---

[36] See, for instance, HRW, 'Joint Civil Society Statement', n. 8.

there are important nuances to be noted here. Firstly, this is a body of only 47 states, which is only a fraction of the 193 states represented in the General Assembly, excluding the permanent observers. Secondly, during the 2008 debate, the delegate from South Africa explicitly stated that his country could not join the consensus, but would not call for a vote. In the end, no voting was called for, thus there was adoption by consensus. A similar episode took place in 2011. During the adoption of the GPs, the Ecuadorian representative made a strong statement virtually announcing Ecuador's departure from the consensus, but then stated that Ecuador would not call for a vote 'out of consideration of the five sponsoring countries'.[37] These two examples show that consensus was not really as strong as it was presented to be.[38]

'Plus ça change, plus c'est la même chose'[39] (the more things change, the more they are the same)?

The HRC's adoption of the Framework and the GPs proposed by the SRSG meant political acknowledgement and support of the 'social norm' that requires corporations to respect all rights. The understanding that this was not innovative but a recognition of fact, prompted several leading human rights organisations to state their support for the Framework by welcoming 'the confirmation' of the corporate responsibility to respect all human rights.[40] Thus, for the human rights movement, this was not a truly new or revolutionary concept.

The most important aspect of the HRC's adoption of the Framework and the underlying concept that business corporations have a social responsibility to respect all rights is not the crafting of a new human rights rule, but the adoption itself, which provided a crucial level of political legitimacy from the UN for a document that would otherwise be without much consequence. However, the significance of this act is somehow diminished by problems of substance and process outlined

---

[37] Human Rights Council, 'Council Establishes Working Group on Human Rights and Transnational Corporations and Other Business Enterprises' (16 June 2011), www.ohchr.org/EN/NewsEvents/Pages/DisplayNews.aspx?NewsID=11165&LangID=E (last accessed 11 December 2012).

[38] For a detailed critique, see Chapter 4.   [39] J. A. Karr, Les Guêpes (January 1849).

[40] Human Rights Watch, 'Joint NGO Statement to the Eighth Session of the Human Rights Council: Third Report of the Special Representative of the Secretary-General on Human Rights and Transnational Corporations and Other Business Enterprises' (20 May 2008), www.hrw.org/news/2008/05/19/joint-ngo-statement-eighth-session-human-rights-council (last accessed 11 December 2012).

above. In terms of the process, neither the Framework nor the GPs were negotiated at an inter-governmental level. Rather they are the product of the work of an individual appointed as an expert by the UN. Whether an instrument is the result of negotiation and agreement among states or not is of great significance in international law.[41]

Much more consequential is the question of whether or not the Framework and the GPs provide answers to the fundamental questions that the UN Norms intended to address: the need for enforceable obligations, accountability and remedies. As the report setting out the Framework states, '[f]ailure to meet this responsibility can subject companies to the courts of public opinion – comprising employees, communities, consumers, civil society as well as investors – and occasionally to charges in actual courts'.[42]

Companies can be held accountable in the courts of public opinion, but who would realistically work to hold companies accountable and with reference to which rights or normative parameters they would be held accountable remains unclear. This is another reason why the 'corporate responsibility to respect' is weak as a normative proposition. Any theory or system that proposes a set of rules with normative force should also incorporate a theory of compliance with the norms proposed, which defines the consequences that lack of observance to the norm will entail. In the case of the GPs, compliance with the 'corporate responsibility to respect' is basically left to the market mechanism, for example consumer awareness and preferences.

Civil society groups and human rights advocates are the most likely candidates to fulfil the role of watchdogs of corporate behaviour with reference to the body of internationally recognised rights. But they normally work within the parameters of national laws and institutions shaped largely by reference to the human rights instruments binding on the country in question. Human rights instruments not binding on a country will not normally be enforced within the national legal system of that country. Steps taken by any given state to implement a non-binding

---

[41] Compare, for instance, the status of the 'Basic Principles and Guidelines on the Right to a Remedy and Reparation for Victims of Gross Violations of International Human Rights Law and Serious Violations of International Humanitarian Law', GA Res. 60/147, A/RES/60/147 (21 March 2006) with that of the 'Updated Set of Principles for the Protection and Promotion of Human Rights Through Action to Combat Impunity', E/CN.4/2005/102/Add.1 (8 February 2005) and many other sets of guidelines drafted by individual experts within the United Nations.

[42] SRSG, '2008 Report', n. 4, para. 54.

rule remain fully optional for that country.[43] The GPs could have provided guidance about the rights that national law should protect or offences it should punish, including through a transnational system of police and judicial co-operation, but they did not do so.

Moving beyond CSR and back to legal responsibility

The resilience of the quest for binding human rights norms for companies shows that it touches on an important need of the international human rights community that begs for an appropriate response. Nowhere has this need found clearer expression so far than in the context of litigation in the United States (US) under the Alien Tort Statute (ATS), an eighteenth century statute attributing jurisdiction to the US federal courts over tort cases committed in violation of 'the law of nations'. Numerous cases – mostly concerning corporate complicity with egregious human rights violations – are being litigated in the US courts under this law. One case in particular, *Esther Kiobel* v. *Royal Dutch Petroleum Company* (*Kiobel*), has served as the focus of radically opposite legal opinions about whether corporations are bound to respect international law norms that prohibit serious human rights violations such as crimes under international customary law.[44]

When, in September 2010, the US Court of Appeals for the Second Circuit in the *Kiobel* case ruled by majority that corporations cannot be held legally liable for the kind of violations of international law foreseen in the ATS,[45] shocked rights advocates asked whether corporations can really be allowed to commit or aid and abet torture, genocide or war crimes yet cannot be held legally accountable for these acts. To ascertain whether the 'law of nations' contained a norm binding corporations, the judges in *Kiobel* looked mainly to international customary law. In that respect, their enquiry went beyond the SRSG's own enquiries in his 2006

---

[43] This point can be illustrated by the example of the United Kingdom, which has recently taken a policy decision not to hire private security contractors who have not signed up to and are not certified by the Oversight Mechanism attached to the International Code of Conduct for Private Security Providers. Critics highlight that this is a simple policy decision that could be rolled back any time as long as it is not enacted in law.

[44] *Esther Kiobel* v. *Royal Dutch Petroleum Co.*, Petition No. 10–1491 (Shell). The history and current documents pertaining to this case can be found at http://www.business-humanrights.org/Categories/Lawlawsuits/Lawsuitsregulatoryaction/LawsuitsSelectedcases/Shelllawsuitre Nigeria and http://www.business-humanrights.org/Documents/SupremeCourtATCAReview (last accessed 11 December 2012).

[45] 621 F. 3d 111 (2010).

and 2007 reports. Crucially, human rights advocates argue that the Court of Appeals did not look at other sources of international law, namely, the 'general principles of law recognised by civilised nations' as defined in the Statute of the International Court of Justice.[46] The principles of law followed in most countries of the world accept that legal entities such as corporations can be held legally liable for wrongs that cause harm to others. If the principle of corporate liability for egregious conduct, including actions of the kind envisaged by the term 'law of nations' in the ATS, is generally accepted, why is this principle not also recognised in international law? In March 2012, the US Supreme Court ordered the rehearing of arguments in this case, but also asked to be briefed on a broader set of issues, including the scope of extra-territorial jurisdiction under the ATS and accessory liability. In April 2013, the Supreme Court ruled affirming the decision by the Second Circuit Court of Appeals and dismissing the petition. But while the Court of Appeals had reasoned that the law of nations does not recognise corporate liability, the Supreme Court dismissed the case on the basis of a presumption against extraterritoriality that applies to claims under the ATS.[47]

A number of well-known scholars and other actors had submitted *amicus curiae* briefs to the Supreme Court. The UN High Commissioner for Human Rights, in *amici curiae* in support of plaintiffs, acknowledged that general principles of law support the view that corporations can be held accountable for serious human rights violations, while the US government expressed the view that nothing in federal law nor in international law requires a distinction between individuals and corporations for the purposes of the application of the ATS.[48] The US filed a supplementary brief taking a more nuanced view this time about the territorial scope of ATS application.[49] During the first oral hearing, the

---

[46] See '*Esther Kiobel* v. *Royal Dutch Petroleum Co.*, Brief of Amici Curiae International Human Rights Organizations and International Law Experts in Support of Petitioners', No. 10–1491 (December 2011), http://www.scotusblog.com/case-files/cases/kiobel-v-royal-dutch-petroleum/ (last accessed 11 December 2012).

[47] *Esther Kiobel* v. *Royal Dutch Petroleum Co.*, 133 S. Ct. 1659 (2013).

[48] '*Esther Kiobel* v. *Royal Dutch Petroleum Co.*, Brief for the United States as Amicus Curiae Supporting Petitioners', 20, www.americanbar.org/content/dam/aba/publications/supreme_court_preview/briefs/10-1491_petitioner_amcu_unitedstates.authcheckdam.pdf (last accessed 7 January 2013).

[49] See '*Esther Kiobel* v. *Royal Dutch Petroleum Co.*, Supplemental Brief for the United States as Amicus Curiae in Partial Support of Affirmance', www.americanbar.org/content/dam/aba/publications/supreme_court_preview/briefs/10-1491_affirmanceamcuusa.authcheckdam.pdf (last accessed 7 January 2013).

respondents stated that the GPs and the work of the SRSG suggested that corporations could not violate international law. Shell quoted from the SRSG's 2007 report: 'it does not seem that the international human rights instruments discussed here currently impose direct legal responsibilities on corporations'.[50] However, Ruggie submitted an *amicus* brief in June 2012 stating that the above-mentioned quote misrepresented his position, because the sentence was taken out of context and did not refer to the rest of his conclusions on this subject.[51] In his 2007 report, as in his 2006 report, the SRSG had in fact left open the possibility that corporations might be liable under international law for international crimes.[52] This could be interpreted as an admission that corporations are bound by international law after all. However, Ruggie never elaborated on this statement.

The debate around the *Kiobel* case highlights both the actuality of the question of corporate legal responsibility under international law and the evolving understanding of international law among scholars and states in relation to this issue. This also suggests a growing willingness to move beyond CSR and tackle the fundamental questions underlying the business and human rights equation.

The Framework and the GPs' restatement of the 'social norms' underpinning the corporate responsibility to respect human rights do offer value, in that they provide a policy framework and identify some concrete steps for states and companies to take in protecting and respecting human rights, respectively. This Framework can be useful in promoting change in some respects. It needs to be developed and put

---

[50] Human Rights Council, 'Business and Human Rights: Mapping International Standards of Responsibility and Accountability for Corporate Acts', A/HRC/4/35 (19 February 2007), para. 44 (SRSG, '2007 Report'). This sentence was quoted in the Brief for Respondents, *Esther Kiobel* v. *Royal Dutch Petroleum Co.*, No. 10–1491 (27 January 2012), 28. See also Transcript of Oral Argument at 49:7–15, *Esther Kiobel* v. *Royal Dutch Petroleum Co.*, No. 10–1491 (28 February 2012). The respondents argued that this statement supports the conclusion that 'international-law sources on the specific offenses at issue refute corporate responsibility'.

[51] 'Brief *Amici Curiae* of Former UN Special Representative for Business and Human Rights, Professor John Ruggie; Professor Philip Alston; and the Global Justice Clinic at NYU School of Law in Support of Neither Party' (12 June 2012), www.americanbar.org/content/dam/aba/publications/supreme_court_preview/briefs/10-1491_neutralamcufmrunspecialrepetal.authcheckdam.pdf (last accessed 7 January 2013).

[52] The 2007 report by the SRSG concluded that 'the most consequential legal development' in the 'business and human rights constellation' is 'the gradual extension of liability to companies for international crimes, under domestic jurisdictions but reflecting international standards'. SRSG, '2007 Report', n. 50, para. 84.

into practice through a variety of tools and instruments, one of which is the text of the GPs itself. However, this Framework does not impose liability (in the sense of the legal understanding of 'responsibility') on corporations. To his credit, the author of the Framework – the SRSG – never presented his work as the ultimate response to all or the most fundamental questions, though there have been subsequent attempts to establish his work as the definitive and authoritative global standard in this field.

The SRSG has described the GPs and their due diligence recommendations as a 'game changer' from 'naming and shaming' to 'knowing and showing'.[53] There is no doubt that 'knowing and showing' can help companies avoid and address harms. What is far from clear is whether 'naming and shaming' is irrelevant or unnecessary. In human rights law and practice, investigation, punishment of those responsible and the provision of redress for the victims are fundamental. The Framework is presented as resting on three differentiated, but complementary principles: the state duty to protect, the corporate responsibility to respect 'and access to remedy, because even the most concerted efforts cannot prevent all abuse'.[54] Nevertheless, legal liability in the form of civil or criminal sanctions would presuppose a clear formulation of the rights to be protected, the violation of which the law will sanction with legal responsibility. The mandate given by the HRC to the newly established Working Group on Business and Human Rights could be used as the setting for the exploration and further elaboration of these concepts.[55] However, early actions and plans by this group do not indicate that they will go in that direction.[56]

---

[53] SRSG, 'The "Protect, Respect and Remedy" Framework: Implications for the ILO: Remarks' (3 June 2010), 3, www.ilo.org/wcmsp5/groups/public/@ed_emp/@emp_ent/@multi/documents/genericdocument/wcms_142560.pdf (last accessed 7 January 2013).

[54] SRSG, '2008 Report', n. 4, para. 9. See also para. 82 stating that 'state regulation proscribing certain corporate conduct will have little impact without accompanying mechanisms to investigate, punish, and redress abuses'.

[55] Human Rights Council, '17/4 Human Rights and Transnational Corporations and Other Business Enterprises: Resolution Adopted by the Human Rights Council', A/HRC/RES/17/4 (6 July 2011).

[56] The first report of the Working Group to the HRC focused on reporting instances of uptaking of the GPs by various initiatives and stakeholders, and defining a set of workstreams and methods of work, without considering exploration of options beyond the GPs. Human Rights Council, 'Report of the Working Group on the Issue of Human Rights and Transnational Corporations and Other Business Enterprises', A/HRC/20/29 (10 April 2012).

In a sense, the 'Ruggie process' appears to have ended where it started, with the fundamental question of whether business corporations are bound by international human rights law, and if so, which rights are they bound to respect? A significant difference from the past state of play is that there is now a process in motion. However, the issue remains controversial and consensus remains elusive, an outcome not entirely different from the point at which the process began.

Conclusion

The Framework and the GPs represent an important step, but they are clearly not exempt from conceptual or political weaknesses. More importantly, they do not close the original and long-running debate about corporate human rights obligations. In fact, the debate about corporate legal obligations and corporate accountability is still very much open. States seem to adopt a range of approaches, some openly dissenting with the majority and most ready to seek better ways to regulate and hold companies accountable.

In international relations and law, as in other areas of human interaction, nothing is irreversible or definitive. Not only do social expectations evolve, and more rapidly than one can imagine or sometimes accept, but political consensus can change too. New consensuses are built to replace or complement others.

The consensus around the 2008 Framework was perhaps the closest the international community has got to real unanimity (beyond the state-centric conception of international community and including all relevant global actors). Significant cracks in that consensus appeared again in 2011, when a number of states, NGOs and trade unions opposed or critiqued the GPs at the time of their adoption. Although consensus is not a requirement for operating meaningful changes – on the contrary, significant oppositions are expected – it is nevertheless useful for establishing legitimacy and asserting authoritativeness, which is perhaps precisely why proponents of the GPs have sought to claim that they enjoy unanimous support.

CSR with an added element of human rights seems to be the accepted formula at present, but the evolving understanding and expectations of international law in relation to corporations seem to be moving in directions that can take us beyond CSR and into the realm of legal liability. That will undoubtedly be a better outcome for the victims of corporate human rights abuses.

4

Treating human rights lightly: a critique of the consensus rhetoric and the language employed by the Guiding Principles

SURYA DEVA[*]

Introduction

The Guiding Principles on Business and Human Rights (GPs)[1] represent the culmination of the mandate of Professor John Ruggie, the former UN Secretary-General's Special Representative on the Issue of Human Rights and Transnational Corporations (SRSG). The GPs, which were endorsed by the UN Human Rights Council (HRC) in June 2011,[2] have been widely applauded. They have been praised for breaking 'new ground'[3] and labelled as the 'game changer'[4] as well as a UDHR equivalent for business.[5] The GPs are also proving to be influential in that they have been incorporated into the 2011 update of the OECD Guidelines[6] and

---

[*] I would like to thank Mr Calvin Chun-ngai Ho for providing excellent research assistance.

[1] Human Rights Council, 'Guiding Principles on Business and Human Rights: Implementing the United Nations "Protect, Respect and Remedy" Framework', A/HRC/17/31 (21 March 2011) (SRSG, 'Guiding Principles').

[2] Human Rights Council, 'New Guiding Principles on Business and Human Rights Endorsed by the UN Human Rights Council' (16 June 2011), www.ohchr.org/en/NewsEvents/Pages/DisplayNews.aspx?NewsID=11164&LangID=E (last accessed 17 June 2011).

[3] M. Otero, 'Keynote Address: UN Guiding Principles on Business and Human Rights' (8 December 2011), www.state.gov/g/178545.htm (last accessed 20 September 2012).

[4] S. Jerbi, 'UN Adopts Guiding Principles on Business and Human Rights – What Comes Next?' (17 June 2011), www.ihrb.org/commentary/staff/un_adopts_guiding_principles_on_business_and_human_rights.html (last accessed 20 September 2012).

[5] J. Kallman and M. Mohan, 'Reality Check: Just Tell It Like It Is', *Forbes Indonesia* (August 2011), 37.

[6] 'OECD Guidelines for Multinational Enterprises: Recommendations for Responsible Business Conduct in a Global Context' (25 May 2011), www.oecd.org/daf/inv/mne/48004323.pdf (last accessed 10 June 2011).

the ISO 26000 Guidance on Social Responsibility.[7] The European Commission is also taking several steps to implement the GPs.[8] The SRSG has of course praised, promoted and sold the GPs like a charming marketing executive.[9]

There is, however, always a danger in uncritically embracing the GPs and the ideas that underpin them. This chapter will critically examine whether the GPs may have undermined the goal of making companies legally accountable for human rights violations. I will argue that the GPs may achieve this unintended result by treating human rights too lightly.[10] Two examples will be offered to illustrate *why* and *how* the GPs have not taken human rights seriously. The first example concerns the oft-quoted claim that the GPs represent a 'consensus' on the issue of business and human rights. Apart from exposing the fragility and hollowness of this claim, I will contend that the so-called consensus rhetoric has moved the goalpost. Rather than attempting to develop robust measures to secure corporate accountability for human rights violations,[11] the focus of the SRSG's mandate in the aftermath of the Norms on the Responsibilities of Transnational Corporations and Other Business Enterprises with Regard to Human Rights (UN Norms)[12] shifted to putting in place whatever was acceptable to the Norms'

---

[7] International Organization for Standardization, 'ISO 26000 – Social Responsibility', www.iso.org/iso/home/standards/management-standards/iso26000.htm/ (last accessed 20 September 2012).

[8] European Commission, 'A Renewed EU Strategy 2011–14 for Corporate Social Responsibility', COM(2011) 681 final (25 October 2011), 14–15, www.ec.europa.eu/enterprise/policies/sustainable-business/files/csr/new-csr/act_en.pdf (last accessed 20 September 2012).

[9] Out of numerous instances, see the following: John Ruggie, 'Building on a "Landmark Year" and Thinking Ahead' (12 January 2012), www.ihrb.org/commentary/board/building_on_landmark_year_and_thinking_ahead.html-footnote-2 (last accessed 20 September 2012).

[10] Human rights are treated 'lightly', for instance, when corporate responsibilities are derived from an amorphous notion of social expectations, the scope of corresponding obligations of states and companies is confined to the 'protect' and 'respect' cages, and human rights are not accorded a normative hierarchy over other norms.

[11] The original 2005 mandate had requested the SRSG to, amongst other goals, '*identify and clarify standards of corporate* responsibility and *accountability* for transnational corporations and other business enterprises with regard to human rights'. Commission on Human Rights, 'Promotion and Protection of Human Rights', E/CN.4/2005/L.87 (15 April 2005), para. 1(a) (emphasis added).

[12] United Nations, 'Norms on the Responsibilities of Transnational Corporations and Other Business Enterprises with Regard to Human Rights', UN Doc E/CN.4/Sub.2/2003/12/Rev.2 (13 August 2003) (UN Norms).

antagonists. In other words, the consensus rhetoric partly explains *why* the GPs have treated human rights too lightly.

This brings me to the second example, which will demonstrate *how* the GPs try to dilute, in subtle ways, the human rights responsibilities of business. It is argued that a deliberate use of carefully chosen terms (e.g. 'responsibility' rather than 'duty'; 'impact' rather than 'violation') and concepts (e.g. social expectations and due diligence) has the effect of rolling back the legal concretisation of corporate human rights obligations. For example, the 'responsibility to respect' mould confines the role companies play with respect to human rights to being voluntary (because there are no legally binding obligations) and narrow (because there are no obligations akin to protecting or fulfilling human rights).

The critical analysis presented in this chapter should be useful for a number of reasons. Firstly, it should provide normative support to the voices raised by civil society groups questioning the robustness of the GPs.[13] Secondly, the present analysis should inform the work of a five-member Working Group that the HRC has established to promote the implementation of the GPs.[14] The Working Group is tasked with a number of responsibilities.[15] It is also mandated to develop a regular dialogue and discuss possible areas of co-operation with governments and all relevant actors (such as the UN bodies/agencies, companies, national human rights institutions, representatives of indigenous peoples, civil society organisations) and to guide the work of the annual Forum on Business and Human Rights.[16] The critique of the GPs advanced here will hopefully assist the Working Group in fulfilling its responsibilities, especially the responsibility 'to explore options and make recommendations at the national, regional and international

---

[13] Among others, Human Rights Watch, Amnesty International and the International Commission of Jurists have pointed out that the GPs do not go far enough in dealing with the current situation of corporate impunity for human rights abuses.

[14] Human Rights Council, 'Human Rights and Transnational Corporations and Other Business Enterprises', A/HRC/17/L.17/Rev.1 (15 July 2011), para. 6.

[15] The Working Group has been requested, among others, to promote the effective and comprehensive dissemination and implementation of the GPs; to identify, exchange and promote good practices learned on the implementation of the GPs; to provide support for capacity-building and offer advice regarding the development of domestic legislation and policies relating to business and human rights; to conduct country visits; and to explore options and make recommendations for enhancing access to effective remedies available to victims of corporate human rights abuses. *Ibid.*

[16] HRC, n. 14, paras. 6 and 13.

levels for enhancing access to effective remedies available to those whose human rights are affected by corporate activities'.[17]

Piercing the façade of consensus

The SRSG had noted at the outset that his underlying mandate was to break 'the stalemated debate' over the UN Norms and build a consensus.[18] The SRSG has, therefore, taken a special pride in being able to forge a consensus on business and human rights in the form of the GPs.[19] It also appears that the success of the SRSG's mandate as well as the GPs is being largely measured by the consensus barometer. There are historical reasons for this orientation: the GPs have achieved what the UN Code of Conduct on Transnational Corporations and the UN Norms could not. However, as I try to show below, the claim of consensus is somewhat fragile and hollow on closer scrutiny. It also appears that the consensus was manufactured by managing objections.

What does 'consensus' mean in common parlance as well as in international law-making? The term is defined by the *Oxford English Dictionary* as a '[g]eneral agreement or concord of different parts or organs of the body in effecting a given purpose'; 'the collective unanimous opinion of a number of persons'.[20] According to *Black's Law Dictionary*, 'consensus' simply means a 'general agreement'; 'collective opinion'.[21] 'Consensus' is further defined as follows in the vocabulary guide of the International Organization for Standardization (ISO): 'general agreement, characterized by the absence of sustained opposition to substantial issues by any important part of the concerned interests and by a process that involves seeking to take into account the views of all parties concerned and to reconcile any conflicting

---

[17] *Ibid.*, para. 6(e).

[18] SRSG for Business and Human Rights, 'Opening Statement to United Nations Human Rights Council' (25 September 2006), http://198.170.85.29/Ruggie-statement-to-UN-Human-Rights-Council-25-Sep-2006.pdf (last accessed 20 September 2012).

[19] Out of numerous self-praising instances, see the following observation: the HRC 'in an unprecedented step, endorsed unanimously [the GPs] in June 2011 . . . I enjoyed strong support within all stakeholder groups, including the business community.' J. G. Ruggie, 'Kiobel and Corporate Social Responsibility: An Issues Brief' (4 September 2012), p. 3, www.business-humanrights.org/media/documents/ruggie-kiobel-and-corp-social-reson sibility-sep-2012.pdf (last accessed 20 September 2012).

[20] *Oxford English Dictionary*, 2nd edn (online version, December 2011).

[21] B. A. Garner (ed.), *Black's Law Dictionary*, 9th edn (St Paul, MN: Thompson Reuters, 2009), 345.

arguments . . . Consensus need not imply unanimity'.[22] It is not uncommon to reach decisions by consensus in the international arena.[23] Several international instruments expressly provide for consensual decision-making, implying thereby the lack of any 'formal objection' to the decision.[24]

Taking these definitions into account, 'consensus' in my view should imply the following: (i) there are fundamental differences between various parties on a given issue; (ii) an attempt is made to reconcile differences through free and reasoned exchange of views; (iii) a broad collective agreement is reached amongst the relevant parties on the contentious issue; and (iv) there is no formal objection to the decision reached.[25] A consensual agreement is often reached either because one group may relent from its position (for instance, because of the futility of contest or having been convinced by other sides about the merit of other views) or there might be a 'give and take' from all sides. The other factor that helps in building consensus is the commonality of purpose.

Before we apply this conceptual matrix to assess the extent to which the GPs and the 'Protect, Respect and Remedy' Framework (Framework), on which the GPs are grounded, reflect consensus on the issue of business and human rights, a rider should be noted. Since human rights treaties generally seek to set ideal or aspirational goals, they may not be an ideal candidate for compromises reached through consensus.[26] Also, the Human Rights Committee members have observed that consensual decision-making has the effect of 'not permitting an individual member to hold out for a different position from the large majority' and

---

[22] ISO/IEC, *Standardization and Related Activities – General Vocabulary*, 8th edn (Geneva: ISO/IEC, 2004), 8.

[23] See A. Boyle and C. Chinkin, *The Making of International Law* (Oxford University Press, 2007), 157; R. Sabel, *Procedure at International Conferences*, 2nd edn (Cambridge University Press, 2006), 338–45.

[24] 'The body concerned shall be deemed to have decided by consensus on a matter submitted for its consideration, if no Member, present at the meeting when the decision is taken, formally objects to the proposed decision.' Agreement Establishing the World Trade Organization 1994, Art IX. See also United Nations Convention on the Law of the Sea 1982, Art. 161(8)(d)/(e); Sabel, *Procedure at International Conferences*, n. 23, 336–37.

[25] Contrast these attributes with three main features of consensus highlighted by Aust: '[consensus] is not the same as unanimity, a State can join a consensus even if it could not vote in favour of the treaty, and it is not incompatible with "indicative voting" (a straw poll)'. A. Aust, *Handbook of International Law*, 2nd edn (Cambridge University Press, 2010), 58.

[26] H. J. Steiner, P. Alston and R. Goodman, *International Human Rights in Context: Law, Politics, Morals*, 3rd edn (Oxford University Press, 2008), 676.

'encouraging members holding minority views to go along with a clear trend or dominant opinion'.[27]

Reconciling differences through consultations

Since consensus presupposes differences, what is crucial is the *process* adopted to reconcile those differences. The process should afford all relevant stakeholders a fair opportunity to articulate their positions and exchange views with others. It is equally important that the architect of consensus-building makes a sincere attempt to understand divergent views and accord each of them equal respect, especially dissenting or minority opinions. Giving equal respect to all views may require, for instance, modifying proposals to incorporate interests of divergent stakeholders.[28] Moreover, the consensus facilitator should build the consensus from the bottom up through consultations with all the relevant stakeholders. These process variables are fundamental, because consensus will hardly mean much if all the relevant stakeholders were not given a reasonable opportunity to express their views, the concerns of certain stakeholders are not addressed, or if the consensus exercise was used to secure approval of predetermined views.[29]

Fundamental differences undoubtedly exist amongst states, companies, shareholders, consumers, trade unions, non-governmental organisations (NGOs) and scholars as to the basis, nature and extent of corporate human rights responsibilities. The SRSG deserves praise for leading the process so as to reach out to different stakeholders and trying hard to conduct extensive consultations in order to understand better the different perspectives. One issue of concern here relates to the SRSG's conscious decision not to engage directly with victims of corporate

---

[27] *Ibid.*, 848.

[28] 'Reaching consensus implies that people have worked out their differences and come to a collective decision.' C. Coglianese, 'Is Consensus an Appropriate Basis for Regulatory Policy?' in E. Orts and K. Deketelaere (eds.), *Environmental Contracts: Comparative Approaches to Regulatory Innovation in the United States and Europe* (Kluwer Law International, 2001), 93 at 94.

[29] A Short Guide prepared by the MIT defines consensus as follows: 'it is important that consensus be the product of a good-faith effort to meet the interests of all stakeholders. The key indicator of whether or not a consensus has been reached is that everyone agrees they can live with the final proposal; that is, after every effort has been made to meet any outstanding interests. Thus, consensus requires that someone frame a proposal after listening carefully to everyone's interests.' MIT, 'A Short Guide to Consensus Building', http://web.mit.edu/publicdisputes/practice/cbh_ch1.html (last accesssed 30 December 2012).

human rights violations, thus denying them an opportunity to raise their concerns directly. One of the rationales advanced for this decision – that 'a mandate aimed at producing general principles and guidance for states and business would not mix well with jumping into the middle of specific disputes, which in any case are extremely difficult to resolve from thousands of miles removed'[30] – does not seem convincing. Consultation with victims was desirable not for resolving their specific disputes, but for understanding first-hand the pain and obstacles that they faced in seeking access to justice. If face-to-face consultations could be held with actual (and potential) violators of human rights, there was no reason to remain distant from the victims of such violations.

Although many NGOs working in the field of business and human rights initially supported uncritically the work and proposals of the SRSG, they became more sceptical midway and later openly expressed their disagreements and disappointments with the narrowness and fragility of the final products: the Framework and the GPs.[31] How should the SRSG have dealt with these dissenting voices? As per the process outlined above, the SRSG should have clearly recognised such differences, adequately articulated them in consultation documents and drafts, refined his ideas by taking divergent feedback seriously, and advanced reasons why certain proposals were rejected.

The SRSG did acknowledge differences with NGOs and/or scholars on key aspects. Nevertheless, these differences were neither adequately articulated in consultation papers and reports nor taken seriously. Whereas favourable views of companies, business organisations, states

---

[30] J. G. Ruggie, 'Opening Remarks at Mandate Consultation with Civil Society' (11–12 October 2010), 7, www.reports-and-materials.org/Ruggie-remarks-consultation-civil-society-11-Oct-2010.pdf (last accesssed 30 December 2012).

[31] See, e.g., Amnesty International, 'Comments in Response to the UN Special Representative of the Secretary-General on Transnational Corporations and Other Business Enterprises: Guiding Principles – Proposed Outline' (October 2010), www.amnesty.org/en/library/asset/IOR50/001/2010/en/71401e1e-7e9c-44a4-88a7-de3618b2983b/ior500012010en.pdf (last accesssed 30 December 2012); Human Rights Watch, 'UN Human Rights Council: Weak Stance on Business Standards' (16 June 2011), www.hrw.org/en/news/2011/06/16/un-human-rights-council-weak-stance-business-standards (last accesssed 30 December 2012); Child Rights Information Network, 'Business and Human Rights: CRIN response to adoption of the Guiding Principles' (21 June 2011), www.crin.org/violence/search/closeup.asp?infoID=25245 (last accesssed 30 December 2012); International Federation for Human Rights (FIDH), 'UN Human Rights Council Adopts Guiding Principles on Business Conduct, yet Victims still Waiting for Effective Remedies' (17 June 2011), www.fidh.org/UN-Human-Rights-Council-adopts-Guiding-Principles (last accesssed 30 December 2012).

and academics were splashed all over the media to paint dissenting voices as an insignificant minority, differences were summarily dismissed and people mooting such ideas were shunned. Let me offer one example here. In his opening remarks at the Mandate Consultation with Civil Society held in Geneva in October 2010, the SRSG observed:

> In the end, some of you may continue to disagree with my approach. *I have no problem with that, but let's not spend too much on that. I really do need and value your advice on the immediate task we face: how to move from the framework to viable Guiding Principles, and what viable options I should put before the Council* for how it can best follow up on the mandate when it ends next June.[32]

This statement reflected the SRSG's general attitude that disagreements shown by 'certain' stakeholders – especially if perceived to be 'less powerful'[33] – need not be taken too seriously and accommodated.[34] Nor was it necessary to continue discussion on contentious aspects so as to find a middle ground. However, it is clear that he took differences expressed by business much more seriously, because 'recommendations addressed to business have to find resonance there or they will be resisted or ignored'.[35]

The advice of all stakeholders, including NGOs, was sought and valued, but only within the framework set by the SRSG.[36] In other words, the *core* of the Ruggie project was not open for change and, in fact, hardly changed despite extensive consultations. A comparison of the text of the draft GPs and the final GPs reveals that despite numerous detailed submissions by NGOs and scholars, the final text did not

---

[32] Ruggie, 'Opening Remarks', n. 30, 7–8 (emphasis added).

[33] P. Simons, 'International Law's Invisible Hand and the Future of Corporate Accountability for Violations of Human Rights' (2012) 3:1 *Journal of Human Rights and the Environment* 5, at 11.

[34] In an interview, Ruggie noted: 'If you accommodated everybody you would have nothing left.' J. Ruggie, 'Business and Human Rights: Together at Last? A Conversation with John Ruggie' (2011) 35 *Fletcher Forum of World Affairs* 117, at 119.

[35] 'At the end of the day, the instruments that we proposed as part of the Guiding Principles – for example human rights due diligence as a method for companies to identify and address what their adverse human rights impacts might be – have to make sense inside of a company. Otherwise, it is not going to get done.' Ruggie, 'Together at Last', n. 34, 121. See also J. G. Ruggie, 'The Construction of the UN "Protect, Respect and Remedy" Framework for Business and Rights: The True Confessions of a Principled Pragmatist' (2011) 2 *European Human Rights Law Review* 127, at 128.

[36] See, e.g., SRSG, 'Mandate Consultation Outline' (October 2010), www.reports-and-materials.org/Ruggie-consultations-outline-Oct-2010.pdf (last accessed 26 September 2012).

become much more robust in terms of broadening the scope of corporate human rights responsibilities, enforcement mechanisms, or the removal of barriers experienced by victims in seeking judicial remedies.[37] Consultations do not mean much if the views of certain participants are not to be taken seriously.[38] It is arguable that the SRSG consultations were designed primarily to acquire legitimacy, something which is badly needed when a small group of persons are engaged in the task of international law-making. Stakeholders had the satisfaction that their voices were heard and the SRSG got what he had desired: legitimacy to claim consensus without much tinkering with his regulatory ideas.

In short, as discussed below, the SRSG bypassed controversial issues and ignored dissenting voices in an attempt to sustain a façade of consensus.

Consensus on what?

One potential hazard with consensual decision-making concerns the shelving of the most critical or controversial issues. Coglianese points out: 'Consensus-based processes increase the likelihood that the wrong issues will receive attention. Instead of devoting time and resources to the issues of most importance to the public, a focus on consensus tends to lead to the selection of the most tractable issues, the ones most amenable to agreement.'[39]

There is no doubt that the SRSG was successful in shifting the focus of debate away from core controversial issues that often engulf the business

---

[37] There are some positives, though. For instance, a reference to 'gender-based violence and sexual violence' in Principle 7(b) was not there in Draft Principle 10. At the same time, it seems that the final text of certain principles was polished to make it more business friendly. For example, Principle 2 now does not explicitly refer to 'subsidiaries and other related legal entities' in relation to states encouraging companies to respect human rights throughout their operations, something that was found in Draft Principle 2. Similarly, Principle 11 uses the term 'involved' – rather than 'cause or contribute' as found in Draft Principle 12 – regarding adverse human rights impacts caused by companies.

[38] Commentators noted that the SRSG's 'real interlocutors were major corporations, business associations such as the International Chamber of Commerce and the International Organization of Employers, as well as the legal counsels of these same corporations. As for the other participants in the numerous meetings organized by the Special Representative of the Secretary-General, they were mere onlookers whose opinion was not at all taken into account.' A. Teitelbaum and M. Ozden, 'Transnational Corporations Major Players in Human Rights Violations' (December 2011), 6, www.cetim.ch/en/documents/report_10.pdf (last accesssed 30 December 2012).

[39] Coglianese, 'Is Consensus an Appropriate Basis?', n. 28, 107.

and human rights discourse.[40] In the wake of several differences that existed amongst various stakeholders, the GPs adopted a minimalist (and to some extent escapist) approach in order to steer clear of complex controversial questions. 'Principled pragmatism' was the paradigm used to justify resorting to this consensus-building strategy.[41] So, if the liability of a parent company for human rights violations by its subsidiaries had been a controversial question, it was pragmatic for the GPs not to offer any solution to this problem, beyond identifying it as one of the legal barriers.[42] Similarly, the GPs make no attempt to concretise the principles that could guide corporate behaviour in situations of complicity – again, perhaps, to pre-empt any potential resistance on the part of companies to such moves. The question of when a company should decide to withdraw from or disinvest in a given market is a difficult one,[43] but the GPs do not bother to confront it. Nor was any effort made to think of sanctions for companies that fail to take the recommended due diligence steps or provide remediation mechanisms.

One complex issue is about the formulation of the precise human rights responsibilities of companies. Considering that deep divisions and disagreements had persisted on this question for several decades (and which most recently surfaced at the drafting of the UN Norms),[44]

---

[40] Dhooge alludes to such shift as follows: 'approaches emphasizing corporate compliance with lists of designated rights have been rejected in favor of a process emphasizing due diligence as implemented through impact assessment. The focus of the Framework on due diligence transforms the debate from one of normative compliance to one of corporate governance.' L. J. Dhooge, 'Due Diligence as a Defense to Corporate Liability Pursuant to the Alien Tort Statute' (2008) 22 *Emory International Law Review* 455, at 496.

[41] Principled pragmatism is defined as follows: 'an unflinching commitment to the principle of strengthening the promotion and protection of human rights as it relates to business, coupled with a pragmatic attachment to what works best in creating change where it matters most – in the daily lives of people'. Commission on Human Rights, 'Interim Report of the Special Representative of the Secretary-General on the Issue of Human Rights and Transnational Corporations and Other Business Enterprises', E/CN.4/2006/97 (22 February 2006), para. 81 (SRSG, '2006 Interim Report').

[42] SRSG, 'Guiding Principles', n. 1, Commentary on Principle 26.

[43] See G. Nystuen, A. Follesdal and O. Mestad (eds.), *Human Rights, Corporate Complicity and Disinvestment* (Cambridge University Press, 2011).

[44] Corporate organisations have been quite active and vocal in opposing domestic as well as international initiatives that seek to impose social responsibilities on companies. See, for example, the opposition of the US Chamber of Commerce to the rule proposed by the National Labor Relations Board that requires all US employers to 'post notices informing workers about their legal rights to form a union and bargain on contracts'. S. Armour, 'Employers Must Tell Workers of Rights to Unionize, NLRB Says' (26 August 2011, www.bloomberg.com/news/2011-08-25/employers-must-tell-workers-of-right-to-unionize-nlrb-says-2-.html (last accesssed 30 December 2012).

the GPs adopt a circular approach and make no attempt to clarify the exact contours of the human rights responsibilities of companies. The GPs rather follow an easier path of referring companies to international human rights instruments that were drafted with states as the primary duty-bearers. This process of transplantation is neither easy nor free from conceptual problems.[45] Let us consider a few examples to understand this point. Article 12 of the International Covenant on Economic, Social and Cultural Rights (ICESCR) states that the 'States Parties to the present Covenant recognize the right of everyone to the enjoyment of the highest attainable standard of physical and mental health.' How can this right be translated into responsibilities for business? Would a company breach this right by not providing medical insurance to its employees, not paying them a salary good enough to enable them to obtain decent medical treatment, or by not offering its workers reasonable breaks and weekly rest days? Similarly, it is likely that companies would struggle to distil the implications flowing from rights enumerated in the International Covenant on Civil and Political Rights (ICCPR): for example, everyone shall have the right to hold opinions without interference (Article 19), the right of peaceful assembly (Article 21), or the right and opportunity to vote and to be elected at genuine periodic elections (Article 25). For instance, will Apple Inc. infringe Article 19 if it dismissed an employee for criticising it for profiteering from the exploitation of workers in Chinese factories?

The GPs, thus, by and large, represent a consensus on generally settled business and human rights issues such as the state duty to protect and corporate responsibility to respect human rights. Since any attempt to offer concrete recommendations on remaining controversial issues would have undermined the goal of achieving consensus, the GPs did not take that route. As the primary objective seemingly was to break the stalemate and achieve consensus, it did not really matter if the GPs fell short of delivering a robust framework to promote corporate human rights responsibilities. It is thus questionable if such a consensus is really worth much when deep disagreements remain on critical key issues.

It is also possible that the current consensus on a narrow set of issues might get exposed and the divisive debate resurface if the GPs fail to offer

---

[45] M. Goodhart, 'Human Rights and Non-State Actors: Theoretical Puzzles' in G. Andreopoulos, Z. F. K. Arat and P. Juviler (eds.), *Non-State Actors in the Human Rights Universe* (Bloomfield, CT: Kumarian Press, 2006), 23, 34–35.

the preventive and redressive levels of efficacy expected by the victims of corporate human rights violations.[46] Kamatali argues that:

> limiting enforcement of the corporate responsibility to respect human rights to general social norms and market expectations ... is not sustainable and offers little to the victims of corporate human rights violations. Until the question of whether international human rights law directly imposes legal obligations on corporations has been authoritatively answered, the divisive debate over companies' human rights responsibilities is unlikely to end.[47]

Manufacturing consensus by managing objections

The SRSG and other commentators[48] have stressed the significance and uniqueness of the universal support that the GPs received in the HRC. A real concern, however, is that such a consensus was manufactured by carefully managing dissenting voices and objections.[49] Conscious, continuous and concerted efforts were made to achieve consensus and steamroll differences, so as to give an impression that the 'win-win' situation is beneficial for all parties. Two examples should suffice here. Firstly, although the SRSG did very well in engaging various stakeholders throughout the mandate, it appears that he was not very receptive to or tolerant of ideas that ran against his vision of what human rights responsibilities companies should have or how companies should be regulated. Some of the publicly available 'adversarial' exchanges that the SRSG has had with NGOs illustrate this approach that polarised the debate and had a chilling effect on the possibility of participants holding diverse opinions on contentious issues.[50] The SRSG also actively

---

[46] For the twin (preventive and redressive) levels of efficacy, see S. Deva, *Regulating Corporate Human Rights Violations: Humanizing Business* (London: Routledge, 2012), 47–50.

[47] J. Kamatali, 'New Guiding Principles on Business and Human Rights' Contribution in Ending the Divisive Debate over Human Rights Responsibilities of Companies: Is it Time for an ICJ Advisory Opinion?' (2012) 20 *Cardozo Journal of International and Comparative Law* 437, at 441 (footnotes omitted).

[48] See, e.g., Jerbi, 'UN Adopts Guiding Principles', n. 4. He notes: 'with 28 countries joining the 12 cross-regional co-sponsors of the resolution and passage without a vote, the Human Rights Council's endorsement of the Guiding Principles could not be stronger'.

[49] One can draw an analogy with the 'manufactured consent' thesis of Herman and Chomsky regarding the role of media in propagating a particular viewpoint in the guise of neutrality. E. S. Herman and N. Chomsky, *Manufacturing Consent: The Political Economy of the Mass Media* (New York: Pantheon Books, 1988).

[50] See, for example, exchanges with Amnesty International, Human Rights Watch and FIDH, www.business-humanrights.org/SpecialRepPortal/Home/Protect-Respect-Remedy-Framework/GuidingPrinciples/Submissions (last accesssed 30 December 2012).

encouraged other international organisations engaged in formulating
the social responsibilities of companies to be consistent with his regulatory ideas, concepts and principles.[51]

Secondly, when the HRC was considering a resolution to endorse the
GPs, Alberto Dumont (Argentina) expressed the hope that 'this resolution could be adopted without a vote'.[52] It was a bit surprising that the
focus, at this point, appeared not to be on putting in place an effective
regulatory framework or improving the GPs, but on achieving consensus. Most telling were the following comments made by Mauricio
Montalvo from Ecuador:

> *it [Ecuador] would not stand in the way of consensus out of consideration
> of the five sponsoring countries.* Ecuador noted that its delegation had
> stressed concerns about binding measures throughout the whole process,
> though its comments were not included in the final text of the resolution.
> *Ecuador noted that the resolution swept aside several issues important for
> setting up a binding legal framework* ... The absence of a complaint
> mechanism that people affected by transnational corporations could
> complain to was important. The Guiding Principles were not binding
> standards nor did they wish to be; they were simply guidance; they were
> not mandatory, which was why binding measures were necessary.[53]

It is clear from the comments made by Montalvo that despite having serious
objections against the GPs as well as the text of the resolution, Ecuador did
not vote against the resolution or even abstain. Considering the politics of
international relations, it is conceivable that some diplomatic efforts might
have been made to ensure that the HRC endorsed the GPs unanimously.[54] It
is worth noting here that fundamental reservations were expressed even by
the representative of the United Kingdom, a state that had supported the
GPs, about Pillars 1 and 2 of the Framework:

> The United Kingdom was co-sponsoring this draft resolution with the
> understanding that the Guiding Principles did not necessarily always
> reflect the provisions of international law. *The United Kingdom did not*

[51] See S. Wood, 'The Case for Leverage-Based Corporate Human Rights Responsibility'
(2012) 22:1 *Business Ethics Quarterly* 63, at 69–70; Ruggie, 'Together at Last', n. 34, 122.

[52] Human Rights Council, 'Council Establishes Working Group on Human Rights and
Transnational Corporations and Other Business Enterprises' (16 June 2011), www.
ohchr.org/en/NewsEvents/Pages/DisplayNews.aspx?NewsID=11165 (last accessed 30
December 2012) (HRC, 'Council Establishes Working Group').

[53] *Ibid.* (emphasis added).

[54] Securing consensus, for instance, places greater demands on chairs 'to take an active role
in promoting consensus through informal negotiations and soundings'. Boyle and
Chinkin, *The Making of International Law*, n. 23, 158.

consider that there was a general duty of a State to protect under international law or international customary law. Due diligence standard, although contained in international law, was not its core provision and the United Kingdom did not recognise collective rights in the international law with the exception of the right to self determination.[55]

It seems then that the consensus around the GPs – even in a small representative body like the HRC – was not as clear or genuine as it has been projected to be. Moreover, one has to question if such manufactured consensus is helpful to the realisation of human rights in the longer run, especially when commentators note that the consensus model may not be suitable in negotiating a human rights instrument, as this may result in 'a text that is weaker or more ambiguous than might be thought desirable by some states or NGOs'.[56] As illustrated in the next section, this is exactly what has happened with the GPs: the blind obsession with achieving consensus has resulted in the adoption of weak language concerning the human rights responsibilities of business. While the '[c]larity of communication . . . is a most crucial resource for promotion and protection of human rights',[57] the quest for consensus can lead to 'imprecision' of language and the acceptance of the 'lowest common denominator'.[58]

Playing with human rights terminology casually

This section looks closely at the language (in relation to both terms and legal concepts) used in the GPs and its potential effect on the nature and scope of human rights obligations that companies should have. Language is critical to human rights, because it embodies the basic ethos of human rights[59] and is designed to be used universally.[60] Language has also been one of the lenses for critiquing the politics of inclusion and exclusion in the human rights discourse. Feminist scholars,

---

[55] HRC, 'Council Establishes Working Group', n. 52 (emphasis added).

[56] Boyle and Chinkin, *The Making of International Law*, n. 23, 159.

[57] U. Baxi, *The Future of Human Rights*, 2nd edn (Oxford University Press, 2006), 8. See also, on the power politics and perils surrounding the language of human rights, *ibid.*, xix–xx.

[58] Coglianese, 'Is Consensus an Appropriate Basis?', n. 28, 109–10. See also Baxi, *The Future of Human Rights, ibid.*, 9.

[59] Ochoa notes: 'As with any specialized field of study and work . . . human rights has developed its own "language for a special purpose".' C. Ochoa, 'Advancing the Language of Human Rights in a Global Economic Order: An Analysis of a Discourse' (2003) 23 *Boston College Third World Law Journal* 57, at 58.

[60] B. Orend, *Human Rights: Concept and Context* (Ontario: Broadview Press Ltd., 2002), 15.

for instance, have highlighted the use of language – whether neutral or otherwise – in international human rights instruments to disempower women and exclude them from the ambit of protection.[61]

Another dimension of linguistic hazards is exposed when human rights institutions and advocates communicate with trade or business institutions and individuals. In order to effectively communicate with companies and bring them on board, it may be expedient to use the language and terminology that is commonly adopted by business people.[62] However, such language usage will not always be conducive to promoting human rights. Ochoa cautions against the creation and use of alternative language to describe human rights while negotiating with multinational corporations (MNCs) and international economic institutions.[63] In relation to the International Monetary Fund's interaction with human rights discourse, she writes:

> It is important to note ... the negative implications of allowing an international institution to invent language when it does not fully address the human rights problems to which it claims to be attentive; it potentially could both demote the legal potency as well as obfuscate the global familiarity that human rights language has attained. It is important to retain the character of a particular human right as a right, rather than allowing it to be framed as a 'social issue'.[64]

Against this background, I will try to show how the intentional use of certain terms and concepts in the GPs has resulted not only in narrowing down the nature and scope of corporate human rights responsibilities, but also in diluting the robustness of remedial responses. The infusion of 'business-friendly' terminology within the human rights discourse is also likely to operate as a precedent for such further usage.

---

[61] See, e.g., H. Charlesworth, C. Chinkin and S. Wright, 'Feminist Approaches to International Law' (1991) 85 *American Journal of International Law* 613; N. H. Kaufman and S. A. Lindquist, 'Critiquing Gender-Neutral Treaty Language: The Convention on the Elimination of All Forms of Discrimination Against Women' in J. S. Peters and A. Wolper (eds.), *Women's Rights, Human Rights: International Feminist Perspectives* (London: Routledge, 1995), 114; H. Charlesworth and C. Chinkin, *The Boundaries of International Law: A Feminist Analysis* (Manchester University Press, 2000).

[62] The SRSG was aware of the need to develop 'common vocabulary' so that companies and human rights advocacy groups can talk 'similar languages'. J. Ames, 'Taking Responsibility' (2011) 111 *European Lawyer* 15, at 16.

[63] Ochoa, 'Advancing the Language of Human Rights, n. 59.   [64] *Ibid.*, 109.

All responsibilities, no duties

The GPs frame human rights obligations of states in relation to third parties operating within their territory or jurisdiction in terms of a '*duty* to protect'. The exact nature of the different components of this duty range from 'must' do (Principles 1 and 25) to 'should' do (Principles 2 to 10).[65] However, when it comes to the human rights obligations of companies, *all* of them are construed as part of the '*responsibility* to respect'. While the term 'responsibility' may mean liability in certain contexts,[66] the GPs consciously use it to denote the non-legal duties of companies.[67] Commentary on Principle 12 states that the 'responsibility of business enterprises to respect human rights is distinct from issues of legal liability and enforcement, which remain defined largely by national law provisions in relevant jurisdictions'.

The 'responsibility to respect' matrix appears to be a conscious decision, given the distinction that the SRSG has maintained between corporate responsibility and corporate accountability.[68] The following paragraph of the 2008 report is quite telling:

> Failure to meet this responsibility [i.e. responsibility to respect] *can subject companies to the courts of public opinion* – comprising employees, communities, consumers, civil society, as well as investors – *and occasionally to charges in actual courts*. Whereas governments define the scope of legal compliance, *the broader scope of the responsibility to respect is defined by social expectations* – as part of what is sometimes called a company's social licence to operate.[69]

The SRSG has maintained, explained and defended this distinction beyond reports submitted to the HRC. In an article published in 2011, he wrote: 'I

---

[65] 'Should' implies that states are encouraged to do something, whereas the term 'must' denotes a mandatory obligation on states.

[66] Garner, *Black's Law Dictionary*, n. 21, 1427; International Law Commission, *Draft Articles on Responsibility of States for Internationally Wrongful Acts* (2001), Supplement No. 10 (A/56/10), ch.IV.E.1.

[67] See L. C. Backer, 'From Institutional Misalignments to Socially Sustainable Governance: The Guiding Principles for the Implementation of the United Nations "Protect, Respect and Remedy" and the Construction of Inter-systemic Global Governance' (2012) 25 *Pacific McGeorge Global Business & Development Law Journal* 69, at 124.

[68] Human Rights Council, 'Report of the SRSG – Business and Human Rights: Mapping International Standards of Responsibility and Accountability for Corporate Acts', A/HRC/4/35 (19 February 2007).

[69] Human Rights Council, 'Protect, Respect and Remedy: A Framework for Business and Human Rights: Report of the Special Representative of the Secretary-General on the Issue of Human Rights and Transnational Corporations and Other Business Enterprises, A/HRC/8/5 (7 April 2008), para. 54 (emphasis added).

refer to the corporate *responsibility* to respect rights, rather than duty, to indicate that respecting rights is not an obligation current international human rights law generally imposes directly on companies.'[70]

There are several problematic aspects of the above formulation. The 'responsibility to respect' might give a misleading impression to companies that all of their human rights responsibilities are without any legal consequences. But this may not be the case. Rather than being swayed by the non-liability allurement, companies and corporate executives would have to take into account the ever-evolving judicial decisions in this area and the legalisation of human rights responsibilities under municipal laws. It is also not the case that legal liability always arises by virtue of, and under, national laws. Nor are national laws and international law like two completely distinct baskets of laws with no overlap or interplay. The litigation under the Alien Tort Claims Act 1789 (a national law) indicates how international human rights jurisprudence can influence the contours of legal obligations under domestic law. It is also questionable to ground corporate responsibilities on 'social expectations'.[71] Besides being unsound normatively, it ignores problems inherent in the slippery notion of social expectations.[72] Ruggie himself, as former SRSG, provided a concrete instance of this problem when he questioned the legal strategy of Shell to assail the extra-territorial applicability of the Alien Tort Claims Act to corporations, because Shell has a responsibility to respect human rights.[73]

Let me also allude to the inaccuracy in the claim that 'respecting rights is not an obligation current *international human rights law* generally imposes directly on companies'.[74] The term 'international human rights law' should not be equated with 'international human rights instruments': the former is wider in scope and includes international customary law, which imposes direct legal obligations on companies. The potential hazards in this conceptual imprecision have already been

---

[70] Ruggie, 'The Construction of the UN Framework', n. 35, 130 (emphasis in original).

[71] On this point, see also Chapter 5.   [72] Deva, *Humanizing Business*, n. 46, 109–10.

[73] 'Should the corporate responsibility to respect human rights remain entirely divorced from litigation strategy and tactics, particularly where the company has choices about the grounds on which to defend itself? Should the litigation strategy aim to destroy an entire juridical edifice for redressing gross violations of human rights, particularly where other legal grounds exist to protect the company's interests? Or would the commitment to socially responsible conduct include an obligation by the company to instruct its attorneys to avoid such far-reaching consequences where that is possible?' Ruggie, 'An Issues Brief', n. 19, at 6.

[74] Ruggie, 'The Construction of the UN Framework', n. 35, 130 (emphasis added).

highlighted by the *Kiobel* litigation before the US Supreme Court. Shell relied on the SRSG's 2007 report to contend that corporations cannot be held liable for human rights violations under international law, and consequently the former SRSG had to file an *amicus* and issue an 'issues brief' to explain his position.[75] In the *amicus*, Ruggie concluded that 'corporations may have direct liability under international law for gross human rights abuses',[76] a conclusion that he did not put as clearly in the 2007 report by drawing the distinction between liability for international crimes and a mere responsibility under international human rights instruments.

Cages of 'protect' and 'respect'

In human rights discourse, the duty typology is by and large settled in that states have a duty to respect, protect and fulfil human rights.[77] Each of these duties has a distinct meaning. These three sets of duties, however, are not watertight compartments; rather there is a complementary interrelationship among these duties. While the duty of companies need not be identical to that of states, companies should have all three types of duties (to a varying extent) under certain circumstances,[78] otherwise human rights cannot be realised fully in a free-market economy.[79] For instance, when states have a duty to protect people against third parties committing human rights abuses within their territory or jurisdiction, there is no good reason why parent companies should not be under a similar duty to protect so as to ensure that

---

[75] Supreme Court of the United States (*Esther Kiobel* v. *Royal Dutch Petroleum Co.*), 'Brief *Amici Curiae* of Former UN Special Representative for Business and Human Rights, Professor John Ruggie; Professor Philip Alston; and the Global Justice Clinic at NYU School of Law in Support of Neither Party' (12 June 2012) (SRSG, 'Brief *Amici Curiae*'); Ruggie, 'An Issues Brief', n. 19.

[76] SRSG, 'Brief *Amici Curiae*', *ibid.*, 15.

[77] H. Shue, *Basic Rights: Subsistence, Affluence, and US Foreign Policy*, 2nd edn (Princeton University Press, 1996), 52–53; O. De Schutter, *International Human Rights Law: Cases, Materials, Commentary* (Cambridge University Press, 2010), 242–53. For a critique of this duty typology, see I. E. Koch, 'Dichotomies, Trichotomies or Waves of Duties?' (2005) 5:1 *Human Rights Law Review* 81.

[78] See D. Bilchitz, 'The Ruggie Framework: An Adequate Rubric for Corporate Human Rights Obligations?' (2010) 7:12 *Sur – International Journal of Human Rights* 199, at 204–15; F. Wettstein, *Multinational Corporations and Global Justice: Human Rights Obligations of a Quasi-governmental Institution* (Stanford Business Books, 2009), 305–16.

[79] 'The complete fulfilment of each kind of rights involves the performance of multiple kinds of duties.' Shue, *Basic Rights*, n. 77, 52.

their subsidiaries (and potentially also contractors/suppliers) respect human rights obligations. The scope of duties should be coterminous, in my view, with possible ways in which rights can be breached by companies. In fact, if the responsibility of corporations is limited to respecting human rights, this might encourage them to contract out human rights abuses to their business partners and supply-chain participants. Against this conceptual background, it is doubtful if the responsibility of corporations merely to *respect* human rights will prove adequate in humanising business.

The GPs also impose an artificial limit on the threefold duties of states by merely confining their duty to the 'protect' category.[80] The 'respect' and 'fulfil' types of state duties can be equally relevant in ensuring that companies comply with human rights norms. If there are some companies owned or controlled by states, it is plausible to argue that the state duty to respect should (also) apply to such situations, for such companies are in effect part of the state machinery. Principle 4, however, deals with such a scenario only within the rubric of the state duty to protect against human rights abuses. This is a regressive idea, because public sector companies may already have an *obligation* to respect human rights. For instance, under Indian constitutional law jurisprudence, public companies are obliged to respect fundamental rights enumerated in the Constitution.[81] Similarly, the state duty to fulfil human rights would become relevant in the context of filling in regulatory gaps and/or working in partnership with companies to provide basic services that contribute to the realisation of human rights. Rather than developing this potential inherent in the threefold duties of states, the duty 'cages' created by the GPs – the duty of states only to protect and the responsibility of companies only to respect human rights – inhibit that potential.

'Violation' becomes 'impact'

It is by and large uncontroversial that companies can violate human rights. 'Violation' of a (human) right implies that an entity breached its duties in relation to bearers of rights.[82] However, the GPs never use the term 'violation' in relation to companies. The terms employed by the

---

[80] Deva, *Humanizing Business*, n. 46, 110–11.
[81] See International Commission of Jurists (ICJ), *Access to Justice: Human Rights Abuses Involving Corporations – India* (Geneva: ICJ, 2011), 5–10.
[82] *Black's Law Dictionary* defines 'violation' as follows: '1. An infraction or breach of the law; a transgression . . . 2. The act of breaking or dishonouring the law; the contravention of a right or duty . . .'. Garner, *Black's Law Dictionary*, n. 21, 1705.

GPs are either 'impact' or 'risk'.[83] This seemingly deliberate attempt to replace the *violation typology* with the *impact typology* has the potential to undermine human rights. Unlike 'violation', 'impact' is a neutral term[84] and even qualifying it with the word 'adverse' cannot adequately reflect perspectives of victims whose rights are violated by companies. An interpretive guide prepared by the Office of the High Commissioner for Human Rights states that an adverse human rights impact 'occurs when an action removes or reduces the ability of an individual to enjoy his or her human rights'.[85] This definition clearly shows how the impact terminology shifts the focus from the breach of obligations implicit in the notion of 'violation' to companies merely affecting adversely the ability of a person to enjoy human rights. Furthermore, 'impact' turns the attention away from the deviant behaviour of companies to the fate of victims, which may be the result of multiple factors.

This choice of impact terminology has at least three implications. Firstly, whereas states can violate human rights, companies can only cause adverse impacts. This perpetuates a state-centric human rights ideology under which non-state actors such as companies cannot ordinarily have human rights obligations. Against this background, it makes sense for the GPs to propose that companies only have a responsibility (not a duty) to respect human rights. However, as scholars have argued, it is critical to bring various non-state actors within the loop of human rights obligations to ensure that the goal of human rights realisation is not undermined in a free-market economy.[86]

Secondly, 'impact' appears to devalue both the importance attached to human rights and the consequence of their violation on victims. Language plays an important role in how the experiences of victims are recognised and how human rights abuses suffered by them are remedied. Taking human rights as well as the plight of victims seriously entail that adequately potent concepts are employed to capture the legal

---

[83] One can, though, notice the use of 'infringing' in Principle 11 and 'abuses' in Principle 23.

[84] It is, incidentally, interesting that the term 'impact' is not even found in *Black's Law Dictionary*.

[85] Office of the High Commissioner for Human Rights, *The Corporate Responsibility to Respect Human Rights: An Interpretive Guide* (November 2011), II Key Concepts.

[86] S. Ratner, 'Corporations and Human Rights: A Theory of Legal Responsibility' (2001) 111 *Yale Law Journal* 443; S. Deva, 'Human Rights Violations by Multinational Corporations and International Law: Where from Here?' (2003) 19 *Connecticut Journal of International Law* 1; D. Kinley and J. Tadaki, 'From Talk to Walk: The Emergence of Human Rights Responsibilities for Corporations at International Law' (2004) 44 *Virginia Journal of International Law* 931.

consequences flowing from corporate human rights abuses. It is really doubtful if 'impact' and 'risk' can do justice either to the notion of human rights as trumps or victims as bearers of those rights.

Thirdly, 'impact' is a term with a much wider scope, but lesser rigour than 'violation'. The latter implies an identified set of people and causation of legal injury to them in terms of a breach of human rights. Impact, however, requires neither of these two variables. One's acts or omissions can cause impacts (both adverse and positive) on a large number of people, some of which might not even be contemplated by the actor. Similarly, impact – good or bad – does not always result in a legal injury or violation of a right. Let me offer an example to illustrate this point. If Wal-Mart is allowed to establish stores in India, this would have a significant impact on a range of people – from consumers to farmers, small retailers and suppliers. If some small shopkeepers in India fail to compete with Wal-Mart and are forced to close their businesses, Wal-Mart has definitely caused an adverse impact on them. Does Wal-Mart have a legal responsibility in such a situation? The answer, in my view, should be no. But the same cannot be said if Wal-Mart treats its workers poorly, misuses its position to acquire farmers' land at an extremely low price, or pollutes the environment. The difference between the two scenarios is clear: unlike for small shopkeepers, certain clear legal rights of workers and farmers are at stake.

Hazards lurking in 'due diligence'

Due diligence is the cornerstone of executing the corporate responsibility to respect human rights. Principle 17 sums up what companies should do:

> In order to identify, prevent, mitigate and account for how they address their adverse human rights impacts, business enterprises should carry out human rights due diligence. The process should include assessing actual and potential human rights impacts, integrating and acting upon the findings, tracking responses, and communicating how impacts are addressed.

Human rights due diligence should 'cover adverse human rights impacts that the business enterprise may cause or contribute to through its own activities, or which may be directly linked to its operations, products or services by its business relationships'.[87] It is conceived as an ongoing (rather than a one-time) exercise that will vary from company to company,

---

[87] SRSG, 'Guiding Principles', n. 1, Principle 17(a).

depending on the size, nature and context of operations, and the severity of human rights risk. For MNCs that have a large number of suppliers and contractors spread all over the world, the advice is to prioritise those identified areas where the risk of adverse impacts is most significant.[88] Human rights due diligence might help companies in addressing 'the risk of legal claims against them by showing that they took every reasonable step to avoid involvement with an alleged human rights abuse'.[89]

The first step of a human rights due diligence enquiry involves conducting a human rights impact assessment. Once the impact assessment has been carried out, companies should integrate its findings across relevant internal functions and processes and take appropriate action.[90] If the adverse impact is caused or contributed to by a company, the firm should take the necessary steps to cease or prevent the impact.[91] But if the impact is merely linked to its operations or products/services rendered by another entity, the appropriate steps that the company should take would depend on its leverage over such entity, the severity of the abuse, and whether terminating the relationship with the entity would have adverse human rights consequences.[92] In a situation where the company lacks the leverage over the given entity, it should either try to increase its leverage or consider ending its relationship with the entity.[93]

It is apparent from the above description that the GPs offer several due diligence steps that should help companies in managing risks arising out of potential human rights violations. Due diligence is a process well known to companies, as they routinely conduct such investigations in commercial contexts to assess, pre-empt and manage risks.[94] I shall argue, however, that there are key differences between due diligence in a commercial context and in a human rights context and that, in view of these differences, a blind importation of the due diligence idea might undermine human rights. First of all, whereas a due diligence investigation in commercial contexts focuses on protecting interests of the company in question (self-interest), human rights discourse is not about safeguarding the rights of companies. The

---

[88] *Ibid.*, Commentary on Principle 17.   [89] *Ibid.*   [90] *Ibid.*, Principle 19.
[91] *Ibid.*, Commentary on Principle 19.
[92] *Ibid.* 'Leverage is considered to exist where the enterprise has the ability to effect change in the wrongful practices of an entity that causes a harm.' *Ibid.*
[93] *Ibid.*
[94] See T. Lambooy, *Corporate Social Responsibility: Legal and Semi-Legal Frameworks Supporting CSR* (Deventer: Kluwer, 2010), 279–92; B. Demeyere, 'Sovereign Wealth Funds and (Un)ethical Investment' in G. Nystuen, A. Follesdal and O. Mestad (eds.), *Human Rights, Corporate Complicity and Disinvestment* (Cambridge University Press, 2011), 183 at 211–13.

focus of a human rights due diligence is rather on protecting the rights of people (interests of external parties).

Secondly, the interests protected by resort to due diligence in commercial deals (money or corporate reputation) are quite different in nature from what is at stake in human rights cases (right to life and various liberties). It is often not possible to recoup fully the sufferings experienced by victims of corporate human rights abuses. Different considerations should then apply in weighing the costs and benefits of undertaking, for instance, mining in an indigenous area than when considering whether to acquire another company. However, human rights considerations might not prevail in their clash with potential business gains because the Framework and the GPs admittedly 'do not rely upon any hierarchy of international [human rights] norms' and let companies (as well as states) do the actual balancing in each case 'to resolve the clash of norms'.[95] As Irene Khan rightly pointed out, the GPs should have explicitly stated the primacy of human rights obligations over other kinds of obligations.[96]

Thirdly, unlike situations involving commercial matters, the targets of the due diligence enquiry are not very definite in human rights cases. Companies can foresee and identify certain sections of society that are adversely affected, but they might not be able to conceive beforehand all stakeholders aggrieved by certain business decisions. Therefore, they might not be able to comply fully with their human rights obligations despite undertaking due diligence investigations.

Fourthly, in commercial contexts, companies employ due diligence not only as a strategy to assess and prevent risks but also as a defence against potential liability.[97] However, in applying the due diligence tool to human rights, corporate executives should avoid perceiving human rights as 'risks' and due diligence as a 'defence' to ward off suits alleging human rights abuses.[98] The reason is simple. Companies should be subject to human rights obligations because of their *relation to* and

---

[95] Ruggie, 'The Construction of the UN Framework', n. 35, 130.

[96] I. Khan, 'Keynote Address' (11 October 2010), 2–3, www.ihrb.org/pdf/IreneKhan-SRSGconsultation-11Oct2010.pdf (last accessed 26 September 2012).

[97] 'Due diligence is necessary to protect a company from liability.' P. A. Hunt, *Structuring Mergers and Acquisitions: A Guide to Creating Shareholder Value* (Austin, TX: Aspen, 2007), 686. For the potential of due diligence to offer a defence against complicity liability, see Chapter 9.

[98] But see Dhooge, 'Due Diligence as a Defense', n. 40.

position in society:[99] they have a responsibility to respect human rights as a precondition to doing business and irrespective of whether human rights pose risks or opportunities for them.

In view of these crucial differences, corporate executives would have to possess a different orientation in applying the due diligence tool in the context of human rights. However, even if they do so, there is no guarantee that due diligence will ensure that companies conduct their business operations in conformity with human rights norms. Due diligence is a process and it may or may not achieve the desired outcome – i.e. non-violation of human rights – in all cases. In comparison to private commercial contexts, due diligence under international (human rights) law serves a useful purpose in determining the obligation of states vis-à-vis non-state actors, that is, the conduct of third parties.[100] However, the GPs propose to apply – without any clear differentiation – the due diligence process to one's own human rights violative conduct, where responsibility should be discharged only by achievement of the outcome (i.e. the realisation of human rights) rather than by merely following a process to achieve the said outcome.

Leaving aside doubts as to the conceptual appropriateness of the due diligence approach in pre-empting and remedying corporate human rights abuses, one major operational difficulty might arise as a result of imperfect information flow. The GPs expect companies to engage relevant stakeholders and seek their feedback at various stages of the due diligence process. Some companies – especially those who burnt their fingers in the past for being secretive, for instance, about the identity and conduct of their suppliers – are likely to be more forthcoming. At the same time, it is highly likely that many companies would continue to be selective in releasing information into the public domain, because such information may be sensitive or disparaging and could be used, among others, to sue companies. By failing to provide for any types of sanctions, the GPs do not account for companies that might defy the assumption of conducting due diligence in a transparent and participatory manner.

---

[99] Deva, *Humanizing Business*, n. 46, 146–50.

[100] Demeyere, 'Sovereign Wealth Funds', n. 94, 214–16; R. B. Barnidge Jr., 'The Due Diligence Principle under International Law' (2006) 8 *International Community Law Review* 81, at 91–121; A. Cassese, *International Law*, 2nd edn (Oxford University Press, 2005), 250.

What happened to access to remedy as a 'human right'?

The access to a remedy in itself is recognised as a human right (not merely a duty) in all major international and regional human rights instruments,[101] because the recognition of rights does not mean much in absence of access to effective remedies. Formulating access to remedy as a right means that states are under a duty to take necessary steps to realise this basic right.[102] If these steps corresponding to the respect-protect-fulfil typology are not taken by a state, it can be held liable for infringing the right to remedy.

However, the rich international human rights jurisprudence concerning the right to remedy is not adequately reflected in the GPs because they recognise this pillar as flowing from the state duty to protect human rights rather than imposing a self-standing obligation. While Principle 25 provides that states 'must' take judicial, administrative, legislative or other appropriate steps to ensure access to an effective remedy, it is silent as to what exact remedies victims of corporate human rights abuses can have against companies.[103] This is a significant omission and it is not cured by including some potential remedies in the Commentary on Principle 25. Moreover, Principle 26 departs from the obligatory 'must' language: it merely recommends that states 'should' consider ways 'to reduce legal, practical and other relevant barriers that could lead to a denial of access to remedy'. Why should states not be obliged to remove some of the well-known obstacles that have hampered victims of corporate human rights abuses in seeking redress? In short, while the GPs should be applauded for stressing the need to employ multiple grievance mechanisms to make companies accountable for human rights

---

[101] See, e.g., Universal Declaration of Human Rights (Art. 8); International Covenant on Civil and Political Rights (Art. 2); African Charter on Human and Peoples' Rights (Art. 7); American Convention on Human Rights (Art. 25); and Convention for the Protection of Human Rights and Fundamental Freedoms (Art. 13).

[102] Shue argues that 'basic' rights are those rights the 'enjoyment of [which] is essential to the enjoyment of all other rights'. Shue, *Basic Rights*, n. 77, 19. Access to remedy should satisfy this yardstick.

[103] One may contrast this with paragraph 18 of the UN Norms, which reads: 'Transnational corporations and other business enterprises *shall provide prompt, effective and adequate reparation to those persons, entities and communities that have been adversely affected by failures to comply with these Norms through, inter alia, reparations, restitution, compensation and rehabilitation for any damage done or property taken.* In connection with determining damages, in regard to criminal sanctions, and in all other respects, these Norms shall be applied by national courts and/or international tribunals, pursuant to national and international law.' UN Norms, n. 12 (emphasis added).

abuses,[104] the robustness and consequent efficacy of these mechanisms (especially state-based judicial mechanisms and supra-state mechanisms) is eroded by ignoring the fact that 'access to a remedy' is a human right in itself.

Conclusion

The GPs are the first corporate human rights responsibility initiative ever to be approved by the UN. This in itself should be regarded as an achievement and the SRSG believed that the GPs may achieve the strategic objective of his mandate: 'maximum reduction in corporate-related human rights harms in the shortest possible period of time'.[105] It may not be easy to assess the extent to which the GPs will accomplish this objective in coming years. However, in this chapter I have tried to highlight how the adoption of a consensual and minimalist path to define and enforce corporate human rights responsibilities might cause irreparable harm to the business and human rights project. I have advanced two claims. Firstly, the SRSG has over-emphasised the importance of building consensus. This obsessive focus on consensus-building has not only resulted in resorting to all means to achieve consensus but has also diluted the robustness of the GPs in ensuring that companies comply with their human rights responsibilities. Secondly, in order to achieve consensus (or rather achieve the support of the business community and certain states), the GPs introduced certain terms and concepts which undermine the normative importance attached to human rights. The terminology of 'social expectations', 'impact', 'risk' and 'due diligence' comes with certain hazards that should be guarded against. Human rights are *rights* and demand the performance of duties on the part of states and non-state actors alike. By departing from this conception of rights, the GPs have undervalued the normative value of human rights in their application to non-state actors.

Taking human rights seriously would require, among others, the evolution of a legally binding international instrument that imposes direct obligations on non-state actors. Although the task of putting in place such an instrument might be 'painfully slow',[106] it is regrettable

---

[104] SRSG, 'Guiding Principles', n. 1, Principles 25–31.

[105] Ruggie, 'The Construction of the UN Framework', n. 35, 132.

[106] J. Ruggie, 'Business and Human Rights: Treaty Road Not Travelled' (May 2008) *Ethical Corporation* 42, www.hks.harvard.edu/m-rcbg/news/ruggie/Pages%20from%20ECM%20May_FINAL_JohnRuggie_may%2010.pdf (last accessed 3 February 2013).

that the SRSG did not at least provide a roadmap for developing such a framework in future, especially for egregious human rights violations or for situations that involved conflict-affected or authoritarian states. Rather than doing so, the SRSG seems to have erected barriers to discourage exploring the path of legally binding international obligations.[107] One can only hope that the Working Group tries to move beyond the GPs in order to provide victims with more effective access to a remedy against MNCs.

---

[107] Simons notes that 'the SRSG actually pushed back against calls for binding international human rights obligations for corporate actors'. Simons, 'International Law's Invisible Hand', n. 33, 13.

PART II

Source and justification of corporate obligations

5

A chasm between 'is' and 'ought'? A critique of the normative foundations of the SRSG's Framework and the Guiding Principles

DAVID BILCHITZ*

Introduction

In a world where corporations have large amounts of wealth and power, what are their obligations in relation to human rights?[1] International discourse on this issue has, in recent years, centred around the 'Protect, Respect and Remedy' Framework (Framework) and the Guiding Principles on Business and Human Rights (GPs), which were developed during the mandate of John Ruggie, the Special Representative of the Secretary-General on the Issue of Human Rights and Transnational Corporations and Other Business Enterprises (SRSG). In these documents (and other ancillary reports), the SRSG has taken two strong and highly controversial positions, which will be the focus of this chapter. Firstly, he has claimed that corporations lack any binding legal obligations in relation to human rights; any responsibilities they have flow from social expectations rather than the law itself.[2] Secondly, the SRSG

---

* I would like to thank participants in the Johannesburg conference (mentioned in the preface) for contributing to the thoughtful discussion surrounding this chapter, and Surya Deva for his incisive comments on this piece.

[1] For sake of consistency with the rest of the book, I use the term 'human' rights, though I prefer the term 'fundamental' rights in general. I believe it to be a philosophical mistake to view such rights as only being ascribed to human beings, for all other sentient creatures may be capable of having some of these rights. For a defence of this idea, see D. Bilchitz, *Poverty and Fundamental Rights* (Oxford University Press, 2007), 1–46.

[2] Indeed, the SRSG uses the word 'responsibility' instead of 'obligation' deliberately to indicate that any duties corporations have are not legally binding. See Human Rights Council, 'Business and Human Rights: Further Steps towards the Operationalization of the "Protect, Respect and Remedy" Framework', A/HRC/14/27 (9 April 2010) (SRSG, '2010 Report'), and the quote referred to in n. 36. For a critical analysis of the language used by the SRSG, see Chapter 4.

contended that the responsibilities of corporations in relation to human rights must be distinguished from the obligations of the state: corporations primarily have a responsibility to respect human rights, which essentially means that they must avoid harming such rights. In other words, unlike states, corporations generally lack positive obligations to play an active role in realising or fulfilling those rights.

In this chapter, I seek to evaluate the normative underpinnings of these two positions. I shall argue that the failure to engage with the moral foundations of human rights leads the SRSG to make several mistakes. The first part of the chapter will contest the SRSG's claims relating to the lack of legally binding obligations upon corporations. I shall first provide arguments as to why a deeper understanding of the normative basis of the key international human rights instruments would lead to a different conclusion. These instruments, I argue, imply that corporations are indeed bound by them. I then turn to demonstrate the inadequacy of rooting the responsibilities of corporations in social expectations, as the SRSG seeks to do.

The second part of this chapter engages with the normative basis that the SRSG offers for restricting the scope and ambit of corporate responsibility to avoiding harm to human rights. First, I seek to demonstrate that human rights logically allow some flexibility in determining the allocation of the obligations that flow from them. I then turn to evaluate several objections the SRSG makes to imposing wider positive responsibilities on corporations that are suggestive of particular normative views underpinning his work. I attempt to show that the SRSG's contentions rest on a mistaken conception of the social role of business as well as a limited understanding of democratic legitimacy. The SRSG reports also perpetuate an unhelpful competitive conception of the respective responsibilities of business and the state, rather than a collaborative one that is more likely to lead to the successful realisation of human rights. I conclude that the SRSG has failed to provide an adequate basis for the restrictive conception of corporate responsibilities articulated by the mandate. As such, there is a serious lacuna at the international level which has significant implications given the potential role of business in helping to address important challenges such as global poverty and environmental sustainability. Future work at the international level providing for a more adequate conception of corporate obligations should be rooted firmly in the principled normative foundations of human rights.

Normativity, law and morals in the work of the SRSG

Before I begin engaging with the content of the SRSG's work, it is important to distinguish between two different senses of 'normativity'. The first notion relates to the source of bindingness of rules or principles. Hart, for instance, in his work on the philosophical nature of law recognises the distinctive 'normativity' of law. For him, law is not just a command that can be backed up by forceful sanctions; under such a conception of law, if the system of enforcement broke down, we would no longer have any reason to follow such rules. Instead, legal rules must be sourced in the rules of recognition for law that are accepted in that society: if a law is passed in accordance with such 'secondary rules', then it is justifiable to enforce it.[3] The justifiability of enforcing law thus comes down to its being passed according to a socially legitimate procedure. An important question arises in connection with business and human rights concerning the legitimate source of bindingness of any rules or principles that are developed. I shall refer to this as the question of 'binding normativity'.

The second question involves a different sense of 'normativity', that is, what 'ought' to be the case. Irrespective of whether there is some legitimate source for business to be bound by particular rules or principles, ought corporations, as a question of political morality, to have binding obligations for the realisation of human rights? Such a question requires engagement with moral justification and reasoning. I shall refer to this as 'moral normativity'. Since human rights are essentially rooted in political morality, a conception of moral normativity is often crucial to understanding their content and implications. An understanding of moral normativity also has consequences for binding normativity, as discussed below. I will try to show that the SRSG rarely engaged with the question of moral normativity, which leads to some of the mistakes the mandate makes in this area.

The next section outlines the SRSG's rejection of law as a source of binding normativity in the field of business and human rights. My critical evaluation of his claims in this regard will involve two elements: firstly, I shall show that a proper conceptual understanding of the moral normative basis of human rights entails that these rights impose binding legal obligations upon corporations; secondly, I shall demonstrate the inadequacy of 'social expectations' as a source of binding normativity.

---

[3] H. L. A. Hart, *The Concept of Law*, 2nd edn (Oxford University Press, 1997), 79–99.

Why businesses have legally binding human rights obligations

The SRSG's first report in 2006 outlined his initial conception of the mandate and some of the meta-theoretical issues involved. He recognised that 'the most challenging part of the mandate concerns the issue of standards'.[4] He identified two reasons for this. First, given the flux of the global context, standards in many instances 'do not simply "exist" out there waiting to be recorded and implemented but are in the process of being socially constructed. Indeed, the mandate itself inevitably is a modest intervention in that larger process.'[5] The second problem related to the stalemate that had been reached in connection with the United Nations Norms on the Responsibilities of Transnational Corporations and Other Business Enterprises with Regard to Human Rights (UN Norms).[6] Whilst the UN Norms claimed to represent 'a definitive and comprehensive set of standards',[7] they had led to great division between states, business and human rights groups.

In response to this situation, the SRSG launched a detailed critique of the UN Norms in which he contested two important elements contained therein. Firstly, he rejected the notion that there are legally binding human rights obligations in international law upon corporations: 'there are no generally accepted international legal principles that do so'.[8] Secondly, he rejected the methodology adopted by the UN Norms to draw out obligations that bind business from existing human rights instruments.[9] Here, he made a strong distinction between what 'is' and what 'ought' to be the case: it may, he said, be 'desirable in some circumstances for corporations to become direct bearers of international human rights obligations . . . But these are not propositions about established law; they are normative commitments and policy preferences about what the law should become and that require State action for them to take effect.'[10]

---

[4] Commission on Human Rights, 'Interim Report of the Special Representative of the Secretary-General on the Issue of Human Rights and Transnational Corporations and Other Business Enterprises', E/CN.4/2006/97 (22 February 2006), para. 54 (SRSG, '2006 Interim Report').

[5] *Ibid.*

[6] Commission on Human Rights, Sub-Commission on the Promotion and Protection of Human Rights, 'Norms on the Responsibilities of Transnational Corporations and Other Business Enterprises with Regard to Human Rights', E/CN.4/Sub.2/2003/12/ Rev.2 (26 August 2003) (UN Norms).

[7] SRSG, '2006 Interim Report', n. 4, para. 55.   [8] *Ibid.*, para. 60.   [9] *Ibid.*

[10] *Ibid.*, para. 65.

Human rights treaties as binding sources of normativity

In my view, both prongs of the SRSG's critique of the UN Norms are flawed and in turn provide a shaky normative foundation for the alternative path he seeks to forge in later documents. In relation to the lack of binding human rights obligations for business at international law, I wish to present two important normative arguments which point to the contrary conclusion than that reached by the SRSG. They both arise from the fact that whilst international human rights instruments generally only bind states expressly, binding obligations upon non-state actors can be derived by necessary implication.[11]

It is trite that human rights treaties clearly impose a binding obligation upon states to ensure that all the rights contained therein are guaranteed to all the individuals within their territory and/or jurisdiction and that they take the necessary legislative and other measures necessary to give effect to this duty.[12] As part of fulfilling this duty, states are required to ensure that the rights of individuals are not violated by third parties: this is an essential component of the uncontroversial state duty to protect, which the SRSG embraces as one central prong of his Framework.[13] If states are required by international law to ensure that third parties (including corporations) comply with binding human rights requirements, then this entails that the third parties are themselves obligated to comply with such requirements. Indeed, if the third parties were not

---

[11] Here I go further than Clapham's views which are based on the effectiveness principle: '[i]f international law is to be effective in protecting human rights, everyone should be prohibited from assisting governments in violating those principles, or indeed prohibited from violating such principles themselves'. A. Clapham, *Human Rights Obligations of Non-State Actors* (Oxford University Press, 2006), 80. What Clapham fails to see is that these obligations are not merely a requirement of effectiveness, but flow necessarily from the logic of the human rights treaties themselves under international law.

[12] See, for instance, International Covenant on Civil and Political Rights (entered into force 23 March 1976), 999 UNTS 171 (ICCPR), Art. 2. See S. Joseph *et al.*, *The International Covenant on Civil and Political Rights: Cases, Materials and Commentary* (Oxford University Press, 2000), 24; and A. Clapham, *Human Rights in the Private Sphere* (Oxford: Clarendon Press, 1993), 109–10. A slightly different formulation is used in Article 2 of the International Covenant on Economic, Social and Cultural Rights (entered into force 3 January 1976), 993 UNTS 3 (ICESCR).

[13] See Human Rights Council, 'Protect, Respect and Remedy: A Framework for Business and Human Rights', A/HRC/8/5 (7 April 2008), para. 18 (SRSG, '2008 Framework'). The existence of this responsibility and some of its incidents were outlined in *Velásquez Rodríguez* v. *Honduras* (1989) 28 I.L.M. 291; (1988) Inter-A. C. H. R. (Ser. C) No. 4, paras. 166–77.

bound by international law to comply with such requirements, then there would be no reason for the state to ensure that they do so. The state can only be required to enforce an obligation that is already recognised – expressly or implicitly – by the international treaties themselves. The logic of the state 'duty to protect' at international law thus necessarily entails the notion that non-state actors, including corporations, in fact have binding legal obligations with respect to the human rights contained in these treaties.[14]

Binding international law obligations upon corporations also follow from another argument concerning the nature of what it is to have human rights under international law: 'they are the rights that one has simply because one is human'.[15] The International Covenant on Civil and Political Rights (ICCPR) and the International Covenant on Economic, Social and Cultural Rights (ICESCR) both contain this central idea in their Preambles, which state that the rights contained therein 'derive from the inherent dignity of the human person'.[16] Two important principles are derived from this foundation. Firstly, if rights flow from the inherent dignity of human beings, then they must apply equally to all human beings and are thus universal in nature.[17] Secondly, the derivation of human rights from human dignity also means that they cannot be 'renounced, lost or forfeited, human rights are inalienable'.[18] Given these principles, it is clear that the recognition of human rights in international law means that individuals are entitled to basic protections for their

---

[14] This results in what has been termed the 'third-party applicability' of the human rights regimes at international law. Clapham, *Human Rights Obligations*, n. 11, 111. In relation to the ICCPR, Clapham states that '[t]he use of the phrase "third-party applicability" goes beyond the application of the Covenant to positive obligations on the State in the private sphere and confirms that the Covenant can be used directly against private bodies in the national legal order where that order recognizes the direct effect and self-executing nature of the right in the Covenant'. For a contrary view concerning the third-party applicability of human rights law, see R. Provost, *International Human Rights and Humanitarian Law* (Cambridge University Press, 2002), 62–64.

[15] J. Donnelly, *International Human Rights*, 2nd edn (Colorado: Westview Press, 1998), 18. See also the classic work by M. Cranston, *What are Human Rights?* (London: Bodley Head, 1973), 7.

[16] ICCPR, n. 12; ICESCR, n. 12.

[17] Donnelly, *International Human Rights*, n. 15, at 18. Dicke also argues that human dignity provides the basis for claims as to the universality of human rights. K. Dicke, 'The Founding Function of Human Dignity in the Universal Declaration of Human Rights' in D. Kretzmer and E. Klein (eds.), *The Concept of Human Dignity in Human Rights Discourse* (The Hague: Kluwer International, 2002), 118.

[18] Donnelly, *ibid.*, at 18.

human interests simply by virtue of the fact that they are human beings.[19] As such, the primary concern from the perspective of human rights law is that these entitlements on the part of individuals are realised and that their interests in this regard are not abrogated. This understanding of rights renders it in fact incoherent to suggest that only states are bound not to violate human rights and all other entities may violate such rights at will.[20] Since human rights flow from the very foundational dignity of the individual, all agents are bound not to violate them and to play a role in ensuring they are realised.[21]

These arguments flow from understanding the implications of the existing recognition of human rights in international law, the structure of deontic relations as well as the normative underpinnings of these rights. The SRSG, in his 2006 report recognised that '[w]hatever other differences may exist in the world, starting with the 1948 Universal Declaration of Human Rights, human rights have been the only internationally agreed expression of the entitlements that each and every one of us has simply because we are human beings'.[22] If the implications of this statement had been carefully thought through, the SRSG may have reached a different conclusion in that very report concerning whether businesses have binding legal obligations in relation to human rights. Yet, even in this statement, the SRSG focuses on the fact that human rights standards are agreed, rather than on their content and deeper justificatory base. Indeed, the SRSG's work is striking for just how little he engages with the concept of human rights and their normative foundation. If the SRSG had thought more about the implications of an existing strong legal entitlement that flows from the dignity of individuals, he may have been more cautious about concluding that existing international human rights instruments do not bind

---

[19] See *Velásquez Rodríguez*, n. 13, para. 144, where it was stated that human rights are 'higher values that "are not derived from the fact that (an individual) is a national of a certain state, but are based upon attributes of his human personality"'. For a justification of rights rooted in the fundamental interests of individuals, see D. Bilchitz, *Poverty and Fundamental Rights*, n. 1, 6–101.

[20] 'If human rights are aimed at the protection of human dignity, the law needs to respond to abuses that do not implicate the state directly.' S. Ratner, 'Corporations and Human Rights: A Theory of Legal Responsibility' (2001) 111 *Yale Law Journal* 443, at 472.

[21] The third section of the chapter, 'Do corporations only have a responsibility to respect human rights?' will address the question of allocating positive obligations that flow from these rights.

[22] SRSG, '2006 Interim Report', n. 4, para. 19.

corporations.[23] This demonstrates the important relationship that exists between 'binding' and 'moral' normativity in relation to human rights, a matter I now proceed to consider further in relation to the second prong of the SRSG's critique of the UN Norms.

The relationship between binding and moral normativity in international law

The SRSG, as we have seen, tries to make a sharp distinction between the arguments for thinking that corporations 'ought' to have binding legal obligations in relation to human rights at international law (the question of moral normativity) and the fact that they do not currently have such obligations (the question of binding normativity). However, very little thought or attention is given by him to the process by which international law develops. When this process is understood, it becomes clear that there is a much closer relationship between moral normativity and binding normativity than the SRSG is prepared to acknowledge. The failure to consider this relationship led the SRSG to ignore the necessary implications of existing human rights treaties (as discussed above) and the manner in which customary international law can develop in this area.

In understanding how new norms become part of customary international law, an analogy used by De Visscher is apposite: he likens the development of custom to the gradual formation of a road across a vacant plot of land. Whilst initially uncertain as to its direction, most of the users begin to recognise the same path across the land. Quickly thereafter, this path is transformed into a road that is accepted as the main path across the territory, even though it may not be possible to state at exactly which point this latter change occurs.[24] In other words, custom does not crystallise at a particular moment, but develops gradually. We may be able to see a developing trend concerning the emergence of a rule without being able to state at exactly which point that rule has become

---

[23] The fact that human rights standards are binding at international law does not automatically mean that international adjudicative bodies would be able to hold corporations liable. The enforcement agents of such international obligations would often be states at the domestic level who could nevertheless use international human rights law as the basis for holding corporations accountable (as in the case of the Alien Tort Claims Act in the United States, for instance).

[24] C. De Visscher, *Theory and Reality in Public International Law*, 3rd edn (Princeton University Press, 1957), 149; M. Shaw, *International Law*, 4th edn (Cambridge University Press, 1997), 62.

law. The analogy also suggests that an understanding of what ought to be the case (the best route for the road) can help entrench a new status quo (the actual route of the road).

Accordingly, when we look at the UN Norms themselves, it is possible to see that the position they adopted concerning the nature of corporate obligations under international law was more complex than what the SRSG had suggested. The Preamble stated that the UN Norms reaffirm 'that transnational corporations and other business enterprises, their officers, and their workers have, inter alia, human rights obligations and responsibilities and that these human rights norms will contribute to the making and development of international law as to their responsibilities and obligations'.[25] The UN Norms thus asserted both the claim that corporations have existing human rights responsibilities and the proposition that the nature of such responsibilities at international law was in the process of being developed. Therefore, the UN Norms were neither the invention of something entirely new nor were they the expression of something that had always existed. The UN Norms themselves were part of a process that can best be described as involving the 'emergence' of more concrete binding legal responsibilities of corporations. 'Emergence' at international law is neither purely descriptive nor purely normative. It is the bridge between what is and what ought to be.

This process of emergence in relation to the UN Norms can be linked to the relationship between the codification of international law and the progressive development thereof.[26] Lauterpacht, for instance, in discussing the work of the International Law Commission, has stated that '[c]odification which constitutes a record of the past rather than a creative use of the existing materials – legal and others – for the purpose of regulating the life of the community is a brake upon progress'.[27] Boyle and Chinkin argue that 'all codification contains significant elements of progressive development and law reform, and the real question is how far it is politic or prudent to go'.[28] The UN Norms could be seen as an attempt to codify some of the existing responsibilities of corporations for

---

[25] UN Norms, n. 6, Preamble.

[26] See A. Boyle and C. Chinkin, *The Making of International Law* (Oxford University Press, 2007), 166.

[27] H. Lauterpacht, 'UN Survey of International Law in Relation to the Work of the International Law Commission', A./CN.4/1/Rev.1 (1949), para. 13, in M. Anderson et al., *The International Law Commission and the Future of International Law* (British Institute of International and Comparative Law, 1998), 76.

[28] Boyle and Chinkin, *The Making of International Law*, n. 26, 174.

the realisation of human rights, whilst progressively developing this area of law in the process.[29] Although the UN Norms were not ultimately adopted, the process envisaged therein was neither foreign to international law nor, in my view, should it be avoided in the manner the SRSG has sought to do. As we have seen above, corporations must, by virtue of the logic of human rights, be bound by their provisions: the drawing out of this necessary implication is a matter that requires express recognition.

Explicitly recognising the human rights obligations of corporations under existing international law does not end the need for progress in this area: the exact nature of such obligations requires further clarification and progressive development. Both these matters require a strong understanding of human rights and their normative foundations. As we have seen, what 'ought' to be the case helps to guide and determine what 'is' the legal position where clearer norms are in the process of 'emergence' as in the field of business and human rights. The SRSG's attempt to separate clearly 'is' from 'ought' is thus misguided in this area. Arguably, his lack of engagement with the moral and conceptual foundations of human rights has led to flawed conclusions about the lack of binding standards on corporations at international law.

Moreover, instead of pushing international law in the direction of more determinate corporate obligations, the SRSG has adopted the position that no such obligations currently exist at international law, except in the most egregious of cases.[30] He claimed that the only way for binding responsibilities to be imposed upon corporations would be for states to reach agreement on a treaty that expressly binds corporations in this regard. Apart from failing to take into account the contrary scholarly opinion in this area,[31] the SRSG's conclusions may in fact impede the

---

[29] Lauterpacht quotes a report from the codification committee which is apposite: 'For the codification of international law, the Committee recognized that no clear-cut distinction between the formulation of the law as it is and the law as it ought to be could be rigidly maintained in practice. It was pointed out that in any work of codification, the codifier inevitably has to fill in gaps and amend the law in the light of new developments.' Lauterpacht, 'UN Survey', n. 27, para. 3.

[30] Human Rights Council, 'Business and Human Rights: Mapping International Standards of Responsibility and Accountability for Corporate Acts', A/HRC/4/35 (19 February 2007), para. 44 (SRSG, '2007 Report').

[31] Diverse views, for instance, were evident at a consultation held by the SRSG with legal experts. Human Rights Council, 'Addendum: Corporate Responsibility under International Law and Issues in Extraterritorial Regulation: Summary of Legal Workshops', A/HRC/4/35/Add.2 (15 February 2007), para. 12.

emergence of more detailed, robust and direct obligations for corporations at international law. Given that the SRSG mandate was the main UN initiative at the international level for six years, tasked with investigating the legal issues relating to corporations and human rights, the community of nations is taking the views expressed by the mandate very seriously. As a result of the state of uncertainty that has prevailed in this area, the SRSG's reports may be taken by some to capture accurately the existing state of international law. The mandate could in fact have assisted in helping to push the relatively vague and undefined state of international law in the direction of stronger legal accountability for corporate human rights abuses under international law. Instead, the firm position the SRSG articulates on the lack of international norms surrounding corporate responsibility could hamper the process through which new norms of international law concerning corporate obligations were developing.[32] His work has failed not only to take into account the complexity surrounding the existing state of international law in this field but also to reflect sensitivity towards the way in which emerging norms crystallise over time into hard law.[33]

As we have seen, the SRSG rejects the notion that corporations have legally binding human rights obligations under international law. Yet, the Framework and the GPs recognise that corporations have a

---

[32] For instance, a majority judgment of the United States Court of Appeals for the Second Circuit in *Kiobel* v. *Royal Dutch Petroleum* 621 F.3d 111 (2nd Cir. 2010) held that customary international law had not developed to the point where corporations could be held liable for human rights violations. On appeal to the Supreme Court, lawyers for Shell used the SRSG's 2007 report to contend that the position articulated in the majority's judgment is correct. The former SRSG responded in an *amicus* brief, emphasising the fact that, in his view, there may be corporate liability under international law for gross human rights abuses, including international crimes such as genocide, slavery, crimes against humanity and torture. The brief though continues to assert that human rights treaties do not bind corporations directly, a matter I discuss in this chapter. See 'Brief *Amici Curiae* of Former UN Special Representative for Business and Human Rights, Professor John Ruggie; Professor Philip Alston; and the Global Justice Clinic at NYU School of Law in Support of Neither Party' (12 June 2012), 6–7. The United States Supreme Court avoided deciding the question of corporate liability under the Alien Tort Statute (ATS), preferring to focus instead on the question of the extra-territorial application of the ATS. *Esther Kiobel* v. *Royal Dutch Petroleum Co.*, 133 S. Ct. 1659 (2013).

[33] In the 2007 Report, the SRSG attempts to deal with soft law and, on the face of it, expresses his understanding of the standard-setting role of soft law. SRSG, '2007 Report', n. 30, paras. 45–49. Yet, he fails to advance adequately the process whereby soft law changes into harder norms of international law in relation to corporate responsibility. On the question of soft law, see Chapter 6.

responsibility to respect human rights. What then is the source of binding normativity for the responsibility to respect? The next section will focus on this question and evaluate the SRSG's understanding thereof.

Social expectations as a source of binding normativity?

Having rejected the idea that corporations are obligated by legal standards in relation to human rights, the SRSG stated: 'we should bear in mind that companies are constrained not only by legal standards but also by social norms and moral considerations ... distinguishing what companies must do, what their internal and external stakeholders expect of them and what is desirable'.[34] This line of thought became central to the SRSG's work and reached fruition in the Framework and the GPs. In the Framework, the SRSG explained that the baseline corporate responsibility to respect human rights

> can subject companies to the courts of public opinion – comprising employees, communities, consumers, civil society, as well as investors – and occasionally to charges in actual courts. Whereas governments define the scope of legal compliance, the broader scope of the responsibility to respect is defined by social expectations – as part of what is sometimes called a company's social license to operate.[35]

In the 2010 report, the SRSG explained the use of the term 'responsibility' instead of 'duty' as follows:

> respecting rights is not an obligation that current international human rights law generally imposes directly on companies, although elements may be reflected in domestic laws. At the international level, the corporate responsibility to respect is a standard of expected conduct acknowledged in virtually every voluntary and soft-law instrument related to corporate responsibility, and now affirmed by the Council itself.[36]

Finally, the GPs state that '[t]he responsibility to respect human rights is a global standard of expected conduct for all business enterprises wherever they operate'.[37] Moreover, international human rights instruments are 'benchmarks against which other social actors assess the human rights impacts of business enterprises. The responsibility of business

---

[34] SRSG, '2006 Interim Report', n. 4, para. 70.

[35] SRSG, '2008 Framework', n. 13, para. 54.   [36] SRSG, '2010 Report', n. 2, para. 55.

[37] Human Rights Council, 'Guiding Principles on Business and Human Rights: Implementing the United Nations' "Protect, Respect and Remedy" Framework', A/HRC/17/31 (21 March 2011), para. 11 (SRSG, 'Guiding Principles').

enterprises to respect human rights is distinct from issues of legal liability and enforcement.'[38] The latter proposition essentially articulates the strange position that what are in essence legal human rights instruments at the international level – both treaties and customary international law – become simply social standards for assessing corporate conduct that lack any legal bite.[39] The SRSG, however, cannot have it both ways: to refer to these human rights instruments as a source of social expectations that guide corporate conduct, yet deny their legally binding nature. If these instruments are relevant to judging corporate conduct – as the SRSG admits – then, as I have argued above in the section on human rights treaties as binding sources of normativity, they, by necessary implication, create legally binding obligations for corporations in this area.

Moreover, it is surprising that the SRSG appears content for human rights to remain binding upon corporations simply as a matter of social expectation. Indeed, even if the SRSG believed that corporations lack legally binding obligations in relation to human rights under existing international law, the work of the mandate was never meant simply to be descriptive. As the SRSG recognises at various points, the Framework is a normative one (in the sense of moral normativity) that is designed to enable the UN to 'lead intellectually' and to help set 'expectations and aspirations'.[40] Thus, it is puzzling that no mention is made of shifting corporate obligations from the domain of 'social expectation' (as the mandate views it) into the realm of law.

What then are the problems with the position that human rights only bind corporations as a matter of social expectation? It is important to recognise that social expectations provide an inadequate grounding for corporate obligations in this regard for several reasons.[41]

---

[38] *Ibid.*, Commentary on Principle 12.

[39] Lane argues that legal accountability should be supplemented by a moral dimension to corporate accountability. M. Lane, 'The Moral Dimension of Corporate Accountability in Global Responsibilities' in A. Kuper (ed.), *Global Responsibilities: Who Must Deliver on Human Rights?* (New York: Routledge, 2005), 229. She does not, however, argue that it should supplant the development of greater legal obligations upon corporations and acknowledges that '[a]ccountability in its fullest sense can only be demanded of corporations by and through the law'. Lane, *ibid.*, at 233.

[40] SRSG, '2008 Framework', n. 13, para. 107.

[41] The connection between social expectations and law has been the subject of much jurisprudential discussion. See, for instance, Hart, *The Concept of Law*, n. 3. Nevertheless, for the reasons given in the text, I do not believe that corporate obligations relating to human rights should be sourced in social expectations alone.

Firstly, if corporate responsibilities are not obligations of law, are we entitled to demand that corporations perform them? Joel Feinberg famously explained that '[r]ights are not mere gifts or favors, motivated by love or pity, for which gratitude is the sole fitting response. A right is something a man can *stand* on, something that can be demanded or insisted upon without embarrassment or shame.'[42] Therefore, the question arises whether, in terms of the Framework, we have a right to demand that corporations respect human rights or whether this is simply a matter of an expectation that they will be 'generous' or 'decent'. If it is the latter, then we have eliminated the sense in which corporations truly have obligations for the realisation of human rights and their actions in this area would merely become a matter of their benevolence. This is inconsistent with the logic of human rights, which entails duties upon those who have the capacity to violate them or assist in their realisation.[43] Furthermore, appeals to benevolence alone are particularly problematic in the context of the corporation, which is often understood to be the exemplar par excellence of an entity that is focused upon profit maximisation for shareholders.[44] As a result, claims relating to human rights often need to be translated into arguments concerning why it is in the corporation's own self-interest to avoid harming rights and to contribute towards their realisation.[45] Indeed, the SRSG often links the notion of social expectations to the self-interest of the corporation: in outlining the Framework, for instance, he writes about how failure to meet this responsibility can subject companies to the 'courts of public opinion' and deprive them of a 'social licence to operate'.[46] These arguments, if seen as the basis for not violating rights, ultimately weaken the normative force of those rights. Moreover, if respecting rights is

---

[42] J. Feinberg, *Social Philosophy* (Englewood Cliffs: Prentice-Hall, 1973), 58–59.

[43] 'A right or claim, then, is the legal position created through the imposing of a duty on someone else.' M. Kramer, N. Simmonds and H. Steiner, *A Debate over Rights* (Oxford University Press, 1998), 9.

[44] One of the most famous proponents of this view is M. Friedman: 'The Social Responsibility of Business is to increase its Profits' in T. Beauchamp *et al.* (eds.), *Ethical Theory and Business*, 8th edn (Englewood Cliffs: Prentice Hall, 2009), 55.

[45] This is often referred to as the 'business case for human rights'. Some key arguments are laid out succinctly in L. Amis, P. Brew and C. Ersmarker, 'Human Rights: It is Your Business' (2005), http://commdev.org/files/1154_file_Human_Rights_It_Is_Your_Business.pdf (last accessed 5 December 2012).

[46] SRSG, '2008 Framework', n. 13, para. 54. See also Human Rights Council, 'Business and Human Rights: Towards Operationalizing the "Protect, Respect and Remedy" Framework', A/HRC/11/13 (22 April 2009), paras. 46 and 81 (SRSG, '2009 Report').

contingent upon bringing benefits to the company, then directors may judge, in many cases, that they need not fulfil their responsibilities in relation to rights as the costs to the company outweigh the benefits that may be achieved. Furthermore, it is the shortcomings of such an essentially voluntary approach that have provided the motivation for initiatives to create more binding legal obligations upon corporations.[47]

Secondly, it is important to consider how we are able to determine what social expectations require, particularly in a global world marked by competing interests and ideologies.[48] In this regard, it is important to note that human rights admit of some 'indeterminacy' and that there is a need consequently to interpret them in order to determine specific obligations of particular agents in concrete situations. Indeed, one of the shortcomings of the SRSG's work appears to be the lack of understanding of this point. He simply refers, for instance in Guiding Principle 12, to the list of human rights in international instruments as 'benchmarks against which other social actors assess the human rights impact of business enterprises' without recognising the interpretive work required to relate abstract standards to concrete contexts. International human rights bodies and municipal courts have made much progress in adopting doctrinal approaches towards the interpretation of such rights, though there remains a lack of clarity as to the exact obligations of business. If the concrete meaning of human rights for corporations is to be ascertained in light of wide-ranging social expectations (rather than having reference to a deeper moral basis as well as the legal standards that have been developed), rights protection can be weakened significantly.

Take, for instance, the debate surrounding carbon emissions which relates to the developing field of environmental rights. In certain states with powerful environmental movements, there may be strong social

---

[47] A number of these problems are outlined in D. Kinley and J. Tadaki, 'The Emergence of Human Rights Responsibilities for Corporations at International Law' (2004) 44 *Virginia Journal of International Law* 931, at 949–52; and D. Bilchitz, 'Corporate Law and the Constitution: Towards Binding Human Rights Responsibilities for Corporations' (2008) 125 *South African Law Journal* 754, at 760–71.

[48] Hart recognised that one of the primary problems with societies that use social expectations as the primary mode of creating social obligation is the resulting uncertainty. Such a mode of determining social rules is also, Hart claims, only likely to succeed for a 'small community closely knit by ties of kinship, common sentiment, and belief, and places in a stable environment'. Hart, *The Concept of Law*, n. 3, 92. If we accept this, social expectations do not, therefore, provide a promising model for the regulation of corporations in today's globalised world.

expectations that corporations should seek to reduce their carbon emissions so as to protect the environment now and for future generations. On the other hand, in states with developing industrial and manufacturing sectors, social expectations may focus upon the duty of corporations to industrialise further so as to increase employment and help address the dire poverty in those societies: consequently, harm to the environment is often seen as less important in that context or as a necessary corollary of development.[49] Similarly, if we consider the strongly conflicting positions taken by corporations, governments and civil society groups in relation to the UN Norms,[50] it would seem to be very difficult to determine a detailed, common set of social expectations surrounding corporate responsibilities in relation to human rights. Thus, it is unclear how we are to determine social expectations in this area and to make authoritative statements in this regard. It is not sufficient – as the SRSG does – to recognise a variety of voluntary initiatives that essentially embrace a corporate obligation to respect. The problem lies in giving more detailed content to this obligation, which the notion of social expectations does not seem well suited to do, except perhaps in the case of the most grievous violations.

Finally, it is not only a problem of definition that arises in this context. Take, for example, a population that has been subjected to authoritarian rule for a lengthy period. The people in this state might have become used to the status quo, and, as a result, have low expectations concerning the regime's compliance with human rights norms.[51] Yet, those very norms exist at the international level precisely to highlight the unacceptable actions of the state in instances such as this and to require compliance with these international standards despite the reduced social expectations of the people living under such a regime. If the normative human rights standards we adopt are based simply upon low societal

---

[49] Louka states that 'developing countries are content to sacrifice more of their environmental protection in the pursuit of their development goals. Developing countries often have argued that developed countries were allowed to despoil their environment in order to develop and that they, developing countries, should achieve some level of development before they implement environmental measures.' E. Louka, *International Environmental Law: Fairness, Effectiveness and World Order* (Cambridge University Press, 2006), 29.

[50] See J. Ruggie, 'Business and Human Rights: The Evolving International Agenda' (2007) 101 *American Journal of International Law* 819, at 821.

[51] This is often referred to in political philosophy as the 'adaptive preference problem'. See the discussion in M. Nussbaum, *Women and Human Development* (Cambridge University Press, 2000), 111–66.

expectations, then we will land up replicating the status quo – that involves large-scale human rights violations – rather than developing a world in which the universal human rights of all individuals are adequately protected.

This point is of particular importance in relation to the debate concerning the obligations of corporations for the realisation of human rights and, in particular, whether they have responsibilities to contribute to the alleviation of poverty. In large parts of the world, expectations of corporations may be low given their poor track record in the past.[52] The binding normative basis for our determination of corporate obligations – whether moral or legal – should thus not be found in some amorphous concept of 'social expectations'. Instead, such obligations should be sourced in the requirements placed upon corporations that can be derived from the existing normative commitments of the international community as expressed in the international human rights treaties.[53] There has been much work on this body of law, which considers the range of individual interests that require protection as well as the kinds of obligations that such instruments impose.[54] Understanding binding normativity in this way will assist in giving greater content to corporate obligations: it then becomes possible to draw upon existing treaties, commentaries, cases and principles in order to determine the particular obligations of corporations for the realisation of human rights. Given that there will be the need to develop existing principles relating to human rights in the context of corporate obligations, inevitably it will also be necessary to have a conception of the moral normative basis of these rights. No doubt, at times there will be strong disagreement in seeking to render 'vague' rights more determinate. The focus of this disagreement, however, should be on the legal and moral notions underpinning human rights, rather than on attempting to articulate the lowest common denominator of social expectations in our world.

---

[52] The CorpWatch website monitors corporate activity and violations in this regard. CorpWatch, 'CorpWatch Holding Corporations Accountable' (2012), www.corpwatch.org/ (last accessed 5 December 2012).

[53] These could be said to be the 'social expectations' of the international legal community, but they are nevertheless legal instruments with a certain degree of determinate content that are binding upon the international community.

[54] The General Comments of the treaty bodies formed in relation to the ICCPR and ICESCR, for instance, are designed to provide guidance concerning the content and scope of particular rights.

Do corporations only have a responsibility to respect human rights?

The lack of an adequate engagement with the moral normative foundations of rights not only leads to mistaken conclusions concerning the legally binding nature of human rights for corporations. It also has an impact on the way in which the extent of corporate responsibilities is conceptualised by the SRSG, who claims that the main responsibilities of corporations are to avoid harming rights and to address adverse human rights impacts with which they are involved.[55] In the face of the human rights violations that flow from global poverty, his assertion is startling.

Global poverty and human rights

One of the most pressing problems of our world today lies in the unequal distribution of wealth and the consequences flowing from this for the poor. Some individuals have an almost unlimited capacity to acquire whatever they want, whilst others lack even the ability to obtain the most basic resources necessary to survive. Those in the latter category suffer from a variety of ills such as homelessness, hunger, thirst, ill health and lack of education. It is not supposed to be this way: indeed, the Universal Declaration of Human Rights guarantees everyone the right to an adequate standard of living.[56] That right, which includes an entitlement to adequate food, housing and clothing, is repeated in the ICESCR.[57] Yet, these rights are abrogated on a daily basis in large parts of the developing world. Under the ICESCR, the state has an obligation to provide a minimum core of these rights and beyond that progressively to realise them.[58]

Many developing states have failed to make significant progress in this regard for a variety of reasons, including incapacity, corruption and political conflicts. Yet, under the complex economic system that has developed in our world, the state is not the whole story. Corporations can have a negative role in exacerbating poverty. Amongst other problems, they often lack a long-term strategy of engagement with a society,

---

[55] SRSG, 'Guiding Principles', n. 37, para. 11.
[56] Universal Declaration of Human Rights (entered into force 17 March 1949), 1438 UNTS 51, Art. 25 (UDHR).
[57] ICESCR, n. 12, Art. 11.
[58] Committee on Economic, Social and Cultural Rights (CESCR), 'General Comment No. 3: the Nature of State Parties' Obligations', E/1991/23 (14 December 1990).

pay poorly, affect local businesses in a negative manner when they cannot compete, and harm the environment.[59] On the other hand, corporations can also help alleviate poverty: they often bring much-needed skills to a society, help train and improve the life chances of individuals, provide jobs and thus raise incomes.[60] In order to determine whether corporations will have a positive or negative effect on poverty, active consideration and engagement with the issues involved are necessary. Corporations should be required to integrate these considerations into their business activities, which often requires positive action on the part of these entities.

At the outset of the mandate, the SRSG in his 2006 report recognised the crucial role businesses can play in addressing these important global challenges. He stated there that 'in individual issue areas, whether the aim is providing access to medicines in poor countries, meeting the Millennium Development Goals, mitigating climate change or curing human rights abuses, civil society actors and policymakers increasingly appreciate the fact that active corporate involvement is an essential ingredient for success'.[61] However, when it came to articulating the responsibilities of business, the SRSG failed to address adequately the potentially positive role companies can play in alleviating poverty. Instead, the responsibility of business is seen to be limited to avoiding harm. The SRSG has, in subsequent reports, clarified that this duty requires companies to conduct a human rights due diligence process to ensure that they are aware of, can prevent and address the adverse human rights impacts of their activities.[62] They are also required to put in place certain mechanisms and grievance procedures to enable them to deal adequately with human rights concerns.[63] Avoiding harm will no doubt require some consideration of the negative effects corporations may have upon socio-economic rights, an issue to which the SRSG mandate devotes very little attention. Nevertheless, if global poverty has a chance of being addressed, a more positive role for corporations must be developed.

---

[59] A summary of some of these negative objections in the wide-ranging literature on this topic is contained in A. Kolk and R. van Tulder, 'Poverty Alleviation as Business Strategy? Evaluating Commitments of Frontrunner Multinational Corporations' (2006) 34 *World Development* 789, at 790. See also J. Madeley, *Big Business, Poor Peoples: How Transnational Corporations Damage the World's Poor* (London: Zed Books, 1999), and J. Stiglitz, *Globalisation and its Discontents* (London: Penguin Books, 2002).
[60] See Kolk and van Tulder, *ibid.*, 791. [61] SRSG, '2006 Interim Report', n. 4, para. 18.
[62] SRSG, '2008 Framework', n. 13, para. 56. [63] SRSG, '2009 Report', n. 46, para. 59.

The ambit of corporate human rights obligations

Do corporations have a duty to go beyond a responsibility to respect and actively to help contribute towards realising the rights of individuals in communities where, for instance, there is large-scale poverty? The SRSG denies that any such responsibility exists as a general matter of moral obligation (or social expectation).[64] Companies, he claims, may of course undertake additional commitments 'voluntarily or as a matter of philanthropy ... [b]ut what is desirable for companies to do should not be confused with what is required of them. Nor do such desirable activities offset a company's failure to do what is required, namely, to respect human rights throughout its operations and relationships.'[65] The SRSG here makes a distinction between what is 'desirable' and what is 'required': the former may be good to do (supererogatory), but are not obligatory. Such actions go beyond what is required; they are actions that do not flow from rights that impose obligations. Is the SRSG correct in this regard?

If we look at the normative underpinnings of rights, they are generally understood (as argued above in the section on normativity, law and morals in the work of the SRSG), in both law and political philosophy, to be entitlements that flow from the very moral worth or dignity of individuals. This dignity is disrespected if certain human interests are not given protection. Understanding the rootedness of human rights in dignity requires recognising that they flow from what may be termed the 'perspective of recipience'. This means that human rights are focused on the individuals who have the entitlements and to whom obligations are owed. This perspective can be contrasted with the 'perspective of agency', where the focus is on the agents that are responsible for performing particular actions rather than on those claiming the entitlements.[66] O'Neill, for instance, argues that the perspective of recipience is a

---

[64] I will not deal with two other cases where additional responsibilities arise according to the SRSG: the additional requirements are imposed by operating conditions (protecting employees in conflict-affected areas and where a company performs public functions). These are cases of specially assumed obligations and are not general obligations of companies.

[65] SRSG, '2009 Report', n. 46, para. 62.

[66] I have previously discussed the issue of recipience and agency in Bilchitz, *Poverty and Fundamental Rights*, n. 1, 72–74. I have considered the implications for corporations of these ideas in D. Bilchitz, 'Corporations and Fundamental Rights: What is the Nature of their Obligations, if Any?' in C. Lutge (ed.), *Handbook on the Philosophical Foundations of Business Ethics* (Dordrecht: Springer, 2012), 1053, at 1059.

weakness of rights discourse because the failure to focus on the agents who must realise these rights provides a recipe for empty promises.[67] Moreover, the obligations rights impose are underspecified and there is no allocation of responsibility to specific agents for the fulfilment of these rights.[68]

However, instead of being a weakness, it can be argued that the focus on the entitlements of individuals is a strength of rights discourse, which provides it with an inherent flexibility. Indeed, the context of much historical discussion of human rights has been focused on the harms that states cause to individuals through repressive actions. If the focus philosophically had simply been on agents and their obligations, it is likely that only the obligations of the state would have been considered. In our current world, of course, placing human rights requirements on states is still relevant given the significant power they exert over individuals. Yet, other agents also possess the ability to affect significantly the human interests of individuals. The logic of human rights thus pushes us towards imposing obligations on all agents who pose a threat to human rights. Obligations can then be allocated according to the power and ability of various agents to impact upon human rights. If non-state actors are increasingly able to impact significantly upon human rights, then we need to grapple with how to ensure that they play a positive (and not harmful) role in ensuring their realisation. The openness of human rights discourse concerning the agents responsible for their realisation allows for an inherent flexibility in allocating these obligations on a basis that will ensure the effective realisation of these rights.

Understanding these points means that rights realisation is the responsibility of multiple duty-bearers, all of whom may be capable of affecting rights positively or negatively. The logic of human rights would not provide any general reason to restrict the obligations of a particular class of agents (especially with the powers possessed by corporations) simply to the negative obligation to avoid harm to such rights. Nevertheless, the SRSG is correct to point out that there is a need to determine a principled normative basis upon which to allocate different levels of obligation between differing agents. The logic of rights pushes us towards recognising that a key criterion for any such allocation must be the impact it will have on human rights and whether it will be likely to

---

[67] O. O'Neill, *Towards Justice and Virtue: A Constructive Account of Practical Reason* (Cambridge University Press, 1996), 135.
[68] *Ibid.*

lead to their effective realisation. Clearly, the fairness of any allocation must also be considered. The SRSG provides three reasons why, in his view, the responsibilities of business should be restricted to 'respecting' rights. In the following sections I examine and evaluate these specific reasons, and, in the process, demonstrate why the SRSG is mistaken in this regard.

Positive corporate obligations: between the state and individuals?

The SRSG contends that there is a need to distinguish between the responsibilities of the state and of business in relation to human rights:

> While it may be useful to think of corporations as 'organs of society' as in the preambular language of the Universal Declaration, they are speci-alized organs that perform specialized functions. They are not a micro-cosm of the entire social body. By their very nature, therefore, corporations do not have a general role in relation to human rights as do States; they have a specialized one.[69]

We may term this the 'argument from the nature of the corporate entity'. The SRSG, at various stages, repeats his assertion of the need to differ-entiate between the social role of corporations and of states. Indeed, it forms the very basis of the Framework, which is founded upon the idea of 'differentiated but complementary responsibilities'.[70]

The problem, however, is that in order to justify differential responsi-bilities, there is a need to have a clear conception of the respective roles of the corporation and the state. The SRSG at no stage outlines a systematic account of the role of the corporation. Apart from the statements quoted above about the 'specialised' role of corporations, the SRSG speaks about how wider social obligations upon corporations may undermine 'the company's own economic role and possibly its commercial viability'.[71] This suggests that the specialised role the SRSG refers to is an *exclusively* economic one; it is hard to see though why this should exclude corpo-rations from contributing as economic agents towards the realisation of rights. The concern about commercial viability could be addressed in determining limits on the extent of the obligations upon corporate

---

[69] SRSG, '2006 Interim Report', n. 4, para. 66.
[70] SRSG, '2008 Framework', n. 13, para. 9.   [71] SRSG, '2010 Report', n. 2, para. 64.

entities.[72] Thus, without further development, the SRSG's assertions that corporations lack positive obligations to contribute towards the realisation of rights lack an adequate normative grounding.[73]

In fact, understanding the normative moral foundations of human rights leads us towards the opposite conclusion. As discussed above, the logic of human rights does not automatically identify the actors responsible for their realisation. Indeed, the obligations they impose are of such a foundational nature that there would need to be very good reasons to exempt corporations from some form of positive obligations to assist in realising such rights.

Ratner, in his well-known discussion of corporate obligations, conceives of such entities as lying in some sense between the state and individuals.[74] When we work out the obligations of corporations, he suggests that we work *'down* from state responsibility and *up* from individual responsibility ... [s]uch a methodology acknowledges that, in general terms, a corporation is, as it were, more than an individual and less than a state'.[75] Although this method of proceeding seems plausible, Ratner too concludes (with very limited discussion) that corporations should not in general have positive obligations. He notes that doing so would be to 'ask too much of the corporation, especially at this stage of the international legal process, when the broad notion of business duties in the human rights area is just emerging'.[76]

Ratner's reasoning appears to be strategic rather than flowing from deep principles of ethics and political morality, but it leads us to ask the important question: would imposing positive obligations upon corporations be asking too much? Using Ratner's own methodology, in my view, leads to a different conclusion than that of the SRSG on this issue, particularly considering that the SRSG is concerned with obligations that flow from social expectations (and are a matter of moral or political rather than legal obligation). Indeed, if we start with individuals, it is by

---

[72] It may well be, for instance, that positive obligations are limited to the extent that they do not threaten the very commercial viability of the enterprise. Clearly, the notion of commercial viability is itself contestable and requires further specification.

[73] I have argued that the SRSG in fact appears to work with a 'libertarian' conception of the corporation. I have critiqued this idea and outlined a different understanding of the purpose of the corporate entity and, on this basis, provided two normative moral arguments why corporations do indeed have positive obligations in relation to human rights. D. Bilchitz, 'Do Corporations have Positive Fundamental Rights Obligations?' (2010) 125 *Theoria* 1.

[74] Ratner, 'A Theory of Legal Responsibility', n. 20, 488.   [75] *Ibid.*, 496.

[76] *Ibid.*, 517. Ratner goes on to say that to require proactive steps to promote human rights 'seems inconsistent with the reality of the corporate enterprise'. *Ibid.*, 518.

no means clear that they lack any positive obligations for the realisation of rights. Intuitively, if a starving woman approaches a well-off individual for some food, there is a strong case that the individual is obligated to provide such assistance if able to do so.[77] Even if one rejects such direct individualised obligations, there is a strong case to be made that individuals are required positively to contribute to institutional mechanisms that would provide such a person with relief from starvation (and prevent them from starving in the first place).[78] On this account, whilst individuals would not have the obligation to feed every poor person in society, they would not be free from some responsibility to contribute to ensuring that, at least, a minimum basic level of entitlements is guaranteed to all. Having an obligation to contribute towards the realisation of rights is not equivalent to placing the whole responsibility upon one agent.

Indeed, difficult problems arise in drawing the limits of the obligations upon individuals in such cases. Peter Singer, for example, has made a strong but controversial case that well-off individuals are required to contribute substantial portions of their income to famine relief.[79] Despite some difficulty in delineating the exact nature and extent of

---

[77] Both the two main schools of moral normative thinking – Kantian and Utilitarian – would reach this conclusion. I. Kant, 'Groundwork for the Metaphysics of Morals' in M. J. Gregor (ed.), *Immanuel Kant: Practical Philosophy* (Cambridge University Press, 1996), 75. For an examination of the implications of Kantian ethics for global hunger, see O. O'Neill, *Faces of Hunger: An Essay on Poverty, Justice and Development* (London: Allen and Unwin, 1986). Similarly, utilitarianism requires individuals to act in such a way that will promote the greatest happiness of the greatest number: this will often require extensive positive duties of assistance. See P. Singer, 'Famine, Affluence and Morality' (1972) 1 *Philosophy and Public Affairs* 229–43. In his recent book, Dworkin also recognises duties to aid which flow from the principle to treat everyone's life as being of equal objective importance (often seen as the underlying principle supporting human rights). R. Dworkin, *Justice for Hedgehogs* (Cambridge: Belknap Press, 2011), 271–84. In the context of analyzing the right to food, J. Dreze ('Democracy and the Right to Food' in P. Alston and M. Robinson, *Human Rights and Development: Towards Mutual Reinforcement* (Oxford University Press, 2005), 55–56) envisages a similar case where a well-off individual comes across someone dying of starvation in the street.

[78] Rawls focuses upon ensuring that the basic structure of society is just. This requires that, at least, certain minimum socio-economic entitlements are realised and that the difference principle is met. In order to meet these conditions, wealthier individuals will have positive obligations to contribute towards societal institutions such that they are able to meet the principles of distributive justice. J. Rawls, *A Theory of Justice* (Cambridge, MA: Harvard University Press, 1971), 6–7.

[79] Singer, 'Famine, Affluence and Morality', n. 77, 229–43. For a response, see A. Kuper, 'More than Charity: Cosmopolitan Alternatives to the "Singer Solution"' (2002) 16 *Ethics and International Affairs* 107.

such obligations, there is nevertheless no good reason to conclude that individuals lack some positive obligations to contribute financially or otherwise to help realise the rights of other individuals.[80] If this is true of individuals, then it would appear that *a fortiori* it must be true of corporations, which often provide financial rewards to significant numbers of individuals and possess significant power to help contribute towards the realisation of rights of other individuals.[81] Although here again there is a problem of drawing limits (which needs further investigation and research), this problem does not entail that there are no such obligations upon corporations. Indeed, the SRSG arguably sought to avoid these complexities by focusing on the negative obligations of corporations; in so doing, however, he failed to fulfil a key element of the task set for him by the UN, which was to clarify the scope and limits of corporate human rights obligations – and which cannot be justifiably limited to avoiding harm.

If we approach the matter from the point of view of state obligations, it is generally recognised in international human rights law (and in many domestic systems) that the state bears positive obligations in relation to human rights. Such positive obligations are often classified as involving a duty to protect individuals from being harmed by third parties, a duty to promote an understanding of human rights through education, and a duty to fulfil or actively provide goods and resources, where individuals cannot gain access to them through their own efforts.[82] Since the corporation is clearly not the state, its burdens in this regard will need to be reduced. Nevertheless, there is no reason to conclude, as a result, that corporations lack any such obligations. Also, the obligations concerned may not necessarily involve direct welfare provision of resources or services. Often, positive obligations can simply require corporations to take such measures as paying decent wages to their employees, considering development priorities in the society when engaging in their own planning, awarding contracts to companies in the host state, and

---

[80] G. Cullity, *The Moral Demands of Affluence* (Oxford University Press, 2004), for instance, attempts to develop principled limits to positive obligations whilst still claiming that we have duties of beneficence.

[81] On the implications of Rawls's theory for corporations and the duties of assistance that flow from it, see N. Hsieh, 'The Obligations of Transnational Corporations, Rawlsian Justice and the Duty of Assistance' (2004) 14 *Business Ethics Quarterly* 643.

[82] This typology of duties has been recognised in several General Comments of the CESCR. See, for instance, CESCR, 'General Comment No. 14: The Right to the Highest Attainable Standard of Health', E/C.12/2000/4 (11 August 2000).

contributing towards training and skills development in the societies in which they operate.[83] Absolving corporations from having obligations to take such positive measures is a wasted opportunity to harness the possibilities a key economic actor holds for advancing many human rights in society. In the future evolution of norms in the area of business and human rights, the focus on positive corporate obligations as a fundamental prong should be placed squarely on the agenda.

The legitimacy argument

The second problem raised by the SRSG with regard to positive obligations concerns the 'legitimacy' of corporate involvement in this area. The SRSG is concerned that, without a clear principled differentiation between the nature of the obligations of the state and corporations, the allocation of obligations to these differing parties will come to be grounded upon their respective capacities to address human rights problems. 'On that premise, a large and profitable company operating in a small and poor country could soon find itself called upon to perform ever-expanding social and even governance functions.'[84] Such provisioning by a company may lack democratic legitimacy and 'undermine efforts ... to make governments more responsible to their own citizenry'.[85] The SRSG here raises the spectre of corporations performing a wide range of social functions and, in some cases, taking over responsibilities that are the domain of governments.

The SRSG does not expand on the concerns relating to 'democratic legitimacy'. However, if we try and draw out what is at issue, it would appear to be the fact that people in society do not elect corporations. Consequently, the argument seems to be that they have no rightful claim to govern or to perform wider social functions without the consent of the people.

Legitimacy, in this context, can be understood to involve the moral right of a corporation to perform the functions that it does. It can be said to involve two elements. The first is 'participatory legitimacy', which involves the important question as to whether people in the community consent to the exercise of a particular power. The second is the question of 'normative legitimacy' concerning whether the exercise of any power complies with the human rights of individuals, which are the basic norms governing the morality of a decent political community seeking

---

[83] See, for instance, Kolk and van Tulder, 'Poverty Alleviation', n. 59, 794.
[84] SRSG, '2010 Report', n. 2, para. 64.   [85] SRSG, '2006 Interim Report', n. 4, para. 68.

to arrange itself on terms of fair co-operation that all can reasonably accept.[86] There is some tension between these two elements, which I will explore below in the context of corporate actions.

It is quite unclear that a corporation will always lack 'participatory legitimacy' if it performs social functions. The key question here is whether the corporation performs its functions with the consent of the people. This may expressly involve the consent of the government in well-functioning democracies, which seems likely to be forthcoming if they are unable to meet their positive obligations. Unfortunately in many countries (and, in particular, weak and failing states, which appear to be the focus of the SRSG's concerns in relation to legitimacy) the government may not necessarily express the will of the people. If, for instance, a government is placing obstacles in the way of a corporation building a hospital and the community clearly demonstrates its wish for that hospital (through protests, negotiations with the corporation, etc.), it seems perfectly legitimate (from a participatory point of view) for the company to build the hospital. Clearly, this means that corporations must engage in good faith with individuals in the community and exhibit a sincere desire to understand what people in the community want.[87]

There may also be times where it is legitimate to act even in the face of majority disapproval of a particular action. This raises the question of 'normative legitimacy'. Indeed, part of the problem with too simple a notion of 'legitimacy' is that it fails to take account of state institutions that are not elected, such as the judiciary. Many societies allow unelected judges to strike down laws of parliament and actions of the executive where they do not conform with a bill of rights. Judicial review of this kind (whilst controversial) is nevertheless not regarded as illegitimate by members of those societies. The reasons for this lie in the understanding that the courts, in such instances, are acting to protect the very integrity of the democracy itself as well as the foundational normative principles

---

[86] The scope of this chapter does not allow a full exploration of the notion of legitimacy. I draw on certain strands of liberal thought in relation to this concept. See, for instance, J. Rawls, *Political Liberalism* (New York: Columbia University Press, 1993), 393. Dworkin also states that '[n]o government is legitimate that does not show equal concern for the fate of all those citizens over whom it claims dominion and from whom it claims allegiance'. R. Dworkin, *Sovereign Virtue* (Cambridge, MA: Harvard University Press, 2000), 1.

[87] Clearly, there are complexities here, particularly where there are competing demands from members of the community in question. The limited length of this chapter means that I cannot hope to address this issue in any detail, but it is a matter that is worthy of further research.

underlying any decent political community, such as the entitlement of all individuals to treatment that exhibits equal concern and respect for all.[88]

In a similar vein, there may be circumstances where it is 'legitimate' for a corporation to act even in the face of majority disapproval. If a minority, for instance, is being persecuted and denied healthcare in public hospitals, a company would be perfectly within its rights to treat members of the minority in its own hospitals, even against the wishes of the majority. The actions and sentiments of the majority violate the basic norms of a decent political community and fail to treat the members of the minority with equal concern and respect. As such, the actions of the majority (or perhaps their authority structures) are not themselves normatively legitimate and a corporation may justifiably disregard them. Of course to do so openly may be difficult for corporations and place their operations at risk; however, it is often possible to take some measures to counteract unjust policies without attracting too much negative attention (which can be a form of passive resistance). In short, if corporations exercise positive obligations to assist in the realisation of rights, this would not necessarily violate the various components of democratic legitimacy, provided corporate actions take place under the conditions described above.

Would positive obligations for corporations undermine efforts to make the government more responsible to its citizenry? It is hard to accord much weight to this objection. In circumstances of developed democracies, it seems unlikely that this would happen, given the wide-ranging mechanisms of accountability that exist. In the developing world, corporations often have to perform significant social functions as a result of a breakdown in the system of governance or conditions of severe distributive inequality that make it impossible for the government to fulfil its duties. Once the particular problems are addressed, the government could rightfully be required to take over functions that had been performed by a corporation. To suggest that, where corporations can assist, they should not be obligated to do so and allow people to suffer from extreme desperation hardly provides a clear recipe for successfully restoring responsible and effective government. Corporate involvement – where there is such a breakdown – can also be directed towards creating the conditions for the restoration of adequate

---

[88] For two classic academic positions relating to judicial review, see J. Waldron, *Law and Disagreement* (Oxford: Clarendon Press, 1999) and R. Dworkin, *Freedom's Law: The Moral Reading of the American Constitution* (Oxford University Press, 1996).

governance, which will be beneficial both for the corporation and other citizens.

These 'legitimacy' objections appear to articulate a notion that somehow corporate positive obligations in some sense 'compete' with government duties in this area. Yet, the extent of human rights violations in the world currently requires a range of actors to contribute towards alleviating the plight of so many people. Instead of a competitive conception of the corporation and the state, which the SRSG appears to employ, we should consider a collaborative conception in which both work together towards the goal of human rights realisation. It does not mean that there will be no need to allocate duties between various actors; what it does signify is that involvement of one party should not be seen to undermine the responsibilities of another.

Capacity and gaming

The point about working together to remedy the violation of rights in our world is also of importance in addressing a further objection by the SRSG. He suggested that placing positive obligations on business can allow states to shirk their role of building sustainable capacity. This is no doubt a risk as the state can transfer its responsibilities to business and avoid addressing its own problems. Yet again, however, the SRSG turns to a risk that emerges from not fully considering the possibility of collaboration between the two parties. Indeed, it is hard to see why the solution to possible shirking on the part of the state is to relieve business of its responsibilities. If business is a partner with the government in addressing deficits in human rights realisation, programmes could be designed to build sustainable capacity, and address deficits in the state capacity to meet its own obligations. In taking over some social functions in failing states, corporations can help develop sustainable local capacity with a plan to assist failing governments to meet their own obligations in the medium term. Corporations, at times, also hinder the development of sustainable capacity (particularly in developing countries) through, for instance, attracting highly skilled workers away from the public sector with high salaries. Placing positive obligations upon them can thus be essential to *ensure* that sustainable capacity is built in the public sector. Again, understanding the arguments for positive obligations means recognising that the state cannot seek to place all social provisioning obligations upon corporations. The SRSG makes the mistake of thinking that imposing *some* positive obligations on corporations requires them to take over *all* such obligations. Corporations and the business sector have limited positive obligations, but these can potentially assist the state in realising its own obligations. The state retains a crucial role in this regard; indeed, arguably, corporate involvement in the field of rights realisation may be hampered without planning and co-ordination, which the state is well designed to perform.[89]

This analysis also provides a response to another of the SRSG's objections: that positive obligations upon corporations would lead to endless 'strategic gaming' between the state and corporations.[90] The SRSG has never explained this point in any detail. The answer to this is, again, not to relieve corporations of all forms of positive obligation; rather, greater attention to the allocation of responsibilities is required. A process-based solution could also be devised allowing an arbiter, such as the judiciary, to adjudicate disputes surrounding the allocation of such responsibilities (based on the range of normative factors involved in such a decision). Again, large gaps are evident in the SRSG's work; instead of engaging with the admittedly difficult questions in determining the positive obligations of corporations and proposing possible solutions for debate and discussion, the mandate simply avoided them with simplistic objections. The agenda for the future of business and human rights thus continues to have plenty of issues to resolve.

Conclusion

In introducing the GPs, the SRSG makes the following statement: '[t]he Guiding Principles' normative contribution lies not in the creation of new international law obligations but in elaborating the implications of existing standards and practices for States and businesses; integrating them within a single, logically coherent and comprehensive template; and identifying where the current regime falls short and how it should be improved'.[91] This chapter has sought to show that the SRSG's contribution has not succeeded in achieving what he claims to have done. The first part argued that existing standards in human rights law provide the basis for drawing out strong legally binding obligations for corporations instead of the weak 'responsibilities' recognised by the SRSG. The

---

[89] See the examples of the pitfalls of corporate social responsibility projects, implemented without proper planning and co-ordination, detailed in J. Frynas, *Beyond CSR: Oil, Multinationals and Social Challenges* (Cambridge University Press, 2009), 116–30.

[90] SRSG, '2006 Interim Report', n. 4, para. 68; and SRSG, '2010 Report', n. 2, para. 68.

[91] SRSG, 'Guiding Principles', n. 37, para. 14.

approach he adopts towards corporate responsibilities is also not logically coherent and comprehensive as it does not adequately engage with the legal and moral normative basis of human rights. This basic flaw in failing to articulate a clear moral normative approach that guides his work has also led him to conclude mistakenly that corporations only have negative obligations for the realisation of human rights. I have argued against these positions, which fundamentally limit the possibility of realising human rights and meeting some of the most pressing rights challenges in the twenty-first century.

The basis for any further developments should, I contend, be rooted in the legal and moral normative underpinnings of human rights. Understanding these entails that business cannot claim to lack obligations in this regard; human rights obligations have a strong binding force and should flow from international human rights law itself. The nature of these obligations must be sourced in the nature of human rights as well as the social role of corporations in society. Corporations can be considered as having obligations that are more extensive than those of private individuals, but less onerous than those of the state. Given that the corporations achieve social benefits largely through conducting business, there is a need to develop an understanding of their obligations that is mindful both of the need to realise rights and the role of business in society as an economic actor. In moving beyond the SRSG's Framework and GPs, the international community should adopt a normative vision that sees the multiple social actors as being collaborators in the crucial task of realising human rights. Doing so will require recognising more extensive obligations upon corporations, so that their significant capacity and power can be harnessed to assist in meeting the most pressing global challenges of our time.

The corporate responsibility to respect human rights: soft law or not law?

JUSTINE NOLAN

Introduction

In June 2011 the United Nations (UN) Human Rights Council endorsed the Guiding Principles on Business and Human Rights (GPs).[1] The GPs are the culmination of six years' work by the Special Representative for Business and Human Rights (SRSG) and are designed to operationalise the 'Protect, Respect and Remedy' Framework (Framework) established by the SRSG in 2008.[2] Both the Framework and the GPs highlight the corporate responsibility to respect human rights as a baseline expectation for all companies.[3] The GPs note that the corporate responsibility to respect 'means that they [companies] should avoid infringing on the human rights of others and should address adverse human rights impacts with which they are involved'.[4] It is arguable that the limitations of this concept – that of a corporation's responsibility (not obligation) to respect (but not protect) rights – are more readily apparent than its promise. To some, the notion of the responsibility to respect rights

---

[1] Human Rights Council, 'Human Rights and Transnational Corporations and Other Business Enterprises', UN Doc. A/HRC/RES/17/4 (6 July 2011), www.business-humanrights.org/media/documents/un-human-rights-council-resolution-re-human-rights-transnational-corps-eng-6-jul-2011.pdf (last accessed 16 August 2012).

[2] Human Rights Council, 'Protect, Respect and Remedy: A Framework for Business and Human Rights: Report of the Special Representative of the Secretary-General on the Issue of Human Rights and Transnational Corporations and Other Business Enterprises', A/HRC/8/5 (7 April 2008) (SRSG, '2008 Report').

[3] Human Rights Council, 'Guiding Principles on Business and Human Rights: Implementing the United Nations "Protect, Respect and Remedy" Framework: Report of the Special Representative of the Secretary-General on the Issue of Human Rights and Transnational Corporations and Other Business Enterprises', A/HRC/17/31 (21 March 2011) (SRSG 'Guiding Principles'), Guiding Principle 11 [II.A.11] at 13.

[4] *Ibid.*

based on social expectations is an inadequate approximation of the nature and scope of business's relationship with human rights and simply reinforces the acceptance of a 'world where companies are encouraged, but not obliged, to respect human rights'.[5] In the last thirty years, attempts to regulate the negative impact of business activities on human rights have increased. While a range of diverse tactics has been employed (with varying degrees of success) there has been a wide degree of reliance on soft law mechanisms both to prevent and monitor corporate rights violations. The SRSG commented in 2011 that the corporate responsibility to respect rights is a notion that has been gradually emerging and is 'acknowledged in virtually every voluntary and soft-law instrument related to corporate responsibility, and now affirmed by the Human Rights Council itself'.[6] The development of such soft law instruments to police corporate conduct has been marked by the involvement and increasing 'regulatory'[7] role played by non-state actors such as non-governmental organisations (NGOs), trade unions and corporations themselves. While there is no entrenched definition of what constitutes soft law, in the context of international law it might commonly include an 'international instrument other than a treaty that contains principles, norms, standards or other statements of expected behaviour'.[8] In the business and human rights field it might also include widely accepted codes of conduct that have been developed by a group of stakeholders as a mechanism to prevent corporate rights abuses.[9]

Soft law has played a prominent role in the development of the SRSG's concept of why and how a corporation might be responsible for human rights. Both the Framework and the subsequent GPs stress that the corporate responsibility to respect human rights is based on social expectations (rather than a legal obligation).[10] Such reliance on soft law to ground a

---

[5] A. Ganesan (Human Rights Watch), 'UN Human Rights Council: Weak Stance on Business Standards' (16 June 2011), www.hrw.org/news/2011/06/16/un-human-rights-council-weak-stance-business-standards (last accessed 10 October 2012).

[6] SRSG, 'The UN "Protect, Respect and Remedy" Framework for Business and Human Rights' (September 2010), http://198.170.85.29/Ruggie-protect-respect-remedy-framework.pdf (last accessed 4 December 2012).

[7] Regulation as referred to in this chapter incorporates both formal and informal mechanisms or techniques designed to influence or at times coerce corporations to better respect and/or protect human rights.

[8] D. Shelton, 'Normative Hierarchy in International Law' (2006) 100 *American Journal of International Law* 291, at 319.

[9] See further discussion at n. 25.

[10] SRSG, '2008 Report', n. 2, para. 54; and SRSG, 'Guiding Principles', n. 3, Guiding Principle 11 [II.A.11].

corporation's responsibility for human rights reflects the SRSG's pragmatic view that any road toward developing an international treaty, which would place binding obligations on business with respect to human rights, was one better not travelled at the present time.[11] The GPs thus appear to be the latest in a long line of soft regulatory techniques used to encourage, but not require, a corporation to comply with human rights.

This chapter is primarily focused on examining the role (and effectiveness) of soft law in regulating businesses with respect to human rights. The first section grapples with developing a general definition of soft law, and in doing so, examines both the advantages and limitations of soft law regulation. The second provides an overview of the significant soft law developments in the business and human rights field. Given the diversity of the principal constituents in this sector – states, corporations and NGOs – it is perhaps not surprising that soft law has been a principal default mechanism for connecting human rights and business in recent decades. The third section focuses on the SRSG's concept of the corporate responsibility to respect as embodied in the GPs, and its status and significance. If considered soft law, then what distinguishes it from prior soft law instruments and to what extent is it likely to be more or less effective than previous attempts to curb corporate human rights violations?

While this chapter highlights the many limitations of using soft law to hold corporations to account for human rights, it also recognises that reliance on soft law can result in incremental change. Soft law is not necessarily commensurate with soft results. Achieving something, even if not perfect, can be preferable to achieving nothing. However, for soft law (and in particular the corporate responsibility to respect as set out in the GPs) to be an effective and sustainable rights protection mechanism, I argue that there is a need for a more intimate connection to 'hard' – that is legally binding – law. This could be achieved in various ways, but one is to require states to oblige corporations to comply with the due diligence component of the responsibility to respect. In its current format the corporate responsibility to respect embodies a high degree of fragility and flexibility, but what is needed most urgently in this field is greater robustness and uniformity that not only encourages but requires corporations to, at a minimum, respect human rights.

---

[11] J. Ruggie, 'Treaty Road not Travelled' (May 2008), www.hks.harvard.edu/m-rcbg/news/ruggie/Pages%20from%20ECM%20May_FINAL_JohnRuggie_may%2010.pdf   (last accessed 9 October 2012).

Soft law or not law?

Over a decade ago Muchlinkski argued that 'a climate of expectation as to proper corporate conduct should be built up through both "soft law" and "hard law" options. Developments in "soft law" through corporate and NGO codes of conduct are already creating a climate in which it might be expected that the management of MNEs [multinational enterprises] includes a conscious assessment of … human rights implications'.[12] However, what has been apparent since Muchlinkski's statement in 2001 is that while developments in the soft law regulation of corporations with respect to human rights have continued to expand and build up this climate of expectation, the development of hard law has lagged behind. The increasing relevance of soft law in this sector is symptomatic of a broader 'worldwide shift from government to governance' and is marked by 'the ascendancy of a new system in which regulation is produced in a participatory fashion by public and private actors collaborating with each other'.[13] This is particularly true in the business and human rights field where corporations, NGOs and states are all influential (though not necessarily equal to each other) in the formulation of guidelines, codes and principles that detail the relevance of human rights standards to business activities. Soft law tends to embody a diffusion of governance which does not render governments powerless but 'nevertheless throw[s] up challenges of coordination and regulation'.[14]

Commentators vary in their opinions as to the indicators that might be used in classifying particular instruments as soft law. As Chinkin notes, '[t]here is a wide diversity in the instruments of so-called soft law which makes the generic term a misleading simplification'.[15] Shelton agrees that the line between what might be loosely defined as law and not-law is blurred, but attempts a definition of soft law by noting that it 'usually refers to any international instrument other than a treaty that contains principles, norms, standards or other statements of expected behaviour'.[16] Others argue for the inclusion of some treaties as soft law,

---

[12] P. Muchlinkski, 'Human Rights and Multinationals: Is there a Problem?' (2001) 77 *International Affairs* 31, at 46.

[13] L. Baccaro and V. Mele, 'For Lack of Anything Better? International Organizations and Global Corporate Codes' (2011) 89 *Public Administration* 451.

[14] C. Scott, F. Cafaggi and L. Senden, 'The Conceptual and Constitutional Challenge of Transnational Private Regulation' (2011) 38 *Journal of Law and Society* 1, at 2.

[15] C. M. Chinkin, 'The Challenge of Soft Law: Development and Change in International Law' (1989) 38 *International and Comparative Law Quarterly* 850, at 850.

[16] D. Shelton, 'Normative Hierarchy in International Law', n. 8, at 319.

albeit only those treatises with soft obligations.[17] For some, it is easier to adopt a negative approach and attempt to define soft law by what it is not rather than what it is. Boyle argues, for example, that soft law can be determined by the status of the obligations it imposes. He suggests that soft law is not (legally) binding, consists of general norms or principles but not rules, and is not readily enforceable through binding dispute resolution mechanisms. However he also concedes that any clear demarcation between hard and soft law is challenging.[18] It is particularly difficult to achieve a clear definition in the human rights arena (although such complexities are not exclusive to human rights, and also occur, for example, in the field of international environmental law),[19] where treaties are apt to include 'soft' obligations such as undertakings to strive to co-operate or agree to take steps, which further blur the line between soft and hard. What is clear is that the differentiation between soft and so-called hard (or legally binding) law is not binary, but one that should be viewed as developing on a continuum.

Soft law may develop partly by default and partly by design. Reliance on soft law, whether in this field or others, has not emerged simply because there is a lack of anything better (although there is no denying that can be – and indeed has been in this field – a significant factor in the development of soft law). The use of soft law can be a deliberate choice and often more attractive to the relevant stakeholders (in this case particularly to business and governments alike) because it may contain aspirational goals that aim for the best possible scenario with few constraints if such goals are not met. Thus, it is easier to achieve consensus in drafting a document that outlines these types of 'commitments'.

Following from the political divisiveness generated by the debate around the UN Norms,[20] achieving consensus was highly prized by the SRSG throughout his term.[21] Part of his preference for a soft law approach in developing the corporate responsibility to respect was

---

[17] C. M. Chinkin, 'The Challenge of Soft Law', n. 15, at 851; also see generally S. Freeland, 'For Better or For Worse? The Use of "Soft Law" within the International Legal Regulation of Outer Space' (2011) *XXXVI Annals of Air and Space Law* 409.

[18] A. E. Boyle, 'Some Reflections on the Relationship of Treaties and Soft Law' (1999) 48 *International and Comparative Law Quarterly* 901, at 901–2.

[19] *Ibid.*, at 902–7.

[20] United Nations Sub-Commission on the Promotion and Protection of Human Rights, 'Norms on the Responsibilities of Transnational Corporations and Other Business Enterprises with Regard to Human Rights', E/CN.4/Sub.2/2003/12/Rev.2 (2003) (UN Norms). See also the discussion at n. 46.

[21] See Chapter 4.

perhaps because the informal nature of soft law allows for a broader group of participants (including non-state actors) in both its development and enforcement.[22] Soft law can generally be formed in a far more timely manner than a treaty: this is perhaps exemplified by the field of business and human rights where waiting for the development of a comprehensive treaty holding corporations accountable for human rights abuses might be akin to waiting for Godot.[23] Soft law can serve as a precursor to the introduction of hard law. For example, it might be used as a testing ground for the development of new mechanisms of accountability and thus function as a useful and necessary tool for the development of hard law that formally binds parties.

This chapter opts for a broad definition of soft law that includes those instruments categorised as 'non-binding or voluntary resolutions and codes of conduct formulated and accepted by international and regional organisations, along with statements prepared by individuals or groups in a non-government capacity, but which purport to promote international principles'.[24] This would include, for example, codes of conduct developed not only at an international level but also at a more micro-level such as by multi-stakeholder groups that rely on and profess to promote international rights. The chapter excludes treaties from soft law on the basis that from the outset they set out to impose legally binding obligations. The definition of soft law embraced here distinguishes treaties from instruments such as resolutions, principles and codes because unlike a treaty they are deliberately cast in a non-legally binding framework. Thus Boyle's point that soft law can be characterised by the status of the obligations it imposes – distinguishing between an intention to legally bind (or not bind) stakeholders – is a useful one. While over time the effectiveness of soft law instruments in 'binding' stakeholders to an agreement or an agreed course of action may be commensurate with, or exceed, that of hard law regulatory mechanisms (such as treaties), the relevant point of distinction here is the intention (or not) to legally bind parties to the instrument at the time of its conception.

---

[22] Although such involvement can also be incorporated within the treaty-making process. For example, civil society was strongly involved in the development and drafting of an international treaty that led to the establishment of the International Criminal Court: the Rome Statute of the International Criminal Court.

[23] *Waiting for Godot* is a play by Samuel Beckett, in which two characters, Vladimir and Estragon, wait endlessly and in vain for someone named Godot to arrive.

[24] Chinkin, 'The Challenge of Soft Law', n. 15, at 851.

The binding/non-binding nature of soft law is contentious. Characterising soft law as non-binding might be regarded by some as accurate only in the strict legal sense. Soft law can include 'mechanisms [that] provide guidelines and principles which, while not legally binding, have force by virtue of the consent that governments, companies, and other civil society actors accord them'.[25] Codes of conduct, developed by multistakeholder groups in the business and human rights field, might be reflective of the varying norms and societal expectations concerning corporations and their responsibilities, and while not legally binding may have 'force' by the degree of consensus and acceptance linked to them.

Thus to argue that soft law is simply not-law is perhaps too simplistic. The evolution of soft law instruments in the business and human rights sector has created, at minimum, standards of expected conduct that, while not setting out to be legally binding, may have normative value that is intended to prescribe expected standards of behaviour. Widespread acceptance of a particular instrument may not turn soft law into legally binding principles but may nevertheless establish standards which 'socially bind' corporations to human rights. How effective this is in regulating corporate behaviour with respect to human rights is a key question. In the absence of legally binding characteristics, the potential 'law-making quality' of soft law is linked to its 'authority', which will in turn influence the likely impact and longevity of the instrument. Does the instrument create an obligation to do or not do something? Is there apparent consent by relevant stakeholders drafting or using the instrument, to be 'bound' by it, and if so, how might such soft law be enforced? The authority of the soft law is intrinsically linked to its binding nature.

In attempting to assess the authority of soft law it is useful to examine a particular instance of such regulation from a number of perspectives. Firstly, consider why this particular mode of 'law' was chosen. For example, does it complement and/or extend existing law on the subject or is it standing in place of such law? If the soft law is acting as a complement to existing law, the combination of the two modes of 'law' might serve to create a greater sense of authority for the soft law than if it stands alone. Secondly, given the mode chosen, does it have the potential to generate compliance, whether by states or other relevant parties? Or to put it another

---

[25] Institute for Human Rights and Business, 'From Red Flags to Green Flags: The Corporate Responsibility to Respect Human Rights in High-Risk Countries' (2011), www.ihrb.org/pdf/from_red_to_green_flags/complete_report.pdf (last accessed 10 October 2012), 39.

way, what is its normative potential? In answering this question, one should consider the process of the development of the soft law, including how it was drafted and the degree of consensus that was reached regarding the final product. For example, in what institutional setting was it formulated and what processes are there for follow-up mechanisms at both international and domestic levels? Also relevant here is the substantive text of the soft law – does it employ the language of obligation or revert to 'should' rather than 'shall'?[26] Each of these factors is a useful indicator of the 'binding' nature of the soft law and its latent power or authority to drive improved adherence to human rights standards.

The consistent use of soft law in the business and human rights field is indicative of the emergence of and reliance on a notion of 'networked governance'[27] that places corporate behaviour under the scrutiny of not only states, but also NGOs, unions and other stakeholders. Soft law, as it is being used to regulate business, transcends the traditional and formal role played by states as the primary regulator and not only encourages, but heavily relies on, the 'marketplace' to police the problem. The effectiveness of this system of governance, and therefore soft law mechanisms more generally, is strongly dependent on the perceived authority of a particular instrument to create change. There is little doubt that '[s]oft law in its various forms can of course be abused, but so can most legal forms'.[28] The key to developing effective soft law is in developing and establishing its 'bindingness' to a point where compliance is widespread and consistent.

No 'silver bullet' or single solution to curbing corporate human rights violations

To understand the development and predominant reliance on soft law in regulating corporate adherence to human rights, it is necessary to recount a little political history, including the role of the UN in the process. The UN has long recognised the need to increase corporate awareness of human rights, and has flitted between adopting a stern regulatory-type approach to the problem, and using a more promotional/awareness-raising style of linking business and rights. More recently, the SRSG has repeatedly stated

---

[26] C. Jochnick, 'Making Headway on Business and Human Rights' (11 February 2011), http://politicsofpoverty.oxfamamerica.org/2011/02/11/making-headway-on-business-and-human-rights/ (last accessed 10 October 2012). See examples from SRSG, 'Guiding Principles', n. 3 at n. 79.

[27] Baccaro and Mele, 'International Organizations', n. 13, at 453.

[28] Boyle, 'Some Reflections', n. 18, at 913.

that there is no 'silver bullet'[29] that will provide a systemic solution to reducing the incidence of business-related human rights abuses. For much of the past few decades a plethora of tactics have been adopted in attempts to regulate or at least minimise the negative impact business can have on human rights, with varying levels of success.

The reason that soft law-type codes and initiatives have developed in such numbers in the past few decades is that there remain very few direct legal obligations dealing with human rights that bind corporations operating transnationally.[30] This lack of clear legal liability has been central to the creation of a permissive international 'human rights free' environment[31] in which some corporations now operate, and the parallel increase in the development of soft law mechanisms to regulate corporate behaviour. The traditional understanding of international human rights law is that it binds only states, a matter which was largely uncontested for many years partly because states have long been viewed as the principal protagonists in human rights abuses. This focus on states as the bearers of human rights responsibilities has meant that some corporations, in particular transnational corporations (TNCs), have been able to operate largely in a legal vacuum, devoid of obligations at the international level.

In the last twenty to thirty years, a variety of soft law instruments have attempted to fill or at least partially address this legal lacuna. In the 1970s work began within the UN on drafting an international code of conduct to regulate the activities of TNCs.[32] In 1975, the UN established a Centre on Transnational Corporations, which by 1977 was co-ordinating the negotiation of a Draft Code of Conduct on Transnational Corporations.[33] Over subsequent years the negotiators managed to

---

[29] Human Rights Council, 'Business and Human Rights: Mapping International Standards of Responsibility and Accountability for Corporate Acts', A/HRC/4/035 (4 February 2007) (SRSG, '2007 Report'), para. 7.

[30] There is a diversity of opinions on the extent to which international human rights law currently binds (directly or indirectly) corporations. See, for example, Chapter 5.

[31] O. De Schutter, 'Extraterritorial Jurisdiction as a Tool for Improving the Human Rights Accountability of Transnational Corporations' (2006), www.corporatejustice.org/IMG/pdf/Extraterritorialityreport_DeSchutter.pdf (last accessed 16 August 2012).

[32] P. Utting, 'UN-Business Partnerships: Whose Agenda Counts?' (Paper presented at a seminar on Partnerships for Development or Privatization of the Multilateral System?, Oslo, 8 December 2000), 2, www.unrisd.org/unrisd/website/document.nsf/d2a23ad2d50cb2a280256eb300385855/a687857bd5e36114c1256c3600434b5f/$FILE/utting.pdf (last accessed 30 January 2013).

[33] S. J. Rubin, 'Transnational Corporations and International Codes of Conduct: A Study of the Relationship between International Legal Cooperation and Economic Development' (1995) 10 *American University International Law Review* 1282.

agree that TNCs should respect host countries' developmental goals, observe their domestic laws, respect fundamental human rights, adhere to socio-cultural objectives and values, abstain from corrupt practices, and observe consumer and environmental protection objectives. Negotiations lingered until the 1990s, but the now-defunct United Nations Centre on Transnational Corporations met serious political and business opposition, not unlike that which the UN Norms were to encounter just over a decade later. The draft Code was viewed as an attempt by the UN to meddle in the affairs of business. The involvement of the UN in corporate affairs was viewed (by companies and some governments) as an unnecessary and unwanted effort to regulate business.

In the 1980s, the UN's policy towards TNCs changed course. Instead of trying to regulate foreign direct investment, UN agencies sought to facilitate developing countries' access to investment.[34] The 1990s was a period when globalisation gathered force and corporate lobbying effectively undermined multilateral attempts at addressing their power. Corporate self-regulation was the key buzz phrase, and the development of codes of conduct in various forms from 1991 (when Levi Strauss first introduced its code) to the end of that decade was explosive. At the same time, UN–business relations entered a new era (continuing today) as the international body strove to develop partnerships with large corporations or establish long-term projects funded by corporate philanthropists.[35] The UN is clear in its belief concerning the positive role business can play in 'being part of the solution to the challenges of globalisation'.[36]

Throughout this period when the UN started to change course and develop a more user-friendly (and softer regulatory) relationship with business, there were ongoing efforts to continue the development of soft

---

[34] P. Utting, 'Rethinking Business Regulation: From Self Regulation to Social Control' (September 2005), www.unrisd.org/unrisd/website/document.nsf/ab82a6805797760f80 256b4f005da1ab/f02ac3db0ed406e0c12570a10029bec8/$FILE/utting.pdf (last accessed 11 December 2012).

[35] A. Zammit, *Development at Risk: Rethinking UN-Business Partnerships* (Geneva: UNRISD, 2003), Ch. III. Also see P. Utting, 'UN-Business Partnerships', n. 32, at 3. Recent examples include the establishment of the UN Foundation with a $1 billion grant from CNN founder Ted Turner and the establishment of the Global Alliance for Vaccines and Immunizations whose contributors include the Bill and Melinda Gates Foundation.

[36] See United Nations Global Compact, www.unglobalcompact.org (last accessed 9 October 2012).

law mechanisms to guide improvements in corporate behaviour. Since the 1970s a number of inter-governmental organisations have formed voluntary guidelines, declarations and codes of conduct to guide the activities of corporations, with two of the most notable early efforts being those of the Organisation for Economic Co-operation and Development (OECD) and the International Labour Organization (ILO).[37]

Parallel to the development of these high-level, broad inter-governmental soft guidelines were efforts developed at a more micro-level, focusing specifically on regional issues or particular industries. In 1977, the Sullivan Principles,[38] directed at the behaviour of American companies operating in South Africa, were established, and, in 1984, the MacBride Principles[39] were created with the aim of influencing the behaviour of US firms in Northern Ireland. Both of these soft law initiatives were drafted as codes that might 'voluntarily' be adopted by businesses in an attempt to avoid the potential of harsher external regulation (the threat of US legislation, for example) that would require companies to disinvest from South Africa and Northern Ireland.

The 1990s saw intense media attention focused on supply chain production, and the manufacturing processes of brands such as Gap and Nike were highlighted along with an increasing Western-driven consumer demand for corporations to assume greater responsibility for the manner in which their goods were produced, whether it be on home soil or offshore. In the absence of any international legal regulation governing supply chain production, hundreds of corporate codes of conduct were developed along with several multi-stakeholder initiatives aimed at integrating human rights into corporate practices.[40] An important aspect of the evolution of the global economic system has been the increased reliance by companies, TNCs in particular, on a global supply chain. This reliance is especially obvious in low-wage, labour-intensive

---

[37] OECD Guidelines for Multinational Enterprises, www.oecd.org/daf/internationalinvestment/ guidelinesformultinationalenterprises/48004323.pdf (last accessed 27 January 2013); and the ILO Tripartite Declaration of Principles Concerning Multinational Enterprises and Social Policy (MNE Declaration), 4th edn, www.ilo.org/empent/Publications/WCMS_094386/ lang–en/index.htm (last accessed 12 October 2012).

[38] L. Sullivan, 'The Sullivan Principles' (1977), http://www1.umn.edu/humanrts/links/ sullivanprinciples.html.

[39] S. McManus for the Irish National Caucus, 'The MacBride Principles' (1984), http:// www1.umn.edu/humanrts/links/macbride.html.

[40] Examples include: the Fair Labor Association's Workplace Code of Conduct and monitoring scheme, Social Accountability 8000, the Ethical Trading Initiative, the Global Reporting Initiative and the Voluntary Principles on Security and Human Rights.

industries like clothing and footwear. 'In a world of 80,000 transnational corporations, ten times as many subsidiaries and countless national firms, many of which are small-and-medium-sized enterprises', any attempt to regulate corporate behaviour will always be a challenge.[41] Such regulation has become progressively more complicated given the decentralised and complex supply chains that produce so many of today's consumer goods, and gives rise to particular challenges when employing soft law to protect human rights.

In 2000, the UN re-entered the fray and launched the Global Compact, which 'asks companies to embrace, support and enact, within their sphere of influence, a set of core values in the areas of human rights, labour standards, the environment and anti-corruption'.[42] The Global Compact has since gone on to garner support from over 7,000 businesses who have signed up to its ten principles. During this time, however, it has also attracted some significant criticism relating to the very soft commitments required of its participants.[43] At around the same time as the Global Compact was being developed, another initiative within the UN was also taking root. In 1998, the UN Sub-Commission on the Promotion and Protection of Human Rights (a twenty-six-member group of experts which reported to the then Commission on Human Rights) established a working group on the activities of transnational corporations which, in 2001, was asked to '[c]ontribute to the drafting of relevant norms concerning human rights and transnational corporations and other economic units whose activities have an impact on human rights'.[44] The working group formulated the Norms on the Responsibilities of Transnational Corporations and Other Business Enterprises with Regard to Human Rights (UN Norms), which were subsequently adopted by the UN Sub-Commission on the Promotion

---

[41] Human Rights Council, 'Business and Human Rights: Further Steps towards the Operationalization of the "Protect, Respect and Remedy" Framework', A/HRC/14/27 (9 April 2010) (SRSG, '2010 Report'), para. 82.

[42] See UN Global Compact, www.unglobalcompact.org/AboutTheGC/TheTenPrinciples/index.html (last accessed 9 October 2012).

[43] S. Deva, 'The UN Global Compact for Responsible Corporate Citizenship: Is it Still too Compact to be Global?' (2006) 2 *Corporate Governance Law Review* 145; J. Nolan, 'The United Nations' Compact with Business: Hindering or Helping the Protection of Human Rights?' (2005) 24 *University of Queensland Law Journal* 445; and Baccaro and Mele, 'International Organizations', n. 13, at 460.

[44] UN Sub-Commission on the Promotion and Protection of Human Rights, 'The Effects of the Working Methods and Activities of Transnational Corporations on the Enjoyment of Human Rights', E/CN.4/Sub.2/RES/2001/3 (15 August 2001).

and Protection of Human Rights in August 2003. The draft Norms were considered by the Commission on Human Rights in April 2004 and again in 2005, but it did not adopt (nor expressly reject) them.

The UN Norms were not universally welcomed and were viewed by some as an unwelcome and unwarranted attempt to privatise human rights.[45] Their introduction prompted heated debate within the business and human rights domain, creating strong divisions between and within the various stakeholder groups, including companies, NGOs, labour unions, governments and industry bodies.[46] Prompted by the widespread interest in the UN Norms (both positive and negative), the UN Human Rights Commission resolved in April 2005 to request the UN Secretary-General to appoint a Special Representative on the issue of business and human rights,[47] reflecting a growing interest internationally in the role companies might play with respect to human rights and the need to clarify the standards of corporate responsibility. The SRSG quickly distanced himself from what he termed the 'train wreck' of the UN Norms and subsequently declared them 'dead',[48] but the debate around the UN Norms did not dissipate quite so quickly. The development of the UN Norms had sparked a revival in the decades-old discussion about the merits of 'hard' (that is, legally binding) vs. 'soft' mechanisms that might be employed to curb corporate violations of human rights. The form and content of the UN Norms harked back to the UN's earlier unsuccessful attempt in the 1970s to draft a more

[45] J. Nolan, 'With Power comes Responsibility: Human Rights and Corporate Accountability' (2005) 28 *University of New South Wales Law Journal* 581, at 585; and D. Kinley, J. Nolan and N. Zerial, 'Reflections on the United Nations Human Rights Norms for Corporations' (2007) 25 *Companies and Securities Law Journal* 30, at 34–37.

[46] See generally D. Kinley, J. Nolan and N. Zerial, 'Reflections', n. 45.

[47] Commission on Human Rights, Agenda Item 17, E/CN.4/2005/L.87 (15 April 2005); and United Nations, 'Secretary-General Appoints John Ruggie of United States Special Representative on Issue of Human Rights, Transnational Corporations, Other Business Enterprises', SGA/A/934 (28 July 2005), www.un.org/News/Press/docs/2005/sga934.doc. htm (last accessed 12 October 2012). On 28 July 2005, the UN Secretary-General appointed Professor John Ruggie as the UN Special Representative. Professor Ruggie had previously served as UN Assistant Secretary-General and senior adviser for strategic planning from 1997 to 2001. He was one of the main architects of the United Nations Global Compact, and he led the Secretary-General's effort at the Millennium Summit in 2000 to propose and secure the adoption of the Millennium Development Goals.

[48] J. Ruggie, Remarks delivered at a Forum on Corporate Social Responsibility Co-Sponsored by the Fair Labor Association and the German Network of Business Ethics (Bamburg, Germany, 14 June 2006), www.reports-and-materials.org/Ruggie-remarks-to-Fair-Labor-Association-and-German-Network-of-Business-Ethics-14-June-2006.pdf (last accessed 9 October 2012).

prescriptive, 'regulatory' code of conduct for companies, with the UN Norms considered by some activists as a potential precursor to developing a human rights treaty on the subject. This prescriptive approach can be contrasted with the 'softer' style of the Global Compact, an initiative with which the newly appointed SRSG had been intimately involved.

During his initial three-year term, the SRSG spent time mapping both the plethora of mechanisms used to attempt to prevent corporate rights abuses as well as the rights abuses themselves. His early annual reports[49] to the UN Human Rights Council (which were drafted after extensive consultations with stakeholders large and small) framed the problem and examined existing responses, but it was not until 2008 that his new course was revealed. In that year the SRSG presented a 'conceptual and policy framework' to the UN Human Rights Council that he suggested would 'anchor the business and human rights debate and . . . help guide all relevant actors'.[50] The Framework rests on three pillars: 'the State duty to protect against human rights abuses by third parties, including business; the corporate responsibility to respect human rights; and the need for more effective access to remedies'.[51]

The way forward, it seemed, rested not just upon a new Framework but also upon a more conciliatory, less prescriptive approach towards business in particular. To understand fully the SRSG's approach, one needs to consider it in the context of his appointment and the debates that preceded it. A key part of the SRSG's methodology was focused on overcoming the failure of agreement triggered by the introduction of the UN Norms, and his approach from the outset was characterised by 'principled pragmatism'[52] as a means of achieving broader consensus. The SRSG's term was extended in 2008 for another three years and, in 2011, with his final report to the UN Human Rights Council, the SRSG endeavoured to 'operationalise' the Framework and proposed the GPs. In July 2011 the UN Human Rights Council endorsed the GPs and announced the formation of a Working Group 'to promote the effective and comprehensive dissemination and implementation of the Guiding Principles'.[53]

---

[49] The reports are easily accessible at www.business-humanrights.org/SpecialRepPortal/Home (last accessed 12 October 2012).
[50] SRSG, '2008 Report', n. 2, at 1.   [51] *Ibid.*
[52] See discussion at n. 60 for an explanation of principled pragmatism.
[53] Human Rights Council, Seventeenth Session, Agenda Item 3, 'Promotion and Protection of All Human Rights, Civil, Political, Economic, Social and Cultural Rights, including the Right to Development', A/HRC/RES/17/4 (6 July 2011), para 6(a), www.business-humanrights.org/

The GPs emerged from decades of reliance on soft measures to prevent and police corporate human rights violations that were primarily designed to guide corporate behaviour but not necessarily to bind it legally. The engagement of business with human rights drew in some companies earlier than others, with some adopting a proactive approach while others remained essentially reactive. The Body Shop, for example, has long promoted itself as much more than just a beauty company. More than thirty years ago, The Body Shop pioneered its simple idea that businesses have the power to do good, and it has continued very visibly to promote human rights as one of its essential platforms for doing business. Subsequent to the emergence of this somewhat radical 'do-gooder' notion of corporate responsibility (that challenged Milton Friedman's argument of the time that the only social responsibility of business is to increase its profits),[54] there was an increasing awareness among companies about the need to formalise, or perhaps more accurately regularise, their approach to incorporating human rights issues in their operations. The development of and reliance on thematic or sector-specific codes emerged as a *de facto* choice for a large number of companies, particularly those in industries with poor social or environmental track records, such as the extractive industries and the clothing, footwear and toy industries. Codes continue to be widely used in supply chain production as a mechanism for attempting to achieve corporate compliance with human rights standards. Such codes, which are increasingly likely to originate from a multi-stakeholder forum, are a means of providing soft sector-specific guidance on the applicability of human rights to that corporate sector and endeavour to achieve a degree of consensus, consistency and credibility that is often lacking in single-enterprise, corporate-driven codes. Such codes are in essence akin to 'law' for those companies that adopt them, albeit a soft and selective form of law that acts as a type of privatised regulation.[55]

While the protection of individuals from corporate human rights violation is complex in all sectors, it is particularly problematic where global supply chains are relied upon to produce goods. Global supply chains were first developed to reduce the costs of labour-intensive production processes such as clothing and footwear, but they continue to expand as more products and

---

media/documents/un-human-rights-council-resolution-re-human-rights-transnational-corps-eng-6-jul-2011.pdf (last accessed 9 October 2012).

[54] Milton Friedman, 'The Social Responsibility of Business is to Increase its Profits', *New York Times* (13 September 1970), 32.

[55] See also Chapter 12.

services – from computer chips to medical research – are provided by lower-cost production solutions. This has been accompanied by the development of a global labour market that has outstripped the traditional forms of labour market regulation. Global supply chains stretch across multiple jurisdictions but are effectively regulated by none. This lack of regulation, combined with the vagaries of global competition, predictably leads to frequent abuses of human rights more generally and labour rights in particular. In response, civil society organisations have often resorted to using one of the only weapons they have, namely information, to expose abuses of labour rights and embarrass the brand-name buyers involved. One technique has been to try and get the company to sign up to a particular code or guideline that would provide some form of external accountability for how the production process functions. Such codes, while lacking the legally binding nature of domestic law, nevertheless can provide a platform for monitoring and assessing a company's performance with regard to human rights.

In his first interim report to the UN Human Rights Council, the SRSG acknowledged the challenges in attempting to curb human rights violations by the corporate sector and identified a number of soft law initiatives that had attempted to police and minimise corporate human rights abuses, some particularly focused on supply chain production.[56] In his report the SRSG noted that while monitoring adherence to a code of conduct can be useful in curbing corporate human rights violations, such codes have their limitations both in terms of standard-setting and enforcement. He explained:

> [T]here can be little doubt but that these arrangements have weaknesses as well. One is that most choose their own definitions and standards of human rights, influenced by but rarely based directly on internationally agreed standards. Those choices have as much to do with what is politically acceptable within and among the participating entities than with objective human rights needs. Much the same is true of their accountability provisions. Moreover, these initiatives tend not to include determined laggards, who constitute the biggest problem – although laggards, too, may require access to capital markets and in the long run face other external pressures. Finally, even when taken together, these 'fragments' leave many areas of human rights uncovered, and human rights in many geographical areas poorly protected. The challenge for the human rights community, then, is to make the promotion and protection of human rights a more standard and uniform corporate practice.[57]

---

[56] Commission on Human Rights, 'Interim Report of the Special Representative of the Secretary-General on the Issue of Human Rights and Transnational Corporations and Other Business Enterprises', E/CN.4/2006/97 (22 February 2006), para. 53 (SRSG, '2006 Interim Report').

[57] Ibid.

While the proliferation of soft law initiatives – whether company specific or as part of a multi-stakeholder initiative – in the last few decades has meant that hundreds of companies have now publicly committed to upholding basic human rights, the challenge is to ensure that these soft law standards espoused in codes or guidelines adopted by business are consistent, comprehensive and implemented. With this abundance of soft law, along with the challenges reliance on soft law regulation imposes, one obvious question is how do the SRSG's three-pillared Framework and its accompanying GPs stand apart from the others? In particular, is this continuing recourse to soft law (specifically, to anchor the second pillar of the Framework, namely, the corporate responsibility to respect rights) likely to be an effective mechanism for preventing corporate human rights abuses? One might legitimately argue that relying on the good faith of corporate actors to adopt and adhere to soft law regulation has worked somewhat sporadically so far, so what is it about the UN Framework and GPs that indicates it will work more effectively in the future?

The 'binding' nature of the corporate responsibility to respect

From the outset, it was clear that the SRSG was looking to overcome the turbulence and 'doctrinal excesses'[58] of the UN Norms and develop a plan based on consensus and pragmatism. To move ahead, as the SRSG noted, with 'an unflinching commitment to the principle of strengthening the promotion and protection of human rights as it relates to business, coupled with a pragmatic attachment to what works best in creating change where it matters most – in the daily lives of people'.[59] However, sometimes a desire to reach a result in the short term can lead not only to compromise but to compromised standards.[60] Historically, when political leaders have spoken of pragmatism it has often been code for subordinating ideals to other strategic and geopolitical priorities. Where solutions are endorsed on the basis of their pragmatism, the 'softer' short-term solution needs to be weighed against the viability of achieving a longer-term 'harder' resolution.

Emphasis on the practical, in this case, has resulted in the extension of a consensual regime of softly developed regulation that encourages but does

---

[58] *Ibid.*, para. 59.   [59] *Ibid.*, para. 81.
[60] P. Orchard, 'Protection of Internally Displaced Persons: Soft Law as a Norm-Generating Mechanism' (2010) 36 *Review of International Studies* 281, at 286.

not require (in a legally binding sense) corporations to respect human rights. Can principled pragmatism be effective in bringing corporations to account? The corporate responsibility to respect, as embodied in the GPs, is, taken at face value, unobjectionable,[61] but is it a 'game-changer'?[62] Is it simply more soft law or a consolidated and definitive version of the numerous codes and guidelines that have preceded it that will reshape and redefine businesses' approach to human rights going forward? It is only, in my view, likely to be the latter if certain aspects of the GPs harden to require more consistency in the application and understanding of the corporate responsibility to respect rights.

The corporate responsibility to respect is defined in the GPs as meaning businesses 'should avoid infringing on the human rights of others and should address adverse human rights impacts with which they are involved'.[63] The explanatory Commentary accompanying the GPs states that 'the responsibility to respect human rights is a global standard of expected conduct for all business enterprises wherever they operate [and that] [i]t exists independently of States' abilities and/or willingness to fulfil their own human rights obligations, and does not diminish those obligations'.[64]

Its content (as to what rights should be respected) is defined by reference to a litany of international human rights laws (see Guiding Principle 12) but, interestingly, the SRSG chose to ground its source of obligation not in this law but in a more inchoate and softer source.[65] The decision to couch the responsibility to respect rights as a responsibility, not an obligation (in contrast to the State *duty* to protect human rights) was a deliberate one. It is grounded in social expectation not legal obligation and it is the 'courts of public opinion'[66] that are relied on to 'enforce' such expectations. The decision to frame it as 'not-law' elevated the odds of achieving governmental consensus and business backing, but it is a sticking point for many NGOs.[67]

---

[61] D. Kinley, *Civilising Globalisation* (Cambridge University Press, 2009), 198.

[62] Remarks by SRSG John Ruggie, 'The "Protect, Respect and Remedy" Framework: Implications for the ILO', International Labour Conference (Geneva, 3 June 2010), 3, www.ilo.org/wcmsp5/groups/public/@ed_emp/@emp_ent/@multi/documents/generic document/wcms_142560.pdf (last accessed 11 December 2012). Also, see the 'Interview with Professor John Ruggie, Special Representative of the UN Secretary-General on Business and Human Rights – Transcript', International Bar Association, www.ibanet.org/Article/Detail.aspx?ArticleUid=4b5233cb-f4b9-4fcd-9779-77e7e85e4d83 (last accessed 9 October 2012).

[63] SRSG, 'Guiding Principles', n. 3, at Guiding Principle 11 [II.A.11].   [64] *Ibid.*

[65] See also in this regard Chapter 5.   [66] SRSG, '2008 Report', n. 2, para. 54.

[67] See, for example, the comments of Ganesan, 'UN Human Rights Council', n. 5.

The concept of due diligence is introduced as a mechanism by which companies might discharge their responsibility to respect rights and reflects the continued reliance on a largely self-regulatory process to curb corporate human rights violations. Guiding Principle 17 notes the parameters of the recommended due diligence process:

> In order to identify, prevent, mitigate and account for how they address their adverse human rights impacts, business enterprises should carry out human rights due diligence. The process should include assessing actual and potential human rights impacts, integrating and acting upon the findings, tracking responses, and communicating how impacts are addressed. Human rights due diligence:
>
> (a) Should cover adverse human rights impacts that the business enterprise may cause or contribute to through its own activities, or which may be directly linked to its operations, products or services by its business relationships;
> (b) Will vary in complexity with the size of the business enterprise, the risk of severe human rights impacts, and the nature and context of its operations;
> (c) Should be ongoing, recognizing that the human rights risks may change over time as the business enterprise's operations and operating context evolve.

Guiding Principle 18 recommends the process should 'draw on internal and/or independent external human rights expertise [and] involve meaningful consultation with potentially affected groups and other relevant stakeholders'.

One of the limitations of this 'unobjectionable' process is that it is not coupled with binding law to enforce this responsibility. There is no legal obligation to conduct the due diligence. The due diligence may or may not be undertaken largely internally by the company, alongside 'meaningful consultation' with external stakeholders. There is no legal obligation either to conduct such an assessment or to publish its results. Relying on the courts of public opinion to protect victims from corporate violations of human rights was the mode of the late 1990s, but limited progress has been made since that time in moving along the continuum from self-regulation to legal obligation. Domestic governments, ideally, should reinforce these 'societal expectations' to respect human rights by, at a minimum, legally requiring due diligence to be conducted and the results made public, but whether they will choose to do so may in part depend on the binding nature of this latest instrument. The GPs were drafted as principles, not law, knowingly. One might legitimately argue that from the perspective of 'practitioners, governments and inter-governmental organisations, there is not a continuum of instruments from soft to hard, but a binary system in which an instrument is entered into as law or not-law'.[68] The consensus on the GPs in the UN Human Rights Council was achieved precisely because they were viewed as not-law and the corporate responsibility to respect rights is not what one might think of as a traditional or formal legal obligation.

But as noted earlier, to argue that soft law is simply not-law can be simplistic. As one commentator notes, 'the challenge lies in appreciating fully the declining reliability of formal criteria of international law as guideposts as to what actually constitutes international law'.[69] In assessing the 'authority' or bindingness of the corporate responsibility to respect, it is useful to examine it in the context of the factors raised earlier.[70] In particular, what is the significance of housing this responsibility in soft law, and, given the mode chosen, does it have the potential to generate compliance by significant stakeholders (including states and business)?

As discussed earlier, soft law will be at its most effective when it 'stands not in isolation' but 'instead, [as] it is used most frequently either as a precursor to hard law or as a supplement to a hard-law instrument',[71] and from this it might obtain a certain element of bindingness. Soft law standing alone can lack legitimacy if not coupled with any binding law for either the source of the obligation or its enforcement mechanisms. The linkage between the rights and the responsibility to respect them, as set out in the GPs, is amorphous and not grounded in legal obligation.[72] On this point, the development of the GPs can be contrasted with the establishment of the

---

[68] D. Shelton, 'Normative Hierarchy', n. 8, at 321.

[69] G. F. Handl, W. M. Reisman, B. Simma, P. M. Dupuy and C. Chinkin, 'A Hard Look at Soft Law' (1988) 82 *American Society of International Law Procedure* 371, at 372.

[70] See discussion in the text relating to nn. 25–26.

[71] D. Shelton, 'Normative Hierarchy', n. 8, at 320.

[72] In terms of the GPs acting as the basis for future hard law, it can be said that the SRSG has effectively closed (but perhaps not slammed) the door on developing a general or comprehensive treaty governing corporations' responsibilities to human rights (with the exception of corporate liability for international crimes). See J. Ruggie, 'Treaty Road not Travelled', n. 11, but in respect of a narrower area, that of corporate liability for international crimes, the SRSG has recognised such liability, and arguably a treaty in this area would be more politically feasible. See also SRSG, '2007 Report', n. 29, paras. 19–32; and P. Simons, 'International Law's Invisible Hand and the Future of Corporate Accountability for Violations of Human Rights' (2012) 3 *Journal of Human Rights and the Environment* 5, at 12.

UN Guiding Principles on Internal Displacement.[73] For similar reasons to those proposed by the SRSG in eschewing a treaty form for business, UN Special Representative Francis Deng favoured casting the Guiding Principles for internally displaced persons (IDPs) in its 'softer' form because it was more timely and likely to achieve a broader degree of consensus. However, with respect to IDPs, it was also recognised that existing treaties already covered many of the rights and obligations associated with IDPs and that Deng was essentially 'graft[ing] soft law onto a hard law foundation'.[74] This is a point of distinction between the two sets of GPs. The second pillar of the Framework, the corporate responsibility to respect, is not grounded by the SRSG in hard law, being based instead on societal expectations, which has the effect of reducing its normative value and making it softer and more inchoate than what might be required.

In considering the normative potential (and thus bindingness) of the corporate responsibility to respect, one relevant factor to consider is the forum in which the Principles were developed and adopted. The fact that the GPs have the endorsement of the UN Human Rights Council and grew out of a collaborative process managed and monitored by the then UN Commission on Human Rights, and now the Council, adds to their authoritative status and moves them up the continuum from soft to a more potentially binding form of law. In theory, given the degree of consultation and consensus (of governments) sought and achieved by the SRSG during his mandate, there is the potential to generate state compliance. '[A] central property of soft law as a norm-generating mechanism is its ability to contribute to the internalisation of new norms within States by becoming entrenched in domestic legislation.'[75] The internalisation of the Guiding Principles on Internal Displacement in numerous domestic laws has been a significant factor in maintaining compliance with them. It is critical to the success of the GPs that states might be willing and ready to recognise their authority and incorporate them into domestic law.

Whether states will similarly internalise the GPs may be influenced by the authoritative nature of the content and language of the Principles.

---

[73] United Nations, 'Handbook for the Protection of Internally Displaced Persons, Provisional Release 2007' (Annex 1), E/CN.4/1998/53/Add2(1998): www.unhcr.org/cgi-bin/texis/vtx/home/opendocPDFViewer.html?docid=47949b3f2&query=guiding%20principles%20internal%20displacement (last accessed 9 October 2012).
[74] P. Orchard, 'Protection of Internally Displaced Persons', n. 60, at 293.   [75] *Ibid.*, at 286.

Depending on your viewpoint, the corporate responsibility to respect either offers the necessary flexibility for companies to 'know and show'[76] their respect for human rights, or allows 'for too much wiggle room [and includes] too many "shoulds" in place of "shalls"'.[77] The language used in the GPs when framing the corporate responsibility to respect human rights is generally non-authoritative, and in itself unlikely to provoke a normative response.[78] The SRSG's emphasis on pragmatism has dictated the framing of the language throughout the GPs, but is nowhere more evident than in relation to the second pillar, the corporate responsibility to respect rights. The ambiguity of the language is likely to be welcomed by some stakeholders in that it allows for specific idiosyncratic tailoring of responses at an industry and state level. On the other hand, the looseness of the language is perhaps more likely to invite inaction and a business-as-usual approach from companies that remain hesitant about their responsibility to act.

The fact that the GPs were endorsed by the UN Human Rights Council means that their status ranks far beyond that of a code such as, for example, that of the Fair Labour Association, which is adopted by thirty-seven companies.[79] The institutional setting of the UN is important but not determinative. The UN Global Compact had the backing of the UN Secretary-General, yet it is difficult to find a less binding version of soft law than the Compact. However, the endorsement of the GPs by the UN Human Rights Council has strengthened their position as an authoritative instrument of soft law. In addition, the revision of the Organisation for Economic Co-operation and Development's (OECD) Guidelines for Multinational Enterprises in 2011 was heavily influenced by the work of the Special Representative, indicating some convergence internationally behind the GPs. In July 2011, the UN Human Rights Council decided to establish a Working Group 'to promote the effective and comprehensive dissemination and implementation of the Guiding

---

[76] See SRSG interview, n. 62.

[77] C. Jochnick, 'Making Headway on Business and Human Rights', n. 26.

[78] For example, Guiding Principle 11: 'Business enterprises ... *should address* adverse human rights impacts ...'; or Guiding Principle 13: 'The responsibility to respect human rights requires that business enterprises: ... (b) *Seek to* prevent or mitigate adverse human rights impacts'; or Guiding Principle 23: 'In all contexts, business enterprises *should*: ... (b) *Seek* ways to honour the principles of internationally recognized human rights when faced with conflicting requirements'; or Guiding Principle 24: 'business enterprises *should first seek* to prevent' (emphasis added).

[79] Fair Labor Association, www.fairlabor.org (last accessed 9 October 2012).

Principles' which consists of five independent experts, of balanced geo-graphical representation, for a period of three years. The Council also decided to establish a Forum on business and human rights under the guidance of the Working Group, to meet annually to discuss trends and challenges in the implementation of the GPs and promote dialogue and co-operation on issues linked to business and human rights.[80] The Working Group and the annual Forum are the principal follow-up mechanisms established following the end of the SRSG's term, but the open-ended wording of the Council's resolution focuses on further consensus-building, prizing dialogue and information-gathering over accountability. This does not bode well for developing a process to harden the corporate responsibility to respect, and thus set up a mech-anism to ensure greater robustness and uniformity in protecting indi-viduals from corporate violations of human rights.

Conclusion

Highlighting the limitations of soft law in holding corporations to account for human rights violations is a straightforward task, particu-larly if one focuses on the selective nature of the standard-setting and participants involved, and the lack of strong accountability enforcement measures. But the clamour for hard international law is a difficult process and not one that necessarily resolves all these issues. International human rights law is not renowned for its enforceability, and the path to a treaty requires political commitment that is not currently forthcoming in this field. There is no doubt that what is required is both a mix of soft and hard law (both domestic and interna-tional), but if heavy reliance is to be placed on soft law it should be done in such a manner that will generate consistent and uniform compliance in generating greater corporate respect for human rights. The most recent soft law initiative that speaks to a corporation's responsibility toward human rights – the GPs – needs more clearly defined parameters and less 'wiggle room' for business. Formulating and adopting coherent policies and gathering them into an international soft instrument is a positive step, but not sufficient. One of the major challenges for interna-tional standard-setting is ensuring compliance, and it is in this area that the GPs are weakest. The fact that the source of the corporate

---

[80] Human Rights Council, 'Human Rights and Transnational Corporations and Other Business Enterprises', A/HRC/RES/17/4 (6 July 2011).

responsibility is inchoate and the language adopted to frame the second pillar is ambiguous leads to the development of a non-authoritative 'pillar' that is unlikely to induce strong normative change.

Given the political climate in which the SRSG was appointed, the pragmatic approach and reliance on soft law with regard to a corporation's responsibilities toward human rights is understandable, but inadequate. While the SRSG has successfully sought to craft a framework of guidelines palatable to states and business, the path of principled pragmatism has led to the development of soft law guidelines that prize dialogue and consensus over ambition. However, a harder edge could be given to this soft law approach in order to develop a more robust framework that not only encourages, but requires, corporations to respect human rights. Legally mandating and clarifying what is required of the due diligence component of the corporate responsibility to respect is a task that should be undertaken by states as part of their duty to protect human rights. The source of the corporate responsibility to respect rights should also be linked to international human rights law and not left to the whim of society.

As has been evident from the past, securing the engagement of business in human rights issues as part of a soft form of regulation is not a fool-proof method for obtaining success, nor is it a straightforward process. Writing in 1999, Addo commented that 'only a selected few among private corporations are likely to willingly submit to new responsibilities without being legally compelled to do so'.[81] Over a decade later, Addo's comment still rings true. While the number of corporations prepared to adopt human rights policies may have risen, the few mechanisms for enforcing such policies remain largely embedded in soft law, that unless hardened, will have a very limited effect in preventing future violations of human rights by corporations.

---

[81] M. K. Addo, 'Human Rights and Transnational Corporations – An Introduction' in M. K. Addo (ed.), *Human Rights and Transnational Corporations* (The Hague: Kluwer Law International, 2001), 11.

7

Closing the governance gap in the business and human rights arena: lessons from the anti-corruption movement

ANITA RAMASASTRY

Introduction

In 2011, the UN Human Rights Council (HRC) unanimously endorsed a soft law instrument, the UN Guiding Principles on Business and Human Rights (GPs).[1] The GPs incorporate the 'Protect, Respect and Remedy' Framework (Framework), which rests on three pillars: the duty of states to protect against human rights abuses by businesses; the corporate responsibility to respect human rights; and greater access for victims to effective remedies. The GPs were the culmination of more than five years of work of the UN Special Representative to the Secretary-General on Business and Human Rights (SRSG), John Ruggie.

As for the 'respect' pillar, the GPs note that businesses have a *responsibility* to respect human rights in their activities. This responsibility comes not from a binding legal requirement – but rather from social expectations regarding how corporations should behave while operating at home and abroad. This means that unless states regulate TNCs to constrain their behaviour, there are no consequences if they fail to respect human rights while operating abroad.

Many policy-makers and businesses applaud the GPs for the pragmatic approach that is contained therein to a thorny issue. Some human rights non-governmental organisations (NGOs) and other civil society groups remain wary or critical of the GPs – for providing too light a touch. Instead of a binding treaty, the SRSG opted for voluntary principles. At the time of their adoption, this led to an open debate on

---

[1] Human Rights Council, 'UN Guiding Principles on Business and Human Rights', A/HRC/17/31 (16 June 2011) (SRSG, 'Guiding Principles').

the matter – including sparring between Professor Ruggie and human rights groups via letters in the *Financial Times*. Ruggie explicitly disavowed a treaty in the short term. Does this mean that a treaty mechanism is out of reach? He did not foreclose the idea of a treaty or treaties – but insisted that the time for a treaty was not now.

Given the experience of negotiating treaties that attempt to bind TNCs, in my view Ruggie's principled pragmatism was on the mark. Before states initiate treaty discussions, several key elements need to be in place before they can negotiate successfully for rules that will bind businesses with respect to human rights.

This chapter addresses the issue of how a treaty focused on corporations and human rights might evolve, through continued advocacy and state practice. It also examines why it is more likely that a series of narrower treaties will emerge, focused on specific ways states might regulate corporations as a means of preventing harm. While this does not create a universal human rights framework governing TNCs, it does offer a regulatory approach to reducing the risk of human rights harms and providing for mitigation.

As a point of comparison, the author examines the anti-corruption movement – which began with a US law prohibiting foreign bribery and led to the 2005 United Nations Convention Against Corruption (UNCAC).[2] The analysis of anti-corruption is instructive because it is another area where law is aimed at directly changing the behaviour of corporations. Corporations are perceived to be major actors in transnational bribery of foreign officials. They are considered important stakeholders – both in terms of causing harm but also in the fight to prevent the harm from occurring.

UNCAC did not arise overnight – indeed, it took over twenty-five years for states to achieve consensus around what a treaty might look like. The international anti-corruption movement began with one state (the USA) as a 'first mover' and champion in the fight against foreign bribery. Along the way, the building blocks for a treaty were developed. This chapter examines the evolution of anti-corruption norms and how this might be a predictor of how civil society and states might work towards more binding corporate regulation. It also examines the role of civil society as 'norm' entrepreneurs, who can campaign to embed consistent rules within national legislation as a way of creating international consensus around global TNC regulation.

---

[2] United Nations Convention Against Corruption (entered into force 14 December 2005), 2340 UNTS 41 (UNCAC).

The first section of this chapter examines the SRSG's reasons for fore-going a treaty in lieu of the GPs. The second section traces the process leading to the emergence of an international treaty against transnational bribery, which initially commenced with a statute enacted in the USA. The third section of the chapter analyses how the business and human rights movement is already beginning to show evidence of binding rules at national levels, and how those binding rules might pave the way for treaty mecha-nisms in the future. Such treaties, however, may address how states might regulate corporations only in specific contexts. Treaties focused on narrower regulatory prescriptions will not serve fully to provide victims of human rights abuse with access to justice or hold corporations to a comprehensive set of human rights obligations. Regulatory measures, however, may none-theless prevent many particular forms of corporate human rights abuses.

Business and human rights: the treaty road not (yet) travelled

The business and human rights movement has been in existence since the late 1990s, focusing on the human rights impacts of businesses (mostly TNCs) in their global operations. The main gap identified by the SRSG arises when businesses operate in 'host' states.[3]

In such 'host' states, a governance gap often arises when a government is unwilling or unable to provide its citizens with access to remedies for human rights violations caused by businesses, including TNCs. Those same states may also lack regulation that would prevent human rights abuses from occurring. In many instances, businesses in host states are not direct perpetrators of human rights violations but instead are seen as possible accomplices to such violations. Hence in the late 1990s the term 'corporate complicity' came to be used – businesses were advised to avoid being 'complicit' in the human rights violations of others.[4]

The quest to regulate TNCs in their overseas investment should be put in a broader historical context. States in the global South and various

---

[3] The law of international investment refers to 'home states' and 'host states'. A 'home' state is the state where an investor (often a TNC) is domiciled and has its legal place of incorporation, and a 'host' state is the state where the investor has made its investment. See generally, M. Sornorajah, *The International Law of Foreign Investment*, 3rd edn (Cambridge University Press, 2010).

[4] A. Ramasastry, 'Corporate Complicity: From Nuremberg to Rangoon – An Examination of Forced Labor Cases and their Impact on the Liability of Multinational Corporations' (2002) 20 *Berkeley Journal of International Law* 91, at 92; A. Clapham and S. Jerbi, 'Categories of Corporate Complicity in Human Rights Abuses' (2001) 24 *Hastings International and Comparative Law Review* 339, at 341.

civil society organisations became concerned during the 1970s that TNCs, because of their size, had vast power to affect national policies in countries at differing stages of economic development. The annual revenues of a corporation like General Motors, for instance, in the 1970s exceeded the gross national product of all but twenty-two independent states. Estimates made in the early 1970s suggested that in the future some three hundred to four hundred TNCs would control 60 to 70 per cent of the industrial assets of the world.[5]

Attempts to establish developing-country unity had their origins in the Bandung Conference in 1955 that led to the creation of the Non-Aligned Movement of States in 1961. Subsequently, the Declaration for the Establishment of a New International Economic Order (NIEO) was adopted by the UN General Assembly in 1974.[6] The NIEO sought to change the international economic system in the interests of developing countries.

Within this context, TNCs became viewed as new colonisers, representing their (and their shareholders') own economic interests through foreign direct investment. This phenomenon has been described as 'neo-colonialism'. In response, the earliest attempts at international TNC regulation focused on economic development and equitable principles of investment. Thus, it was quite understandable that host states would call for international corporate regulation to ensure that TNCs would not frustrate national development strategies. Others have perceived the TNC as an instrument that perpetuates an inequitable allocation of resources. The TNC was regarded as widening disparities not only between nations, but also between economic classes within a nation, while simultaneously destroying indigenous cultural practices.

The concerns of developing countries intensified, and before long they were taken up at the UN General Assembly as part of a larger trade and development agenda. The UN created a Center on Transnational Corporations in 1977, and its main task was to draft a code of conduct for TNCs that would focus on responsible and equitable investment

---

[5] S. J. Rubin, 'Transnational Corporations and International Codes of Conduct: A Study of the Relationship between International Legal Cooperation and Economic Development' (1981) 30 *American University International Law Review* 903, at 906–07; see also T. J. Biersteker, 'The Illusion of State Power: Transnational Corporations and the Neutralization of Host-Country Legislation' (1980) *Journal of Peace Research* 207.

[6] UN General Assembly, 'Declaration on the Establishment of a New International Economic Order', A/RES/S-6/3201 (1 May 1974); see also J. N. Bhagwati (ed.), *The New International Economic Order: The North-South Debate* (Cambridge, MA: MIT Press, 1977).

practices.[7] Home state governments and TNCs objected to the efforts of the UN. Such concerns eventually led to the demise of the Center and the abandonment of the code project in the early 1990s. In short, historical attempts to set forth binding comprehensive international frameworks to regulate TNCs have seen no success.[8]

With the death of a binding treaty, major exporting countries (as the home states of large TNCs) developed a set of voluntary guidelines for Multinational Enterprises. The Organisation for Economic Co-operation and Development (OECD) Guidelines for Multinational Enterprises (OECD Guidelines) are intended to help steer businesses towards good social and economic conduct. Adopted in 1976, the Guidelines set forth investment-related principles meant to govern how TNCs behaved when operating abroad. They are meant to facilitate better development outcomes in host countries.[9]

With the focus on globalisation in the last two decades, there has been a renewed interest in the economic and political power that TNCs possess.[10] In the 1990s, NGOs turned their attention to the impact of transnational trade and investment on human rights in host states. NGOs, for example, have drawn attention to the role of business in facilitating armed conflict.[11] As a result, in 1998, at the Rome Conference of state parties to draft a statute establishing the International Criminal Court (ICC), the governments of France and the Solomon Islands tabled a proposal to include corporations (referred to as legal persons) within the jurisdiction of the court. This would have made corporations subject to

---

[7] UN Intellectual History Project, 'The UN and Transnational Corporations' (July 2009), www.unhistory.org/briefing/17TNCs.pdf (last accessed 3 February 2013); see also T. Sagafi-nejad and J. H. Dunning, *The UN and Transnational Corporations: From Code of Conduct to Global Compact* (Indiana University Press, 2008).

[8] R. A. Hedley, 'Transnational Corporations and their Regulation: Issues and Strategies' (1999) 40 *International Journal of Comparative Sociology* 215, at 222.

[9] OECD Guidelines for Multinational Enterprises (Paris: OECD Publishing, 2011).

[10] See, for instance, K. Cowling and P. R. Tomlinson, 'Globalization and Corporate Power' (2005) 24 *Contributions in Political Economy* 375; D. C. Korten, *When Corporations Rule the World*, 2nd edn (San Francisco: Berrett-Koehler Publishers, 2001); Rubin, 'Corporations and International Codes of Conduct', n. 5, 907.

[11] An example of this was Global Witness's report on the role of the diamond trade in the armed conflict in Angola and Sierra Leone. Global Witness, 'A Rough Trade' (1 December 1998), www.globalwitness.org/library/rough-trade (last accessed 3 February 2013); see also K. Ballentine and J. Sherman, 'Beyond Greed and Grievance: Policy Lessons from Studies in the Political Economy of Armed Conflict' (International Peace Academy Policy Report, October 2003), 12–15, www.gpia.info/files/u16/ Ballentine_Beyond.pdf (last accessed 3 February 2013).

potential prosecution at the ICC for involvement in international crimes. At first, such an idea may seem far-fetched – but one can look to conflict situations such as the trade of blood diamonds in Sierra Leone,[12] or the relationship between banana companies and Colombian paramilitary groups,[13] to see that businesses are often implicated in mass atrocity. The ICC proposal was rejected – because state parties could not agree on particular standards for how to attribute liability to a company.[14]

In the run-up to the World Summit on Sustainable Development, held in Johannesburg in 2002, international NGOs called publicly for binding international regulation of TNCs.[15] Human rights groups highlighted examples of alleged TNC wrongdoing that suggested the international regulatory regime was failing to deter harmful behaviour. Several Northern and Southern NGOs joined forces and campaigned for an international convention that aimed to ensure future TNC activities would not undermine social, environmental and human rights. Some called for the establishment of a new global watchdog that would focus on corporate human rights abuses. Others proposed the revival of the UN Center on Transnational Corporations.[16]

To date, however, the efforts to get TNCs to address the human rights impacts of their overseas economic activities have been developed

---

[12] Global Witness, 'A Rough Trade', *ibid.*

[13] US Department of Justice Press Release, 'Chiquita Brands International Pleads Guilty to Making Payments to a Designated Terrorist Organization and Agrees to Pay $25 million fine' (19 March 2007), www.justice.gov/opa/pr/2007/March/07_nsd_161.html (last accessed 3 February 2013). (Chiquita admitted that it had made payments over many years to the violent, right-wing terrorist organization United Self-Defense Forces of Colombia.)

[14] A. Clapham, 'Question of Jurisdiction under International Criminal Law over Legal Persons: Lessons from the Rome Conference on an International Criminal Court' in M. T. Kamminga and S. Zia-Zarifi (eds.), *Liability of Multinational Corporations under International Law* (The Hague: Kluwer Law International, 2000), 139–95.

[15] Peter Utting, 'Corporate Responsibility and the Movement of Business' (2005) 15 *Development in Practice* 375, at 384–85. Prior to the Summit, NGOs called for the creation of a new Corporate Accountability Code.

[16] While there was mounting pressure for international regulation of TNCs on the ground, national law was being utilised to hold corporations to account. At the height of the Summit, twenty cases were being brought against TNCs in US courts under the Alien Tort Statute. R. C. Thompson, A. Ramasastry and M. B. Taylor, 'Translating Unocal: The Expanding Web of Liability for Business Entities Implicated in International Crimes' (2009) 40 *George Washington International Law Review* 841, at 841–42; see also D. Everett, Comment, 'New Concern for Transnational Corporations: Potential Liability for Tortious Acts Committed by Foreign Partners' (1998) 35 *San Diego Law Review* 1123.

through soft law and voluntary codes of conduct.[17] In addition to the OECD Guidelines, the UN Global Compact sets out ten human rights norms or 'principles' which apply to corporations. It aims to encourage companies to comply with these principles voluntarily. There are no repercussions for companies failing to abide by the promises they make – which include promises to avoid being complicit in human rights abuses in their operations.

As for binding rules focused on human rights broadly – the one recent attempt to create such an instrument has failed. In 2003 the UN Sub-Commission on the Promotion and Protection of Human Rights (the precursor to the UN Human Rights Council) issued for comment its draft Norms on the Responsibilities of Transnational Corporations and Other Business Enterprises with Regard to Human Rights (UN Norms).[18] The UN Norms represented a restatement of existing human rights obligations, found in diverse treaties, and an application of those principles to corporations.[19]

The UN Norms stated that virtually every human right gives rise to a wide range of duties on virtually every corporation. Although neither the Sub-Commission nor the Commission had the authority to make the UN Norms legally binding, if adopted by the Commission they were meant to become the basis for a later binding instrument or to become a restatement of customary international law in the making.[20] The UN

[17] Over the past few decades, there has been code proliferation. Levi Strauss is usually credited as the first TNC to establish a code with comprehensive principles regarding its global sourcing and operations, in 1991. Since then, company codes of conduct have become more common. A recent World Bank estimate put the number of company codes at around 1,000. In this regard, see Chapter 12, and F. McLeay, 'Corporate Codes of Conduct and the Human Rights Accountability of Transnational Corporations – A Small Piece of a Large Puzzle' (2005) *Global Law Working Papers*, www.law.nyu.edu/global/workingpapers/2005/index.htm (last accessed 3 February 2013); see also R. Jenkins, 'Corporate Codes of Conduct: Self-Regulation in a Global Economy' (2001) UN Research Institute for Social Development: Technology, Business and Society Programme Paper No. 2, http://digitalcommons.ilr.cornell.edu/codes/10/ (last accessed 3 February 2013).

[18] Sub-Commission on the Promotion and Protection of Human Rights, 'Draft Norms on the Responsibilities of Transnational Corporations and Other Business Enterprises with Regard to Human Rights', E/CN.4/Sub.2/2003/12 (26 August 2003).

[19] McLeay, *Corporate Codes of Conduct*, n. 17; D. Weissbrodt and M. Kruger, 'Norms on the Responsibilities of Transnational Corporations and Other Business Enterprises' (2003) 97 *American Journal of International Law* 901–22.

[20] J. Gelfand, 'The Lack of Enforcement in the UN Draft Norms: Benefit or Disadvantage?' (2005) *Global Law Working Papers* 1; D. Weissbrodt and M. Kruger, 'Norms on the Responsibilities', *ibid.*, at 913–14.

Norms were controversial. They had not been 'negotiated' by states, but rather represented a document prepared by academic experts.

While human rights groups strongly supported them, TNCs opposed them. The governments on the Human Rights Commission decided not to adopt them and tabled them indefinitely. Instead, in 2005, the Commission requested the UN Secretary-General to appoint a Special Representative (SRSG) on human rights and transnational corporations and other business enterprises, with a mandate to clarify existing standards and elaborate on the role of states in effectively regulating corporations.[21]

Kofi Annan named John Ruggie, a Harvard professor who had helped to establish the UN Global Compact, as his SRSG. Ruggie was explicit from the outset that he had a different approach from that of the UN Norms. He criticised the Norms' 'exaggerated legal claims' that human rights law directly imposes broad human rights duties on corporations.[22] He took the position that, with the potential exceptions of 'the most heinous human rights violations amounting to international crimes, including genocide, slavery, human trafficking, forced labor, torture, and some crimes against humanity', human rights law does not currently impose direct obligations on corporations or any other non-state actors.[23] The SRSG also made it clear that he would not try to convince states to adopt a new treaty that would impose direct obligations.

As early as 2008 the SRSG explained why he was not in favour of a binding treaty but favoured a principles-based approach. He published an article in *Ethical Corporation*, entitled 'The Treaty Road Not Travelled'. The SRSG noted that the GPs 'lay out a strategic policy framework for better managing business and human rights challenges'.[24]

The SRSG stated that while the Framework is meant to provide a basis for greater policy coherence –'there is one thing the report does not do: recommend that states negotiate an overarching treaty imposing binding

---

[21] J. G. Ruggie, 'Business and Human Rights: The Evolving International Agenda' (2007) 101 *American Journal of International Law* 819.

[22] Commission on Human Rights, 'Interim Report of the Special Representative of the Secretary-General on the Issue of Human Rights and Transnational Corporations and Other Business Enterprises', E/CN.4/2006/97 (22 February 2006), para. 41 (SRSG, '2006 Interim Report'); see also A. Ramasastry and R. C. Thompson, *Commerce, Crime and Conflict: Legal Remedies for Private Sector Liability for Grave Breaches of International Law* (Norway: FAFO, 2006), 16.

[23] SRSG, '2006 Interim Report', n. 22, para. 61.

[24] J. G. Ruggie, 'Business and Human Rights: Treaty Road Not Travelled' (May 2008) *Ethical Corporation* 42–43, www.hks.harvard.edu/m-rcbg/news/ruggie/Pages%20from%20ECM%20May_FINAL_JohnRuggie_may%2010.pdf (last accessed 3 February 2013).

standards on companies under international law' – his rejection of a treaty mechanism was not perpetual:

> [t]reaties form the bedrock of the international human rights system. Specific elements of the business and human rights agenda may become candidates for successful international legal instruments. But it is my carefully considered view that negotiations on an overarching treaty now would be unlikely to get off the ground, and even if they did the outcome could well leave us worse off than we are today.[25]

The SRSG offered three main reservations in his salvo. Firstly, treaty-making can be painfully slow, while the challenges of business and human rights are immediate and urgent. Secondly, and worse, a treaty-making process now risks undermining effective shorter-term measures to raise business standards on human rights.[26] And thirdly, even if treaty obligations were imposed on companies, serious questions remain about how they would be enforced. He emphatically states: '[w]e cannot simply tell victims of human rights abuses that rescue will be on the way in the year 2030 – if all goes well'.[27]

In his essay, the SRSG also answered his critics' question about why he declined to recommend initiating a treaty-making process as part of his mandate. He takes a pragmatic approach to the matter: '[w]here states are reluctant to do very much in the first place, as is the case for quite a few states in the business and human rights area, they may invoke the fact of treaty negotiation as a pretext for not taking other significant steps, including changing national laws – arguing that they would not want to "preempt" the ultimate outcome'.[28] The SRSG is also concerned that a treaty might dilute standards applied to corporations, rather than raise the bar.

As for a new UN treaty body to administer such a treaty, the SRSG reminds his critics that unlike States (which exist in the hundreds), there are thousands of TNCs in existence, which would pose a challenge for the monitoring of treaty compliance:

> Do the math if this is the preferred approach, then the arithmetic needs to be explained. There are 77,000 transnational corporations, with about

---

[25] *Ibid.*

[26] The SRSG notes, for example, that human rights treaties can take a long time to negotiate, and still longer to come into force. For example, the Declaration on the Rights of Indigenous Peoples, adopted by the General Assembly last year, was twenty-two years in the making. *Ibid.*

[27] *Ibid.*   [28] *Ibid.*

800,000 subsidiaries and millions of suppliers – Wal-Mart alone has 62,000. Then there are millions of other national companies. The existing treaty bodies have difficulty keeping up with 192 member states, and each deals with only a specific set of rights or affected groups. How would one such committee handle millions of companies, while addressing all rights of all persons?

Human rights NGOs, however, took a different view of the GPs. The *Financial Times* published, in January 2011, a strongly worded statement by Amnesty International, Human Rights Watch and five other human rights groups, arguing that the current draft should not be adopted by the Human Rights Council because it failed to outline clearly enough how governments should regulate business activity, and how companies should avoid abusing human rights. 'In their current form, [the SRSG's proposals] . . . risk undermining efforts to strengthen corporate responsibility and accountability for human rights,' the groups argued.[29]

The SRSG replied to this criticism with his own letter to the *Financial Times*.[30] In it he wrote, '[t]hese same organizations keep telling the world that there are currently no global standards in the area of business and human rights, causing both governments and business enterprises to fall far short of desired practices. In contrast, the UN framework and guiding principles elevate standards of conduct significantly'.

The SRSG did not pull his punches. He states:

> Amnesty and the others would have a lot to answer for if they actually were to oppose Human Rights Council endorsement of this hard-won initiative. In 2004, they heavily promoted a scheme for regulating companies that had no champions among governments and triggered the vehement and unified opposition of the business community. What was the result? Victims of corporate-related human rights harm, for whom these organizations claim to speak, got nothing. Now, seven years later, we have a proposal on the table that enjoys broad support from governments, business associations, individual companies, as well as a wide array of civil society and workers' organizations.
>
> Do Amnesty and the others really urge its defeat – delivering 'nothing' to victims yet again? How much longer will they ask victims to wait in the name of some abstract and elusive global regulatory regime when practical results are achievable now?

---

[29] H. Williamson, 'Rights Groups Slam UN Plan for Multinationals', *Financial Times* (17 January 2011).

[30] SRSG J. Ruggie, Letter to the Editor, 'Bizarre Response by Human Rights Groups to UN Framework Plan', *Financial Times* (19 January 2011).

The SRSG is referring to the UN Norms when he speaks of the scheme that triggered the 'vehement and unified' opposition of the business community. And when he speaks of an elusive global regulatory regime, he is alluding to what he views as the dim prospects of an international treaty.

Amnesty responded to the SRSG with its own letter in the *Financial Times*. It replies:[31]

> At Amnesty International our researchers regularly investigate human rights abuses committed by corporations. We work with victims – from the Niger Delta to India, Netherlands to Papua New Guinea. We campaign for their rights and work with them to seek reparations. We do not believe the draft guiding principles effectively protect victims' rights or ensure their access to reparations.
>
> Let's be frank – the real opposition to effective guiding principles does not come from Amnesty International but from business interests. The draft guiding principles enjoy broad support from business, precisely because they require little meaningful action by business.
>
> Prof. Ruggie has acknowledged that governments often fail to regulate companies effectively, and that companies working in many countries evade accountability and proper sanctions when they commit human rights abuses. The fundamental challenge was how to address these problems. His draft guiding principles fail to meet this challenge. Amnesty International believes they must be strengthened.

This public debate signalled a rift between the SRSG and civil society groups. While Amnesty and other human rights organisations were initially critical, they have participated more actively in the implementation of the GPs. At the same time, they still explore the concept of binding global rules. At the first UN Forum on Business and Human Rights held in Geneva in December 2012, a group of NGOs held an alternative forum to discuss how to keep up momentum for a treaty rather than a voluntary framework.

From state practice to multilateral treaty: the anti-corruption experience

The FCPA as a catalyst for a treaty

In 2013, states and civil society do not have a binding international treaty as a tool to influence TNC behaviour globally. To date, attempts at a large

---

[31] W. Brown, Amnesty International, Letter to the Editor, 'Stronger UN Draft Norms on Human Rights Abuses', *Financial Times* (20 January 2011).

and broad treaty that regulates TNCs have failed – in part perhaps because they attempt to constrain TNC conduct too broadly, which leads to no global consensus. And the question still remains on the table – how would states successfully negotiate a binding treaty focused on business and human rights? This is where an examination of the international anti-corruption movement is illustrative as a form of gradualised regulation.

The genesis of anti-corruption treaties did not involve a wide range of issues. Rather, states agreed to focus on a particular harm – bribery and related corrupt acts. The treaty mechanism then required states to prohibit bribery and to penalise persons and corporations who engaged in the prohibited act. This is a narrower approach to TNC regulation, and focuses on regulation as a means of preventing a specific harm.

Can one draw a parallel between preventing transnational corporate bribery and preventing transnational corporate human rights abuses? In part, the answer is yes. Corruption does not stop at national borders: TNCs bribe government officials to get them to buy useless medicines and faulty equipment for public hospitals; global trafficking rings bribe immigration authorities to let them transport women and children across borders and force them into slavery; and government officials divert public money to offshore accounts leaving poor people without schools.

Corruption also impacts citizens in ways that involve human rights. As Secretary-General Ban Ki Moon noted:

> Corruption undermines democracy and the rule of law. It leads to violations of human rights. It erodes public trust in government. It can even kill – for example, when corrupt officials allow medicines to be tampered with, or when they accept bribes that enable terrorist acts to take place . . . It has adverse effects on the delivery of basic social services. It has a particularly harmful impact on the poor.[32]

For any country to succeed in fighting corruption, it has to co-operate and co-ordinate with other countries. To this end, governments have adopted global and regional anti-corruption conventions. The most comprehensive anti-corruption convention is UNCAC, approved by the UN in 2005.

---

[32] UN Secretary-General Ban-Ki Moon, 'Remarks at Launch of Stolen Asset Recovery Initiative', SG/SM/11161 (17 September 2007), www.un.org/News/Press/docs/2007/sgsm11161.doc.htm (last accessed 3 February 2013).

As stated above, UNCAC is one example of an international treaty mechanism that binds corporations with respect to their transnational conduct and the harms they cause. UNCAC clearly involves the private sector – as the so-called 'supply' side of bribery (i.e. actors that pay bribes are often TNCs that engage in foreign bribery in order to secure a market advantage). The UN Convention contains criminal prohibitions aimed at corporations with respect to their overseas activities. In addition, it also contains a chapter focused on the private sector and its role in fighting and preventing corruption.

The road to a binding international convention began with one state, the USA, as a 'first mover'. The USA created a law in 1977 that penalised foreign bribery – not only of US companies, but other companies trading on US stock exchanges – by including an overt extraterritorial application of its laws.[33] As a result, the US Foreign Corrupt Practices Act (FCPA) had an impact on TNCs domiciled in other states, who feared prosecution in US courts. It also prompted US companies to lobby for treaty-based mechanisms to level the playing field for their OECD counterparts.[34]

The US law had its origins in the Watergate investigation that led to the resignation of President Richard Nixon and the prosecution of several companies and executives for using slush funds to make illegal political contributions to American politicians.[35] It was a unique moment in US history and one where the question of business ethics took on a new resonance.

Stanley Sporkin, the Securities and Exchange Commission's (SEC's) enforcement director from 1974 to 1981, had watched the Watergate hearings on television and wondered how US companies had accounted for their illegal political contributions. During his investigations, he found that some companies also dipped into secret funds to pay off foreign officials, with an eye to landing government contracts abroad. More than 400 US companies admitted making questionable payments totalling more $300 million to foreign government officials and politicians.[36]

---

[33] For useful background, see S. Rep. No. 95–114.

[34] G. C. Lodge and C. Wilson, *A Corporate Solution to Global Poverty: How Multinationals can help the Poor and Invigorate their own Legitimacy* (Princeton University Press, 2006), 64.

[35] J. Palazollo, 'From Watergate to Today: How the FCPA became so Feared', *Wall Street Journal* (10 October 2012).

[36] *Ibid.*; see also H. R. Rep. No. 95–640 (1977), www.justice.gov/criminal/fraud/fcpa/history/1977/houseprt-95-640.pdf (last accessed 3 February 2013).

These corporations included some of the largest and most widely known public companies in the USA; over 117 of them ranked in the top Fortune 500 industries. The abuses ranged from bribery of high-ranking foreign officials in order to secure some type of favourable action,[37] to so-called 'facilitation' payments that allegedly were made to ensure that government functionaries discharge certain ministerial duties, like granting a licence or clearing imports through customs. Pharmaceuticals, healthcare, oil and gas were among the sectors implicated.

Senator Frank Church, one of the main proponents of the legislation, conducted the first hearings on foreign bribery in 1975, under the auspices of the US Senate Select Committee to Study Governmental Operations with Respect to Intelligence Activities (the 'Church Committee').[38] Church believed US companies were undermining the nation's Cold War-era foreign policy, and also impeding fair competition and free enterprise by encouraging corruption among US allies.

The legislative background to the FCPA (as introduced in the House of Representatives) emphasised bribery as a harmful act:

> The payment of bribes to influence the acts or decisions of foreign officials, foreign political parties or candidates for foreign political office is unethical. It is counter to the moral expectations and values of the American public. But not only is it unethical, it is bad business as well. It erodes public confidence in the integrity of the free market system. It short-circuits the marketplace by directing business to those companies too inefficient to compete in terms of price, quality or service, or too lazy to engage in honest salesmanship, or too intent upon unloading marginal products. In short, it rewards corruption instead of efficiency and puts pressure on ethical enterprises to lower their standards or risk losing business.[39]

After carefully considering all the testimony, the Church Committee concluded that bribery should be criminalised rather than legalised through disclosure. The Committee believed that criminalisation of bribery would

---

[37] 'Multinational Corporations and United States Foreign Policy: Hearings Before the Subcomm. on Multinational Corps. of the S. Comm. on Foreign Relations', 94th Cong. 1 (1975); see also H. R. REP. No. 95–640, n. 36; US SEC, 'Report of the Securities and Exchange Commission on Questionable and Illegal Corporate Payments and Practices' (1976), repr. in Sec. Reg. & L. Rep. No. 353, at 2 (19 May 1976).

[38] Palazzollo, 'From Watergate to Today', n. 35; M. Koehler, 'The Story of the Foreign Corrupt Practices Act' (2012) 73 Ohio State Law Journal 930, at 933–34.

[39] H. R. REP. No. 95–640, n. 36, 2.

be the most effective deterrent, the least burdensome on business, and no more difficult to enforce than disclosure of bribe payments.[40]

The SEC, which oversees corporate disclosures, initially wanted no part in enforcing a law prohibiting bribery overseas, and the State Department opposed one, fearing that it would be perceived abroad as a sign of US moral exceptionalism.

Despite his agency's reservations, Sporkin worked closely with the late Senator William Proxmire, chairman of the Committee on Banking, Housing and Urban Affairs, on the legislation. Senator Proxmire did pursue criminal measures in his bill – outlawing foreign bribery in addition to requiring corporate disclosure of foreign payments.[41] President Jimmy Carter signed the bill into law in December 1977, creating the FCPA. The FCPA applied not only to US TNCs that bribed officials overseas, but also to international companies listing on US securities markets. As such, its impact and reach were broad. The new rules also applied to all types of businesses, regardless of size or sector.

Once the USA had established a domestic statute, it turned its sights on partner countries and began to lobby for regional conventions addressing corruption.[42] The Inter-American Convention Against Corruption entered into force in 1997 followed by the OECD Anti-Bribery Convention, which entered into force in 1999. The Council of Europe Conventions on Corruption, both Civil and Criminal, entered into force in 2002. The African Union Convention on Preventing and Combating Corruption entered into force in 2006. UNCAC, which is much broader than the FCPA, entered into force in 2005 and currently has 140 signatories, including the USA, which ratified UNCAC in 2006.[43]

At present, the obligation of states in terms of both law-making and law enforcement to prevent corruption is governed by two major international frameworks, which together address both the supply and demand side of bribery. In terms of international reach and effect, the leading conventions on corruption are the OECD Convention and UNCAC.

It took twenty years from the passing of the FCPA before other developed nations adopted an anti-bribery convention, in 1997. While

---

[40] SEC Report, 'Questionable Payments and Practices', n. 37.

[41] Koehler, 'The Story of the Foreign Corrupt Practices Act', n. 38, 980–88.

[42] For a list of relevant anti-corruption treaties, see Georgetown Law Library, 'International Anti-Corruption Law Research Guide', www.law.georgetown.edu/library/research/guides/intlcorruption.cfm#selected-treaties (last accessed 3 February 2013).

[43] UN Office of Drugs and Crime, 'UNCAC Ratifications as of 24 December 2012', www.unodc.org/unodc/en/treaties/CAC/signatories.html (last accessed 30 January 2013).

other regional conventions are significant, the OECD Anti-Bribery Convention was the first to regulate TNCs from major exporting countries in an attempt to curtail the supply side of bribery.

It took concerted US pressure as well as the collapse of the Soviet Union and the increasing globalisation of the world economy for major exporting nations to come together. Despite US overtures to the UN to follow its lead, a movement to ban international bribery via a global treaty went nowhere. Then eleven years after the FCPA was passed, the law faced its first crisis. In 1988, under pressure from US businesses, the Reagan administration considered relaxing the anti-bribery law, arguing that it put American companies at a competitive disadvantage.[44]

But instead of weakening the law, the USA reached out to its international competitors to see if they were prepared to level the playing field by implementing their own anti-bribery laws. The OECD's work on international bribery began in 1989, when US companies, constrained by the FCPA, complained of a recurring disadvantage as compared to global competitors.[45]

The Soviet bloc was beginning to dissolve, and new markets were opening up. Businesses all over the world feared that bribery and unfair business practices would determine who could sell soft drinks to Ukraine or computers to Russia. This growing unease about unfair, corrupt competition, particularly in accessing these new markets, prompted thirty-seven countries, including most of the EU, Canada, Australia and Japan, to sign the original OECD Anti-Bribery Convention,[46] which all member countries ratified between 1999 and 2001.[47]

The OECD Convention targets those who pay bribes to public officials to win or maintain business abroad, in effect internationalising the

---

[44] When Ronald Reagan took over as president in 1981, FCPA enforcement dwindled – the SEC settled just two cases during his eight years in office. PBS *Frontline/World*, 'Corruption in the Crosshairs: A Brief History of International Anti-Bribery Legislation' (7 April 2009), www.pbs.org/frontlineworld/stories/bribe/2009/04/time line.html (last accessed 3 February 2013).

[45] K. W. Abbott and D. Snidal, 'Filling in the Folk Theorem: The Role of Gradualism and Legalization in International Cooperation to Combat Corruption' (30 August 2002), www. international.ucla.edu/cms/files/Duncan_Snidal.pdf (last accessed 3 February 2013).

[46] OECD Convention on Combating Bribery of Foreign Public Officials in International Business Transactions (entered into force 15 February 1999), 37 ILM 1.

[47] *Ibid.* The US was also able to exert political pressure on European states. E. K. Spahn, 'Multijurisdictional Bribery Law Enforcement: The OECD Anti-Bribery Convention' (2012) 53 *Virginia Journal of International Law* 1, at 7–11; see also K. W. Abbott and D. Snidal, 'Values and Interests: International Legalization in the Fight against Corruption' (2002) 31 *Journal of Legal Studies* 141.

FCPA. The thirty-seven parties, which include all thirty OECD countries and seven non-member countries, collectively account for 76 per
cent of world gross domestic national income and 84 per cent of world
trade. The Convention requires parties to create sanctions for bribery
that are 'effective, proportionate and dissuasive' and that countries
establish liability for legal persons with respect to corruption offences.[48]

With OECD member states now subject to a framework, the USA
turned its attention back to the UN and a global treaty.[49] In December
2000, the UN General Assembly recognised that an effective international
legal instrument against corruption, independent of the United Nations
Convention against Transnational Organized Crime (Resolution 55/25,
Annex I), was desirable and decided to establish an *ad hoc* committee
for the negotiation of such an instrument in Vienna at the headquarters
of the United Nations Office on Drugs and Crime.[50]

UNCAC was opened for signature during the High Level Political
Conference of the United Nations in Mexico in 2003.[51] The Convention
was a landmark development for global action against corruption, establishing jointly agreed norms and methods for international co-operation.
It was open for ratification more than twenty-five years after the FCPA
was enacted.

As civil society and human rights activists look for models, the anti-
corruption story highlights the steps they take to achieve consensus
around the types of private sector behaviour that should be criminalized.
UNCAC represents a consensus around global anti-corruption norms –
what types of bribery and related use of influence are wrong and thus
should be penalised. Some scholars have referred to this as a process of
gradual 'legalization'.[52] It was not an easy task, as states and societies
have differing perceptions of what types of payments or exchanges are

---

[48] See, for example, OECD, 'Anti-Bribery Convention', n. 46, Art. 2 'On the Responsibility
of Legal Persons'. ('Each Party shall take such measures as may be necessary, in
accordance with its legal principles, to establish the liability of legal persons for the
bribery of a foreign public official.')

[49] P. Webb, 'The United Nations Convention against Corruption: Global Achievement or
Missed Opportunity?' (2005) 8 *Journal of International Economic Law* 191.

[50] A. Argandoña, 'The United Nations Convention against Corruption and its Impact on
International Companies' (2006), www.iese.edu/research/pdfs/DI-0656-E.pdf (last
accessed 3 February 2013).

[51] *Ibid.*

[52] Abbott and Snidal, 'Filling in the Folk Theorem', n. 45, at 2 (in this article, the authors
discuss the creation of the OECD Anti-Bribery Convention and note that it emerged
through a 'gradualized and legalized process').

ethically wrong. With human rights, the norms exist – as they are already enshrined in existing treaties. What those norms mean in practice for corporations, however, is still contested.[53]

The OECD Convention and UNCAC require parties and states, respectively, to promulgate and enforce laws for the purpose of regulating the behaviour of public and private actors. Therefore, the Conventions are designed to regulate the actions of the parties and states, which in turn regulate the actions of their nationals. The effectiveness of the Conventions is therefore based on the extent to which the parties and states are actually willing, or in some cases able, to alter the behaviour of their society, rather than a simple question of whether the parties and states have implemented the required laws, policies and procedures.

And even with UNCAC and the OECD Convention, states still lag in terms of the enforcement of their laws. Transparency International (TI) highlights the under-enforcement problem in its 2012 Progress Report on state implementation of the OECD Convention. TI reported that eighteen countries have little or no enforcement at all, and have not yet brought any criminal charges for major cross-border corruption by companies. Together these countries represent 10 per cent of world exports. Only seven out of thirty-seven countries are actively enforcing foreign bribery law.[54]

Anti-corruption treaties use regulatory requirements to prevent transnational harm

Although globalisation has turned corruption into a global phenomenon, which also requires a global governance approach, implementation is still largely at the national level and requires states to implement regulatory measures as a means of restraining TNC activity. UNCAC and other treaties set up frameworks whereby nations should create sanctions for corrupt acts, and institutions designed to prevent and prosecute such acts. Since national implementation is the critical

---

[53] See Chapter 5, in which the author argues that existing human rights treaties may bind corporations. Even if this is so, however, there is still important work to be done in determining the exact obligations corporations are required to perform.

[54] Transparency International, 'Exporting Corruption? Country Enforcement of the OECD Anti-Bribery Convention, Progress Report 2012' (2012), www.transparency.org/whatwedo/ pub/exporting_corruption_country_enforcement_of_the_oecd_anti_bribery_convention (last accessed 3 February 2013).

element, states relied on the existence of state practice as a means of understanding what could be achieved through a treaty, and in what way it was possible to bind corporations through such a mechanism.

Anti-corruption treaties, however, impact upon corporations in very discrete ways. The FCPA and subsequent treaties criminalise foreign bribery – inducing corporations to act in certain ways to prevent harm or suffer legal consequences for their non-compliance. Under Article 16 of UNCAC, for example, bribery constitutes an offence.[55] This prohibition applies to legal persons (corporations). Unlike the UN Norms, described above, anti-corruption treaties focus on narrow prohibitions rather than broad corporate duties and obligations. The focus is also on prohibitions rather than affirmative duties. 'Do not bribe' is the key mantra.

The USA, through its FCPA enforcement actions, provided examples of how legislation could be used to deal with transnational corporate bribery. As such, the anti-corruption story is as much about global governance as it is about reliance on existing state practice to shape treaty rules. What the treaty does, however, is signal to TNCs that there are common global rules and corresponding legal expectations of universal behaviour on their part.

The international framework around anti-corruption is still fragile. The USA is still the leading enforcer of anti-bribery laws, and the US Department of Justice (DOJ) carries out the lion's share of criminal investigations of US and other TNCs alleged to have engaged in corrupt practices.[56] Because of heightened enforcement and the global recession, the US Chamber of Commerce and other business stakeholders have started to lobby to roll back or amend the FCPA.[57] To date, Congress has not done so. The existence of at least one robust national law serves to keep other states and the private sector engaged in compliance and risk mitigation.

---

[55] According to Art. 16 of UNCAC, 'bribery of foreign public officials' constitutes a criminal offence, when committed intentionally, that prohibits 'the promise, offering or giving, to a foreign public official, directly or indirectly, of an undue advantage, for the official himself or herself or another person or entity, in order that the official act or refrain from acting in the exercise of his or her official duties, in order to obtain or retain business or other undue advantage in relation to the content of international business'.

[56] Transparency International, 2012 Progress Report, n. 54.

[57] US Chamber of Commerce, 'Restoring Balance: Proposed Amendments to the Foreign Corrupt Practices Act' (2010), www.uschamber.com/reports/restoring-balance-proposed-amendments-foreign-corrupt-practices-act (last accessed 3 February 2013).

The role of civil society and business as partners in the anti-corruption movement

At the international level, the push for a treaty was bolstered in part by the role of civil society. This includes having the business community as part of coalitions.

In the 1990s, as the price of bribery in proportion to the contract's value continued to escalate, companies found it increasingly difficult to compete internationally.[58] Civil society – represented by business, trade unions and anti-corruption NGOs – all pushed for the OECD treaty.

Within this context, the OECD Business and Industry Advisory Council (BIAC) and Trade Union Advisory Council (TUAC), as well as the International Chamber of Commerce (International Chamber) and Transparency International, continuously advocated against international bribery. Each organisation had a different perspective and approach. BIAC and the International Chamber advanced pro-competitiveness arguments to justify the need to fight international bribery from the private sector perspective. TUAC encouraged the mobilisation of trade unions, showing the links between corruption and abuses of freedom of association and other core labour standards.

Finally, the fight against corruption in international business transactions was TI's primary *raison d'être*. TI's founders saw these practices as causing great economic and political damage to developing countries. These four organisations, supported by their constituencies, helped generate the needed political will to criminalise the bribery of foreign public officials.

TI made regular interventions in the media in favour of the OECD's work. In 1997, it sent a letter endorsing the work of the OECD to European governments. The letter was prepared under the auspices of TI and the International Chamber, and signed by sixteen of the most important European business leaders.[59]

The support from representatives of the business community was particularly important as it countered the widely accepted idea that companies were the first to benefit from the existence of corruption in international transactions.[60]

---

[58] OECD, 'Fighting Corruption: What Role for Civil Society? The Experience of the OECD' (Paris: OECD Publishing, 2003).

[59] *Ibid.*

[60] M. Chene and G. Dell, TI, 'UNCAC and the Participation of NGOs in the Fight against Corruption' (8 April 2008), www.u4.no/publications/uncac-and-the-participation-of-ngos-in-the-fight-against-corruption/ (last accessed 3 February 2013).

TI was actively involved in advocacy for UNCAC as well. It serves as the Secretariat to the UNCAC Coalition, a group of more than 310 civil society organisations and individuals in over 100 countries that pressures governments to ratify and comply with UNCAC.[61] The private sector has also been important to the UNCAC process, with business leaders, including the International Chamber, calling for implementation and ratification of UNCAC by states.[62]

Peter Eigen, the founder of TI, wrote at the time the OECD Convention was being negotiated:

> the [OECD] has specifically asked Transparency International to officially accompany the process of drafting an anticorruption convention. By also including the private sector – through the International Chamber of Commerce – the OECD is perhaps the best example for the path-finding that is needed to involve governments, the private sector and civil society.[63]

Civil society will be central to a continued business and human rights agenda.[64] NGOs need to explore how to engage business as part of the governance process. When the FCPA was enacted, business opposed regulation. US companies became champions of extending the US regulatory regime once national legislation had been put in place. Peter Eigen has also noted that civil society has a role in helping business see the 'business case' for reform:

> It would be the natural role of civil society to convince the private sector that action is better than inaction and that corruption does not have to be accepted as a necessary evil. Civil society can help the private sector to understand that it is in its own interest to lobby government for greater openness.[65]

---

[61] Transparency International, 'Our Work on Conventions' (2011), www.transparency. org/whatwedo/activity/our_work_on_conventions (last accessed 3 February 2013).

[62] See, for example, UN Global Compact, TI, International Chamber of Commerce and World Economic Forum, CEO Letter in Support of UNCAC (1 May 2009), www.unglobalcompact. org/Issues/transparency_anticorruption/CEO_Letter.html (last accessed 3 February 2013).

[63] P. Eigen, 'The Role of Civil Society' in UN Development Program, *Corruption and Integrity Improvement Initiatives in Developing Countries* (1998), http://mirror.undp. org/magnet/Docs/efa/corruption/Chapter05.pdf (last accessed 30 January 2013).

[64] For a useful discussion of the role of TI in setting an international and national agenda see J. Martinsson, 'Global Norms, Creation, Diffusion and Limits' (August 2011), http:// go.worldbank.org/RNG0D86E40 (last accessed 3 February 2013).

[65] *Ibid.*

In short, there are several key points one can make about the anti-corruption movement that may inform the business and human rights movement. Firstly, beyond the obvious fact that international treaty-making takes years, is the fact that strong state practice and a dominant state champion were critical components of the movement towards a binding international treaty. National regulation also turned reluctant businesses into potential champions for global governance. Secondly, state practice also helped states to understand what the contours of treaty provisions might look like and how such provisions would work in practice. States were better able to understand what it meant to prohibit certain types of corrupt acts, once they saw evidence of state prosecutions. Thus, even for more technical reasons of legal drafting, the existence of state practice will better inform the business and human rights debate. Thirdly, civil society also needs to be engaged – but this means inclusion of business as well as broader civil society representation. While the entire private sector may not advocate for a business and human rights treaty, some champions that see the importance of ethical business may be a necessary ingredient.

Finally, the debate is one focused not only on harm, but also on the integrity of markets and on free and fair competition. Human rights advocates may consider how to frame the business and human rights agenda in terms of harm to states and their economies from the costs created by companies that permit or cause human rights abuses in their global operations. Companies that have strong human rights compliance (especially those that may be subject to regulation already in their own home states) may seek global prescriptions that require compliance by a broader swathe of corporations. Responsible corporations and NGOs can demonstrate that the cost of mitigating such harms will be born by host states, if there are no binding rules in place, and that certain TNCs will suffer economically if forced to compete with unethical business.

Business and human rights: the emergence of state practice in home state regulation

As we look at the potential for a binding treaty in the area of corporate human rights violations, the question arises of what that treaty might contain. Consequently, the anti-corruption movement points us to national legislation as an important source of potential global norms as applied to corporations.

With the advent of the UN GPs, states are starting to examine discrete human rights impacts caused by TNC business activity. As a result, two phenomena are occurring. Firstly, home states are starting to enact legislation addressing the human rights impacts of their TNCs. Secondly, other states are then looking to these 'first-mover' states and attempting to replicate their regulation. Policy-makers are beginning to see the evolution of governance norms in the business and human rights arena. These norms are focused on regulations that prohibit specific corporate conduct as a means of preventing harm. Thus, these examples mainly offer regulatory prescriptions to address harm, as opposed to larger frameworks governing corporate activity broadly.

NGOs are playing a key role in these new legislative campaigns. By forging coalitions and working across jurisdictions, such NGOs become norm entrepreneurs – moving from one state to the next in order to try and close the human rights governance gap. Thus, while a treaty campaign may be important, it is equally important for NGOs to focus on how to move a legislative/regulatory agenda forward in multiple jurisdictions.[66]

As norms (around what business activity should be prohibited) become embedded in national laws, it becomes easier to envisage what subjects might be encompassed by regional or international treaties with a regulatory emphasis. I shall consider three examples of this. Firstly, I will consider the issue of illegal logging and the importation of illegally harvested timber. Secondly, I shall consider the issue of conflict minerals in global supply chains for electronic products. Finally, I shall consider how states have dealt with embedding international crimes into domestic criminal laws, and extending their jurisdiction to corporations as well at the national level. This third example is the one that attempts to hold corporations to the same standards with respect to a universal set of norms.

Illegal logging

Illegal logging occurs across the globe in all types of forests, from Brazil to Canada, Cameroon to Kenya and Indonesia to Russia. Illegal logging

---

[66] Martinsson, n. 64; N. Shawki, 'Global Norms, Local Implementation – How are Global Norms Translated into Local Practice?' (2 September 2011) 26 *Globality Studies Journal*, https://globality.cc.stonybrook.edu/?p=221 (last accessed 3 February 2013). An example of civil society co-ordination is found in the illegal logging area. See Forest Law Enforcement, Governance and Trade, 'Briefing Note: Local Civil Society Organizations Join EU Battle against Illegal Logging' (July 2012), www.fern.org/publications/results/type/briefing-note-183 (last accessed 3 February 2013).

refers to situations where timber is harvested in contravention of national and international laws on cutting, processing, transporting or exporting wood.[67] The definition also covers exporting endangered plant/tree species, and falsifying official documents. In addition, it includes situations where companies break licence agreements, avoid paying taxes, bribe government officials involved in the timber trade, and interfere with access and rights to forest areas.[68]

Illegal logging has a devastating impact on some of the world's most valuable remaining forests and the people that live in them. Its environmental effects include deforestation and the loss of biodiversity. Its direct impacts on people include violence and human rights abuses, the fuelling of corruption and exacerbation of poverty. In some cases it has even funded armed conflict. Furthermore, it limits the ability of states to implement sustainable forest management. As Human Rights Watch points out:

> Human rights violations are frequent and may include forced labor, sexual abuse, and violence against indigenous groups and forest-dependent communities. Forestry sector corruption has widespread spillover effects on governance and human rights. The individuals responsible for the losses are rarely held accountable by law enforcement and a judiciary deeply corrupted by illegal logging interests, undermining respect for human rights.[69]

The USA has exercised leadership to address and prevent illegal logging. The US Lacey Act was amended in 2008 to thwart illegal logging. In its 2008 Farm Bill, Congress included a measure that made it a violation of US law to traffic in products made from wood that is harvested, transported or sold in violation of laws in the country of origin, such as forest management laws and regulations in Indonesia. An extension of the Lacey Act of 1900, previously used primarily to prohibit the trade of illegally trafficked endangered species, the new provisions require importers to demonstrate the species and origin of the wood and that it was legally harvested.[70]

Manufacturers, exporters, importers and retailers of goods made with suspect timber could face forfeiture, penalties and even imprisonment for

---

[67] World Wildlife Fund, 'Illegal Logging', http://wwf.panda.org/about_our_earth/about_forests/deforestation/forest_illegal_logging/ (last accessed 3 February 2013).

[68] *Ibid.*

[69] Human Rights Watch, '"Wild Money": The Human Rights Consequences of Illegal Logging and Corruption in Indonesia's Forestry Sector' (December 2009), at 39, www.hrw.org/reports/2009/12/01/wild-money-0 (last accessed 3 February 2013).

[70] *Ibid.*, 65.

violations. While companies may face higher penalties for willingly trafficking in stolen timber, liability attaches regardless of whether individuals or companies know about illegalities in the sourcing of their wood. This provision creates an incentive for importers to conduct rigorous due diligence enquiries about the provenance of their supply.

A recent agreement between the US Department of Justice and the Gibson Guitar Corporation provides an example of the types of penalties companies face under the Lacey Act.[71] In August 2012, Gibson Guitars entered into a criminal enforcement agreement with the USA, resolving a criminal investigation into allegations that the company violated the Lacey Act by illegally purchasing and importing ebony wood from Madagascar and rosewood and ebony from India. The criminal enforcement agreement defers prosecution for criminal violations of the Lacey Act and requires Gibson to pay a penalty of $300,000.[72]

In response to the US timber legislation, the EU also moved to address illegal timber.[73] Human rights and environmental groups co-ordinated on policy proposals and campaigned for reform in both the USA and the EU. EU Regulation No. 995/2010 of the European Parliament and of the Council of 20 October 2010 sets forth the obligations of operators who place timber and timber products on the market. The Regulation, also known as the (Illegal) Timber Regulation, counters the trade in illegally harvested timber through three key obligations. It (1) prohibits the placing on the EU market of illegally harvested timber and products derived from such timber; (2) requires EU traders who place timber products on the EU market for the first time to exercise 'due diligence'; and (3) facilitates the traceability of timber products. So-called timber 'traders' will have an obligation to keep records of their suppliers and customers. The Timber Regulation became effective on 3 March 2013.

Australia has also enacted laws to prevent illegal logging.[74] In 2012, Australia's parliament passed laws to ban the import and trade of illegally

---

[71] US Department of Justice Press Release, 'Gibson Guitar Corp. Agrees to Resolve Investigation into Lacy Act Violations' (6 August 2012), www.justice.gov/opa/pr/2012/August/12-enrd-976.html (last accessed 3 February 2013).

[72] *Ibid.*

[73] Regulation 995/2010 of the European Parliament and of the Council of 20 October 2010 Laying Down the Obligations of Operators who Place Timber and Timber Products on the Market, 2010 O.J. (L 295) 23.

[74] J. Grubel and D. Fogarty, 'Australia Passes Illegal Logging Laws, Joins EU, US' (19 November 2012), www.reuters.com/article/2012/11/19/us-australia-logging-idUSBRE8AI0CF20121119 (last accessed 3 February 2013).

logged timber. The Australian laws impose fines, jail and forfeiture of goods, and oblige importers to carry out mandatory due diligence on timber and timber products sourced from overseas. The Australian government says about 10 per cent of the more than $4.12 billion of timber imported annually is illegal and that illegal logging globally causes environmental and social damage estimated at $60 billion a year.

Conflict minerals

Armed groups in eastern Democratic Republic of Congo (DRC) have illegally used proceeds from the minerals trade to fund their armed conflict in a brutal civil war that has lasted for over fifteen years. These minerals – tin, tungsten, tantalum and gold – are used in products sold to consumers, but few companies actually carry out checks on their supply chains to find out whether their purchases are causing harm. Civil society groups in both the EU and the USA have actively campaigned for regulation that would require companies to know if the minerals used in various products, such as mobile phones, include minerals that are sourced from conflict zones or are, in fact, 'conflict free'.[75]

In 2010, the USA, through the Dodd-Frank Wall Street Reform and Consumer Protection Act, passed a law to require companies to disclose publicly their use of conflict minerals that originated in the DRC or an adjoining country.[76] Dodd-Frank directed the US Securities and Exchange Commission (SEC) to issue rules requiring certain companies to disclose their use of conflict minerals, if those minerals are 'necessary to the functionality or production of a product' manufactured by those companies.[77] Companies are required to provide this disclosure on a new form to be filed with the SEC called Form SD.

The EU commenced discussions on whether to develop a conflict minerals-type regulation during a 5 December 2012 internal workshop. Within the European Commission, the Directorate-General for Trade

---

[75] The International Corporate Accountability Roundtable (ICAR), for example, is a coalition of human rights NGOs that have supported the enactment of the US conflict minerals legislation. 'ICAR, Disclosure and Transparency', http://accountabilityroundt able.org/campaigns/conflict-minerals/ (last accessed 3 February 2013).

[76] Public Law 111–203, 124 Stat. 1376 (2010) (codified as amended at 15 U.S.C.A. § 78u-6 (West 2012)).

[77] Conflict Mineral Disclosure, 77 Fed. Reg. 56274 (Sept. 12, 2012) (to be codified at 17 C.F. R. pts. 240, 249, and 249b), http://rwebgate.access.gpo.gov/cgi-bin/getpage.cgi?posi tion=all&page=56274&dbname=2012_register (last accessed 3 February 2013).

(DG Trade) is leading this effort and has requested input from industry, academia and NGOs.[78] DG Trade is considering implementing regulations that mimic either the OECD Due Diligence Guidelines or the US Dodd-Frank rules.[79]

Liability of corporations for international crimes

As noted above, states rejected a proposal to include legal persons within the jurisdiction of the ICC. At the same time, states that are parties to the Rome Statute have amended their domestic criminal laws to include international crimes among those that may be prosecuted in national courts.[80] Indeed, states contemplate that the majority of prosecutions of international crimes will occur in national courts, leaving the ICC to prosecute only the most serious of cases in the tribunal based in The Hague.

It is true that the impetus for national legal reform comes from an international treaty – but, in reforming their laws, some states have done so in a way that permits them to prosecute corporations as well as individuals for international crimes. This is true for countries like the UK, Australia, the Netherlands, Norway and France. To date, of course, no corporation has been prosecuted in a domestic court for international crimes, although there have been referrals made by human rights groups to domestic authorities in Norway, Australia and Canada with respect to TNCs alleged to have been complicit in war crimes and crimes against humanity while operating abroad.

Thus, the existence of state penal laws that hold corporations accountable for international crimes may pave the way for the development of state practice and, in turn, the amendment of the Rome/ICC Statute to include corporations within its scope.

Conclusion

A broader business and human rights treaty, would, of course, provide the global community with a wider set of aspirational universal norms that would hold businesses to account for human rights duties. And from such a document might come a framework for enforcement. Such a treaty would also give victims and the public a larger sense of justice.

[78] S. Sanders and A. J. Renacci, 'EU Considers Implementing Conflict Minerals Regulation' (10 December 2012), www.lexology.com/library/detail.aspx?g=1cc1c43a-d8a5-4013-9d53-8781fffd64c9 (last accessed 3 February 2013).
[79] *Ibid.*   [80] Ramasastry and Thompson, *Commerce, Crime and Conflict*, n. 22.

But it may be possible to embed human rights norms into regulatory mechanisms. For example, laws focused on preventing illegal logging might provide mechanisms for victims in affected communities to seek restitution from companies that are illegal importers. Administrative fines could be used not only for bolstering state finances but also for providing victims with redress.

The three examples of state regulation of business activities discussed in this chapter indicate the ways in which states may choose to regulate and address problems where human rights are being adversely affected. Of course, each of these regulatory responses arises because of a governance gap – where host states have been unable to stop relevant human rights abuses and home states have seen the need to constrain the behaviour of their TNCs.

Two of the examples focus on human rights due diligence and transparency as mechanisms for preventing harm, whereas the other focuses on criminal penalties for harms caused by corporations. It is difficult to imagine embedding these different approaches and substantive problem areas in one treaty. Instead, it may be that the emergence of state practice leads to international frameworks or conventions focused on more discrete problems that arise with respect to TNCs and business and human rights.

With that in mind, it is important to remember that the treaty road will take years to traverse, and while it has not been travelled yet for business and human rights, the emergence of state practice is a necessary first step. Civil society can also pave the way for improved regulation through legislative reform in multiple jurisdictions. This does not mean that NGOs should abandon the quest for a greater and more universal set of norms, but it does mean that risk prevention via regulation can achieve many human rights objectives.

PART III

Nature and extent of corporate obligations

8

Business, human rights and gender: a legal approach to external and internal considerations

BONITA MEYERSFELD

Introduction

The emerging area of business and human rights in international law seeks, in part, to address the power disparity between developed countries, multi-national corporations (MNCs) and developing world societies. Attempts to deal with this power disparity have, ironically, sidelined another well-documented imbalance of power, namely, gender inequality. Inequality between women and men is one of the oldest manifestations of discrimination.[1] The World Health Organization considers violence against women a pandemic.[2] The majority of impoverished people worldwide are women.[3] Globally, women have fewer employment opportunities than men, have less access to credit and endure a range of social restrictions that impede their economic independence.[4]

International human rights law has developed specific, nuanced and increasingly effective principles to eliminate all forms of discrimination

---

[1] For an overview of discrimination against women, see B. C. Meyersfeld, *Domestic Violence and International Law* (Oxford: Hart Publishing, 2010), 124–26.

[2] E. G. Krug *et al.*, *World Report on Violence and Health* (Geneva: WHO, 2002), 99. See also A. Sen, 'Missing Women' (1992) 304 *British Medical Journal* 586.

[3] 'The majority of the 1.5 billion people living on 1 dollar a day or less are women. In addition, the gap between women and men caught in the cycle of poverty has continued to widen in the past decade, a phenomenon commonly referred to as "the feminization of poverty". Worldwide, women earn on average slightly more than 50 per cent of what men earn.' Division for the Advancement of Women, 'The Feminization of Poverty: Fact Sheet No. 1' (May 2000), www.un.org/womenwatch/daw/followup/session/presskit/fs1.htm (last accessed 26 December 2012). See also International Bank for Reconstruction and Development (IBRD) and World Bank, *Women, Business and the Law: Removing Barriers to Economic Inclusion* (Washington, DC: IBRD and World Bank, 2012).

[4] The Economist Intelligence Unit, *Women's Economic Opportunity: A New Pilot Index and Global Ranking – Findings and Methodology* (June 2010), 4, http://graphics.eiu.com/upload/WEO_report_June_2010.pdf (last accessed 26 December 2012).

against women. Almost every sub-category of international human rights law identifies the importance of understanding discrimination against women and tries to determine how such discrimination manifests. From children's rights to government torture, from principles of access to justice to food availability, experts have identified the discriminatory distinction between women and men as a pervasive issue that requires attention. Sadly, the general finding is that within any one area of human rights concern, women's experience is at best different and, more often, worse than that of men. This is not because of some essentialising vulnerability of women; rather, the difference between women and men based on sex has led to a distinction between the two sexes in social relations, communal development and the laws that regulate them. It is the latter – the socially constructed rules and norms regarding an individual's sex – that constitutes the term 'gender' and is the basis for persistent discrimination against women. Where an individual's talents, abilities and role in life are predetermined by their sex, this constitutes gender-based discrimination.

Lawyers and activists are trying to change the social and legal constructs that insist that because someone is a woman, she may not inherit property, choose her life partner, earn a wage, decide on her political representation or pursue leadership positions in her community. Many of these constraints no longer exist for a large number of women. In many parts of the world, women may vote, represent their communities in parliament, run businesses and choose if and when to reproduce. At the same time, however, certain social and legal differences persist. At first blush, these may appear to be gender neutral, but in reality, laws and rules exist that have a disproportionately negative impact on women. Women represent the highest number of internally displaced persons;[5] they are the poorest segments of the world's indigent population and dominate the informal and vulnerable employment sector;[6] they experience the highest rates of intimate violence; women in sub-Saharan Africa are the fastest growing population to contract HIV;[7] and having

---

[5] UN Women, *Progress of the World's Women, 2011–2012: In Pursuit of Justice* (2011), 84, http://progress.unwomen.org/pdfs/EN-Report-Progress.pdf (last accessed 12 January 2013).

[6] *Ibid.*, 8. See also The Global Poverty Project, 'Global Poverty Info Bank: Women and Poverty', www.globalpovertyproject.com/infobank/women (last accessed 12 January 2013).

[7] UNESCO, 'Regional Overview: Sub-Saharan Africa' (2008), 1, http://unesdoc.unesco.org/images/0015/001572/157229e.pdf (last accessed 24 January 2013).

a baby or living with a man are two of the most dangerous and life-threatening activities for women.[8] While we may be tired of the dogged insistence that women's rights require special attention, the continued harm, fear and poverty that women experience in every part of the world is, sadly, unabated.

It is against this background that the UN Human Rights Council (HRC) mandated John Ruggie, the Special Representative of the Secretary-General on the Issue of Human Rights and Transnational Corporations and Other Business Enterprises (SRSG), to ensure that he considered the issue of discrimination against women in his mandate. Three broad questions arise from this gender-specific mandate. Firstly, is it necessary for the business and human rights debate to include an analysis of gender? Secondly, why should the experience of women receive special consideration and not also that of children, the disabled and indigenous groups, for example? Thirdly, if a gendered analysis is necessary, what is the scope and content of such analysis?

The SRSG did address gender in the Guiding Principles on Business and Human Rights (GPs), which are discussed in further detail below.[9] The GPs, for example, call for states to guide business enterprises, *inter alia*, on 'how to consider effectively issues of gender, vulnerability and/or marginalization, recognizing the specific challenges that may be faced by indigenous peoples, women, national or ethnic minorities, religious and linguistic minorities, children, persons with disabilities, and migrant workers and their families'.[10] The GPs also expect states to provide 'adequate assistance to business enterprises to assess and address the heightened risks of abuses, paying special attention to both gender-based and sexual violence' in conflict-affected areas.[11] Companies should use gender-disaggregated data to track the effectiveness of their response to adverse human rights impacts.[12]

This chapter engages these developments and the three questions which led to their inclusion in the GPs. The objective of this analysis is

---

[8] Meyersfeld, *Domestic Violence*, n. 1, 125. See also A. Buchanan, *Justice, Legitimacy, and Self-Determination* (Oxford University Press, 2006), 79; M. C. Nussbaum, *Women and Human Development* (Cambridge University Press, 2000), 1; and A. Sen, *Development as Freedom* (New York: Random House, 2000), 15.

[9] Human Rights Council, 'Guiding Principles on Business and Human Rights: Implementing the United Nations' "Protect, Respect and Remedy" Framework', A/HRC/17/31 (21 March 2011), 12 (SRSG, 'Guiding Principles').

[10] *Ibid.*, Principle 3 Commentary.   [11] *Ibid.*, Principle 7(b).

[12] *Ibid.*, Principle 20 Commentary.

to justify and explore the full integration of gender into the business and human rights discussion.

Backdrop of gender's entry into the SRSG's work

International law has seen a rapid development of the norms relating to business and human rights.[13] This area of law was triggered by the increasing power, both fiscal and political, of corporations engaging in cross-border activities.[14] Relatively speaking, this is a new and unique phenomenon in international law. Traditionally, international law has focused on the rights and obligations of states. Only in the last half-century has international law seriously engaged the role of individuals and non-state actors.[15]

In July 2005, the SRSG was appointed to propose an international legal framework governing transnational corporations and the protection of human rights. The objective of his work, in part, was to identify and remedy governance gaps caused by the accelerated growth of globalised, trans-border commerce. The SRSG's challenge was to devise a framework that would provide an effective regulatory response to the global activities of MNCs and which would find favour with the international community.

When the HRC renewed Ruggie's mandate in June 2008, it explicitly required him '[t]o integrate a gender perspective throughout his work and to give special attention to persons belonging to vulnerable groups,

---

[13] See S. Ratner, 'Corporations and Human Rights: A Theory of Legal Responsibility' (2001) 111 *Yale Law Journal* 443; Nicola Jägers, *Corporate Human Rights Obligations: In Search of Accountability* (Antwerp: Intersentia, 2002); S. Deva, *Regulating Corporate Human Rights Violations: Humanizing Business* (London: Routledge, 2012); O. De Schutter (ed.), *Transnational Corporation and Human Rights* (Oxford: Hart Publishing, 2006); D. Bilchitz, 'Do Corporations have Positive Fundamental Rights Obligations?' [2010] *Theoria* 1; and generally B. C. Meyersfeld, 'Institutional Investment and the Protection of Human Rights: A Regional Proposal' in L. Boulle (ed.), *Globalisation and Governance* (Cape Town: Siber Ink, 2011).

[14] The turnover of some MNCs dwarfs the economies of many countries, with the result that they have greater political influence. See Ratner, 'Corporations and Human Rights', n. 13, 461–62; S. Joseph, *Corporations and Transnational Human Rights Litigation* (Oxford: Hart Publishing, 2004), 1–14; S. Chesterman, 'The Turn to Ethics: Disinvestment from Multinational Corporations for Human Rights Violations: The Case of Norway's Sovereign Wealth Fund' (2008) 23 *American University International Law Review* 577, at 594–95; B. J. Richardson, *Socially Responsible Investment Law: Regulating the Unseen Polluters* (Oxford University Press, 2008), 5.

[15] See generally Meyersfeld, *Domestic Violence*, n. 1, 194–204.

in particular children'.[16] For many people this seemed counter-intuitive. Gender was seen as a discrete, separate issue that could be addressed once the 'main' issues surrounding business and human rights had been fleshed out. Notwithstanding this uncertainty, the SRSG took the HRC's instruction on board. In his preliminary workplan, he stated that '[i]n keeping with the Council resolution, all work streams will consider how best to integrate a gender perspective and to give special attention to persons belonging to vulnerable groups'.[17]

In June 2009, an expert consultation was held with the SRSG on the subject of integrating a gender perspective into his work.[18] Two issues became evident during this consultation: the SRSG's team was open to gender but uncertain about how to engage this as a cross-cutting theme in their work; and existing international law norms regarding gender could not provide all the answers. A great deal of work was needed to identify and attenuate the intersection between corporate conduct and gender relations. When the SRSG released the draft GPs in 2010, a group of gender specialists submitted a joint response as to how gender should be incorporated into the final GPs.[19] These proposals, some of which found their way into the final GPs, posited gender as a lens through which all business and human rights work must be examined.[20]

While this approach was innovative in respect of business and human rights, a gendered analysis has occupied international human rights law for several decades. Today, almost every international and regional

---

[16] Later on, the HRC renewed the SRSG's mandate for another three years, i.e. until June 2011. Human Rights Council, 'Resolution 8/7: Mandate of the Special Representative of the Secretary-General on the Issue of Human Rights and Transnational Corporations and Other Business Enterprises', A/HRC/RES/8/7 (18 June 2008), para. 4(d).

[17] See Human Rights Council, 'Preliminary Work Plan: Mandate of the Special Representative on the Issue of Human Rights and Transnational Corporations and Other Business Enterprises: 1 September 2008 – 30 June 2011' (10 October 2008).

[18] 'Integrating a Gender Perspective into the UN "Protect, Respect and Remedy" Framework: Consultation Summary' (New York, 29 June 2009), www.valoresociale.it/detail.asp?c=1&p=0&id=307 (last accessed 26 December 2012). The author participated in this consultation.

[19] K. Dovey et al., 'Comments on the Draft "Guiding Principles" for the Implementation of the "Protect, Respect and Remedy" Framework: Integrating a Gender Perspective' (January 2011), www.business-humanrights.org/media/documents/ruggie/joint-submission-re-guiding-principles-integrating-a-gender-perspective-jan-2011.pdf (last accessed 26 December 2012).

[20] Ibid. For example, the final GPs included reference to gender-disaggregated data (SRSG, 'Guiding Principles', n. 9, Principle 20 Commentary) and in general distinguished 'gender' from other 'vulnerable groups'.

human rights body has a policy regarding gender, empowerment and women's rights. In order for the business and human rights agenda to be a meaningful one, it must join other areas of international law and engage the power imbalance between women and men. The justifications for this analysis and a proposed approach to gender, business and human rights are discussed below.

Need for integrating gender analysis into the business and human rights debate

The protection of human rights in international law has always struggled to ensure that its application is rich, effective and fair. Over the last fifty years, individuals and groups have identified that the network of generic international human rights instruments does not address the needs and rights of women.[21]

Theorists and activists have long argued that women endure a particular form of harm due to their gender, which intersects with their ethnicity, race or religion. Theorists called on international law to 'recharacterize internationally protected human rights to accommodate women's experience of injustice'.[22] In 1991, Hilary Charlesworth, Christine Chinkin and Shelly Wright observed that '[i]nternational law is a thoroughly gendered system'.[23] This was a bold statement in a time marked by 'the immunity of international law to feminist analysis',[24] and with it came a range of feminist commentary on the substance, procedures and politics of international law and women.

Over the same period, it became increasingly clear that the differentiation between women and men – the allocation of gendered roles – had (and sadly continues to have) a disproportionately negative impact on women. The socially constructed differences attributed to women and men benefited men in the realisation of their potential but impeded women in the fulfilment of theirs. The link between differentiation and discrimination has led to worldwide attempts to change the way law and society respond to women and their human rights.

---

[21] See generally Meyersfeld, *Domestic Violence*, n. 1.
[22] R. J. Cook, 'Women's International Human Rights Law: The Way Forward' (1993) 15 *Human Rights Quarterly* 230, at 231.
[23] H. Charlesworth, C. Chinkin and S. Wright, 'Feminist Approaches to International Law' (1991) 85 *American Journal of International Law* 613, at 614.
[24] *Ibid.*

Within the realm of international human rights law, it was established that generic principles do not provide the type of social and physical protection that women often require by virtue of differences in bodily, reproductive and cultural functions.[25] While the provisions of international human rights instruments could arguably be extrapolated to apply to gender-based violations, many maintain that this is insufficient and that human rights principles had been moulded from a purely male perspective.[26] The call for precise and express rights for women resulted in the development of international instruments, bodies and organisations that specifically address the rights of women in international law. It has also led to the integration of women's rights specifically into otherwise mainstream human rights principles and laws. For example, the UN committees responsible for the Torture Convention[27] and the Race Convention,[28] the Special Rapporteur on the independence of judges and lawyers,[29] and the Millennium Development Goals[30] have all included specific principles relating to the protection of women. This is not because there is something essentially vulnerable about women, but rather because the human rights principles that exist to protect political, cultural, civil, social and economic rights have been refined to respond to the reality of sex and gender discrimination that characterises every society and country, to varying degrees.

As an emerging area within international law and with new institutional structures, business and human rights is ripe for a gendered analysis. Corporate conduct that appears to have a gender-neutral

---

[25] A. Sen, 'Gender Inequality and Theories of Justice' in M. C. Nussbaum and J. Glover (eds.), *Women, Culture and Development: A Study of Human Capabilities* (Oxford: Clarendon Press, 1995), 259 at 270.

[26] See, for example, Charlesworth, Chenkin and Wright, 'Feminist Approaches', n. 23. See also C. Romany, 'Women as Aliens: A Feminist Critique of the Public/Private Distinction in International Human Rights Law' (1993) 6 *Harvard Human Rights Journal* 87, 98–99. For a general discussion about the need for specificity in international law, see Meyersfeld, *Domestic Violence*, n. 1, 144–47.

[27] Human Rights Council, 'Report of the Special Rapporteur on Torture and Other Cruel, Inhuman or Degrading Treatment or Punishment, Manfred Nowak: Promotion and Protection of All Human Rights, Civil, Political, Economic, Social and Cultural Rights, Including the Right to Development', A/HRC/7/3 (15 January 2008).

[28] Human Rights Council, 'Report of the Secretary-General on the Implementation of Resolution 2005/42, Integrating the Human Rights of Women throughout the United Nations System', A/HRC/4/104 (15 February 2007), para. 36.

[29] *Ibid.*, para. 40.

[30] General Assembly, '55/2 United Nations Millennium Declaration', A/Res/55/2 (18 September 2000).

impact on a community may cause – or exacerbate – discrimination against women because of pre-existing gendered roles and structures within that community. In keeping with almost every other area of international human rights law, business and human rights lawyers need to consider the extent to which the human rights principles governing business affect, exclude and potentially harm women.

Women's experiences versus special consideration for children, the disabled and indigenous groups

Gender-based discrimination, violence and harm cut across every aspect of international human rights law. This reflects the fact that gender-based discrimination and harm cut across every aspect of life. The manifestation of a seemingly generic human rights violation may be different for women depending on the communal, social or state policies that define women's experiences in society. In other words, a human rights violation that affects a community may impact differently on women than men because of the pre-existing differentiation between men and women. For example, the violation of a political dissident's human rights may be very different depending on the individual's sex. A man imprisoned for political dissidence may be treated differently from a woman who is also imprisoned: rape being a key example of women's unique experience of political detention. There are certainly similarities in their experiences but there are seminal differences, which must be addressed by international law. The most widely understood difference is in the form of sexual harm, where the phenomenon of political rape has developed as a uniquely gendered form of torture.[31]

The imperative to consider gender does not mean that women's experiences are more important than harm perpetrated against children, the disabled or racially discrete groups. Rather, the meaning of gender – namely, the socially constructed roles based on sex – and the harm perpetrated as a result of such role allocation occur in addition to and

---

[31] 'Since it was clear that rape or other sexual assault against women in detention were a particularly ignominious violation of the inherent dignity and the right to physical integrity of the human being, they accordingly constituted an act of torture.' Commission on Human Rights, 'Report of the Special Rapporteur, Mr Nigel S. Rodley, submitted pursuant to Commission on Human Rights Resolution 1992/32: Question of the Human Rights of All Persons subjected to any Form of Detention or Imprisonment, in Particular: Torture and Other Cruel, Inhuman or Degrading Treatment or Punishment', E/CN.4/1995/34 (12 January 1995), para. 16, citing E/CN.4/1992/SR.21, para. 35.

irrespective of an individual's race, religion, age or abilities. Black and Hispanic women in the United States, for example, experience discrimination differently from – and similarly to – men in their communities.[32] Disabled women report an array of harm that differs from the experience of men with similar disabilities.[33] Therefore, the assumption that gender is irrelevant is dangerous; ignoring the different experiences threatens to whitewash the distinctive harm. The result is that legal remedies may be developed to address the generic experience, leaving the particular experiences of women unaddressed.

The gender analysis is not a sub-stratum of an otherwise universal human rights framework. Rather, it is a lens of analysis through which all human rights considerations should be examined. Not only is gender-based harm and discrimination relevant to every human rights analysis, it is also an important analytical tool to pry open situational problems in order to reveal the realities and vicissitudes of otherwise invisible harm occurring in a particular context.

This analytical methodology is at the heart of the UN's inclusion of gender in all its human rights work, including the work of the General Assembly, the Secretary-General and treaty-monitoring bodies. Specific examples are: the General Assembly's statement on the effect of macro-economic policies and the role of the Bretton Woods institutions in reducing gender-based violence;[34] the Secretary-General's report to the HRC on the activities of the human rights treaty-monitoring bodies regarding gender equality and women's rights requiring the integration of the human rights of women throughout the United Nations system;[35] and the importance of recognising and addressing gender-based harm among indigenous peoples.[36]

The field of business and human rights requires a similarly integrated analysis of women's and men's experiences. Such analysis is not yet evident in this field. The SRSG's 'Protect, Respect and Remedy' Framework (Framework) operates at a level of abstraction so that it may find its home within the language of international relations and

---

[32] See, for example, B. Hooks, *Feminist Theory from Margin to Center* (Boston, MA: South End Press, 1984) and C. L. Moraga, *A Xicana Codex of Changing Consciousness: Writings, 2000–2010* (Durham, NC: Duke University Press, 2011).

[33] See WomenWatch, 'Women with Disabilities' (2006–2011), www.un.org/womenwatch/ enable/ (last accessed 26 December 2012).

[34] General Assembly, '61/143 Intensification of Efforts to Eliminate All Forms of Violence against Women', A/RES/61/143 (30 January 2007).

[35] Human Rights Council, 'Implementation of Resolution 2005/42', n. 28.   [36] *Ibid.*

international human rights policy. In that sense, it is divorced from the personal and does not attempt to assess or provide for differential impacts companies may have on different individuals and their circumstances. This universal approach is normal and, to varying degrees, appropriate in international law – a body of law that is based more on consensus than coercion. However, just as broad international law has developed specific standards in respect of gender, the same manifestation should occur in respect of this new burgeoning field.

As discussed below, the GPs include some references to gender. However, gender is not integrated throughout the GPs as a theme that recognises that generic principles may operate differently in practice for women and men. This position not only fails to reflect the reality that women are the majority of the population with specific group experiences, but it is also out of sync with the rest of the UN system in developing specific principles regarding the eradication of gender-specific harm throughout international human rights law.

Scope and content of gender analysis

Scope: internal operations, external impacts and the informal sector

The scope of a gender analysis may be divided into three broad categories: internal operations, external impacts and the informal sector.

Traditionally, the consideration of women's rights in corporate activity has revolved around employment equity. This relates to issues that are *internal* to the corporation and includes equal pay for equal work, equal opportunities, positive discrimination, sexual harassment and, in certain circumstances, affirmative action measures. This area of international women's rights law is well canvassed and forms the subject of many international instruments.[37]

Equality in the workplace is indeed a human rights issue, but it is only one aspect of women's human rights that a corporation might affect. There are other ways in which corporations may affect women's human rights that are

---

[37] See, for example, Equal Remuneration Convention (ILO No. 100) (entered into force 23 May 1953), 165 UNTS 303; Social Security (Minimum Standards) Convention (ILO No. 102) (entered into force 27 April 1955), 210 UNTS 131; Discrimination (Employment and Occupation) Convention (ILO No. 111) (entered into force 15 June 1960), 362 UNTS 31; and Maternity Protection Convention (ILO No. 183) (entered into force 7 February 2002), 214 UNTS 321.

external to the operations and running of the corporation. In the same way that a corporation's activities may affect human rights of a community, it may also affect the human rights of women who are not its employees. For example, large-scale infrastructure projects often require the resettlement of a community with concomitant compensation. Such resettlement may have differential impacts on women and men, and consequently the envisaged compensation scheme should take this into account. In many communities, women and men often have distinct family responsibilities, economic opportunities and childcare responsibilities. If, in relocating a community, a compensation scheme envisages cash compensation to heads of households for family-held plots of land, this could have different consequences for women and men. A gender-neutral approach to compensation can exacerbate existing gender inequalities by paying compensation solely to the male head of the household and not to female-headed households, single or widowed women. As such, inequality may arise or existing inequalities may be exacerbated. Attention must also be paid to compensation for loss of livelihood or provision of alternative livelihoods in recognising that women worldwide have fewer opportunities to obtain remunerated, formal work.

External violations may include corporate complicity in conflict where women may be targeted by armed forces; harm that occurs as a result of changes to the environment in which the corporation operates, e.g. a change in access to water, for which women tend to bear the primary responsibility in many agrarian-based economies;[38] loss of existing employment without creation of new employment;[39] changes in industry or changes to city structures that may cause the transfer of certain industries from women to men; and changes due to new technologies and skills.[40] For example, the textile industry in India was once female dominated. The presence of MNCs led to the centralisation of textile work in the cities and employment of more men than women at the formal level of the textile industry. The result is that unemployment affected women more than men and the jobs that are now available to

[38] Rehabilitation, for instance, may have an adverse impact on women's access to water. See N. Bugalski and J.Medallo, 'Derailed: A Study on the Rehabilitation of the Cambodian Railway' (Bridges Across Borders Cambodia, 2012), 7–8, 17, www.babcam-bodia.org/derailed/derailed.pdf (last accessed 24 January 2013).

[39] See R. Jhabvala and S. Sinha, 'Liberalization and the Woman Worker' (25 May 2002), 2, www.sewa.org/images/Archive/Pdf/Liberlization_Women_Worker.pdf (last accessed 26 December 2012).

[40] *Ibid.*, 2.

women in the textile industry tend to be lower paid, informal and with-out legal protection or employment benefits.[41]

Corporations that seek to comply with human rights standards must give attention to all these factors, both internal and external. Although critically important, it is not enough to have gender representation on boards and in senior management. It is equally vital that the range of rights that a corporation's external activities may impact be considered and steps are taken to attenuate gender-based harm.

Corporations, together with states, are also responsible for and may exacerbate the phenomenon of a female-dominated informal employ-ment sector. All over the world women work disproportionately in the informal employment sector, where they have less-secure jobs, worse working conditions and lesser pay.[42] This, in turn, contributes to women's disproportionate impoverishment globally (the so-called fem-inisation of poverty) – a serious issue of gender inequality in the business and human rights context. There is a role for both states and MNCs to play regarding the informal employment sector and eliminating gender-based obstacles to formal work. Additionally, where corporate supply chains rely on workers in the informal sector, this will have implications for how they pursue their 'responsibility to respect'. The informal employment sector and the associated obstacles to formal employment should receive specific attention.

The three categories discussed here are not a closed list of ways in which women's rights may be impeded by corporate activity; they are merely a method of categorising and understanding what it means to take a gendered approach to business and human rights. The next question is what steps both corporations and states should take to safeguard against the perpetuation of discrimination against women.

A preliminary structure of safeguards

The international law discussion regarding MNCs and human rights now oscillates around the SRSG's three-pillar Framework.[43] The first

---

[41] Ibid.

[42] Women who move from informal to formal employment usually enjoy an increase in earnings. See The Economist Intelligence Unit, *Women's Economic Opportunity*, n. 4, 6.

[43] Human Rights Council, 'Protect, Respect and Remedy: A Framework for Business and Human Rights: Report of the Special Representative of the Secretary-General on the Issue of Human Rights and Transnational Corporations and Other Business Enterprises', A/HRC/8/5 (7 April 2008), para. 3 (SRSG, '2008 Report').

pillar focuses on the state duty to protect its citizens from the harmful conduct of third parties, including non-state actors such as MNCs. The second focuses on the responsibility of corporations to respect human rights, and the third pillar addresses the need for access to remedies when violations occur.

In this section, I focus on the first and second pillars of the Framework for the purpose of proposing a structure within which to adopt a gender perspective on the business and human rights debate. However, I raise an important caveat. Underlying the second pillar is the notion that business enterprises should 'avoid infringing on the human rights of others and should address adverse human rights impacts with which they are involved'.[44] Although this responsibility applies to all rights, this is not a legally binding concept under international law. Rather it is a standard of performance implemented through the process of due diligence.

It is arguable that international law, operating in a new global market-place, should impose strict legal obligations on corporations, either through the development of a normative framework around corporate liability or through the application of extraterritorial state obligations. In the absence of global law, the only oversight of corporate activity is in voluntary guidelines. These are useful as they set industry standards and aspire towards a form of business practice that is in harmony with human rights, environmental sustainability and development. They are, however, voluntary and depend almost entirely on the integrated factors of goodwill and reputational concern.[45] Therefore, I am of the view that in the long term there is scope for the due diligence standard to become binding and mandatory.

I now turn to discuss the first and second pillars of the Framework in respect of gender.

---

[44] SRSG, 'Guiding Principles', n. 9, Principle 11.

[45] For discussions of the advantages and disadvantages of voluntarism in business, see F. McLeay, 'Corporate Codes of Conduct and the Human Rights Accountability of Transnational Corporations: A Small Piece of a Larger Puzzle' in O. De Schutter (ed.), *Transnational Corporations and Human Rights* (Oxford: Hart Publishing, 2006), 219; E. Westfield, 'Globalization, Governance, and Multinational Enterprise Responsibility: Corporate Codes of Conduct in the 21st Century' (2002) 42 *Virginia Journal of International Law* 1075; International Council on Human Rights Policy, *Beyond Voluntarism: Human Rights and the Development of International Legal Obligations of Companies* (Versoix: ICHRP, 2002), 23–25, 34; E. E. Macek, 'Scratching the Corporate Back: Why Corporations Have No Incentive to Define Human Rights' (2002) 11 *Minnesota Journal of Global Trade* 101.

State duty to protect

The Convention on the Elimination of All Forms of Discrimination against Women (CEDAW)[46] and other women's rights instruments place a positive obligation on states to ensure that the rights of women are not violated either by states or non-state actors.[47] The notion of state responsibility for the protection of harm by third parties, including MNCs, is particularly relevant to the protection against gender-based harm.

The state is responsible not only for directly violating women's rights, but also for failing to take reasonable steps which would prevent discrimination or harm against women. How does one judge what reasonable steps are and at what stage can one say that a state has done enough? In response to this question, international law has developed the due diligence standard (not as enunciated by the SRSG's second pillar, but as defined according to international human rights law). The positive obligation of states to protect individuals from third party harm is moored in the developing notion of 'due diligence'.[48]

First articulated in *Velásquez-Rodríguez* v. *Honduras*,[49] the due diligence standard requires states to take active measures to protect against, prosecute and punish private actors who commit human rights violations.[50] This standard is at the core of states' responsibilities in respect of

[46] Convention on the Elimination of All Forms of Violence against Women (entered into force 3 September 1981), 1249 UNTS 13 (CEDAW), Art. 2(e) (requiring states to take measures to eliminate discrimination against women 'by any person, organization or enterprise').

[47] Declaration on the Elimination of Violence against Women (entered into force 23 February 1994), A/RES/48/104 (DEVAW), Art. 4(c) (requiring states to prevent, investigate and punish acts of violence against women whether perpetrated 'by the State or by private persons'). For an extensive discussion on the responsibility of states for the actions of non-state actors, see Meyersfeld, *Domestic Violence*, n. 1, 194–203.

[48] See, for example, Council of Europe Convention on Preventing and Combating Violence against Women and Domestic Violence (opened for signature 11 May 2011), CETS No. 210, Art. 5.

[49] *Velásquez Rodríguez* v. *Honduras* (1989) 28 I.L.M. 291. The due diligence standard was resuscitated by the first Special Rapporteur on Violence against Women, its Causes and Consequences, R. Coomaraswamy. Commission on Human Rights, 'Preliminary Report Submitted by the Special Rapporteur on Violence against Women, its Causes and Consequences, Ms. Radhika Coomaraswamy, in Accordance with the Commission on Human Rights Resolution 994/5: Further Promotion and Encouragement of Human Rights and Fundamental Freedoms, Including the Question of the Programme and Methods of Work of the Commission: Alternative Approaches and Ways and Means within the United Nations System for Improving the Effective Enjoyment of Human Rights and Fundamental Freedoms', E/CN.4/1995/42 (22 November 1994).

[50] For a discussion of this standard, see Meyersfeld, *Domestic Violence*, n. 1, 151.

preventing third party actors, such as corporations, from causing or exacerbating gender inequality.[51]

The fulfilment of the due diligence standard, however, is amorphous and difficult to measure. Traditionally, the due diligence test asks whether 'a more active and more efficient course of procedure might have been pursued' to avoid a particular type of harm.[52] This test is similar to the standard negligence test: would a reasonable actor, in that situation, have taken steps which could have changed a harmful outcome? The Explanatory Report to the new Council of Europe Convention on Preventing and Combating Violence against Women and Domestic Violence maintains that due diligence is not designed as 'an obligation of result, but an obligation of means'.[53] Parties must 'organise their response[s]' to violence against women to ensure that authorities 'diligently prevent, investigate, punish and provide reparation for such acts of violence'.[54] Failure to do so incurs state responsibility 'for an act otherwise solely attributable to a non-state actor'.[55]

When read as a theme that applies to state conduct, one begins to see the due diligence standard as a standard of performance. The standard does not prescribe specific steps; rather, states may take an array of possible steps, provided that they act thoroughly and effectively. For example, a state that signs and ratifies CEDAW has a range of obligations to protect women's right to work. Article 11(1) of CEDAW requires states to 'take all appropriate measures to eliminate discrimination against women in the field of employment in order to ensure, on a basis of equality of men and women, the same rights'.[56] These rights include the right to the same employment opportunities as men,[57] the right freely to choose one's profession and employment without discrimination,[58] and the right to equal pay for equal work.[59] CEDAW further requires states to take positive steps to ensure that corporations do not unfairly dismiss women employees on grounds of pregnancy,

---

[51] *Opuz* v. *Turkey* (2009) 48 I.L.M. 909.

[52] A. V. Freeman, *The International Responsibility of States for Denial of Justice* (New York: Longmans, Green and Co., 1938), 380. See also Commission on Human Rights, 'The Due Diligence Standard as a Tool for the Elimination of Violence against Women: Report of the Special Rapporteur on Violence against Women, its Causes and Consequences, Yakin Ertürk', E/CN.4/2006/61 (20 January 2006), para. 15.

[53] Council of Europe, 'Convention on Preventing and Combating Violence against Women and Domestic Violence, Explanatory Report', CM(2011)49addfinalE (7 April 2011), para. 59.

[54] *Ibid.* [55] *Ibid.* [56] CEDAW, n. 46. [57] *Ibid.*, Art. 11(1)(b).

[58] *Ibid.*, Art. 11(1)(c). [59] *Ibid.*, Art. 11(1)(d).

marital status or family responsibilities.[60] These are all obligations which, by definition, require some type of intervention into the affairs of corporations to ensure the fulfilment of these provisions. A failure to intervene effectively and properly regulate corporate conduct in this regard may constitute a breach of a state's international obligations and an internationally wrongful act. This broadly is what is meant by the injunction to 'act with due diligence'.

Very few states can be said to comply with their international human rights obligations in respect of women's rights to equality in the workplace. With an average worldwide pay gap of 15 per cent and continued pay disparity between male- and female- dominated industries, Article 11 of CEDAW remains an aspiration.[61] However, the underlying principles are largely not contentious. States have a duty to ensure that women are not discriminated against in the workplace and this is an obligation of result or outcome. The indicators of equality are not in policies or laws but in the extent to which policies or laws have reduced discrimination against women.[62] How this is implemented and the extent of this obligation usually fall within the state's margin of appreciation.[63]

In the context of business and human rights, however, the application of this obligation is problematic. Governance gaps between developed and developing countries often result in inconsistencies between gender equality in the workplace of a corporation's home state and that in the workplace of its host state. These governance gaps allow for the exploitation of women in host state countries in a manner that would be unlawful in the home state of the corporation. As is widely documented, host states often fail to provide effective statutory and other protection

---

[60] *Ibid.*, Art. 11(2).

[61] 'Women, on average, earn 75% of their male co-workers' wages, and the differences cannot be explained solely by schooling or experience.' The Economist Intelligence Unit, *Women's Economic Opportunity*, n. 4, 4.

[62] A. Facio and M. I. Morgan, 'Equity or Equality for Women? Understanding CEDAW's Equality Principles' (2009) *International Women's Rights Action Watch Asia Pacific Occasional Papers Series No. 14*, 14.

[63] For a discussion of this margin of appreciation and the extent to which states may design their response to employment equity, see the views of the Committee on the Elimination of Discrimination against Women under Art. 7, para. 3, of the Optional Protocol to the Convention on the Elimination of All Forms of Discrimination against Women (entered into force 22 December 2002), Communication No. 3/2004, Ms. Dung Thi Thuy Nguyen (views adopted on 14 August 2006, Thirty-Sixth Session), regarding employment equity, maternity pay and margin of appreciation.

against such exploitation, clearly failing in their duty to protect against the violation of, *inter alia*, Article 11 of CEDAW.

A developing and important exploration of closing these gaps is the principle of extraterritorial application of a state's international human rights obligations. Principle 2 of the GPs captures the rules of international law relating to jurisdiction and notes that states should set out clearly the expectation that all business enterprises domiciled in their territory and/or jurisdiction respect human rights throughout their operations.[64] The recently devised Maastricht Principles on Extraterritorial Obligations of States in the area of Economic, Social and Cultural Rights (Maastricht Principles)[65] confirm that '[a]ll States have obligations to respect, protect and fulfil human rights, including civil, cultural, economic, political and social rights, both within their territories and extraterritorially'.[66] The Maastricht Principles define extraterritorial obligations as including 'obligations relating to the acts and omissions of a State, within or beyond its territory, that have effects on the enjoyment of human rights outside of that State's territory'.[67] This may appear contentious at first blush: how could a state exercise authority over activity taking place in a foreign jurisdiction? The reality is that states regularly exercise extraterritorial authority over the conduct of their nationals abroad. For example, many states have laws prohibiting their nationals from the manufacture, use of and trade in weapons of mass destruction, *irrespective of where such use, manufacture or trade occurs.*[68] The United States Peace Corp volunteer programme will apply US laws prohibiting sexual abuse of children to their volunteers who commit such crimes abroad.[69] During the apartheid era, US corporations operating in South Africa were called upon to ensure that the South African workers they employed were treated equally and in accordance with the same standards of equal protection applicable in the United

---

[64] For a critical analysis, see Chapter 11.

[65] Maastricht Principles on Extra-territorial Obligations of States in the Area of Economic, Social and Cultural Rights (28 September 2011).

[66] *Ibid.*, General Principle 3.   [67] *Ibid.*, General Principle 8 (a).

[68] See L. Andros, 'Chemical Weapons Proliferation: Extraterritorial Jurisdiction and United States Export Controls: When Too Much is Not Enough' (1992) 3 *New York Law School Journal of International and Comparative Law* 257.

[69] US Department of Justice, 'Peace Corps Volunteer Charged with Sexually Abusing Children in South Africa' (4 August 2011), http://multimedia.peacecorps.gov/multimedia/pdf/about/leadership/ig/PCV_Charged_with_Sexually_Abusing_Children_in_SA_080411.pdf (last accessed 26 December 2012).

States.[70] These examples show that the extraterritorial application of human rights obligations is neither new nor overly contentious.[71]

In reality, extraterritoriality does not interfere with the jurisdictional sovereignty of another state. It merely allows for the exportation of a state governance regime over the actions of its citizens, including MNCs, abroad. It is, therefore, entirely viable and, I propose, in keeping with the principle of state sovereignty that a state's duty to protect against violations of women's rights applies to the operations of a corporation abroad. So, for example, a British corporation that operates in Saudi Arabia ought to be subject to the UK's laws on gender equality. Although the difficulties of private international law apply, they are not insurmountable.[72]

The theme of extraterritoriality is certainly in keeping with the protection and advancement of women's rights. CEDAW and other women's rights instruments place a positive obligation on states to ensure that the rights of women are not violated by both state and non-state actors.[73]

A state must exercise due diligence to prevent, prosecute and punish instances of women's rights violations, including where such are perpetrated by non-state actors such as corporations. The most common form of corporate regulation by the state in respect of women's rights is in the form of employment equity legislation and equal pay. International law requires corporations to implement employment strategies that eliminate discrimination against, and harassment of, women (and other marginalised groups, including employees of alternative sexual orientations and employees with disabilities). Broadly, these strategies may include: equal pay audits; affirmative action or positive discrimination; recognising the pay difference

---

[70] See H. J. Richardson III, 'Two Treaties, and Global Influences of the American Civil Rights Movements, through the Black International Tradition' (2010) 18 *Virginia Journal of Social Policy and the Law* 59, at 66; 'Reverend Leon Sullivan's Principles, Race, and International Law: A Comment' (2001) 15 *Temple International and Comparative Law Journal* 55, at 57–58.

[71] For a thorough and succinct discussion of this developing area of international law, see R. McCorquodale and P. Simons, 'Responsibility beyond Borders: State Responsibility for Extraterritorial Violations of Corporations of International Human Rights Law' (2007) 70 *Modern Law Review* 598.

[72] For a brief, but pertinent, discussion of this complexity, see R. Grabosch, 'Prospects of Legal Redress for Victims of Corporate Human Rights Violations in a Globalised World' in L. Boulle (ed.), *Globalisation and Governance*, n. 13, 166–69.

[73] For an extensive discussion on the responsibility of states for the actions of non-state actors, see Meyersfeld, *Domestic Violence*, n. 1, 94–203.

between traditionally female-dominated industries, such as nursing, and traditionally male-dominated industries, such as construction, and remedying industry-based pay discrimination; policies to eliminate sexual harassment; policies regarding maternity and paternity leave; policies regarding promotion and advancement; and policies regarding equal opportunities for advancement to management and ownership.

These policies could apply to the conduct of corporations within a state's jurisdiction and to such corporations' subsidiaries operating abroad. A hypothetical example of this scenario could be as follows: a British corporation enters into a contract with a Syrian authority to manufacture in Saudi Arabia a type of weapon which is prohibited under UK law. This corporation will be in contravention of UK law, notwithstanding that the prohibited conduct does not take place within the UK. The corporation, its head office or its agents (this is where matters become very complicated) will be in contravention of UK law and subject to the relevant punitive consequences.

It seems a reasonable requirement that a corporation that operates, either directly or through a subsidiary, in a foreign jurisdiction (the host state) should be subject to the highest standard of gender equality in its operations.[74] Where such standards are absent in the host state, but applicable in the home state, the home state standards should apply. Failure to apply them should lead to the same consequences of non-compliance for the corporate activity abroad as it would for such prohibited corporate activity at home.

The extraterritorial application of laws is not a particularly gendered approach. However, peculiarly, while states' prohibitions against racism, slavery, terrorism or arms trading, for example, have been applied extraterritorially, the same is not true of gender equality and employment equity.

In brief, the state's duty to protect against the violation of women's rights applies to both state and non-state actors, including corporations.[75] The extent to which a state is required to protect individuals is moored in the due diligence standard that requires an active approach by the state to guide and constrain corporate conduct, if necessary. Where governance is absent in that a host state does not provide that protection and an MNC exploits such rights-free zones, the home state of such

---

[74] The GPs contemplate the possibility of the 'requirements on "parent" companies to report on the global operations of the entire enterprise'. SRSG, 'Guiding Principles', n. 9, Principle 2 Commentary.

[75] See Meyersfeld, *Domestic Violence*, n. 1, 203.

corporation should apply its standards of gender equality to the conduct of the corporation abroad.

The corporate responsibility to respect

It is well documented that the power, both financial and political, of MNCs exceeds that of many states.[76] The *de facto* role of MNCs in many respects mirrors the powers and capabilities of governments. The non-application of international human rights law to MNCs is, at least, discordant with the nature of their activities, the impact of their activities on human rights violations and the need to enforce human rights standards. The reality, however, is that international law theorists (with some exceptions) and states themselves have not concluded that MNCs are subjects of international law. While there is a strong and important debate about the application of international law to non-state entities,[77] it is a debate and not law. Therefore, for the time being, we must examine gender within the non-binding notion of the Framework's second pillar: the responsibility to respect.

The SRSG proposes that the 'corporate responsibility to respect human rights means avoiding the infringement' of the rights of others and addressing adverse impacts that may occur'.[78] This is achieved by adopting a due diligence process, which is different from the notion of a due diligence process discussed above. The SRSG's due diligence process envisages three steps: an analysis of the country context in which the proposed business operation will take place, to highlight specific human rights challenges; an evaluation of what human rights impacts the corporation's own activities may have on the country in question; and determining whether the corporation might contribute to the human rights violations through the relationships connected to its activities.[79] Among others, Principle 17 of the GPs elaborates this process further, referring to the assessment of actual and potential human rights impacts,

---

[76] See the materials cited in n. 14.

[77] See S. Deva, 'Human Rights Violations by Multinational Corporations and International Law: Where from Here?' (2003) 19 *Connecticut Journal of International Law* 1, at 48–56.

[78] Human Rights Council, 'Business and Human Rights: Further Steps Toward the Operationalization of the "Protect, Respect and Remedy" Framework: Report of the Special Representative of the Secretary-General on the Issue of Human Rights and Transnational Corporations and Other Business Enterprises', A/HRC/14/27 (9 April 2010), para. 57 (SRSG, '2010 Report').

[79] SRSG, '2008 Report', n. 43, para. 57.

integrating and acting upon the findings, tracking responses and communicating how impacts are addressed.

The three due diligence steps identified by the SRSG could and should incorporate gender-specific considerations. How should this be done? Ertürk, the former UN Special Rapporteur on violence against women, devised a useful framework in which to identify possible violations of women's rights and to take steps to attenuate those violations.[80] This is a three-tiered approach, which looks at the possibility of violence against women at the individual, communal and state level. Ertürk also examines the international level, which I omit for the purpose of this analysis because the Framework's primary focus is on national policies to be adopted by MNCs. MNCs could adopt this tiered approach to ensure the protection of women's human rights in the activities they undertake. The analysis for MNCs would operate in reverse: looking at the state, communal and then individual levels.

At the state level, a corporation should determine whether the proposed corporate activity would create, encourage, reinforce or exacerbate existing gender-based inequalities. This level of analysis is particularly important in trying to reduce the number of women in the informal sector. The informal sector is often dangerous and susceptible to exploitation. The fact that this sector is dominated by women is a clear manifestation of discrimination against women. It would be unrealistic to suggest that MNCs alone are responsible for ending the predominance of women in the informal employment sector. Nevertheless, an MNC seeking to operate in a foreign jurisdiction should consider whether that jurisdiction has a high rate of women in the informal employment sector, a situation that might be exacerbated by its presence. An example of this is the textile industry, where the use of supply chains in unregulated jurisdictions has had a disproportionately negative effect on women. Corporations investing in such jurisdictions should be careful not to exploit the unregulated informal sector and ensure that their supply chains are subject to strict gender considerations.

The above is only one example of the state-level enquiry. Corporations should identify possible inequalities in other areas, consider how their presence may exacerbate such inequalities, and explore the steps that they should take to avoid harm and advance equality.

At the communal tier, corporations should consider whether the proposed corporate activity would create, encourage, reinforce or

[80] Commission on Human Rights, 'The Due Diligence Standard', n. 52, para. 29.

exacerbate existing gender-based inequalities within discrete communities. This examination would arise, for example, in the context of large-scale infrastructure projects or mining. These endeavours often have an impact on discrete, contained communities. Corporations are generally required to engage some form of free, prior and informed consent (or consultation), the standard enunciated for all corporate engagement with local communities.[81] Who is engaged is of particular importance at this level. In order to unearth potential gender-based harm, a corporate analysis should insist on engagement with female members of the community and the involvement of female trade union representatives and local women's rights organisations.

The final tier is the most personal and difficult to navigate: the level of the family. The question for corporations in this regard is whether the proposed corporate activity creates, encourages, reinforces or exacerbates existing gender-based inequalities at the individual level or within the family.[82]

In addition to engagement, at each level a corporate analysis should include sector-specific considerations. For example, the garment industry may have a particular impact on women operating in the informal sector. The analysis should also include the exigencies in the informal economy and factors that may lead to women predominating in it, for example the agricultural industry in Africa, which is dominated by unremunerated women workers. Moreover, it should include unintended consequences of any course of action, for example triggering higher rates of domestic violence.

In short, a corporation which seeks to meet international standards for the protection and advancement of women's human rights would need to consider: (i) internal and external violations; (ii) the gender-specific aspect of generic human rights violations; and (iii) the gender-specific impact of seemingly gender-neutral policies.

The spectre of culture

A problem that often arises for both state and non-state actors relates to dealing with diverse cultural norms. This is a problem for international human rights law generally, which faces the challenge of prescribing and implementing a set of uniform norms for the protection of individuals in

---

[81] See, for example, R. Goodland, 'Free, Prior and Informed Consent and the World Bank Group' (2004) 4 *Sustainable Development Law and Policy* 66.

[82] Commission on Human Rights, 'The Due Diligence Standard', n. 52, paras. 85–99.

very diverse contexts and cultures. At the same time, international human rights law protects the rights of groups to practise and enjoy their cultural autonomy.[83] The result is that some general human rights norms may conflict with cultural practices of groups.

Some autonomous groups have claimed that their cultural heritage includes differentiation between men and women and that this practice of gender distinction trumps international standards of sex equality. They propose that the status of women and men is framed by cultural, religious, political or social imperatives, which may preclude certain individual rights of women for the benefit of family order, discipline or other communal imperatives. In some instances, even where a practice is physically harmful, there are those who insist on its role as an essential part of a larger communal practice, the abolition of which will destroy the communal system.[84] MNCs are now being asked to respect and protect human rights within this context.

Theorists have had to refute this argument without subscribing to the cultural imperialism of the so-called Western powers that have wreaked havoc among thousands of cultures and groups throughout the world. The response to this problem has become more sensitive and sophisticated, balancing the importance of culture against the need to protect the individual.

One approach is to reconsider the narrow definition of culture. Traditionally, academics have perceived culture as petrified in a snapshot moment of time.[85] While this may be the view of people encountering certain cultures for the first time, it is short-sighted to believe that a culture has not evolved, influenced to greater or lesser degrees by externalities. This is not to say that because a culture has transmogrified in the

---

[83] International Covenant on Civil and Political Rights (entered into force 23 March 1976), 999 UNTS 171 (ICCPR), Art. 27.

[84] See K. Bowman, 'Comment: Bridging the Gap in the Hopes of Ending Female Genital Cutting' (2005) 3 *Santa Clara Journal of International Law* 132 (citing the former President of Kenya and his view of female genital cutting). See also E. Pagels, 'The Roots and Origins of Human Rights' in A. Henkin (ed.), *Human Dignity: The Internationalization of Human Rights* (Washington, DC: Aspen Institute for Humanities Studies, 1979), 1. The issue of cultural relativism came before the CEDAW committee in 1984 during Egypt's country report. General Assembly, 'Official Records of the General Assembly, Thirty-Ninth Session, Supplement No. 45: Report of the Committee on the Elimination of Discrimination against Women, Volume I (Second Session)', A/39/45 (27 June 1984), para. 209.

[85] For a discussion regarding cultural relativism, see Meyersfeld, *Domestic Violence*, n. 1, 103–04.

past, it is therefore legitimate to compel it to change in the future. What is clear, however, is that integrating global human rights norms into certain discrete cultures is not antithetical to the perpetuation of, or respect for, the integrity of those cultures. If anything, the gender analysis enables a more honest and deeper understanding of a community and how best to ensure that an MNC does not undo its systemic fabric.

Taking an unfiltered, pejorative view of certain cultural practices is dangerous, not only because the value of tradition deserves respect, but also because disregarding the cultural context of practices feeds a rift between communities, business and the international human rights system.[86] Nevertheless, culture or tradition cannot justify harm, especially where the cultural entity is open to change in other respects. Culture, after all, is not a justification for slavery, racism or other prohibited practices. If the cultural relativism debate continues to oscillate around the hub of gender equality, we need to ask why it is that to hate a black man is a prejudice but to hate a woman is a custom.[87]

MNCs are in a precarious situation where they are, by definition of their intervention, going to morph into and contribute to the change of culturally insulated communities. The very presence of the corporation in such a setting requires a delicate balance between respecting culture, ousting cruelty and advancing corporate interests. Current scholarship and international law maintain that diversity does not bar the formulation of principles that could be universally adopted within the contours of a group's specific cultural and traditional imperatives.[88]

This is an important balance that must be struck by both states, in the fulfilment of their international obligations, and corporations. There is no simple solution to the difficulty of balancing general human rights norms with cultural norms practised by certain groups. However, corporations could be guided by basic human rights principles relating to equality. If a corporation would oppose, for example, systematised racial inequality or slavery, it should adopt a similar approach to promoting gender equality.

---

[86] See, for example, Rio Tinto, 'Why Gender Matters: A Resource Guide for Integrating Gender Considerations into Communities Work at Rio Tinto' (2009), 5, www.riotinto.com/documents/ReportsPublications/Rio_Tinto_gender_guide.pdf (last accessed 24 January 2013).

[87] Meyersfeld, *Domestic Violence*, n. 1, 103–04.

[88] See S. E. Merry, 'Constructing a Global Law – Violence against Women and the Human Rights System' (2003) 28 *Law and Social Inquiry* 941, at 952.

Conclusion

This chapter has highlighted why a gender analysis is critical to human rights discourse, including the emerging area of business and human rights. The gender analysis is not about creating a parallel universe of considerations and policies. It is about an honest assessment of the ways in which gendered roles and expectations fuel differentiation and harm. It is this harm, a reality in almost every country in the world, which can be exacerbated by corporate activities. It can also be ameliorated by corporate policies and practices which, in turn, have the potential to enhance profit through a non-sexist approach to companies' operations.

Integrating a gender perspective into the development of the business and human rights principles is consistent with both international law and sustainable business operations. I have argued that a gendered analysis is not only about prioritising women; it is also about prying open hidden power disparities that may impede effective community engagement and business operations. This chapter has proposed a methodology for business entities to pursue a gendered approach to business and human rights.

An important step has been taken to include gendered considerations, albeit in a limited manner, in the GPs. It is now necessary to import specificity into the broad proposals and concretise international standards expected of companies in respect of gender equality, just as are demanded of corporations in respect of slavery or racism. This proposal is not merely about human rights standards or some altruistic call to equality. The non-sexist approach to a workforce and an approach that respects the nuanced needs of all affected by corporate activity may be commensurate with the long-term profitability of business. Corporate engagement with the goal of gender equality is indispensable to the realisation of human rights.

9

Due diligence and complicity: a relationship in need of clarification

SABINE MICHALOWSKI[*]

Introduction

In the context of corporate accountability, due diligence and complicity are two important concepts. The Merriam-Webster dictionary defines due diligence as 'the care that a reasonable person exercises to avoid harm to other persons or their property'. In the business context, due diligence refers to the 'research and analysis of a company or organization done in preparation for a business transaction',[1] or the 'duty of a firm's directors and officers to act prudently in evaluating associated risks in all transactions'.[2] Complicity, on the other hand, is described as 'association or participation in ... a wrongful act'.[3]

Due diligence and complicity are thus different notions. This chapter will explore the various possible connections between these two concepts. Questions arising in this respect include, for example, whether the assessment and avoidance of the risk of complicity is part of a company's due diligence responsibility. If so, can complicity liability arise even though the company acted with due diligence, but harm nevertheless occurs? And can due diligence responsibilities help to define the elements of complicity liability, with regard to both the question of which acts might result in liability of the company for third party wrongdoing, and which mental element is necessary in order to hold the corporation

[*] I would like to thank David Bilchitz and Judith Schönsteiner for insightful comments on previous drafts of this chapter, and Diana Guarnizo Peralta for her valuable research assistance.

[1] Merriam Webster Dictionary, www.merriam-webster.com/dictionary/due%20diligence (last accessed 17 October 2012).
[2] Business Dictionary, www.businessdictionary.com/definition/due-diligence.html (last accessed 17 October 2012).
[3] See www.merriam-webster.com/dictionary/complicity (last accessed 17 October 2012).

to account in such circumstances? Or does complicity liability define the content and scope of due diligence responsibilities?

These are complex questions, some of which the Special Representative of the Secretary-General on the Issue of Human Rights and Transnational Corporations and Other Business Enterprises (SRSG) touched upon at various stages of his mandate. In his report of April 2008, the SRSG suggested that

> the relationship between complicity and due diligence is clear and compelling: companies can avoid complicity by employing the due diligence processes described above – which, as noted, apply not only to their own activities but also to the relationships connected with them.[4]

This implies that compliance with the due diligence requirements set out by the SRSG prevents the occurrence of complicity. This could give rise to the assumption that, as a logical consequence, the exercise of human rights due diligence excludes liability for complicity if human rights violations nevertheless occur. Due diligence could thus be seen to serve as a defence against complicity charges.[5] However, in his Commentary to Principle 17 of the Guiding Principles (GPs), the SRSG explains that

> [c]onducting appropriate human rights due diligence should help business enterprises address the risk of legal claims against them by showing that they took every reasonable step to avoid involvement with an alleged human rights abuse. However, business enterprises conducting such due diligence should not assume that, by itself, this will automatically and fully absolve them from liability for causing or contributing to human rights abuses.[6]

This clarifies that even though human rights due diligence is regarded as a tool to assist with avoiding complicity in human rights violations, and might count in favour of a corporation when determining its liability for complicity, due diligence is not envisaged as providing a full legal defence against complicity charges. However, the Commentary is rather

---

[4] Human Rights Council, 'Protect, Respect and Remedy: A Framework for Business and Human Rights', A/HRC/8/5 (7 April 2008) (SRSG, '2008 Framework'), para. 81.

[5] For such an approach see, in particular, L. J. Dhooge, 'Due Diligence as a Defense to Corporate Liability Pursuant to the Alien Tort Statute' (2008) 22 *Emory International Law Review* 455.

[6] Human Rights Council, 'Guiding Principles on Business and Human Rights: Implementing the United Nations "Protect, Respect and Remedy" Framework', A/HRC/17/31 (21 March 2011) (SRSG, 'Guiding Principles').

unhelpful when it comes to shedding light on what, exactly, the relationship of complicity and due diligence is considered to be, and how companies can avoid complicity liability if compliance with the SRSG's due diligence framework is not, in itself, sufficient to guarantee the achievement of that goal.

This chapter will examine how the various documents issued by the SRSG perceive the relationship between complicity and due diligence. After introducing the concepts of complicity, the duty to respect human rights, and due diligence, I will analyse to what extent due diligence can act as a tool to avoid complicity in human rights violations, and whether due diligence can provide a defence against complicity actions.

The definition and interaction of the concepts of complicity, the duty to respect human rights, and due diligence in the SRSG framework

Part of the mandate of the SRSG was to 'research and clarify the implications for transnational corporations and other business enterprises of concepts such as "complicity"'.[7] This is not an easy task, as complicity is not a clearly defined notion. In the SRSG's 2007 report, corporate complicity was defined as 'an umbrella term for a range of ways in which companies may be liable for their participation in criminal or civil wrongs'.[8] The 2008 report elaborated that '[c]omplicity refers to indirect involvement by companies in human rights abuses – where the actual harm is committed by another party, including governments and non-State actors'.[9] A 2008 report that was specifically dedicated to 'Clarifying the Concepts of "Sphere of Influence" and "Complicity"' highlighted that

> [i]t is conceived as indirect involvement because the company itself does not actually carry out the abuse. In principle, complicity may be alleged in relation to knowingly contributing to any type of human rights abuse, whether of civil or political rights, or economic, social and cultural rights.[10]

---

[7] UN Office of the High Commissioner for Human Rights, 'Human Rights and Transnational Corporations and Other Business Enterprises', E/CN.4/RES/2005/69, para. 1(c).

[8] Human Rights Council, 'Business and Human Rights: Mapping International Standards of Responsibility and Accountability for Corporate Acts', A/HRC/4/035 (4 February 2007) (SRSG, '2007 Report'), para. 31.

[9] SRSG, '2008 Framework', n. 4, para. 73.

[10] Human Rights Council, 'Clarifying the Concepts of "Sphere of Influence" and "Complicity"', A/HRC/8/16 (15 May 2008) (SRSG, '2008 Complicity Report'), para. 30.

The concept of complicity is integrated into the Ruggie framework through the corporate responsibility to respect human rights, which requires businesses to 'avoid infringing on the human rights of others',[11] and includes a responsibility to avoid complicity in human rights violations.[12] In this respect, the SRSG explains that

> the key tools companies use to determine their human rights impacts for the purpose of fulfilling the responsibility to respect, whether human rights policies, impact assessments, integration policies and/or practices for tracking performance, should focus not only on the company's own business activities, but also on the relationships associated with those activities, to ensure that the company is not complicit, or otherwise implicated in human rights harms caused by others.[13]

This is where due diligence comes in, as '[t]o discharge the responsibility to respect requires due diligence',[14] which includes 'assessing actual and potential human rights impacts, integrating and acting upon the findings, tracking responses, and communicating how impacts are addressed'.[15] The responsibility to respect is thus not envisaged merely as a negative duty, as it requires human rights due diligence and thus positive acts.[16] Due diligence, in turn, is perceived as a tool which assists corporations in fulfilling their responsibility to respect human rights.

At first sight, one could think that the SRSG surpasses here the concept of the duty to respect which is usually understood to describe a duty not to cause harm. This is because the duty to avoid complicity could be understood as creating responsibility for third party behaviour, which resembles the duty to protect rather than the duty to respect.[17] However, the responsibility to avoid complicity refers to the avoidance of harm through one's own complicit behaviour. Any responsibility to

---

[11] SRSG, 'Guiding Principles', n. 6, Principle 11.

[12] SRSG, '2008 Framework', n. 4, para. 73; SRSG, '2008 Complicity Report', n. 10, para. 26; and SRSG, 'Guiding Principles', n. 6, Commentary to Principle 17.

[13] SRSG, '2008 Complicity Report', n. 10, para. 72.

[14] SRSG, '2008 Framework', n. 4, para. 56. See also SRSG, 'Guiding Principles', n. 6, Principle 17.

[15] SRSG, 'Guiding Principles', n. 6, Commentary to Principle 17.

[16] Human Rights Council, 'Business and Human Rights: Towards Operationalizing the "Protect, Respect and Remedy" Framework', A/HRC/11/13 (22 April 2009) (SRSG, '2009 Report'), para. 59.

[17] See D. Bilchitz, 'The Ruggie Framework: An Adequate Rubric for Corporate Human Rights Violations?' (2010) 7 SUR International Journal on Human Rights 199, at 204–05.

prevent harm caused by others is limited to that harm whose occurrence is facilitated or exacerbated by the acts of the company itself.

Due diligence refers to 'the steps a company must take to become aware of, prevent and address adverse human rights impacts'.[18] While due diligence thus primarily seems to be a procedural concept, its link with the duty to respect brings in a substantive side which requires that 'companies should look, at a minimum, to the international bill of human rights and the core conventions of the ILO' when determining the scope of their due diligence responsibilities.[19] This element has found expression in Guiding Principle 12. Guidance on how such a far-reaching responsibility can, in practice, be fulfilled with regard to the plethora of rights that need to be respected, is not provided.

It is not easy to determine how, exactly, the SRSG sees the relationship between complicity and due diligence. The Commentary to Guiding Principle 17 states that '[c]onducting appropriate human rights due diligence should help business enterprises address the risk of legal claims against them by showing that they took every reasonable step to avoid involvement with an alleged human rights abuse'. This seems to apply the general idea of due diligence as a tool which assists corporations in fulfilling their obligation to respect human rights to the particular case of the responsibility to avoid complicity. Two separate questions which are, to some extent, related, need to be addressed in this context: firstly, what can due diligence achieve as a tool to avoid complicity; and, secondly, what is the role of due diligence when a corporation is faced with complicity charges?

Due diligence as a tool to avoid complicity

Due diligence responsibilities are directed at risk management and, in the business and human rights context, are triggered by the realisation that carrying out business operations can create human rights-related risks. When considering the relationship between due diligence and complicity, the SRSG seems to focus primarily on the idea that complicity in human rights violations can be avoided by exercising appropriate due diligence. As part of the exercise of due diligence, companies should consider 'whether they might contribute to abuse through the

---

[18] SRSG, '2008 Framework', n. 4, para. 56. This is reflected in SRSG, 'Guiding Principles', n. 6, Principles 17–19.

[19] SRSG, '2008 Framework', n. 4, para. 58.

relationships connected to their activities, such as with business partners, suppliers, State agencies, and other non-State actors ... How far or how deep this process must go will depend on circumstances.'[20] Thus, an assessment of potential complicity as a consequence of its activities is part of a corporation's due diligence responsibilities. Indeed, to exercise human rights due diligence is promoted as '[t]he appropriate corporate response to managing the risks of infringing the rights of others ... That very process helps companies address their responsibilities to individuals and communities that they impact.'[21] The envisaged responsibilities are far reaching, as human rights due diligence requires 'a comprehensive, proactive attempt to uncover human rights risks, actual and potential, over the entire life cycle of a project or business activity, with the aim of avoiding and mitigating those risks'.[22] The reason why applying due diligence might help to avoid complicity is that 'companies can become aware of, prevent and address risks of complicity by integrating the common features of legal and societal benchmarks into their due diligence processes'.[23]

The scope of the due diligence responsibility to avoid complicity

While this sounds fairly straightforward, it raises the question of whether the concept of complicity is defined clearly enough to allow for an assessment of complicity risks as part of due diligence processes. The various SRSG documents that engage with the question of complicity consistently stress that complicity has a legal as well as an extra-legal social meaning. According to the SRSG, the two are not identical, as the social understanding of complicity goes beyond its legal definition.[24] To evaluate the risk of complicity is further complicated by the fact that '[w]hat constitutes complicity in both legal and non-legal terms is not uniform, nor is it static'.[25] Instead:

> Owing to the relatively limited case history, especially in relation to companies rather than individuals, and given the substantial variations

---

[20] SRSG, '2008 Complicity Report', n. 10, para. 19.
[21] Human Rights Council, 'Business and Human Rights: Further Steps Toward the Operationalization of the "Protect, Respect and Remedy" Framework', A/HRC/14/27 (9 April 2010) (SRSG, '2010 Report'), para. 79.
[22] SRSG, '2008 Complicity Report', n. 10, para. 71.   [23] Ibid., para. 32.
[24] SRSG, 'Guiding Principles', n. 6, Commentary to Principle 17; SRSG, '2007 Report', n. 8, paras. 31–32; and SRSG, '2008 Framework', n. 4, paras. 76–78.
[25] SRSG, '2008 Complicity Report', n. 10, para. 70.

in definitions of complicity within and between the legal and non-legal spheres, it is not possible to specify definitive tests for what constitutes complicity in any given context.[26]

Therefore, 'an appreciation of how both the law and various social actors might view company contributions to human rights abuse and the possible consequences of those views ... may seem a daunting task'.[27] However:

> Despite this messy reality, the evidence to date lends itself to several conclusions. First, knowingly providing a substantial contribution to human rights abuses could result in a company being held accountable in both legal and non-legal settings. Second, being seen to benefit from abuse may attract the attention of social actors even if it does not lead to legal liability. Third, and similarly, mere presence in contexts where abuses are taking place may attract attention from other social actors but is unlikely, by itself, to lead to legal liability. In short, both operating in contexts where abuses occur and the appearance of benefiting from such abuses should serve as red flags for companies to ensure that they exercise due diligence, adapted for the specific context of their operations.[28]

This makes clear that the scope of due diligence responsibilities varies according to the circumstances.[29] Operating in contexts with an increased risk that complicity might occur, such as conflict zones, heightens the need for assessing the risk of complicity. The statement also shows that a corporation's responsibility to avoid complicity goes further than potential legal obligations in this respect. Indeed, for the SRSG, to avoid 'complicity is part and parcel of the responsibility to respect human rights, and entails acting with due diligence to avoid knowingly contributing to human rights abuses, *whether or not there is a risk of legal liability*' (emphasis added).[30]

Due diligence responsibilities thus do not primarily focus on avoiding legal liability for complicity, but rather on preventing the occurrence of human rights violations through refraining from complicit behaviour. Under the SRSG framework, corporations should adopt a wide-ranging definition of complicity when setting in place their due diligence policies, whatever the precise scope of the legal obligations in this respect.

---

[26] SRSG, '2008 Framework', n. 4, para. 76.
[27] SRSG, '2008 Complicity Report', n. 10, para. 32.
[28] *Ibid.*, para. 70. See also SRSG, '2008 Framework', n. 4, paras. 73–74.
[29] See also SRSG, 'Guiding Principles', n. 6, Principle 23 and Commentary.
[30] SRSG, '2008 Complicity Report', n. 10, para. 71.

However, the SRSG's statements concerning the definitions of complicity are very vague.[31] It is, for example, not discussed at all under what circumstances, if any, behaviour such as mere silence,[32] mere presence in a country, or benefiting from abuse committed by others could amount to non-legal complicity. This makes it difficult to define the scope of due diligence that is required and to determine which corporate activities, and which consequences thereof, need to be avoided.

When examining the boundaries of due diligence responsibilities in the context of complicity, it seems important to unpack the various potential meanings of complicity and which of these might result in legal liability as opposed to 'mere' moral complicity and social disapproval. One possible way to approach this issue is the differentiation of direct, beneficial and silent complicity adopted by the Global Compact and referred to by the SRSG in one of his reports.[33] Direct complicity 'occurs when a company knowingly assists a State in violating human rights';[34] beneficial complicity, where 'a company benefits directly from human rights abuses';[35] and silent complicity refers to the situation where a company fails 'to raise the question of systematic or continuous human rights violations in its interactions with the appropriate authorities'.[36]

Silent complicity could thus be triggered through presence and investment in a country where large-scale gross human rights abuses occur.[37] In this type of scenario, it will often be difficult to establish a link

---

[31] The Commentary to Guiding Principle 19 shows the complexity of some of the related issues rather than providing useful advice, given the vagueness of the reflections presented.

[32] On this point, see the in-depth analysis provided in Chapter 10.

[33] SRSG, '2008 Complicity Report', n. 10, para. 58, quoting Commentary on Principle 2 from the Global Compact, www.unglobalcompact.org/AboutTheGC/TheTenPrinciples/Principle2.html (last accessed 17 October 2012).

[34] Ibid.   [35] Ibid.

[36] Ibid. The distinction between these three forms of complicity has also found its way into the academic legal discussion of complicity; see, for example, A. Ramasastry, 'Corporate Complicity: From Nuremberg to Rangoon – An Examination of Forced Labor Cases and their Impact on the Liability of Multinational Corporations' (2002) 20 Berkeley Journal of International Law 102–04; J. Clough, 'Punishing the Parent: Corporate Criminal Complicity in Human Rights Abuses' (2008) 33 Brooklyn Journal of International Law 909–10; E. Engle, 'Extraterritorial Corporate Criminal Liability: A Remedy for Human Rights Violations?' (2006) 20 Saint John's Journal of Legal Commentary 297–98; and A. Triponel, 'Business and Human Rights Law: Diverging Trends in the United States and France' (2007) 23 American University International Law Review 855, at 899–903.

[37] Ramasastry, 'Corporate Complicity', n. 36, 104.

between the violations that are committed and the corporate behaviour in question that would be sufficient to trigger legal responsibility.[38] Nevertheless, a moral duty to speak out, and, in extreme cases, even to divest, might exist, particularly where gross violations occur on a large scale;[39] where the corporation has a close relationship with the victims; or where it exercises a strong influence on the wrongdoer.[40] In these situations, due diligence responsibilities could be heightened.

Beneficial complicity can, for example, arise where governments violate human rights in order to secure investments or suppress protest directed against a corporation,[41] but also when the company takes advantage of the poor human rights situation in the country because this provides the opportunity of making use of cheap labour, as was the case in South Africa under apartheid.[42] Even though it has been argued that legal liability should be extended to situations where knowledge of the large-scale human rights violations is combined with 'acceptance of direct economic benefit arising from the violations and continued partnership with a host government',[43] this form of complicity will primarily give rise to social rather than legal consequences.[44]

Direct complicity best fits the legal definition of complicity, though with the caveat that legal complicity can take different forms in different countries, and also might vary depending on whether the liability is based in criminal or tort law.[45] In several of his reports, the SRSG attempted to undertake some analysis of the legal notion of complicity. When describing its contours, he mainly referred to the principles governing liability for aiding and abetting international crimes.[46] Their

---

[38] *Ibid.* See also Triponel, 'Business and Human Rights Law', n. 36, 903. The International Commission of Jurists, 'Report of the Expert Legal Panel on Corporate Complicity in International Crimes: Corporate Complicity and Accounting Liability', vol. 1: 'Facing the Facts and Charting a Legal Path' (Geneva: International Commission of Jurists, 2008), 14–15 (ICJ, 'Complicity Report'), suggests that under certain limited circumstances even legal liability might be a possibility.

[39] Ramasastry, 'Corporate Complicity', n. 36, 104; and A. Triponel, 'Business and Human Rights Law', n. 36.

[40] ICJ, 'Complicity Report', vol. 1, n. 38, 15.

[41] See Commentary on Principle 2 from the Global Compact, n. 33; and Ramasastry, 'Corporate Complicity', n. 36, 102.

[42] Triponel, 'Business and Human Rights Law', n. 36, 901–02.

[43] Ramasastry, 'Corporate Complicity', n. 36, 150.

[44] Clough, 'Punishing the Parent', n. 36, 910; and ICJ, 'Complicity Report', vol. 1, n. 38, 15.

[45] ICJ, 'Complicity Report', n. 38, vols. 1–111.

[46] SRSG, '2008 Complicity Report', n. 10, paras. 34–44, with particular reference to the principles developed by the *ad hoc* international criminal tribunals, such as *Prosecutor*

relevance stems from case law in the US where courts rely on principles of international criminal law to determine civil liability in the context of litigation under the Alien Tort Claims Act (ATCA) against corporations for complicity in violations of the law of nations, including violations of certain human rights.[47] While corporations can, to some extent, face complicity liability under the domestic law of certain countries,[48] the significance attached by the SRSG to the ATCA seems justified on the basis that the most prominent examples of litigation to hold corporations accountable for their complicity in human rights violations have taken place in the USA under this legislation.

The ATCA provides that '[t]he district courts shall have original jurisdiction of any civil action by an alien for a tort only, committed in violation of the law of nations or a treaty of the United States'.[49] It was enacted as part of the Judiciary Act of 1789 to deal with cases such as piracy.[50] For about 200 years the statute lay forgotten until it was rediscovered by human rights lawyers and tested in *Filartiga v. Pena-Irala*, where the court determined that the ATCA allowed victims to sue in US courts for serious violations of international human rights law.[51] A string of lawsuits for gross human rights violations followed, including against multinational corporations.[52]

The future of the ATCA as a vehicle to achieve corporate accountability for complicity in human rights violations is currently uncertain. In April 2013, the US Supreme Court decided in *Kiobel* v. *Royal Dutch Petroleum Co.* that because of a presumption against the extraterritorial

---

v. *Furundzija*, Case No. IT-95–17/1, Trial Chamber Judgment (10 December 1998); *Prosecutor* v. *Vasiljevic*, Case No. IT-98–32-A, Appeals Judgment (25 February 2004); *Prosecutor* v. *Blaskic*, Case No. IT-95–14-A, Appeals Judgment (29 July 2004); and *Prosecutor* v. *Simic*, Case No. IT-95–9-A, Appeals Judgment (28 November 2006).

[47] See, for example, *Doe* v. *Unocal Corp.*, 395 F.3d 932 (9th Cir. 2002); *Khulumani* v. *Barclay National Bank*, 504 F.3d 254 (2nd Cir. 2007).

[48] See, in this regard, Chapter 14.

[49] Alien Tort Claims Act (ATCA), 28 U.S.C. § 1350 (2006).

[50] *Sosa* v. *Alvarez-Machain*, 542 US 692 (2004), 724, per Justice Souter.

[51] *Filartiga* v. *Pena-Irala*, 630 F.2d 876 (2nd Cir. 1980), 880.

[52] For example, *Sosa* v. *Alvarez-Machain*, n. 50. Talisman Energy was sued for aiding and abetting genocide and other gross human rights violations committed by the Sudanese government in the context of the development of oil concessions in southern Sudan (*Presbyterian Church of Sudan* v. *Talisman Energy, Inc.*, 2009 WL 3151804 (2nd Cir. 2009)); and Shell Oil Company for complicity in the repression of Ogoni protests against the environmental damages caused by oil platforms and in the execution of Ken Saro-Wiwa (*Wiwa* v. *Royal Dutch Petroleum*, 2002 WL 319887 (SDNY. 2002).

application of US legislation, the ATCA in principle does not apply to human rights violations that occurred outside of the USA.[53] '[E]ven where the claims touch and concern the territory of the United States, they must do so with sufficient force to displace the presumption against extraterritorial application.'[54] Under what circumstances a sufficient link exists that will allow future claims against corporations under the ATCA to succeed remains to be tested. However, whether or not corporate liability under the ATCA will continue to exist, a closer look at the principles developed by US courts might shed light on corporate legal responsibilities beyond the narrow context of the ATCA itself, given that these courts have interpreted and applied the relevant international criminal law principles to corporate complicity, and, as a result, have highly influenced the debate on corporate complicity in recent years worldwide.[55]

Among US courts, agreement seems to exist that 'the *actus reus* of aiding and abetting in international criminal law requires practical assistance, encouragement, or moral support which has a *substantial effect* on the perpetration of the crime'.[56] Less straightforward is how to apply this rather abstract definition, which stems from the context of individual criminal liability for aiding and abetting atrocious crimes, to corporate civil liability. Many courts seem to find it counter-intuitive to impose liability on corporations for an act that could, in the abstract, be regarded as an ordinary business transaction. Where the acts a company is accused of are not 'inherently criminal or wrongful',[57] but rather facially neutral, the *actus reus* analysis of liability is complicated, as the harmful effect of the corporate acts can then only be determined by a

---

[53] *Kiobel* v. *Royal Dutch Petroleum Co.*, 2013 WL 1628935, para. 9.   [54] *Ibid.*, para. 10.

[55] See, for example, ICJ, 'Complicity Report', n. 38 vol. iii, n. 38.

[56] *Khulumani* v. *Barclay National Bank*, 504 F.3d 254, n. 47, 277, per Judge Katzman; *In re South African Apartheid Litigation*, 617 F.Supp.2d 228 (SDNY 2009), 257. See also *Presbyterian Church of Sudan* v. *Talisman Energy, Inc.*, 374 F.Supp.2d 331 (SDNY 2005), 337–38 and 340; *Doe* v. *Unocal Corp.*, n. 47, 951. Courts in ATCA cases tend to derive this standard from international criminal law cases such as *Prosecutor* v. *Furundzija*, Case No. IT-95-17/1, n. 46, para. 235; *Prosecutor* v. *Tadic*, Case No. IT-94-1-T, Trial Chamber Judgment ('*Tadic I*'), para. 688 (7 May 1997); *Prosecutor* v. *Blagojevic and Jokic*, Case No. IT-02-60-A, Appeal Judgment, paras. 127 and 134 (9 May 2007); and *Accord United States* v. *Von Weizsacker* ('*The Ministries Case*'), in *Fourteen Trials of War Criminals Before the Nuremberg Military Tribunals*, 478 (1950).

[57] *The Presbyterian Church of Sudan* v. *Talisman Energy, Inc.*, n. 56, 261.

thorough case-by-case analysis. Instead of rising to this task and evaluating whether the relevant corporate acts amounted to practical assistance that had a substantial effect on the violations committed – and thereby providing guidance to corporations with regard to the distinction between acceptable and unlawful business practices – some courts simply forego the *actus reus* analysis and rest their judgment decisively on an assessment of the mental state with which the acts of assistance were carried out.[58]

The issue was, however, discussed in some detail in the context of the South African apartheid litigation against a variety of multinational corporations for aiding and abetting the international law violations committed by the apartheid regime. On appeal to the Second Circuit, Judge Korman (dissenting) regarded the complaints as being about nothing other than condemning the defendants for having done business with the apartheid regime,[59] something which in itself would not be sufficient to trigger legal liability for complicity. Indeed:

> It is (or should be) undisputed that simply doing business with a state or individual who violates the law of nations is insufficient to create liability under customary international law. International law does not impose liability for declining to boycott a pariah state or to shun a war criminal. Aiding a criminal 'is not the same thing as aiding and abetting [his or her] alleged human rights abuses'.[60]

However, corporate legal complicity liability may arise if it can be established that a corporation facilitated 'the commission of human rights violations by providing the principal tortfeasor with the tools, instrumentalities, or services to commit those violations'.[61] In the apartheid litigation case, the complaints were upheld in the District Court to the extent that the services and goods supplied by the defendant corporations were specifically designed for harmful purposes or provided the direct means for carrying out gross human rights violations. The provision of goods, such as money, that are inherently neutral, and which

---

[58] The decision in *Presbyterian Church of Sudan v. Talisman Energy, Inc.*, n. 56, provides a good example of this.

[59] *Khulumani* v. *Barclay National Bank*, n. 47, 294.

[60] *In re South African Apartheid Litigation*, n. 56, 257; and *Mastafa* v. *Australian Wheat Board Ltd and Banque Nationale de Paris Paribas*, 2008 WL 4378443 (SDNY), 4.

[61] *Khulumani* v. *Barclay National Bank*, n. 47, 289–90, per Judge Hall.

cannot, by their very nature, provide the instrument with which violations are carried out, was, on the other hand, found to be too remote to
amount to substantial assistance by the companies in the crimes of the
apartheid regime.[62]

This is where it becomes particularly apparent that due diligence
responsibilities envisaged by the SRSG surpass existing legal obligations
to refrain from complicit behaviour. While courts stress that doing
business with a regime that commits gross human rights violations in
and of itself is not sufficient to create legal complicity liability of corporations, the SRSG observes that

> [a] company should ensure that it is not implicated in third party harm to
> rights through its relationships with such parties. This possibility can
> arise from a company's business activities, including the provision or
> contracting of goods, services, and even non-business activities, such as
> lending equipment or vehicles. Therefore, a company needs to under-
> stand the track records of those entities with which it deals in order to
> assess whether it might contribute to or be associated with harm caused
> by entities with which it conducts, or is considering conducting business
> or other activities. This analysis of relationships will include looking at
> instances where the company might be seen as complicit in abuse caused
> by others.[63]

Thus, due diligence responsibilities are based on the assumption that
mere business relationships can have an adverse human rights impact
which needs to be avoided, even though it would not give rise to legal
complicity liability. Due diligence responsibilities consequently not only
include forms of complicity, such as silent and beneficial complicity, that
are widely outside the scope of legal complicity, but moreover apply a
broader approach to the definition of direct complicity than is covered
by legal obligations.

Due diligence responsibilities to avoid complicity thus complement
legal complicity liability. First, while there is some overlap between the
two concepts, legal complicity liability seems to set no more than a
minimum standard of the kind of complicit behaviour that needs to be
avoided. Moreover, the focus of the two concepts is different. Legal
complicity liability is reactive as it aims to remedy a violation that has

---

[62] See also *In re South African Apartheid Litigation*, n. 56, 258. For a critical analysis of this
approach see S. Michalowski, 'No Complicity Liability for Funding Gross Human Rights
Violations?' (2012) 30:2 *Berkeley Journal of International Law* 451, at 459–70.

[63] SRSG, '2008 Complicity Report', n. 10, para. 22.

already occurred and determines the circumstances in which the corporate actor can be sufficiently linked to the harm caused by the third party, in order to justify the imposition of some form of legal responsibility towards the victims of violations. Due diligence responsibilities, on the other hand, are forward-looking and preventive. Given the reactive nature and limitations of legal complicity liability, due diligence responsibilities that require avoiding legal as well as extra-legal forms of complicity therefore allow for a much wider approach to the prevention of human rights violations by third parties than legal complicity liability can achieve. From a victim perspective this is a big improvement, as both the narrow legal definition of complicity and difficulties regarding the burden of proving a sufficient impact of the company's activities on violations committed by third parties, make it difficult to succeed with legal complicity claims.

Despite these positive aspects of due diligence responsibilities to avoid complicity, it is a problem that the violation of due diligence responsibilities does not have enforceable consequences. Victims will rather have to rely on the corporation's willingness to provide remediation.

Moreover, the contours of extra-legal forms of complicity need further clarity in order to provide guidance to corporations as to the exact nature of the behaviour they need to avoid. It is particularly confusing that it seems as if, for the SRSG, 'being seen to benefit from abuse', or being seen to contribute to adverse human rights impacts,[64] can trigger complicity. According to the SRSG's definition of complicity, the concept of complicity 'refers to indirect involvement by companies in human rights abuses – where the actual harm is committed by another party'.[65] It is clearly misleading to suggest that being seen to be involved, rather than being involved, in abuses carried out by third parties, can amount to any type of complicity. What might be possible is that where a sufficiently close relationship between a corporation, corporate activities and the wrongdoer exists, a suspicion of complicity may arise. This, however, is different from actual complicity. To conflate the two creates the impression that corporations should be more concerned with avoiding reputational damage than with avoiding complicit behaviour, and that this might be the primary purpose of human rights due diligence.[66]

---

[64] *Ibid.*, para. 70.   [65] SRSG, '2008 Complicity Report', n. 10, para. 30.
[66] See Chapter 4.

Mens rea *considerations*

As due diligence is a concept that defines positive responsibilities designed to ensure that the risk of human rights violations is as far as possible avoided or minimised, it requires proactive behaviour which includes, in the words of the SRSG, that the corporation 'become aware of, prevent and address adverse human rights impacts'.[67] It thus includes a responsibility to investigate and obtain information. To the extent that a corporation does not have knowledge it should have had, it is in violation of its due diligence responsibilities.

A comparable standard might apply in cases of civil legal complicity, as many legal systems impose liability where harm was foreseeable, whether or not the accomplice had actual knowledge. As the International Commission of Jurists explains, 'the law of civil remedies will often require a company to undertake a due diligence inquiry: an investigation and inventory of the potential risks to third parties that could be connected with its activities'.[68] Where this is the case, the relationship between legal complicity liability and due diligence responsibilities would work as follows: The scope of due diligence responsibilities would define to what extent the corporation is under a need to investigate and thus should know of risks, while complicity liability would provide legal remedies where due diligence was not carried out and harm occurred as a result.

However, if complicity liability is determined under criminal law standards,[69] in particular according to international criminal law,[70] which is also the standard applied in civil complicity litigation under the ATCA,[71] actual knowledge is necessary. The only US case which regarded it as sufficient that the corporation should have been aware of the consequences of its acts is *Doe* v. *Unocal*,[72] a case in which residents of Myanmar brought actions against several oil companies for aiding and

---

[67] SRSG, '2008 Framework', n. 4, para. 56. See also SRSG, 'Guiding Principles', n. 6, Principle 17.

[68] ICJ, 'Complicity Report', n. 38, vol. III, 18.   [69] *Ibid.*, vol. II, 21–25.

[70] *Prosecutor* v. *Furundzija*, n. 46, paras. 236–49; *Prosecutor* v. *Blaskic*, n. 46, para. 50; *Prosecutor* v. *Mrksic*, Case No. IT-95-13/1-A, Judgment, 5 May 2009, paras. 49 and 159.

[71] See, for example, *Doe, et al.*, v. *Exxon Mobil Corporation, et al.*, 654 F.3d 11 (DC Cir. 2011), para. 19; *Cabello* v. *Fernandez-Larios*, 402 F.3d 1148 (11th Cir. 2005), 1158; *In re 'Agent Orange' Product Liability Litigation*, 373 F.Supp.2d 7 (EDNY 2005), 54; and *Almog* v. *Arab Bank*, 471 F.Supp.2d 257 (EDNY 2007), 291.

[72] 395 F.3d 932 (9th Cir. 2002).

abetting human rights violations perpetrated by the Myanmar military in furtherance of an oil pipeline project. Relying on the *Furundzija* decision of the Trial Chamber of the International Criminal Tribunal for the former Yugoslavia (ICTY), the court set the *mens rea* standard to be one of 'actual or constructive (i.e., "reasonabl[e]") "knowledge that [the accomplice's] actions will assist the perpetrator in the commission of the crime"'.[73] Applying this to the facts of the case, the court regarded it as sufficient that 'Unocal knew or should reasonably have known that its conduct – including the payments and the instructions where to provide security and build infrastructure – would assist or encourage the Myanmar Military to subject Plaintiffs to forced labor'.[74]

However, it is questionable that *Furundzija* can be relied upon to support the 'should have known' standard adopted in *Unocal*. In the relevant paragraph of *Furundzija*, the Tribunal concludes that 'if it were not proven that a driver would reasonably have known that the purpose of the trip was an unlawful execution, he would be acquitted'.[75] This suggests, in line with other ICTY cases, that actual knowledge is required, but can be proved if, based on all known circumstances of the case, it is reasonable to infer that the defendant 'must have known'.[76] Constructive knowledge thus refers to situations where, for evidentiary reasons, the presence of actual knowledge needs to be inferred from all surrounding facts.[77] This is different from a 'should have known' standard which would be satisfied even if no such likelihood can be established, but where the accomplice should have had the relevant knowledge had due diligence been exercised.[78]

Regarding the question of what, exactly, a corporation needs to have known in order to incur complicity liability, an analogy with ICTY case law suggests that the corporation would need to have acted with 'knowledge that the acts performed by the aider and abettor assist the

---

[73] *Ibid.*, 950, quoting *Prosecutor v. Furundzija*, n. 46, para. 245.   [74] *Ibid.*, 953.
[75] *Ibid.*
[76] See, for example, *Prosecutor v. Tadic*, n. 56, para. 659, though not in the context of aiding and abetting liability; *Prosecutor v. Blaskic*, n. 46, para. 599.
[77] *Prosecutor v. Kayishema*, Case No. ICTR-95-1-T, Judgment, 21 May 1999, para. 134; *Prosecutor v. Kordic*, Case No. IT-95-14/2-T, Judgment, 26 February 2001, para. 185. See also *In re South African Apartheid Litigation*, n. 56, 265.
[78] R. Mares, 'Defining the Limits of Corporate Responsibilities against the Concept of Legal Positive Obligations' (2009) 40 *George Washington International Law Review* 1157, 1205–07.

commission of a specific crime by the principal'.[79] However, this does not mean that the corporation would need to have acted with knowledge of 'the precise crime that was intended and which in the event was committed'. Knowledge that 'one of a number of crimes will probably be committed',[80] and thus of the type of crime, is instead sufficient. Therefore, a corporation that knows 'that the equipment the business is selling is likely to be used by a buyer for one of a number of crimes would not escape liability because there is uncertainty as to the exact crime intended'.[81]

Where the *mens rea* requirement for complicity liability is one of actual knowledge, liability decisively depends on the amount of knowledge a corporation can be proven to have had. Corporations are thus invited to stay ignorant about potential complicity in human rights violations in order to avoid complicity liability. This is where due diligence responsibilities to become aware of the human rights impact of corporate activities gain importance. Corporations can then no longer hide behind their ignorance with regard to human rights violations. Due diligence determines the standard of knowledge a corporation is expected to have and, to the extent that no such knowledge exists, imposes a responsibility to collect the necessary information. The mere failure to conduct an assessment of complicity risks, to follow red flags that might be arising in the context of a business relationship, and/or to acquire the relevant information to avoid complicity might therefore violate due diligence responsibilities, but it does not make the corporation complicit in the violations that occur.[82]

Due diligence responsibilities could attain particular relevance in the context of the current uncertainty surrounding legal complicity liability under the ATCA. Even to the extent that corporate complicity cases can still be pursued in the aftermath of the Supreme Court decision in *Kiobel*,[83] another challenge to legal liability for aiding and abetting gross human rights violations under the ATCA is posed by the decision

[79] *Prosecutor* v. *Tadic*, Case No. IT-94-1-A, Judgment, 15 July 1999, para. 229. See also *Prosecutor* v. *Vasiljevic*, Case No. IT-98-32-T, 29 November 2002, para. 71; *Prosecutor* v. *Blaskic*, n. 46, at para. 45.

[80] *Prosecutor* v. *Furundzija*, n. 46, at para. 246; *Prosecutor* v. *Blaskic*, n. 46, at para. 50.

[81] ICJ, 'Complicity Report', n. 38, vol. II, 21.

[82] R. Mares, 'Defining the Limits', n. 78, 1212.

[83] *Kiobel* v. *Royal Dutch Petroleum Co.*, 2013 WL 1628935.

in *Presbyterian Church of Sudan v. Talisman Energy, Inc.*[84] In that case, the court departed from the *mens rea* standard of actual knowledge and instead required that the corporation has to have acted with the primary purpose of facilitating these violations. While companies might sometimes knowingly accept that their activities will almost certainly contribute to gross human rights violations that are being carried out, particularly when working in countries with poor human rights records, or in the middle of armed conflicts, they will only very rarely act with the aim or wish to facilitate them.[85] The controversy among US courts regarding the applicable *mens rea* standard[86] is thus hugely relevant because if the stringent *mens rea* standard of primary purpose prevails, complicity liability under the ATCA would be limited to very extreme cases indeed, and might in practice even approach a 'vanishing point'.[87] To the extent that the primary purpose standard is favoured, due diligence responsibilities might thus become the most important means to avoid the occurrence of and achieve some accountability for corporate complicity.

Due diligence as a defence against complicity charges?

This leaves examination of what happens if due diligence is exercised but a corporation is nevertheless accused of having been complicit in human rights violations carried out by third parties. If due diligence imposes an obligation of conduct rather than result,[88] a corporation that employs

---

[84] *The Presbyterian Church of Sudan v. Talisman Energy, Inc.*, n. 56, 258–59.

[85] But see *In Re: Chiquita Brands International, Inc., Alien Tort Statute and Shareholder Derivative Litigation*, 792 F.Supp.2d 1301 (SD Fla. 2011), and *Sarei v. Rio Tinto*, 2011 WL 5041927 (CA 9 (Cal.)), for cases where the courts accepted that the plaintiffs had sufficiently alleged that the defendant corporations acted with the purpose of facilitating violations of the law of nations.

[86] In favour of a *mens rea* standard of knowledge see, for example, *Doe, et al., v. Exxon Mobil Corporation, et al.*, 654 F.3d 11 (DC Cir. 2011); *Doe v. Unocal*, n. 47, 950–51; *Cabello v. Fernandez-Larios*, n. 71, 1158; *In re 'Agent Orange' Product Liability Litigation*, n. 71, 54; and *Almog v. Arab Bank*, n. 71, 291. A *mens rea* standard of purpose was accepted by *In Re: Chiquita Brands International, Inc., Alien Tort Statute and Shareholder Derivative Litigation*, 792 F.Supp.2d 1301 (SD Fla. 2011). The question was left open in *Sarei v. Rio Tinto*, n. 85, 26.

[87] *Kiobel v. Royal Dutch Petroleum Co.*, 621 F.3d 111 (2nd Cir. 2010), 270, in a decision rejecting an *en banc* rehearing, at 271, per Chief Justice Jacobs.

[88] J. H. Knox, 'Horizontal Human Rights Law' (2008) 102 *American Journal of International Law* 22.

the required human rights due diligence would not be responsible for human rights violations that nevertheless occur, as the responsibility is not directed at preventing their occurrence, but rather at employing the required diligence in attempting to avoid it. Complicity liability, on the other hand, arises where, regardless of the corporation's undertaking of due diligence, its activities had a substantial effect on violations committed by others. This is maybe where the relationship between due diligence and complicity becomes most interesting, as it raises the question of whether, if human rights violations are committed by third parties despite an exercise of due diligence on the part of the company, the latter is exempt from liability for contributing to these violations, or whether liability can nevertheless exist.

This question was addressed in some of the SRSG documents. As already stated, the SRSG report issued in April 2008 suggested, rather categorically, that 'the relationship between complicity and due diligence is clear and compelling: companies can avoid complicity by employing the due diligence processes described above – which, as noted, apply not only to their own activities but also to the relationships connected with them'.[89]

If corporations can avoid complicity by employing human rights due diligence, this seems to suggest that as a consequence of complying with their due diligence responsibilities, corporations cannot be held liable for complicity if human rights violations nevertheless occur. Thus understood, due diligence would serve as a defence against complicity charges.[90] However, in later documents, the SRSG made it clear that this was not how he envisaged the effect of human rights due diligence on complicity charges. In 'Clarifying the Concepts of "Sphere of Influence" and "Complicity"', a report published in May 2008, it was rather emphasised that compliance with due diligence would not automatically award protection against legal liability, although it 'should go a long way in improving the company's ability to recognize and act on risks of complicity, and to highlight to stakeholders that it is serious about not contributing to the abuses of others'.[91]

---

[89] SRSG, '2008 Framework', n. 4, para. 81.
[90] For such an approach see, in particular, Dhooge, 'Due Diligence', n. 5, 455–98.
[91] SRSG, '2008 Complicity Report', n. 10, para. 32.

In his 2010 report, the SRSG addressed the same issue in the following words:

> Conducting due diligence enables companies to identify and prevent adverse human rights impacts ... In Alien Tort Statute and similar suits, proof that the company took every reasonable step to avoid involvement in the alleged violation can only count in its favour. However, the Special Representative would not support proposals that conducting human rights due diligence, by itself, should automatically and fully absolve a company from Alien Tort Statute or similar liability.[92]

The same position was taken in the Commentary to Guiding Principle 17, according to which:

> Conducting appropriate human rights due diligence should help business enterprises address the risk of legal claims against them by showing that they took every reasonable step to avoid involvement with an alleged human rights abuse. However, business enterprises conducting such due diligence should not assume that, by itself, this will automatically and fully absolve them from liability for causing or contributing to human rights abuses.

Thus, apart from the report of April 2008,[93] which might give rise to the contrary assumption, all other documents issued by the SRSG consistently suggest that human rights due diligence is not envisaged as providing a full defence against complicity charges. Due diligence can assist a corporation with improving its human rights record with regard to complicity, and compliance with human rights due diligence requirements might be looked upon favourably by a court if a corporation faces complicity charges. However, while limiting the risk of complicity liability, it will not automatically exempt corporations from it.

The insistence that complicity can be prevented by exercising human rights due diligence is not easy to reconcile with the statement that compliance with human rights due diligence does not provide a guarantee that legal complicity charges can thereby be avoided.[94] Here,

---

[92] SRSG, '2010 Report', n. 21, para. 86; with specific reference to Dhooge, 'Due Diligence', n. 5, thereby clearly rejecting his plea in favour of a due diligence defence against complicity charges.

[93] SRSG, '2008 Framework', n. 4, para. 81.

[94] For a similar point see P. Muchlinski, 'Comments on the Draft Guiding Principles for Business and Human Rights' [DOC] (24 January 2011), www.business-humanrights. org/SpecialRepPortal/Home/Protect-Respect-Remedy-Framework/GuidingPrinciples/ Submissions (last accessed 17 October 2012).

it becomes important to consider more closely what, exactly, due diligence responsibilities to avoid complicity involve. So far, the discussion has mostly focused on due diligence responsibilities to acquire information about potential complicity risks. However, the more significant question in the current context is whether the responsibilities stop there, or whether they go further and include the responsibility to act upon that information in order to avoid the complicity risk from materialising.

According to the SRSG, the due diligence responsibility to avoid complicity extends to acting on risks of complicity,[95] preventing 'adverse human rights impacts' and taking 'every reasonable step to avoid involvement in the alleged violation'.[96] The issue was perhaps most explicitly addressed in his 2009 report, where he emphasised that how the company responds to the information it acquires about complicity risks will determine whether it can avoid complicity liability through its human rights due diligence enquiry. If 'the company gains knowledge of possible human rights violations it may commit or be involved in, does nothing to act on it, [and] the violations occur',[97] it faces the risk of complicity liability.

If this is true, properly carried out human rights due diligence should not leave any room for the occurrence of legal complicity. Calls that due diligence should set a milestone for expected behaviour, with the consequence that due diligence compliance would provide the corporation with a defence against complicity actions, for example under the ATCA,[98] are therefore understandable.[99] However, from a legal perspective, outside of cases where civil complicity liability can be triggered by

---

[95] SRSG, '2008 Complicity Report', n. 10, para. 32.

[96] SRSG, '2010 Report', n. 21, para. 86. See also SRSG, 'Guiding Principles', n. 6, Commentary to Principle 17.

[97] SRSG, '2009 Report', n. 16, para. 82.   [98] Dhooge, 'Due Diligence', n. 5.

[99] Even though the way in which Dhooge conceptualises a defence of due diligence is problematic and objectionable. In favour of a due diligence defence, see also US Chamber of Commerce Institute for Legal Reform, 'Comments on the Draft Guiding Principles for the Implementation of the United Nations "Protect, Respect and Remedy" Framework' (31 January 2011), 27, www.business-humanrights.org/SpecialRepPortal/ Home/Protect-Respect-Remedy-Framework/GuidingPrinciples/Submissions (last accessed 17 October 2012), suggesting that '[a]llowing robust due diligence to serve as a defense, where a company does undertake all reasonable steps consistent with the expectation set out in the Draft Principles, would no doubt encourage businesses to pursue these important pre-emptive measures'.

negligence, complicity liability does not know a defence of reasonable behaviour or of acting with due care and diligence. The limitations of complicity liability are rather achieved through the relevant *actus reus*, *mens rea* and causation standards discussed previously in this chapter. This reflects the idea that it cannot be reasonable knowingly to engage in behaviour that has a substantial effect on the commission of human rights violations by third parties.

Even though due diligence cannot technically provide a defence for complicity charges in these cases, if one aim of due diligence responsibilities is to avoid legal complicity liability, due diligence needs to be conceptualised in a way that it achieves what it sets out to do. This would require that due diligence responsibilities include, as a minimum, to identify the risk of legal complicity and to prevent it from materialising. If the avoidance of legal complicity was part of the due diligence responsibilities, then, where legal complicity occurs, due diligence cannot be said to have been appropriately carried out. Conversely, proper human rights due diligence would, by definition, prevent legal complicity from occurring.

Indeed, one might be inclined to question the adequacy of due diligence standards that are not stringent enough even to prevent legal complicity liability with any certainty. As long as a duly carried out human rights due diligence is not regarded as a sufficiently reliable method through which complicity in human rights violations and resulting legal charges can be avoided, there must be something wrong with the due diligence mechanisms, or with the conceptualisation of the relationship between due diligence and complicity. However, where the scope of the due diligence responsibility to avoid complicity remains as vague as is currently the case in the SRSG's documents, the congruence between due diligence and complicity cannot be achieved.

Only where the scope of due diligence responsibilities overlaps with that of the relevant legal obligation to refrain from complicit behaviour can due diligence provide proof in complicity litigation that 'the company took every reasonable step to avoid involvement in the alleged violation'.[100] Otherwise, to regard due diligence as counting in favour of

---

[100] SRSG, '2010 Report', n. 21, para. 86; M. W. Sheffer, 'Bilateral Investment Treaties: A Friend or Foe to Human Rights?' (2011) 39 *Denver Journal of International Law and Policy* 483; and L. C. Backer, 'On the Evolution of the United Nations' "Protect-Respect-Remedy" Project: The State, the Corporation and Human Rights in a Global Governance Context' (2011) 9 *Santa Clara Journal of International Law* 37, at 59.

corporate defendants in complicity litigation would imply that the corporation might have done everything that can be expected even though it was, in law, complicit in human rights violations. This risks watering down existing legal standards and blurs the line between acceptable and unacceptable corporate behaviour instead of clarifying it.

As a consequence of the fact that within the SRSG framework, human rights due diligence does not provide a defence against complicity charges, compliance with due diligence responsibilities could potentially be counterproductive for corporations in that it might increase the probability of being exposed to legal liability.[101] This is because in the course of abiding by its due diligence responsibilities, a corporation may acquire knowledge which could be held against it in the context of a complicity charge. The more prudent approach might be that of not being too proactive with regard to the due diligence responsibility to become aware of complicity risks.[102] Nevertheless, the SRSG regards this fear of an adverse impact of human rights due diligence on corporations as misplaced, suggesting that 'not knowing is itself a risk, and an unreliable defence'.[103] For him, 'the point of human rights due diligence is to learn about risks that the company would then take action to mitigate, and not to ignore or misrepresent the findings'.[104] While this might be true, it is difficult to reconcile with the fact that human rights due diligence, properly exercised and acted upon, is nevertheless not regarded as a guarantee against legal claims. Again, this problem could be avoided if the scope of the due diligence responsibilities to avoid complicity was clarified according to the suggestions made above.

---

[101] This risk was also acknowledged by Advisory Council to OECD: Joint IOE-ICC-BIAC, 'Comments on the Draft Guiding Principles' (26 January 2011), www.business-humanrights. org/SpecialRepPortal/Home/Protect-Respect-Remedy-Framework/GuidingPrinciples/ Submissions (last accessed 17 October 2012); and Vidar Lindefjeld, Assistant Director, Confederation of Norwegian Enterprise, 'Response from Vidar Lindefjeld' (27 January 2011), 109, http://en.hrsu.org/wp-content/uploads/2011/08/online-forum-re-guiding-principles-nov-2010-to-jan-2011.pdf (last accessed 13 December 2012).

[102] See also Dhooge, 'Due Diligence', n. 5, 488, who suggests that without a due diligence defence to complicity charges, corporations might be safer in ignoring ongoing abuse, as addressing it could be regarded as an admission of complicity. For a discussion see also F. Stevelman, 'Global Finance, Multinationals and Human Rights: With Commentary on Backer's Critique of the 2008 Report by John Ruggie' (2011) 9 *Santa Clara Journal of International Law* 101, at 120. SRSG, '2008 Complicity Report', n. 10, para. 32.

[103] SRSG, '2009 Report', n. 16, para. 81.   [104] *Ibid.*, para. 82.

Conclusions

As has been shown in this chapter, due diligence and complicity are two different concepts which have areas of overlap and the potential to complement and strengthen each other. As long as human rights due diligence is a principle of soft law whose violation does not have enforceable consequences, legal complicity liability is important in order to give victims justiciable remedies where a corporation knowingly provided practical assistance that had a substantial effect on the commission of human rights violations carried out by others. At the same time, given the constraints of the legal definition of complicity, the need to establish a clear link between the complicit behaviour and the harm that occurred, and the fact that complicity liability is reactive and therefore kicks in only after harm has already occurred, due diligence responsibilities to avoid complicity have an important role to play as they address a broader range of complicit behaviour and are forward-looking, aiming to prevent future violations.

In principle, therefore, the introduction of due diligence responsibilities to inquire into and act upon complicity risks is a very positive step towards avoiding the occurrence of corporate complicity in human rights violations. However, it would have been desirable had the relationship between due diligence and complicity been more thoroughly elaborated by the SRSG. For the SRSG, the most important feature of the relationship between the two concepts seems to be that due diligence is a tool to avoid complicity. However, this task is complicated by the unclear definition of complicity. Indeed, the scope and definition of complicity is left rather vague by the SRSG, not only with regard to the difference between complicity as a legal and a social concept, but also concerning the definition of each. This makes it difficult to determine the scope of the due diligence responsibilities with regard to complicity. In particular, the scope of extra-legal complicity needs to be drawn much more clearly to provide companies with guidance regarding which risks they need to avoid and under what circumstances even the mere presence in a country, or the continuation of business relationships, can make them complicit in human rights violations carried out by their business partners. While this is a difficult task, it needs to be tackled. Otherwise, the SRSG's statements that due diligence aims at the avoidance of not only legal but also extra-legal complicity are of little significance.

At the same time, the far-reaching responsibility to acquire information about potential complicity risks is a very welcome addition to complicity liability, which largely requires existing knowledge and does not arise even in cases of wilful ignorance. If, as the SRSG suggests, due diligence responsibilities go beyond collecting information and assessing risks, and include acting upon that information, they have the potential to become an important tool for avoiding complicity. However, a lot would depend on the precise content of the due diligence responsibility to avoid complicity, and on the effectiveness of enforcement mechanisms. It has been argued in this chapter that, as a minimum, these responsibilities must include identifying and acting upon the risk of complicity in the legal sense. If a congruence between due diligence and legal complicity is achieved, properly exercised due diligence would exclude the occurrence of legal complicity, while instances of legal complicity would clearly show a lack of due diligence. This would avoid the unsatisfactory situation that even an adequate exercise of due diligence does not guarantee the exclusion of complicity liability, as the current approach of the SRSG seems to suggest.

10

Making noise about silent complicity: the moral inconsistency of the 'Protect, Respect and Remedy' Framework

FLORIAN WETTSTEIN

Introduction

In 2005, Harvard Professor and Global Compact mastermind John Ruggie became the UN Secretary-General's Special Representative on business and human rights (SRSG). The debate on the Norms on the Responsibilities of Transnational Corporations and Other Business Enterprises with Regard to Human Rights (UN Norms), which were torpedoed by the private sector and subsequently shelved by the UN Commission on Human Rights, illustrated the need for more orientation and guidance within the business and human rights debate. The mandate of the UN Special Representative was put in place in order to provide such a guiding light within the debate.

The mandate of the SRSG concluded in 2011 with the publication of the much anticipated UN Guiding Principles on Business and Human Rights (GPs).[1] Subsequently, it has been replaced with a lower-profile UN Working Group on business and human rights, consisting of five experts on the issue, representing five different geographical areas. The mandate of the Working Group is set for three years and aims, amongst other goals, to promote the effective and comprehensive dissemination and implementation of the GPs, to identify, exchange and promote good practices within this process, and to support it with

---

[1] See Human Rights Council, 'Guiding Principles on Business and Human Rights: Implementing the United Nations "Protect, Respect and Remedy" Framework: Report of the Special Representative of the Secretary-General on the Issue of Human Rights and Transnational Corporations and Other Business Enterprises', A/HRC/17/31 (21 March 2011) (SRSG, 'Guiding Principles').

the promotion of capacity-building and the provision of advice and recommendations.[2]

During the SRSG's tenure, one of the main tasks was to 'research and clarify the implications for transnational corporations and other business enterprises of concepts such as "complicity" and "sphere of influence"'.[3] He presented his findings in two reports published in 2008. The main report introduced the now widely influential 'Protect, Respect and Remedy Framework' (Framework)[4], while the so-called companion report specifically dealt with questions of complicity and sphere of influence.[5] This chapter is concerned predominantly with the notion of complicity as it informs the SRSG's Framework and subsequent GPs. More specifically, it argues that, from a normative perspective, the SRSG's use of the concept is not sufficiently nuanced, which affects the coherence of the entire Framework. The more subtle forms of beneficial and silent complicity are not dealt with, nor, it seems, understood in a sufficiently thorough manner. If these specific concepts received the attention they warrant, the Framework's clear-cut separation of a corporate responsibility to respect human rights and the duty of the state to protect human rights could no longer be upheld. As a consequence, there is a moral inconsistency at the very heart of the SRSG's Framework, which jeopardises the plausibility of its key messages.

My argument will proceed in five steps. First, I will briefly outline the structure of the SRSG's Framework and the logic underlying its strict separation of the state duty to protect and the corporate responsibility to respect human rights. In a second step, I will deal with the SRSG's understanding of complicity in general, while in the third step I will have a look at the implications of silent complicity in particular. Specifically, I will assess the profound conceptual implications of the

---

[2] Human Rights Council, 'Human Rights and Transnational Corporations and Other Business Enterprises', A/HRC/17/L.17/Rev.1 (15 June 2011), para. 6.

[3] Human Rights Council, 'Human Rights and Transnational Corporations and Other Business Enterprises', Human Rights Resolution 2005/69, para. 1c. See also Human Rights Council, 'Clarifying the Concepts of Sphere of Influence and Complicity: Report of the Special Representative of the Secretary-General on the Issue of Human Rights and Transnational Corporations and Other Business Enterprises', A/HRC/8/16 (15 May 2008) (SRSG, '2008 Companion Report'), para. 4.

[4] Human Rights Council, 'Protect, Respect and Remedy: a Framework for Business and Human Rights: Report of the Special Representative of the Secretary-General on the Issue of Human Rights and Transnational Corporations and Other Business Enterprises', A/HRC/8/5 (7 April 2008) (SRSG, '2008 Framework').

[5] SRSG, '2008 Companion Report', n. 3.

concept of silent complicity and how they relate to the SRSG's Framework. In a final step, three of these conceptual implications will be analysed in more detail: I will clarify, first, why silent complicity implies positive, rather than negative responsibilities on the part of corporations; second, why the SRSG's fear of 'can implies ought' is unjustified; and, third, why the Framework is in need of more thorough ethical argumentation.

Dividing responsibility according to the 'Protect, Respect and Remedy Framework'

In July 2008, the SRSG published what is now known as the 'Protect, Respect and Remedy Framework'. The Framework provides an opposing position to the approach taken by the UN Norms five years earlier. The UN Norms, according to the SRSG, limited the catalogue of rights that ought to be relevant for corporations. On the duty side, however, the UN Norms were expansive: corporate responsibilities were seen not only to comprise respect for human rights, but also their protection and promotion. The SRSG saw this as the wrong approach. As economic actors, he argues, 'companies have unique responsibilities', which should not be 'entangled' with state obligations. Adopting this approach would result in more, rather than less, clarity: 'it makes it difficult if not impossible to tell who is responsible for what in practice'.[6] On the other hand, any limited list of rights will, according to the SRSG, 'almost certainly miss one or more rights that may turn out to be significant in a particular instance'. As a result, it will provide 'misleading guidance'.[7] Consequently, the Framework and the subsequent GPs place no limitations on the list of rights applicable to corporations, but do limit the respective corporate duties.

The SRSG asserts that 'all social actors – States, businesses, and civil society – must learn to do many things differently'. Those things, as he argues, 'must cohere and become cumulative' in order to solve the 'institutional misalignments in the business and human rights domain'.[8] The main conclusion that the SRSG derives from this insight seems to be a need for a clear division of responsibilities of such actors. It is this division of responsibilities which is at the very core of the Framework and defines its basic shape and structure.

---

[6] SRSG, '2008 Framework', n. 4, para. 6.   [7] *Ibid.*   [8] *Ibid.*, para. 7.

Hence, the Framework consists of three 'differentiated but complementary' responsibilities.[9] Thus, the separation of duties within the Framework is thought to be clear-cut, rather than fluent and overlapping. The first and primary pillar of the Framework is the state duty to protect human rights from the abuse of third parties. In other words, even in the domain of business and human rights, the primary duty rests with governments. It is their responsibility to protect citizens from corporate abuse, for example by enacting and implementing effective laws and regulations. The second pillar is the corporate responsibility to respect human rights, which also applies importantly in contexts characterised by inadequate laws and governance. Thus, where governance gaps prevail and governments fail to meet their duty to protect human rights, corporations ought to respect human rights beyond what is legally or otherwise mandated. 'The responsibility to respect', as the SRSG asserts, 'is the baseline expectation for all companies in all situations',[10] that is, also in those situations in which clear legal and regulatory boundaries are missing. The third pillar establishes the need for access to effective remedies for the victims of corporate human rights violations. Thus, where corporations were involved in the violation of human rights, it is, among others, the state's duty to put mechanisms in place that help the victims to seek redress.

The separation of duties in the Framework is thought to be programmatic: it aims at anchoring the business and human rights debate and at guiding all relevant actors.[11] As such, it is seen by the SRSG to provide the authoritative focal point which the business and human rights debate allegedly had been lacking in the past.[12]

Corporate complicity and the responsibility to respect in the UN Framework

The corporate responsibility to respect human rights in the Framework is to be understood essentially as a responsibility 'not to infringe on the rights of others – put simply, to do no harm'.[13] The SRSG correctly argues that such a responsibility not to harm spans both direct and indirect human rights violations. As such, it naturally includes avoidance of complicity.[14] Corporations can become complicit in human rights

[9] *Ibid.*, para. 9.   [10] *Ibid.*, para. 24.   [11] *Ibid.*, Summary: 1.   [12] *Ibid.*, para. 5.
[13] *Ibid.*, para. 24; SRSG, '2008 Companion Report', n. 3, para. 3.
[14] SRSG, '2008 Framework', n. 4, para. 81.

violations if they contribute indirectly to human rights violations committed by a primary perpetrator. Thus, complicity, in the SRSG's words, 'describes a subset of the indirect ways in which companies can have an adverse effect on rights through their relationships'.[15] Today, a majority of human rights violations with corporate involvement are indirect.[16]

In the literature on the topic, complicity is commonly defined broadly as aiding and abetting human rights violations committed by third parties.[17] It is commonly argued that in order to be complicit, the company must have provided such assistance *knowingly*. That is, complicity presupposes that the company knows or should (reasonably) have known that its activities may contribute to human rights abuse:

> In essence, complicity means that a company knowingly contributed to another's abuse of human rights ... In principle, complicity may be alleged in relation to knowingly contributing to any type of human rights abuse, whether of civil or political rights, or economic, social and cultural rights.[18]

Furthermore, the literature distinguishes between different types of complicity. There are what can be termed active and passive types of complicity. Active complicity occurs through a company's active involvement in or contribution to the human rights violation. Such active complicity can be further divided into direct and indirect complicity. Direct complicity is defined by a company's direct contribution to certain human rights violations. Indirect complicity, on the other hand, is based on more subtle ways of facilitating the abuse. For example, a corporation may support and bolster the general ability of a (potential) perpetrator to carry out and sustain systematic violations of human rights by maintaining business relationships with it. Some commentators go so far as to argue that even paying taxes in countries with corrupt and despotic governments amounts to indirect complicity. As opposed to active complicity, passive complicity does not require involvement or an active contribution by the corporation. Beneficial and silent

---

[15] SRSG, '2008 Companion Report', n. 3, para. 4.

[16] S. J. Kobrin, 'Private Political Authority and Public Responsibility: Transnational Politics, Transnational Firms and Human Rights' (2009) 19 *Business Ethics Quarterly* 351.

[17] See, for example, A. Clapham and S. Jerbi, 'Categories of Corporate Complicity in Human Rights Abuses' (2001) 24 *Hastings International and Comparative Law Review* 340; S. J. Kobrin, 'Private Political Authority', n. 16, 351; and A. Ramasastry, 'Corporate Complicity: From Nuremberg to Rangoon – An Examination of Forced Labor Cases and their Impact on the Liability of Multinational Corporations' (2002) 20 *Berkeley Journal of International Law* 95.

[18] SRSG, '2008 Companion Report', n. 3, para. 30.

complicity are passive kinds of complicity. Beneficial complicity is based on a company accepting benefits from the violation of human rights committed by others. Silent complicity refers to a company remaining silent in the face of human rights violations despite having some ability to curb the abuse. Often, these two kinds of complicity occur in combination: those who willingly and knowingly benefit from human rights violations over an extended time tend to keep a low profile; and those who remain silent in the face of such abuse often benefit substantially from it. A distinguishing element may be that beneficial complicity often implies an interest of the corporation in maintaining the status quo of the rights violations, depending on how substantially it benefits from it.[19] Silent complicity does not imply such an interest. Thus, while from a moral standpoint we are dealing with two separate reasons or bases for moral blame and thus with two distinct forms of complicity, they often – though not always – occur interdependently and at the same time.

In his main report of 2008, the SRSG adheres to a rather narrow definition of complicity as the 'indirect *involvement* by companies in human rights abuses'.[20] Involvement implies engagement and participation. Thus, defining complicity as involvement would exclude passive types of complicity from the Framework. Consistent with this definition, the SRSG raises doubts about interpreting mere presence in a country, paying taxes, or silence in the face of human rights violations as actual complicity. At least from a legal point of view, as he argues, the basis for such wide interpretations of complicity would not be accepted. Only in very narrow contexts, as he asserts, have omissions led to the legal liability of individuals. This has happened when such omissions legitimised or encouraged the abuse. Commonly, however, the requirement of practical assistance – that is, *involvement* – would likely not be met in such cases.[21]

From the point of view of international criminal law, complicity presupposes a substantial contribution to the crime. Substantiality must be distinguished from indispensability. In order for an agent to become complicit in a human rights violation, its contribution does not need to be indispensable or even essential for the abuse.[22] Thus,

---

[19] I. Tofalo, 'Overt and Hidden Accomplices: Transnational Corporations' Range of Complicity for Human Rights Violations' in O. De Schutter (ed.), *Transnational Corporations and Human Rights* (Oxford: Hart Publishing, 2006), 350.

[20] SRSG, '2008 Framework', n. 4, para. 73, emphasis added.   [21] *Ibid.*, para. 77.

[22] SRSG, '2008 Companion Report', n. 3, paras. 37 and 38; and The International Commission of Jurists, 'Corporate Complicity and Legal Accountability' (Geneva: International Commission of Jurists, 2008), vol. i, 10 speaks of a '*sufficient* level of

complicity of an agent may occur even if the human rights violations would have taken place without his or her contribution. Hence, in order to make a case for holding corporations legally liable for *silent* complicity, one would need to show that an agent's silence contributed in a significant and substantial way to the human rights violation by encouraging and lending moral support to it. Similarly, 'merely' benefiting from a human rights abuse is unlikely to meet this threshold for legal complicity on its own.[23]

Thus, the SRSG may be right with his assessment of the passive types of complicity from a legal point of view. However, he goes on to point out that the concept of complicity 'has legal and non-legal pedigrees' and he asserts that 'the implications of both are important for companies'.[24] In other words, while silent and beneficial complicity may not have any legal implications in the Framework, the SRSG does not explicitly reject or exclude their relevance for the corporate responsibility to respect human rights in a non-legal sense.

The companion report, which specifically deals with complicity and sphere of influence, confirms this particular reading of the main report. In its section on complicity, the SRSG outlines what he calls 'the most relevant considerations underpinning complicity', stressing again that this includes 'both legal and non-legal points of view'.[25] Thus, in addition to the implications deriving from international criminal law, the SRSG sets out to 'explore the key non-legal contexts in which indirect involvement in human rights abuses has carried important implications for companies'.[26] Legal standards, as he asserts, are 'only part of the story' for understanding complicity.

The non-legal contexts to which the SRSG is referring in the reports are framed by 'social expectations'.[27] Such expectations are perceived to be set particularly by organisations such as the UN, public and private investors and human rights advocacy groups.[28] In regard to framing the concept and implications of complicity, the companion report relies heavily on the expectations laid down in the UN Global Compact.[29] In its explanatory statement for Principle 2, the Global Compact points out

---

assistance or encouragement' by 'enabling, exacerbating or facilitating' human rights abuse (emphasis added).

[23] SRSG, '2008 Framework', n. 4, para. 78; and SRSG, '2008 Companion Report', n. 3, para. 41.

[24] SRSG, '2008 Framework', n. 4, para. 73.

[25] SRSG, '2008 Companion Report', n. 3, para. 28.   [26] *Ibid.*, para. 28.

[27] *Ibid.*, para. 54.   [28] *Ibid.*   [29] *Ibid.*, paras. 57–60.

three main forms of complicity. These are direct, beneficial and silent complicity. Thus, with this reference, the SRSG asserts silent complicity as 'part of the story', that is, as among 'the most relevant considerations' for companies from a non-legal point of view – i.e. from the standpoint of social expectations.

The SRSG also relies on the Global Compact for a specific definition of silent complicity:

> **Silent Complicity** describes the way human rights advocates see the failure by a company to raise the question of systematic or continuous human rights violations in its interactions with the appropriate authorities. For example, inaction or acceptance by companies of systematic discrimination in employment law against particular groups on the grounds of ethnicity or gender could bring accusations of silent complicity.[30]

Hence, the SRSG's initial definition of complicity as indirect 'involvement' in human rights violations is too narrow even in comparison to his own elaborations in the companion report. In order to ensure consistency and to signal the importance of non-legal contexts in the definition, he would have to broaden it to include the possibility of passive complicity. However, the problems with the SRSG's work in this area do not stop with this definitional question.[31] In what follows I will argue that the implications deriving from the SRSG's seeming endorsement of silent complicity as a relevant concept for corporate conduct puts the very consistency and coherence of the UN Framework in question.

Understanding silent complicity and its implications

The defining element of silent complicity is its independence from a company's active involvement in and contribution to a human rights violation. Rather, it is seen to derive from a company's inactivity, that is, its silence in the face of such a violation. If silent complicity rests on the passivity of a company in the presence of human rights abuse committed by a third party, avoidance of silent complicity logically requires the company actively to take a stance against that abuse. In other words, if silence is what leads to complicity, speaking out is what is needed to avoid it. Thus, silent complicity derives from omitting to speak out

---

[30] *Ibid.*, para. 58 (bold in the original).
[31] For an examination of further problems that arise in connection with the relationship between the SRSG's understanding of complicity and the responsibility to perform a due diligence, see Chapter 9.

against human rights abuse. However, omitting to speak out can only amount to complicity if one had an actual responsibility or duty to do so. After all, one cannot be blamed for omitting an action, if that action is entirely optional. In sum, silent complicity presupposes a responsibility or a *duty to speak out*. This raises two questions: firstly, what exactly does this duty to speak out entail? Secondly, what else than mere presence are the conditions that give rise to such a duty?

Initially and perhaps intuitively, one could define speaking out in the context of silent complicity simply as taking a stance, publicly, against the violation of human rights. Thus, the company would be expected to issue a clear statement rejecting the abuse, no more and no less. While taking a public stance indeed seems to be essential, silent complicity, as it is commonly defined in the business and human rights discourse and particularly also by the Global Compact and thus by the SRSG, is based on a more demanding interpretation of speaking out. Specifically, as the above definition by the Global Compact makes clear, silent complicity derives not only from not taking a stance, but from the 'failure by a company to raise the question of systematic or continuous human rights violations in its interactions with the appropriate authorities'. Similarly, for Andrew Clapham and Scott Jerbi silent complicity is more than merely speaking out, but 'reflects the expectation on companies that they raise systematic or continuous human rights abuses with the appropriate authorities'.[32] For the former UN High Commissioner for Human Rights, Mary Robinson, silent complicity refers to 'the growing acceptance . . . that there is something culpable about failing to *exercise influence*' in circumstances of 'systematic or continuous human rights abuses'.[33] Finally, for the International Council on Human Rights Policy, silent complicity implies that '[a] company is aware that human rights violations are occurring, but does not intervene with the authorities to *try and prevent or stop the violations*'.[34] Underlying this interpretation, obviously, is the perception that the company ought not merely to disassociate itself from the abuse by publicly condemning it, but to come to the victims' help by raising the issue with and exercising influence over the respective authorities. Speaking out in this sense

---

[32] A. Clapham and S. Jerbi, 'Categories of Corporate Complicity', n. 17, 347–48.
[33] Quoted in A. Clapham, *Human Rights Obligations of Non-State Actors* (New York: Oxford University Press, 2006), 221, emphasis added.
[34] International Council on Human Rights Policy, *Beyond Voluntarism: Human Rights and the Developing International Legal Obligations of Companies* (Versoix: International Council on Human Rights Policy, 2002), 133, emphasis added.

means speaking out *in protection* of the victims of the human rights abuse. The duty to speak out, as a consequence, must be interpreted in terms of a duty to help protect the victims. Summarising these insights, for John M. Kline silent complicity implies 'that a non-participant is aware of abusive action and, although possessing some degree of ability to act, chooses neither to help protect nor to assist victims of the abuse, remaining content to meet the minimal ethical requirement to do no (direct) harm'.[35]

Two implications of relevance for the Framework derive from this conceptual definition. In fact, the two implications point to two interrelated inconsistencies within the Framework. Firstly, the responsibility to avoid silent complicity, that is, the duty to speak out, is based on what Stepan Wood recently called 'leverage-based responsibility'.[36] A leverage-based conception of responsibility holds that an agent's capacity to exert influence or leverage can be a source of responsibility beyond his or her involvement in bringing a specific harm about. Interestingly, the SRSG denies the validity of leverage-based responsibility in an almost categorical manner in his report, holding that companies can only be held responsible for the human rights impact of their conduct, not, however, for the leverage they may have over other actors.[37] This rejection of leverage-based responsibility seems to stand in sharp contradiction to the definition of silent complicity used in the companion report.

Secondly, the duty to speak out, when linked to the concept of silent complicity and as conceived in the definition contained in the Framework, aligns more plausibly with a duty to protect rather than a duty merely to respect human rights. It is precisely because of the rigid separation of these duties in the Framework that the SRSG is hesitant to embrace leverage as a source of responsibility: '[i]mpact falls squarely within the responsibility to respect; leverage may only do so in particular circumstances'.[38] Thus, the duty to speak out in this context is not a negative duty deriving from the 'do no harm' principle, but a positive duty to help protect the victims of human rights abuse. The implications

---

[35] J. M. Kline, *Ethics for International Business: Decision Making in a Global Political Economy* (London; New York: Routledge, 2005), 79.

[36] S. Wood, 'The Case for Leverage-Based Corporate Human Rights Responsibility' (2012) 22 *Business Ethics Quarterly* 63–98.

[37] SRSG, '2008 Framework', n. 4, paras. 68–69; and SRSG, '2008 Companion Report', n. 3, paras. 12–13.

[38] SRSG, '2008 Framework', n. 4, para. 68; and SRSG, '2008 Companion Report', n. 3, para. 12.

of this insight for the moral consistency and inner coherence of the Framework are far reaching: if silent complicity implies a positive duty to protect, then the very separation of duties on which the Framework is based does not hold up anymore.

Let us now have a closer look at the second question raised above, that is, at the conditions which need to be met in order for a company justifiably to be accused of silent complicity.

Conditions for a positive duty to speak out

Leverage-based responsibility, as is implied by the definition of silent complicity, means that a specific agent may not only have a responsibility to exercise power responsibly (i.e. do no harm) but that, under certain conditions, there may be an actual responsibility actively to make use of its power for the benefit of others.[39] Thus, after clarifying the nature of the responsibility to speak out in protection of the victims of human rights abuses, the question now is, what conditions need to be met in order for an agent to actually have such a leverage-based responsibility?

Before we have a look at this particular question, let us briefly distinguish more clearly a positive from a negative responsibility. A negative responsibility, in a nutshell, is a responsibility to do no harm. As outlined above, the SRSG bases the corporate responsibility to respect human rights squarely on this principle. A responsibility to do no harm, and thus a negative responsibility to respect human rights, can be passive or active. A passive responsibility is a responsibility to abstain from harmful actions. An active responsibility, on the other hand, is a responsibility to prevent or mitigate harm that is taking place or threatens to do so. For example, the owner of a private swimming pool has an active negative responsibility to secure his pool properly in order to prevent the neighbour's children from falling in and drowning. The SRSG explicitly asserts this dual interpretation of a negative duty in his reports. "'[D]oing no harm'", as he argues, 'is not merely a passive responsibility for firms but may entail positive steps – for example, a workplace anti-discrimination policy might require the company to adopt specific recruitment and training programmes'.[40] Let us make this distinction very clear: what makes a duty negative is its derivation from the 'do no

---

[39] S. Wood, 'Leverage-Based Corporate Human Rights Responsibility', n. 36, 77.
[40] SRSG, '2008 Framework', n. 4, para. 55.

harm' principle. The requirement of taking positive steps to prevent such harm from occurring does not turn the duty itself into a positive one. Rather, it turns it into an active, instead of a passive, negative duty. A positive duty, on the other hand, is a duty to improve a given state of affairs or to come to the assistance of or help people in need. It is, in other words, a duty to do good, rather than not to harm. As such, it requires an idea of desirable or obligatory ends. Such a duty – perhaps with very few exceptions – requires positive action and, as a consequence, is always active. As opposed to the deontological basis of negative responsibilities, positive responsibilities are grounded in teleological thinking, since, as responsibilities that aim at the improvement of a given state of affairs, they derive from a perspective concerned with consequences and thus hinge on a vision of the good in society. This is why they can be thought of as leverage-based responsibilities. It is this kind of responsibility which the Framework rejects as not relevant for companies in the human rights domain.

Based on this distinction, I would argue that three conditions need to be met in order for companies to have such positive, leverage-based responsibilities.[41] First and most evidently, in order to have a responsibility to exercise influence and pressure on or over the perpetrator, the corporation must be in a position that effectively allows it to do so. In other words, there must be a reasonable and realistic chance that the exercise of influence will in fact lead to an actual improvement of the victims' situation. Thus, such positive duties to come to people's help or to change a given state of affairs presuppose certain capacities, which are not shared by all agents equally. This is why such duties are particular, and not universal: rather than applying to everyone equally and at all times, as does the (passive) negative duty to do no harm, positive duties apply to specific agents in specific contexts and to varying degrees and extents. They become more plausible and more extensive the greater the prospective impact of such action, that is, the greater the influence and power of the respective agent.

Secondly, responsibility, both negative and positive, presupposes autonomy. Thus, a corporation can be blamed for actions or omissions only if those actions or omissions are based on free and voluntary choice. If such actions or omissions derive from external force or coercion, one

---

[41] See F. Wettstein, 'Silence as Complicity: Elements of a Corporate Duty to Speak Out against the Violation of Human Rights' (2012) 22 *Business Ethics Quarterly* 275–83 for a more detailed analysis.

cannot be held responsible for them and, as a consequence, cannot be blamed because of them. In the case of silent complicity, the autonomy of an agent to speak out against the abuse can be severely limited by the threat of retaliation. If retaliation by the perpetrator is likely in a given situation and there is reason to believe that the agent will not be able to withstand it, the existence of a duty to speak out is in question.[42] After all, the normative burden for an agent to have to meet an obligation must not be unreasonably high. It must be reasonable and, with reference to Kant, proportional to the fundamentality of the obligation at stake:

> Subjectively, the degree to which an action can be imputed (*imputabili-tas*) has to be assessed by the magnitude of the obstacles that had to be overcome. – The greater the natural obstacles (of sensibility) and the less the moral obstacle (of duty), so much the more merit is to be accounted for a good deed, as when, for example, at considerable self-sacrifice I rescue a complete stranger from great distress.[43]

Thus, while the first condition was that the exercise of influence must have the potential to improve the situation of the victims, the second condition is that meeting this responsibility must not worsen the situation of the responsibility-bearer to an unreasonable degree. Condition one and in a wider, normative sense also condition two derive from the principle of 'ought implies can'.

Thirdly, having a positive responsibility based on influence requires a morally significant connection between the responsibility-bearer and the human rights abuse, for without such a connection, remedial responsibility for social ills would potentially be limitless. Peter Singer, for example, famously argued that 'if it is in our power to prevent something bad from happening without thereby sacrificing anything of comparable moral importance, we ought, morally, to do it'.[44] This would mean, as Singer points out himself, 'that one reduce oneself to very near the material circumstances of a Bengali refugee'.[45] It takes a most uncompromising consequentialism to defend such a position. To be sure, as shown above, arguing for positive obligations does presuppose a 'teleological' turn and thus requires argumentation that is at least

---

[42] M. Santoro, 'Post-Westphalia and its Discontents: Business, Globalization, and Human Rights in Political and Moral Perspective' (2010) 20 *Business Ethics Quarterly* 292; F. Wettstein, 'Silence as Complicity', n. 41, 46.

[43] I. Kant, *The Metaphysics of Morals*, trans. M. Gregor (Cambridge University Press, 1996), 19.

[44] P. Singer, 'Famine, Affluence and Morality' (1972) 1:3 *Philosophy and Public Affairs* 231.

[45] *Ibid.*, 241.

sensitive to consequences. However, in order not to become (normatively) overbearing, positive obligations must generally be limited in two dimensions. As argued above in relation to condition two, they are limited in regard to their extent, that is, regarding *how much* help is owed to a specific group of people. Rather than the balance of marginal utility gains and losses as in Singer's theory, it is the normative burden caused to the responsible agent which sets the limits for reasonable obligations.[46] However, positive duties are limited also in regard to their scope, that is, in regard to *whom* an agent is required to help. This is why condition three is important; the requirement of a morally significant connection as a condition for remedial obligation narrows or limits the scope of situations for which one can reasonably be held responsible.

A morally significant connection as required by condition three does not imply direct involvement. After all, direct involvement of a company in violations of human rights would raise the (stronger) accusation of direct complicity rather than 'merely' of silent complicity. Thus, in the context of silent complicity we are rather looking at indirect connections, which in a more general way *associate* the corporation with the human rights violation at hand.

These three conditions need to be met in order for corporations to have (positive) remedial human rights obligations beyond the 'do no harm' principle. However, the existence of and subsequent omission to perform a remedial obligation does not in itself imply complicity. One may have a positive duty to come to someone's help without becoming complicit in the misery of those people if such help is not offered. For example, someone who witnesses an accident and chooses not to help the injured despite his capacity to do so, can hardly be said to be complicit in the accident. He can, however, be blamed for omitting to perform a positive duty to help the victims.[47] Thus, in order for the omission of a positive duty to turn into complicity, a fourth condition needs to be met.

---

[46] In principle, the reasonableness of and thus the limits to (positive) human rights obligations are themselves given by the condition of equal human rights (H. Shue, 'The Burdens of Justice' (1983) 80 *The Journal of Philosophy* 606). As responsible agents, all duty-bearers are at the same time also rights-bearers. Obligations are thus limited by a responsible agent's own legitimate claim for personal flourishing and advancement. With reference to Peter Singer's proposition, this threshold must be placed substantially higher than that of a 'Bengali refugee'. Kant even claimed that one not only has a justified claim, but an actual duty to provide 'for oneself to the extent necessary just to find *satisfaction* in living' (I. Kant, *The Metaphysics of Morals*, n. 43, 201, emphasis added).

[47] S. Wood, 'Leverage-Based Corporate Human Rights Responsibility', n. 36, 78–80.

I would argue that apart from the general condition of knowledge which defines cases of complicity in general, silent complicity presupposes, fourthly, a certain social or political status or prestige of an agent. Silent complicity does not merely require that a silent witness tolerates abuse that is taking place in its sphere of influence, but that doing so signals moral support for these morally reprehensible actions. Particularly if one considers substantiality of contribution to be an essential defining element of complicity in general, more is needed than mere toleration. Analogising from international criminal law cases, the SRSG, for example, argues that substantiality can be assumed if a witness's silence in some way *legitimises or encourages* the abuse.[48] For this to be the case, as he goes on, mere presence is not sufficient. What is needed in addition is that the agent's silence carries some moral weight in the public perception. This is the case if the agent enjoys a certain (superior) status:

> [P]resence was only one factor that led to a finding that the individuals' acts or omissions had a legitimizing or encouraging effect on the crime in the specific context, and all of the accused also had some form of superior status.[49]

A similar argument is put forth by Andrew Clapham and Scott Jerbi:

> Presence when combined with authority, can constitute assistance in the form of moral support, that is, the *actus reus* of the offence. The supporter must be of a certain status for this to be sufficient for [criminal] responsibility.[50]

Let me briefly summarise these insights. The question of silent complicity is raised if two interrelated circumstances are met, which, in turn, depend on a total of four conditions: first, the corporation is in a position to help and indeed has a positive responsibility to do so, but chooses to remain inactive. Thus, the first circumstance is that of omitting to perform a positive duty. Three conditions need to be met in order for this to be the case: autonomy, influence and connection. The second circumstance is that the omission of this positive duty legitimises or encourages and thus lends moral support to the abuse. This is the case if a fourth condition is met: the silent witness must enjoy a certain (higher or superior) status or prestige within the wider social or political environment.

---

[48] SRSG, '2008 Companion Report', n. 3, para. 39.   [49] *Ibid.*, para. 40.
[50] A. Clapham and S. Jerbi, 'Categories of Corporate Complicity', n. 17, 344.

One can certainly debate on a more fundamental level to what extent silent complicity ought to be a relevant concept for companies to begin with. However, this would ultimately be irrelevant for this chapter, since all it sets out to show is that there is an inconsistency between the basic structure of the Framework and its assumption that silent complicity is, in fact, a relevant concept in the corporate context. Nevertheless, none of the constitutive circumstances and conditions outlined above rule out, in principle, that the concept can be applied also to the corporate context. Doing so, however, necessarily presupposes that companies can have positive human rights obligations. If that is the case, then the Framework is fundamentally flawed.

Thus, to maintain consistency, the Framework would either have to be relaxed in order to include positive corporate responsibilities in the categories of protecting and realising human rights, or it would categorically have to exclude silent complicity as a relevant and important concept for corporations. Three additional distinctions will help to clarify this argument some more. I will address them in the remainder of the chapter.

First clarification: speaking out as a positive or an active negative duty?

The duty to speak out in protection of victims of human rights abuses as it is commonly defined in connection with silent complicity is a positive duty, based on influence or leverage, rather than a negative duty based on avoiding harm. I have defined and clarified this distinction above.

Based on it, two objections could be launched against the argument put forth in this chapter. Firstly, one could argue that the duty to speak out is not to be interpreted as a positive duty to help protect the victims, but 'merely' as an active negative one for the company to disassociate itself publicly from the human rights abuse. Hence, a responsibility publicly to condemn the abuse could be framed as an active obligation of the negative kind. As such, it would serve the mere purpose of refuting the suspicion of a company's supportive stance toward the perpetrator. However, it would not include an expectation that speaking out assists or contributes to the protection of the victims in any way. Secondly, even if we adhere to the more demanding interpretation of speaking out as exerting influence and putting pressure on the authorities, still one could argue that this duty too may be framed as a negative duty to do no harm. Let me briefly address both objections.

The first objection warrants two responses. Firstly, even if a mere public condemnation was sufficient for an agent to diffuse the accusations of being silently complicit, the definition used in the SRSG's reports, and indeed the definition which seems to be standard in the debate on business and human rights is, as shown above, more demanding than that. Referring to the Global Compact, the SRSG's definition clearly is based on a positive, rather than merely an active negative, responsibility to speak out. Thus, even if, in principle, we decided that silent complicity as a concept is based on the 'do no harm' principle, it would not remedy the inconsistency in the Framework. At the very least it would imply that the definition in the Framework is flawed at a very basic level. Considering that defining complicity and its implications was one of the main tasks in the SRSG's mandate, this would certainly raise questions as to whether the mandate was properly fulfilled.

Secondly, an interpretation of the duty to speak out as an active negative duty is unconvincing, especially in cases in which the second (influence) and fourth (status) of the above conditions are met. Corporations which are powerful enough, both in terms of influence and status, to help prevent and stop human rights violations to which they are connected would likely be considered insincere or hypocritical if they merely issued a public condemnation of those abuses instead of taking positive action to assist in curbing them. One could argue that, at least in certain cases, a public statement would be sufficient to eliminate the third condition (connection), since the corporation would effectively disassociate itself from the abuse. However, it is questionable whether such a statement could eliminate the legitimisation or encouragement condition. One could even argue that a perpetrator might draw increased encouragement from a powerful actor who publicly disapproves of its misdeeds but still does nothing to prevent or stop them. This is why, for an agent who fulfils both the influence and the status conditions, it takes more effectively to disassociate from abuses than merely issuing a disapproving statement.

Let us now come to the second objection, that is, to the claim that even a responsibility actively to raise the issue with the authorities can consistently be derived from the 'do no harm' principle and thus be grounded in a negative obligation. A similar claim has recently been made by Hsieh in connection with the question of whether corporations have an obligation to promote just institutions in contexts in which they are lacking.[51] Hsieh argues that they do, based not on a positive obligation – though he does not rule out that a convincing case for such positive responsibilities could be made – but on the negative duty to do no harm. Hsieh argues that, in contexts which lack just background institutions, corporate activity often unwittingly contributes to harming, rather than benefiting, people. Therefore, corporations ought to promote the creation of an adequate institutional infrastructure, which would effectively eliminate such harmful side-effects. I have shown elsewhere that this argumentation does not hold up to closer scrutiny.[52] I agree with Hsieh that corporations do have such a responsibility, but I doubt that it can be consistently grounded in a negative obligation. What Hsieh does not show in his argument is why the duty to promote just institutions seems to trump a more basic duty for the company to withdraw from the context in question. From the perspective of 'do no harm' this seems implausible, since promoting just institutions would imply the continuation of the harmful activities by the company for an indeterminate amount of time. That is, the company would continue contributing to the harms caused by its presence until the institutions which it is promoting would effectively be put in place. Withdrawing, on the other hand, would eliminate the harmful effects of corporate activity immediately. As a consequence, the reliance on 'do no harm' alone cannot produce convincing reasons for a duty to promote just institutions. A more plausible line of argumentation would have to revert to an influence- or power-based argument. This, however, essentially turns the duty to promote just institutions into a positive obligation.

Second clarification: 'can implies ought' vs. 'ought implies can'

The SRSG presents his caveats against assigning influence- or leverage-based positive human rights responsibilities to corporations on Page 5 of the companion report. 'Anchoring corporate responsibility in influence defined as leverage', as he asserts, 'is problematic, because it requires assuming, in moral philosophy terms, that "can implies ought"'.[53] Thus, according to the SRSG, corporations 'cannot be held responsible for the

---

[51] See N. Hsieh, 'Does Global Business have a Responsibility to Promote Just Institutions?' (2009) 19 *Business Ethics Quarterly* 251–73.

[52] See F. Wettstein, 'For Better or for Worse: Corporate Responsibility beyond Do No Harm' (2010) 20 *Business Ethics Quarterly* 275–83.

[53] SRSG, '2008 Companion Report', n. 3, para. 13.

human rights impacts of every entity over which they may have some leverage because this would include cases in which they are not contributing to, nor are a causal agent of the harm in question'.[54] The SRSG's concern warrants two responses.

Firstly, his claim that such leverage-based responsibility is based on the assumption that 'can implies ought' is mistaken. In fact, the SRSG builds a straw man by arguing against a position which allegedly holds that corporate responsibility occurs whenever corporations may have some leverage. Such an unqualified interpretation of 'can implies ought' would indeed be untenable and is, to my knowledge, not seriously defended by anyone. This is why in this chapter and in all similar accounts of corporate responsibility which I am aware of, leverage (i.e. 'can') implies 'ought' only under certain conditions: a company must be connected to the human rights violation and the normative burden of meeting the obligation must be bearable. Furthermore, any such argument *per se* assumes that corporations are, in principle, directly obligated by human rights at the outset. Thus, the SRSG's objection against positive human rights responsibility loses its argumentative force, for 'can' (i.e. leverage) is only one among other factors that ground and shape the respective obligation. If anything, we are dealing with a qualified version of 'can implies ought', that is, one that is highly dependent on the respective context. However, this is not at all an anomaly in moral philosophy as the SRSG tries to suggest.

Secondly therefore, even if the SRSG's claim was correct, that is, if such an argument was, in fact, based on 'can implies ought', this insight would hardly be sufficient to disqualify this position as baseless without further ado. The SRSG's assumption that any form of 'can implies ought' automatically and *per se* negates the validity of an argument is peculiar and most certainly lacks nuance. According to the SRSG, responsibility *per se* presupposes that an agent either contributed to or is a causal agent of the harm in question. In short, one is only responsible for problems one has helped to bring about. This seems highly counter-intuitive, morally, for there already are various contexts in which responsibility is commonly assumed to go beyond an agent's prior involvement or contribution to outcomes.[55] Examples include role-based responsibility such as that of a parent for a child, or a responsibility to aid those in acute distress.[56] I am not suggesting any analogy between these contexts and

---

[54] *Ibid.*
[55] S. Wood, 'Leverage-Based Corporate Human Rights Responsibility', n. 36, 75.　　[56] *Ibid.*

the responsibility of companies for human rights. Rather, the mere existence of such contexts puts a general question mark behind the SRSG's rather nonchalant and categorical rejection of any form of responsibility beyond contribution or causal involvement.

Third clarification: morality vs. social expectations

In a recent article, Wes Cragg notes that in his defence of corporate human rights responsibilities, the SRSG seems to sideline morality altogether. That is, nowhere in his reports does the SRSG attempt to justify his recommendations 'by suggesting or arguing that the corporate responsibility to respect human rights is an ethical or moral responsibility and should be recognized as such by corporations'.[57] Granted that the SRSG distinguishes between legal and non-legal contexts and asserts that both of them are important for the assessment of corporations' human rights responsibilities, but there is no deliberate or explicit attempt to specify such non-legal contexts in terms of morality. Instead, the SRSG refers to 'social expectations' as the benchmark for corporate human rights responsibility.

The question that the SRSG does not answer is on what basis social expectations give rise to such responsibilities.[58] There are two likely explanations: firstly, they may be seen as the reference point for a purely instrumental interpretation of corporate human rights responsibilities. Secondly, social expectations could be seen as a proxy or a surrogate for moral considerations. Again, let us have a brief look at both interpretations and how they relate to the argument put forth in this chapter.

The SRSG's argument for the justification and promotion of the Framework seems to be instrumental at its core. Corporations ought to respect human rights, as he puts it, because 'failure to meet this responsibility can subject companies to the courts of public opinion'.[59] Thus, it is not the moral legitimacy of claims that ought to guide corporate behaviour, but public opinion, whether or not such behaviour is justified from a moral point of view.[60] Corporations, in other words, ought to avoid negative publicity connected to human rights violations, because it might affect their reputation and, in severe cases, their very 'licence

---

[57] W. Cragg, 'Ethics, Enlightened Self-Interest and the Corporate Responsibility to Respect Human Rights' (2012) 22 *Business Ethics Quarterly* 9, at 10.

[58] See Chapter 5.   [59] SRSG, '2008 Framework, n. 4, para. 54.   [60] See Chapter 4.

to operate'.[61] As Denis Arnold recently confirmed, the main thrust of the SRSG's argument is based on prudential risk management and is thus predominantly strategic or instrumental.[62] The problem with such an instrumental justification of corporate human rights responsibility is that it cannot account for why corporations should care about human rights where they have little public exposure.[63] Furthermore, it naturally suffers from the general normative[64] and empirical[65] shortcomings of instrumental CSR, which are well documented and which shall not be repeated here.[66]

The SRSG does not explicitly endorse instrumental CSR in his reports. Granted that his use of instrumental argumentation is anything but subtle, but it does leave some room for interpretation. It could be argued, for example, that the SRSG's reference to strategic considerations is a mere selling point while the actual justification of the underlying responsibilities is thought to be moral. After all, by speaking of corporate human rights *responsibility*, rather than of mere human rights *considerations*, he does raise an explicitly normative claim. As such, this claim inevitably is based on certain (implicit) assumptions about ethics and morality. Responsibility is a normative concept with evident moral connotations. In other words, the SRSG assumes that for corporations there is a responsibility to respect human rights, which ought to be defended also on instrumental grounds. Social expectations, from this perspective, are relevant not only strategically, but they claim *moral*

---

[61] SRSG, '2008 Framework', n. 4, 54.

[62] D. Arnold, 'Transnational Corporations and the Duty to Respect Basic Human Rights' (2010) 20 *Business Ethics Quarterly* 371–99.

[63] *Ibid.*, 383.

[64] See, for example, L. S. Paine, 'Does Ethics Pay?' (2000) 10 *Business Ethics Quarterly* 319–30; D. Vogel, *The Market for Virtue: The Potential and Limits of Corporate Social Responsibility* (Washington, D.C.: Brookings Institution Press, 2005); F. Wettstein, 'Beyond Voluntariness, Beyond CSR: Making a Case for Human Rights and Justice' (2009) 114 *Business and Society Review* 125; and J.-P. Gond, G. Palazzo and K. Basu, 'Reconsidering Instrumental Corporate Social Responsibility through the Mafia Metaphor' (2009) 19 *Business Ethics Quarterly* 57–80.

[65] See, for example, J. D. Margolis and J. P. Walsh, *People and Profits? The Search for a Link between a Company's Social and Financial Performance* (Mahwah, NJ: Lawrence Erlbaum Associates, 2001).

[66] For a comprehensive conceptual and normative analysis of instrumental CSR in the domain of human rights see F. Wettstein, 'Human Rights as a Critique of Instrumental CSR: Corporate Responsibility Beyond the Business Case' (2012) 18 *Notizie di Politeia* 18–33.

relevance or even authority. Such an interpretation would effectively refute the accusation that the SRSG's Framework lacks a moral basis.

However, turning social expectations into the authoritative reference point of morality comes with its own problems. At the very core of such a positivist account of responsibility is the naturalistic fallacy of turning empirical facts into normative prescriptions. Thus, it does not differentiate between existing norms (morality) expressed, for example, within and through public opinion, and their critical justification (ethics).[67] Two problems derive from this. Firstly, doing so systematically suppresses marginal voices within the public discourse and instead only caters to the dominant ones irrespective of their moral legitimacy. Scherer and Palazzo rightly point out that defining corporate responsibility in such a positivist manner would not be a problem if it could be 'assumed that the signals of stakeholder groups could be considered as legitimate expectations'.[68] But the more pluralistic our societies become, the less certainty there is in this regard. Secondly, such conventional moralities disconnect the source of moral authority from the self and thus diminish the importance of the autonomous judgement of the responsibility-bearer as a moral agent. In other words, they reduce moral conduct to mere compliance with whatever the public's expectations are,[69] and thus empty morality itself of its critical potential. Morality is determined externally and all it takes to act in line with it is to do what one is told. Within such an understanding of morality, moral judgement on the part of the agent is not needed and the moral autonomy of the individual vanishes. This does not sit well with the normative underpinnings of human rights, whose very purpose is to protect precisely this autonomy which constitutes our inherent human quality.[70]

Is this lack of ethical argumentation in the SRSG's Framework of any relevance? Wesley Cragg asserts that it is: '[t]he failure to ground the framework on explicitly moral foundations', he claims, 'makes the framework both pragmatically and intellectually unpersuasive'.[71] Cragg is right. Had the SRSG engaged in more deliberate moral argumentation,

---

[67] A. G. Scherer and G. Palazzo, 'Toward a Political Conception of Corporate Responsibility: Business and Society Seen from a Habermasian Perspective' (2007) 32 *Academy of Management Review* 1099.

[68] *Ibid.*

[69] L. S. Paine, 'Managing for Organizational Integrity' (1994) 72 *Harvard Business Review* 106–17.

[70] On the link between freedom and human rights see, for example, A. Sen, 'Elements of a Theory of Human Rights' 32 *Philosophy & Public Affairs* 315–56.

[71] W. Cragg, 'Ethics, Enlightened Self-Interest and Corporate Responsibility', n. 57, 10.

the inconsistency at the heart of the Framework could have been corrected – not by eliminating silent complicity from the Framework, but by expanding the responsibilities of companies to include the possibility of positive duties beyond those based upon involvement and causal contribution. By this, I do not mean merely a duty to speak out against human rights violations as is implied by silent complicity, but much more general responsibilities in the categories of protecting and realising human rights.

Conclusion

Silent complicity may appear as the least significant form of complicity at a first glance, for it does not imply or presuppose that a company actively contributes to or is involved in the violations of human rights. A closer look at the concept, however, reveals its momentous implications in regard to the responsibilities of corporations for human rights in general. Surprisingly, the SRSG's analysis seems not to take notice of these implications at all. The result is an inconsistency at the very core of the SRSG's Framework. Its constitutive separation of the corporate responsibility to respect and the state duty to protect, as shown above, collapses upon a thorough and holistic analysis of the concept of silent complicity.

The SRSG's limitation of corporate human rights responsibility to a mere (negative) responsibility to do no harm is unconvincing also beyond the context of silent complicity. In an increasingly complex world in which many of the most pressing challenges elude the reach and the capacity of any single agent, lasting and sustainable solutions must increasingly be sought in collaborative approaches between a variety of social, political and economic actors. Against this background, multinational corporations can no longer make do merely with not making the situation worse, but must become a part of the solution. Their proactive and productive participation in such collaborative approaches is not a matter of voluntariness but a moral responsibility that comes with the powerful role they are fulfilling in today's global political economy. What the analysis of silent complicity points to, therefore, is a much broader failure of the Framework to take into account the full range of corporate responsibilities in the human rights domain.[72]

---

[72] On this more general point, see D. Bilchitz, 'The Ruggie Framework: An Adequate Rubric for Corporate Human Rights Obligations?' (2010) 12 *SUR International Journal on Human Rights* 199–228.

There is a growing stream of research in business ethics and beyond which calls for a broader notion of corporate responsibility, that is, for a notion of responsibility that is at least partially detached from involvement and based on social connections and influence.[73] Not too long ago, even John Ruggie called for such a turn in our thinking about corporate responsibility. In a 2007 publication, commenting on 'future direction' of the business and human rights debate, he asserted that its focal point 'needs to expand beyond establishing individual corporate liability for wrongdoing'. 'An individual liability model alone', as he argued, 'cannot fix larger imbalances in the system of global governance'.[74] Unfortunately, such visionary thinking largely disappeared in the reports that established the UN Framework.

Nevertheless, the Guiding Principles on Business and Human Rights (GPs) seem at least partially to depart from the premises laid down in the Framework and also accept responsibility beyond involvement.[75] Principle 13 of the GPs reads as follows:

> The responsibility to respect human rights requires that business enterprises: . . . [s]eek to prevent or mitigate adverse human rights impacts that are directly linked to their operations, products or services by their business relationships, even if they have not contributed to those impacts.[76]

Furthermore, in Principle 19 of the GPs, the SRSG asserts that appropriate action taken by companies to prevent and mitigate adverse human rights impacts will vary, firstly, according to whether a business causally contributes or is 'merely' directly linked to those impacts and, secondly, according to the extent of its leverage in addressing them.[77] In the Commentary to Principle 19, the SRSG reiterates that in situations in which 'a business enterprise has not contributed to an adverse human

---

[73] See, for example, M. A. Santoro, *Profits and Principles: Global Capitalism and Human Rights in China* (Ithaca; London: Cornell University Press, 2000); M. A. Santoro, *China 2020: How Western Business Can – and Should – Influence Social and Political Change in the Coming Decade* (Ithaca; London: Cornell University Press, 2009); I. M. Young, 'Responsibility and Global Labour Justice' (2004) 12 *Journal of Political Philosophy* 365–88; F. Wettstein, *Multinational Corporations and Global Justice: Human Rights Obligations of a Quasi-Governmental Institution* (Stanford University Press, 2009); and S. Wood, 'Leverage-Based Corporate Human Rights Responsibility', n. 36, 63–98.

[74] J. G. Ruggie, 'Business and Human Rights: The Evolving International Agenda' (2007) 101 *American Journal of International Law* 819, at 839.

[75] For a more detailed analysis of this point, see S. Wood, 'Leverage-Based Corporate Human Rights Responsibility', n. 36, 88–93.

[76] SRSG, 'Guiding Principles', n. 1, Principle 13.   [77] *Ibid.*, Principle 19.

rights impact, but that impact is nevertheless directly linked to its operations, products or services by its business relationship with another entity', leverage is among the factors that will enter into the determination of appropriate action. He defines leverage as the 'ability to effect change in the wrongful practices of an entity that causes a harm'.[78] The SRSG even goes a step further in what reads like a full endorsement of leverage-based responsibility: '[I]f the business enterprise has leverage to prevent or mitigate the adverse impact, it should exercise it. And if it lacks leverage there may be ways for the enterprise to increase it'.[79] The SRSG even recommends ending a relationship (i.e. withdrawal) only in situations in which leverage cannot be exerted or increased effectively. With this recommendation, he seemingly even turns 'do no harm' into a subordinate consideration to leverage. Nevertheless, the SRSG attempts to limit the implications of this point by holding on to and reasserting the limitation of corporate responsibility to the (negative) responsibility to respect and its clear separation from the state duty to protect human rights. Having it both ways, however, is impossible. Despite such conceptual inconsistencies, the SRSG's increased openness to leverage as a relevant consideration for corporate responsibility is to be welcomed. The newly appointed UN Working Group on business and human rights is well advised to continue on this path.

---

[78] *Ibid.*, para. 4 in Commentary to Principle 19.
[79] *Ibid.*, para. 7 in Commentary to Principle 19.

PART IV

Implementation and enforcement

11

When human rights 'responsibilities' become 'duties': the extra-territorial obligations of states that bind corporations

DANIEL AUGENSTEIN AND DAVID KINLEY

Introduction

Economic globalisation poses significant challenges to the Westphalian paradigm of human rights protection under national-constitutional and international law that allocates human rights obligations within and between sovereign states. Patterns of economic co-operation and competition across national-territorial borders are creating greater gaps between the operational capacities of global business entities and the regulatory capacities of territorial states. At the same time, the privatisation of state functions tends to shift powers and responsibilities from governments to the market. Accordingly, the traditional preoccupation of human rights law with protecting individuals against the oppressive power of the 'public' and 'territorial' state is increasingly overshadowed by concerns about the human rights impacts of 'private' power that coalesces around globally operating multinational corporations (MNCs). While – as a default rule – human rights are protected against public emanations of the state for the benefit of rights-holders physically located on the state's territory, creating a level playing field between states and globally operating business entities requires extra-territorial protection of human rights in relation to private actors. It is argued that the traditional state-based paradigm fails where it is most needed: for the benefit of individuals in weak host states of corporate investment which lack the capacity (and at times also the willingness) to protect human rights against business operations conducted with the active support or passive connivance of strong home state governments.

The wealth of documentation on positive and negative impacts of global business operations on human rights has over the past decade triggered 'business and human rights' debates in the major international,

European and domestic fora. At the UN level, John Ruggie was appointed as the Special Representative of the Secretary-General on the Issue of Human Rights and Transnational Corporations and Other Business Enterprises (SRSG) in 2005. This was after the failure to adopt the UN Draft Norms on the Responsibilities of Transnational Corporations and Other Business Enterprises with Regard to Human Rights (UN Norms) which pointed towards establishing an international treaty-based system of human rights obligations directly enforceable against private actors.[1] The SRSG developed the 'Protect, Respect and Remedy' Framework (Framework) in a series of reports. It builds on three pillars: (1) the state's duty to protect human rights against violations by third parties (including corporations), through appropriate policies, regulation, adjudication and enforcement measures; (2) the corporate responsibility to respect human rights, meaning to act with due diligence to avoid infringing the rights of others; and (3) greater access to effective remedies, both judicial and non-judicial, for victims of corporate-related human rights abuses. The SRSG's mandate culminated in the formulation of the Guiding Principles on Business and Human Rights (GPs) (endorsed by the UN Human Rights Council in June 2011), which seek to further explicate and operationalise the Framework.[2]

Whatever the attributes of the outputs of the SRSG's mandate – these having enjoyed conspicuous endorsement by many, especially corporations and governments, and attracted much discussion, analysis and criticism – neither the Framework nor the GPs provide much by way of addressing the problem of extra-territorial liability of globally operating business entities. Such liability can be ensured either by directly imposing legal human rights obligations on corporations or by extending existing obligations of states to regulate and control corporate actors beyond their territorial confines. Turning his back on the UN Norms, the SRSG discarded the former option. Distinguishing state obligations to protect human rights (the first pillar of the Framework) from corporate responsibilities to respect human rights

---

[1] Commission on Human Rights, Sub-Commission on the Promotion and Protection of Human Rights, 'Norms on the Responsibilities of Transnational Corporations and Other Business Enterprises with Regard to Human Rights', E/CN.4/Sub.2/2003/12 (26 August 2003). See also D. Kinley and R. Chambers, 'The UN Human Rights Norms for Corporations: The Private Implications of Public International Law' (2006) 2 *Human Rights Law Review* 447.

[2] Human Rights Council, 'Guiding Principles on Business and Human Rights: Implementing the United Nations' "Protect, Respect and Remedy" Framework', A/HRC/17/31 (21 March 2011) (SRSG, 'Guiding Principles').

(the second pillar of the Framework), he indicated that 'respecting rights is not an obligation that current international human rights law generally imposes directly on companies'.[3] At the same time, despite the fact that the problem of extra-territorial state obligations has featured prominently at various stages of the development of the Framework,[4] its resolution was effectively sidestepped by the mandate. Having examined the treaty body commentaries and jurisprudence under the core UN human rights instruments, the SRSG concluded that the extra-territorial dimension of the state duty to protect human rights in relation to business entities remains 'unsettled' in international law.[5] In response to perceived legal-doctrinal and political difficulties in firmly grounding extra-territorial liability in international law, the SRSG shifted the emphasis of debate from states' extra-territorial obligations under human rights law to states' policy rationales to protect human rights in their international relations.

As a consequence, the potential extra-territorial scope of existing territorial state obligations to protect human rights against corporate violations remains underexplored. In fact, the guidance provided by the SRSG on human rights violations in the 'state-business nexus' is

---

[3] Human Rights Council, 'Business and Human Rights: Further Steps towards the Operationalization of the "Protect, Respect and Remedy" Framework', A/HRC/14/27 (9 April 2010), para. 55 (SRSG, '2010 Report').

[4] See SRSG, 'Extra-territorial Legislation as a Tool to Improve the Accountability of Transnational Corporations for Human Rights Violations: Summary Report of Seminar of Legal Experts, Brussels' (November 2006); O. De Schutter, 'Extra-territorial Jurisdiction as a Tool for Improving the Human Rights Accountability of Transnational Corporations', Report Prepared in Support of the Mandate of the SRSG, Brussels (November 2006); Human Rights Council, 'State Responsibilities to Regulate and Adjudicate Corporate Activities under the United Nations Core Human Rights Treaties: An Overview of Treaty Body Commentaries', A/HRC/4/35/Add.1 (13 February 2007), paras. 81–92 (SRSG, 'State Responsibilities to Regulate'); Human Rights Council, 'Corporate Responsibility under International Law and Issues of Extra-territorial Regulation', A/HRC/4/35/Add.2 (15 February 2007) (SRSG, 'Issues of Extra-territorial Regulation'); SRSG, '2010 Report', n. 3, paras. 46–53; J. Zerk, 'Extra-territorial Jurisdiction: Lessons for the Business and Human Rights Sphere from Six Regulatory Areas', Report of the Harvard Corporate Social Responsibility Initiative to Inform the Mandate of the SRSG (June 2010); SRSG, 'Summary Note of Expert Meeting on Exploring Extra-territoriality in Business and Human Rights, Boston' (14 December 2010); H. Ascensio, 'Extra-territoriality as an Instrument', Report Prepared for an Expert Meeting on Exploring Extra-territoriality in Business and Human Rights, Boston (September 2010); and D. Augenstein, 'State Responsibilities to Regulate and Adjudicate Corporate Activities under the European Convention on Human Rights', Report Prepared in Support of the Mandate of the SRSG, Tilburg (April 2011).

[5] Human Rights Council, 'Business and Human Rights: Towards Operationalizing the "Protect, Respect and Remedy" Framework', A/HRC/11/13 (22 April 2009), para. 15 (SRSG, '2009 Report').

somewhat non-committal and avoids the clear language of legal obligations. The GPs generally limit themselves to suggesting that '[s]tates
should take additional steps to protect against human rights abuses by
business enterprises that are owned or controlled by the State, or that
receive substantial support and services from State agencies such as
export credit agencies and official investment insurance or guarantee
agencies, including, where appropriate, by requiring human rights due
diligence'.[6]

It may be unsurprising that the SRSG's approach of 'principled
pragmatism',[7] coupled with his healthy scepticism towards law (and
lawyers), tended him away from the legal-conceptual issues that lie at
the root of the relationship between international human rights protection and economic globalisation. It would be unfair to criticise the
Framework's notably successful strategy to bridge the gaps between the
attitudes of state governments, the business community and human
rights defenders that materialised in the process of burying the UN
Norms for its purported political imprudence.[8] Nevertheless, the emerging consensus on 'business and human rights' between the relevant
stakeholders may prove rather thin, and the endorsement of the GPs
by parts of the business community as 'a unique chance to lay to rest a
long-standing international debate about whether mandatory norms are
required'[9] certainly gives many pause to think. Against this background,
the scant consideration that the GPs give to extra-territorial human
rights obligations of states in relation to globally operating business
entities is an important missed opportunity.

It is to this issue that this chapter is dedicated. Instead of directly
engaging with the problem of corporate human rights obligations under

---

[6] See SRSG, 'Guiding Principles', n. 2, para. 4. The Commentary to this provision hints at
the possibility that negative corporate human rights impacts directly attributable to the
state 'may entail a violation of the State's own international law obligations'.

[7] Defined as 'an unflinching commitment to the principle of strengthening the promotion
and protection of human rights as it relates to business, coupled with a pragmatic
attachment to what works best in creating change where it matters most – in the daily
lives of people'. SRSG, '2010 Report', n. 3, para. 4.

[8] D. Kinley, J. Nolan and N. Zerial, 'The Politics of Corporate Social Responsibility:
Reflections on the United Nations Human Rights Norms for Corporations' (2007) 25:1
Company and Securities Law Journal 30.

[9] BP, 'BP Sustainability Reporting 2010: How We Operate' (2010), 19, www.aral.de/liveassets/
bp_internet/globalbp/globalbp_uk_english/sustainability/bp_sustainability/STAGING/local_
assets/downloads_pdfs/Sustainability2010_HowWeOperate.pdf (last accessed 15 November
2012).

international law – much discussed before and after the formulation of the corporate responsibility to respect in the second pillar of the Framework – we adopt an indirect approach that starts from a more orthodox position. This approach posits that under the Framework's first pillar, states have both direct (vertical) obligations as regards their own actions and indirect (horizontal) obligations to protect individuals within their jurisdiction, both inside and outside their territory, against corporate violations. This indirect approach to legal obligations of business entities to respect human rights in their global operations builds on three major propositions. Firstly, it is generally accepted, including by the SRSG, that states' human rights obligations do in fact entail obligations to protect individuals against corporate violations within their territory. Secondly, despite the fact that corporate responsibility to respect under the Framework's second pillar does not explicitly stipulate 'legal' obligations, business entities are in practice, and can be further, legally bound to respect human rights in their global operations via the medium of state regulation and control. Thirdly, in so far as states are under extra-territorial obligations to protect human rights, such obligations extend to the extra-territorial regulation and control of corporate actors.

In the following two sections, we discuss the SRSG's 'extra-territoriality matrix' in the context of the relationship between extra-territorial jurisdiction under public international law and the extra-territorial reach of international human rights treaties. Considering the SRSG's distinction between 'direct extra-territorial jurisdiction' and 'domestic measures with extra-territorial implications', we submit that in both constellations, extra-territorial human rights obligations are constituted by a *de facto* relationship of power of the state over the individual. The fourth section of the chapter is dedicated to developing the implications of this approach for extra-territorial corporate human rights violations. Emphasising the interdependency between the first and second pillar of the Framework, we argue that, bolstered by extra-territorial state obligations, the corporate responsibility to respect human rights grounded in the corporation's 'social licence to operate' translates into its legal accountability for human rights violations.

From law to policy: the SRSG's extra-territoriality matrix

It is helpful to place the GPs' minimal reference to extra-territorial obligations in the context of earlier research conducted in support of the Framework. Reviewing current state practice on extra-territorial jurisdiction, the SRSG notes that while in certain policy domains (including anti-corruption, anti-trust, securities regulation, environmental protection and general civil and criminal jurisdictions) states have agreed to certain uses of extra-territorial jurisdiction, this is typically not the case in business and human rights.[10] Moreover, the SRSG's examination of treaty body commentaries and jurisprudence under the core UN human rights treaties suggests that 'the extraterritorial dimension of the [state] duty to protect remains unsettled in international law'.[11] Accordingly, the GPs proclaim that:

> At present, states are not generally required under international human rights law to regulate the extra-territorial activities of business domiciled in their territory and/or jurisdiction. Nor are they generally prohibited from doing so, provided there is a recognised jurisdictional basis. Within these parameters, some human rights treaty bodies recommend that home states take steps to prevent abuse by business enterprises within their jurisdiction.[12]

The assertion that states are neither 'generally required' nor 'generally prohibited' to regulate and control business operations outside their territories shapes the SRSG's approach to extra-territorial jurisdiction. Firstly, the GPs focus on the permissibility of the extra-territorial exercise of (legislative, judicial and executive) state powers in accordance with a recognised basis of jurisdiction under public international law. What is at issue is the competence of states, as delimited by general international law, to assert authority over conduct not exclusively of domestic concern. Secondly, the GPs are primarily concerned with the territorial location and/or nationality of the business entity as the perpetrator of extra-territorial human rights violations. The enquiry thus turns on whether a state can exercise jurisdiction over corporate actors violating human rights abroad because they reside within the

---

[10] SRSG, '2010 Report', n. 3, para. 46, with reference to Zerk, 'Extra-territorial Jurisdiction', n. 4.

[11] SRSG, '2009 Report', n. 5, para. 15.

[12] See SRSG, 'Guiding Principles', n. 2, para. 2. This formulation draws on a background report prepared by O. De Schutter in support of the SRSG's mandate. De Schutter, 'Extra-territorial Jurisdiction', n. 4. However, De Schutter also notes that 'the classical view may be changing . . . especially as far as economic and social rights are concerned'. *Ibid.*, at 19. De Schutter has co-authored the recent 'Maastricht Principles on Extra-territorial Obligations of States in the area of Economic, Social and Cultural Rights' (September 2011) that adopt a decidedly more affirmative approach to extra-territorial human rights obligations in relation to globally operating business entities.

state's territory (the territoriality principle) and/or because they can be considered 'corporate nationals' of that state (the nationality principle).[13]

This twofold focus is perpetuated in a further distinction the SRSG introduces, namely between instances of 'direct extra-territorial jurisdiction' and 'domestic measures with extra-territorial implications':

> In the heated debates about extra-territoriality regarding business and human rights, a critical distinction between two very different phenomena is usually obscured. One is jurisdiction exercised directly in relation to actors or activities overseas, such as criminal regimes governing child sex tourism, which rely on the nationality of the perpetrator no matter where the offence occurs. The other is domestic measures with extra-territorial implications; for example, requiring corporate parents to report on the company's overall human rights policy and impacts, including those of its overseas subsidiaries. The latter phenomenon relies on territory as the jurisdictional basis, even though it may have extra-territorial implications.[14]

'Direct extra-territorial jurisdiction' and 'domestic measures with extra-territorial implications', in turn, form the 'rows' of the SRSG's extra-territoriality matrix:

> Indeed, one can imagine a matrix, with two rows and three columns. Its rows would be domestic measures with extraterritorial implications; and direct extraterritorial jurisdiction over actors and activities abroad. Its columns would be public policies for companies (such as CSR and public procurement policies, export credit agency criteria, or consular support); regulation (through corporate law, for instance); and enforcement action (adjudicating alleged breaches and enforcing judicial and executive decisions). Their combination yields six types of 'extraterritorial' form, each in turn offering a range of options.[15]

Whatever the legal-doctrinal virtues and pitfalls of this matrix, its intended political use-value is clear: to emphasise that extra-territoriality 'is not a binary matter' and that not all forms of extra-territoriality 'are equally likely to trigger objections under all circumstances'.[16] This is meant to depolarise the extra-territoriality debate and to mitigate

---

[13] In his earlier work, the SRSG has also explored other bases of extra-territorial jurisdiction under general international law, including the nationality of the victim (i.e. the passive personality principle). See SRSG, 'Issues of Extra-territorial Regulation', n. 4, paras. 35–74.

[14] SRSG, '2010 Report', n. 3, para. 48.   [15] *Ibid.*, para. 49.   [16] *Ibid.*

concerns that extra-territorial jurisdiction may interfere with the sovereign territorial rights of other states.[17]

However, the SRSG's 'critical distinction' between 'direct extra-territorial jurisdiction' and 'domestic measures with extra-territorial implications' obscures another critical distinction, namely between extra-territorial obligations imposed on states by virtue of human rights law and states' policy rationales to protect human rights against extra-territorial corporate violations. While the GPs' marginalisation of the former is the upshot of the SRSG's (negative) assertion that states 'are not generally required … to regulate the extraterritorial activities of businesses', the championing of the latter relates to his (positive) assertion that states are not 'prohibited from doing so, provided there is a recognized jurisdictional basis'.[18] The ensuing shift from law to policy in addressing extra-territorial human rights impacts of MNCs is clearly visible in the passages of the GPs that deal with human rights violations in the state-business nexus: '[t]here are strong policy reasons for home states to set out clearly the expectation that businesses respect human rights abroad, especially when the State itself is involved in or supports those businesses. The reasons include ensuring predictability for business enterprises by providing coherent and consistent messages, and preserving the State's own reputation.'[19]

The SRSG's encouragement of states to improve the quality of their human rights policies and to ensure that other policies do not have adverse impacts on human rights is certainly to be welcomed. However, it is one question whether states are *permitted* to adjust their

---

[17] It is indeed not uncommon for states to object to assertions of extra-territorial jurisdiction on grounds of state sovereignty and to take measures to offset its effects. For example, when the US government, using the Trading with the Enemy Act, ordered the US parent corporation of a French subsidiary to halt the sale of vehicles to China, the French courts appointed administrators to run the subsidiary and carry on with the sale. See *Société Fruehauf* v. *Massardy*, English trans. in (1966) 4 *International Legal Materials* 476. The USA also tried to prevent European subsidiaries of US corporations, and European corporations using US technology, from exporting equipment for the construction of a pipeline carrying gas from the USSR to Western Europe. EU member states protested at the US regulations and, in some cases, passed blocking legislation compelling their companies to carry out the contracts and disregard US law. The European Commission viewed the application of this legislation to European corporations (even if they were subsidiaries of US corporations) as a violation of the territorial jurisdiction of EU member states and an abuse of the nationality principle. See Commission of the European Communities, 'Comments on the US Regulations Concerning Trade with the USSR' (1982) 21 *International Legal Materials* 864.
[18] SRSG, 'Guiding Principles', n. 2, para. 2.   [19] *Ibid.*

policies and regulation to better promote and protect human rights in relation to extra-territorial corporate abuse (what may be termed the 'permissive question'). It is quite a different question whether states are *obliged* to do so as a matter of international human rights law (what may be termed the 'prescriptive question'). The GPs marginalise the 'prescriptive question' in favour of the 'permissive question' – with detrimental consequences for the extra-territorial protection of human rights against corporate violations. On the one hand, the SRSG's own research is evidence that in globalising economies there exists a whole range of domestic policies and regulations governing corporate conduct that *de facto* impact on the human rights of individuals in third countries, including restrictions imposed on the import and export of goods; public procurement and (more or less) socially responsible investment; criminal regimes governing foreign corruption and bribery; and traditional forms of private law regulation, such as the corporate law doctrine of separate legal personality.[20] On the other hand, states remain reluctant to regulate and control these extra-territorial human rights impacts, often with reference to the need to maintain a 'level playing field' for their own corporations, and the exceptional and politically sensitive nature of extra-territorial measures.[21] The SRSG acknowledged as much by noting that in 'several policy domains ... States have agreed to certain uses of extraterritorial jurisdiction. However, this is typically not the case in business and human rights.'[22]

Once the epistemic bias against certain forms of extra-territoriality is dispersed, the real question is not whether states use 'direct extra-territorial jurisdiction' and 'domestic measures with extra-territorial implications', but whether they use them *to protect human rights*. Against this background, an enquiry into the existing obligations of states under international human rights law to protect individuals against extra-territorial corporate violations (the 'prescriptive question') is relevant beyond narrow concerns with enforcement. It turns on the principled issue of the role and standing of human rights

[20] See Zerk, 'Extra-territorial Jurisdiction', n. 4; Ascensio, 'Extra-territoriality', n. 4. For a recent collection of case studies, see F. Coomans and R. Künnemann (eds.), *Cases and Concepts on Extra-territorial Obligations in the Area of Economic, Social and Cultural Rights* (Cambridge: Intersentia, 2012).

[21] See, for example, the UK Government, '"Any of Our Business?" Human Rights and the UK Private Sector: Government Response to the Committee's First Report of Session 2009–10', HL Paper 66 HC 401 (8 March 2010), para. 41.

[22] SRSG, '2010 Report', n. 3, para. 46.

protection in the area of tension between globalising economies and an international *ordre publique* constituted by territorial states. While, as one of us has argued elsewhere, 'human rights must embrace the power of the global economy', this power must also be harnessed 'so as to promote the overarching goals of human rights'.[23]

From policy to law: extra-territorial jurisdiction and international human rights obligations

In the previous section, we suggested that the SRSG's distinction between 'direct extra-territorial jurisdiction' and 'domestic measures with extra-territorial implications' is primarily geared towards mitigating concerns that the extra-territorial regulation of business activities may interfere with the sovereign territorial rights of other states. Moreover, the ensuing preoccupation with states' competence to protect human rights against extra-territorial corporate abuse obscures the problem of corresponding state obligations. Yet, put crudely, the question whether states are obliged to protect the human rights of individuals in third countries against corporate abuse is *not reducible to* the question whether they are permitted to do so pursuant to a recognised basis of jurisdiction under general international law. The 'prescriptive question' cannot be collapsed into the 'permissive question'.

The concept of jurisdiction bears various different meanings in international law. Consider, by way of example, Article 5(1)(a) of the Convention against Torture and Other Cruel, Inhuman or Degrading Treatment or Punishment (CAT), which reads: 'Each State Party shall take such measures as may be necessary to establish its jurisdiction ... [w]hen the offences are committed in any territory under its jurisdiction'. Clearly, the term 'jurisdiction' is used here in two different senses.[24] Article 5(1)(a) provides that a state is under a *de jure* obligation to establish jurisdiction (e.g. by ensuring 'that all acts of torture are offences under its criminal law'[25]) whenever it *de facto* exercises

---

[23] D. Kinley, *Civilizing Globalisation* (Cambridge University Press, 2009), 9.

[24] Otherwise, the provision would stipulate the paradoxical requirement that states should establish jurisdiction in circumstances in which they already have jurisdiction. See also M. Milanović, 'From Compromise to Principle: Clarifying the Concept of State Jurisdiction in Human Rights Treaties' (2008) 8 *Human Rights Law Review* 411.

[25] Convention against Torture and Other Cruel, Inhuman or Degrading Treatment or Punishment (CAT), Art. 4(1).

jurisdiction over 'any territory'.[26] This correlation of effective control and legal obligations can be mapped onto the relationship between extra-territorial jurisdiction as delimited by general international law and jurisdiction under international human rights treaties as constitutive of a state's extra-territorial human rights obligations. The former is a function of state sovereignty and concerns the state's right to exercise jurisdiction abroad.[27] The latter, by contrast, is a function of protecting the rights of individuals and concerns the state's obligations when exercising jurisdiction abroad. Put differently, whereas the purpose of the former is to establish whether a state has legal authority to act extra-territorially, the purpose of the latter is to establish whether a state incurs extra-territorial obligations towards individuals over whom it exercises factual power. Importantly, the existence of extra-territorial human rights obligations is not restricted to situations in which the state is competent to exercise extra-territorial jurisdiction. Any other conclusion would lead to the counter-intuitive result that a state could circumvent its obligations under international human rights treaties by exceeding its jurisdictional competences under general international law.[28] Accordingly, while the concrete prerequisites of extra-territorial human rights obligations remain subject to debate, it seems widely accepted that what is decisive is not a state's *de jure* authority, but its exercise of *de facto* power or control over individuals outside its territory.

According to the UN Human Rights Committee (HRC), 'a State party must respect and ensure the rights laid down in the [International Covenant on Civil and Political Rights (ICCPR)] to anyone within [its] power or effective control . . . even if not situated within the territory of

---

[26] According to the UN Committee against Torture, any territory under a state's juris-diction includes 'all areas where the State party exercises, directly or indirectly, in whole or in part, *de jure* or *de facto* effective control, in accordance with international law'. Committee against Torture, 'General Comment No. 2: Implementation of Article 2 by States Parties', CAT/C/GC/2 (24 January 2008), para. 16.

[27] As Mann puts it, the concept of jurisdiction fulfils 'one of the fundamental functions of public international law', namely 'the function of regulating and delimiting the respec-tive [legislative, judicial and administrative] competences of States'. F. A. Mann, 'The Doctrine of Jurisdiction in International Law' (1964) 111 *Recueil des Cours* 1, at 15. See also M. Gondek, *The Reach of Human Rights in a Globalising World: Extra-territorial Application of Human Rights Treaties* (Cambridge: Intersentia, 2009), Ch. 2.

[28] See, for example, O. De Schutter, 'Globalisation and Jurisdiction: Lessons from the European Convention on Human Rights,' *Centre for Human Rights and Global Justice Working Paper No. 9* (2005).

the State Party ... and regardless of the circumstances in which such power or effective control was obtained'.[29] Similarly, in the case of *Loizidou* v. *Turkey*, the European Court of Human Rights (ECtHR) held that 'the responsibility of a Contracting Party could also arise when as a consequence of military action – whether lawful or unlawful – it exercises effective control of an area outside its national territory'.[30] Having regard to *Loizidou*, the Inter-American Commission of Human Rights considered that '[t]his understanding of jurisdiction – and therefore responsibility for compliance with international obligations – [is] a notion linked to authority and effective control, and not merely to territorial boundaries'.[31] This approach to human rights jurisdiction is not confined to civil and political rights, but also determines the extraterritorial reach of the International Covenant on Economic, Social and Cultural Rights (ICESCR) as well as of the Convention on the Rights of the Child (CRC). For example, in its *Advisory Opinion on the Legality of the Wall in the Occupied Palestinian Territory*, the International Court of Justice (ICJ) reiterated the view of the Committee on Economic, Social and Cultural Rights that 'the State party's obligations under the Covenant apply to all territories and populations under its effective control'.[32] On this basis, the ICJ held that the construction of the wall impeded, *inter alia*, 'the exercise by the persons concerned of the right to work, to health, to education and to an adequate standard of living as proclaimed in the International Covenant on Economic, Social and Cultural Rights and in the United Nations Convention on the Rights of the Child'.[33]

---

[29] Human Rights Committee, 'General Comment No. 31: The Nature of the General Legal Obligation Imposed on States Parties to the Covenant', CCPR/C/21/Rev.1/Add.13 (26 May 2004), para. 10.

[30] *Loizidou* v. *Turkey (Preliminary Objections)*, Judgment of 23 March 1995, ECtHR, para. 61, confirmed at the merits stage, *Loizidou* v. *Turkey*, Judgment of 18 December 1996, ECtHR, para. 52.

[31] *Victor Saldano* v. *Argentina*, Report No. 38/99, OEA/Er.L/V.II.95 Doc. 7 Rev., Judgment of 11 March 1999, Inter-ACHR, para. 19.

[32] International Court of Justice (ICJ), *Legal Consequences of the Construction of a Wall in the Occupied Palestinian Territory: Advisory Opinion* (9 July 2004), 136, para. 112, relying on CESCR, 'Concluding Considerations of the Committee on Economic, Social and Cultural Rights: Israel', E/C.12/1/Add.90 (23 May 2003), paras. 15 and 31.

[33] ICJ, *Advisory Opinion, ibid.*, para. 134. This was applied in *Democratic Republic of Congo* v. *Uganda*, Judgment of 19 December 2005, *ICJ Reports*, 168, para. 216, where the Court held that 'international human rights instruments are applicable "in respect of acts done by a State in the exercise of its jurisdiction outside its own territory", particularly in occupied territories'.

Despite the fact that the ICJ based its judgment on Israel's 'territorial jurisdiction as an occupying power', extra-territorial human rights obligations are not confined to situations of state occupation, with effective control over foreign territory functioning as a proxy of territorial jurisdiction.[34] Rather, what is decisive is that the state asserts *de facto* power and control over an individual physically located in a third country.[35] Effective control over individuals *sans* control over territory has been recognised as an exercise of extra-territorial jurisdiction under international human rights treaties.[36] Furthermore, it is implicit in the very definition of jurisdiction under human rights treaties employed by various international courts and treaty bodies. According to the Inter-American Commission of Human Rights, 'any person subject to [a state's] jurisdiction' in Article 1 of the American Convention of Human Rights refers to:

> conduct with an extraterritorial locus where the person concerned is present in the territory of one state, but subject to the control of another state – usually through the acts of the latter's agents abroad. In principle, the inquiry turns not on the presumed victim's nationality or presence within a particular geographic area, but on whether, under the specific circumstances, the State observed the rights of a person subject to its authority and control.[37]

According to the HRC, the ICCPR's reference to individuals subject to a state's jurisdiction 'is not to the place where the violation occurred, but

---

[34] Thus, presupposing an exercise of state authority with a 'discrete quasi-territorial quality' or a 'strong nexus to state territory'. See, respectively, *R (on the Application of Mazin Jumaa Gatteh Al Skeini and Others) v. Secretary of State for Defence* [2004] EWHC 2911 (Admin) (High Court of Justice (Divisional Court)), para. 270 and S. Miller, 'Revisiting Extraterritorial Jurisdiction: A Territorial Justification for Extraterritorial Jurisdiction under the European Convention' (2010) 20:4 *European Journal of International Law* 1223, at 1236.

[35] Similarly with regard to, respectively, the International Covenant on Civil and Political Rights and the European Convention on Human Rights, M. Scheinin, 'Extraterritorial Effect of the International Covenant on Civil and Political Rights' and R. Lawson, 'Life After Banković: On the Extraterritorial Application of the European Convention on Human Rights', both in F. Coomans and M. T. Kamminga (eds.), *Extraterritorial Application of Human Rights Treaties* (Cambridge: Intersentia, 2004).

[36] See, e.g., *X v. United Kingdom*, Judgment of 15 December 1977, E Comm. HR; *Öcalan v. Turkey*, Chamber Judgment of 12 March 2003 and Grand Chamber Judgment of 12 May 2005, ECtHR; *Alejandre et al. v. Republic of Cuba*, Case 11.589, Report No. 86/99, Judgment of 29 September 1999, Inter-Am. CHR; *Coard et al. v. The United States*, Case 10.951, Report No. 109/99, Judgment of 29 September 1999, HRC; *López Burgos v. Uruguay*, Comm. No. 52/1979, CCPR/C/OP/1, Judgment of 29 July 1981, HRC.

[37] *Coard et al.*, n. 36, para. 37.

rather to the relationship between the individual and the State in relation to a violation of any of the rights set forth in the Covenant'.[38] Similarly, according to the ECtHR,

> the real connection between the applicants and the respondent States is the impugned act which, wherever decided, was performed, or had effects, outside of the territory of those States ('the extra-territorial act'). [The Court] considers that the essential question to be examined therefore is whether the applicants ... were, as a result of that extra-territorial act, capable of falling within the jurisdiction of the respondent States.[39]

The ECtHR's distinction between acts performed outside the state's territory and acts performed inside the state's territory that produce effects outside the state's territory indicates that the relevant test of *de facto* power and control applies not only to what the SRSG has termed 'direct extra-territorial jurisdiction' but also to his category of 'domestic measures with extra-territorial implications'. The classical examples are non-refoulement cases, *à la Soering*, where the responsibility of the extraditing state is engaged, because the person to be removed from the state's territory is likely to be subjected to treatment in violation of Articles 2 and 3 of the European Convention on Human Rights (ECHR) in the receiving State.[40] Arguably, in these cases, the initial location of the victim on the state's territory establishes a presumption of *de facto* control over the individual on the part of that state.

Extra-territorial human rights obligations and globally operating business entities

It is widely accepted that states' human rights obligations entail obligations to protect individuals against corporate violations within their territorial jurisdiction. According to the SRSG, international law imposes obligations on states not only to 'refrain from violating' human

---

[38] *López Burgos*, n. 36, para. 12.2.

[39] *Banković and Others* v. *Belgium and Others*, Grand Chamber Admissibility Decision of 12 December 2001, ECtHR, para. 54. See also *R (Al-Skeini and Others)* v. *Secretary of State for Defence* [2007] UKHL 26, 34 (HL). Having regard to the case law of the ECtHR, Lord Roger remarked: 'It is important therefore to recognise that, when considering the question of jurisdiction under the Convention, the focus has shifted to the victim or, more precisely, to the link between the victim and the contracting state.' *Ibid.*, para. 64.

[40] *Soering* v. *United Kingdom*, Judgment of 7 July 1989, ECtHR; see also *Kindler* v. *Canada*, A/48/50/138, Judgment of 30 July 1993, HRC.

rights, but also 'to "ensure" (or some functionally equivalent verb) the enjoyment or realization of those rights by the rights holders'.[41] The latter obligation 'requires protection by States against other social actors, including business, who impede or negate those rights. Guidance from international human rights bodies suggests that the state duty to protect applies to all recognized rights that private parties are capable of impairing, and to all types of business enterprises.'[42] In this vein, the ECtHR distinguishes between negative state obligations to protect Convention rights against violations by private actors as state agents and positive state obligations to protect Convention rights against violations by private actors as third parties. While in the former case the private act is attributed to the state so that the state is considered to directly interfere with Convention rights, in the latter case the state violates its obligations by failing 'to take reasonable and appropriate measures to secure the applicant's rights'.[43] Similarly, the Inter-American Court of Human Rights in *Velasquez Rodriguez* v. *Honduras* noted that

> [a]n illegal act which violates human rights and which is initially not directly imputable to a State (for example, because it is the act of a private person . . .) can lead to international responsibility of the State, not because of the act itself, but because of the lack of due diligence to prevent the violation or to respond to it as required by the Convention.[44]

It is against this background that we now turn to consider the application of these principles to extra-territorial corporate violations in the light of the general distinction between extra-territorial jurisdiction under public international law and extra-territorial human rights obligations elaborated in the previous section. Our main contention is that the (non-) regulation or control of corporate actors by the state establishes a relationship of *de facto* power between the state and the individual constitutive of extra-territorial human rights obligations. A state's *de jure* authority to exercise extra-territorial jurisdiction under public international law not only delimits the state's lawful competence to regulate and control business entities as perpetrators of extra-territorial

---

[41] SRSG, 'Mandate Consultation Outline' (October 2010), 2, www.reports-and-materials. org/Ruggie-consultations-outline-Oct-2010.pdf (last accessed 20 January 2013).

[42] SRSG, '2009 Report', n. 5, para. 13.

[43] See, for example, *Fadeyeva* v. *Russia*, Judgment of 9 June 2005, ECtHR, para. 89.

[44] *Velasquez Rodriguez* v. *Honduras* (Ser. C) No. 4, Judgment of 29 July 1988, Inter-Am. CtHR, para. 172.

human rights violations, but also constitutes a *de facto* relationship of power of the state over the individual that brings the individual under the state's human rights jurisdiction and triggers corresponding extra-territorial obligations.

The case law of the ECtHR in particular provides various examples of extra-territorial obligations to protect human rights against violations by non-state actors, akin to the SRSG's category of 'direct extra-territorial jurisdiction'. In one of the Cyprus cases, for example, the Court held that Turkey's human rights obligations as an occupying power in Northern Cyprus extended not only to acts of its own soldiers and officials as well as acts of the local administration (the Turkish Republic of Northern Cyprus, TRNC), but also to the acts of private parties violating the rights of Greek and Turkish Cypriots.[45] In the latter context, the Court noted that 'the acquiescence or connivance of the authorities of a Contracting State in the acts of private individuals which violate the Convention rights of other individuals within its jurisdiction may engage that State's responsibility under the Convention. Any different conclusion would be at variance with the obligation contained in Article 1 of the Convention.'[46]

The more recent case of *Isaak* v. *Turkey* indicates that the application of these principles is not confined to situations in which the state, as an occupying power, exercises effective control over foreign territory.[47] *Isaak* concerned a demonstration in the neutral UN buffer zone established between the Turkish and Greek Cypriot ceasefire lines, in the course of which one participant was beaten to death by TRNC policemen and private actors (the 'Turkish mob'). The circumstances of the case precluded any finding of Turkey exercising effective territorial control over the area in question. Nevertheless, having established that 'despite the presence of the Turkish armed forces and other "TRNC" police officers in the area, nothing was done to prevent or stop the attack [by civilian demonstrators] or to help the victim',[48] the Court reiterated its dictum in *Cyprus* that 'the acquiescence or connivance of the authorities of a Contracting State in the acts of private individuals which violate Convention rights of other individuals within its jurisdiction may engage that State's responsibility under the Convention'.[49] In the absence of

---

[45] *Cyprus* v. *Turkey*, Judgment of 10 May 2001, ECtHR.   [46] *Ibid.*, para. 81.

[47] *Isaak and Others* v. *Turkey*, Admissibility Decision of 28 September 2006; confirmed at the merits stage, *Isaak* v. *Turkey*, Judgment of 24 June 2008.

[48] Admissibility Decision of 28 September 2006, *ibid.*, para. 21.   [49] *Ibid.*

effective territorial control, Turkey's extra-territorial obligations are apparently directly grounded in the state's acquiescence in the human rights violations committed by private actors outside the state's territory.[50]

Similarly, in extra-territorial effects cases associated with the SRSG's category of 'domestic measures with extra-territorial implications', the ECtHR considered that the prohibition of extradition stipulated in *Soering* also applies where the threat to Convention rights in the receiving country emanates from private actors.[51] Moreover, the Court's more recent case law indicates that these principles extend beyond the narrow category of non-refoulement cases to instances where the violation of Convention rights in a third country can be linked to a failure of the home state to regulate and control private actors on its own territory.[52] Of particular interest in this context is the case of *Kovačič*, which concerned the domestic regulation of business activities that allegedly violated Convention rights outside the state's territory.[53] The Croatian applicants complained that they were prevented by a Slovenian law from withdrawing funds from their accounts in the Croatian branch of a Slovenian bank. The Slovenian government submitted that its obligation to secure property rights under Article 1 of Protocol 1 of the ECHR was confined to property within its jurisdiction, and that none of the instances of extra-territorial jurisdiction recognised by the ECtHR was applicable in the present case. Indeed, neither did the respondent state exercise 'effective control' outside its territory, nor did the applicants reside at any point within the respondent state's territory. Nevertheless,

---

[50] As Miltner notes in her discussion of the case, it is unlikely that the Court could have established jurisdiction 'without the broadening of the authority and control test via the use of the "acquiescence" device'. B. Miltner, 'Extraterritorial Jurisdiction under the European Convention on Human Rights: An Expansion under *Isaak v Turkey*?' (2007) 2 *European Human Rights Law Review* 172, 181. The principle that not only acts, but also omissions, of the state can constitute an extra-territorial exercise of authority over persons was recognised early by the European Commission of Human Rights: *X v. UK*, Decision of 15 December 1977, Eur. CHR. Similarly, the recently adopted Maastricht Principles on Extra-Territorial Human Rights Obligations in the Area of Economic, Social and Cultural Rights define extra-territorial obligations as 'obligations relating to the acts and omissions of a State, within or beyond its territory, that have effects on the enjoyment of human rights outside of that State's territory'. Maastricht Principles, n. 12, para. 8.

[51] *HLR v. France*, Grand Chamber Judgment of 29 April 1997, ECtHR.

[52] See, for example, *Rantsev v. Cyprus and Russia*, Judgment of 7 January 2010, ECtHR.

[53] *Kovačič and Others v. Slovenia*, Admissibility Decision of 1 April 2004, ECtHR. The case was struck out at the merits stage due to new facts that had come to the Court's attention.

the ECtHR, after reiterating that 'the responsibility of [the High] Contracting Parties can be involved by acts and omissions of their authorities which produce effects outside their own territory',[54] accepted that the banking legislation introduced by the Slovenian National Assembly 'affected' the applicants' property rights in Croatia. 'This being so', the ECtHR found that 'the acts of the Slovenian authorities continue to produce effects, albeit outside Slovenian territory, such that Slovenia's responsibility under the Convention could be engaged'.[55]

Hence, it appears that what is decisive for the determination of extra-territorial human rights obligations to protect against corporate violations is not the state's exercise of *de jure* authority, but its assertion of *de facto* power over the individual rights-holder. More specifically, it is an act or omission of the state in relation to a corporate actor that brings the individual under the power of the state and triggers corresponding obligations to protect his or her human rights against corporate violations.

This view is consistent with the general definitions of human rights jurisdiction developed by international courts and treaty bodies as discussed in the previous section. It finds further support in two more recent ECtHR cases on extra-territorial state obligations. According to the partly dissenting opinion of Judge Loucaides in *Illascu*,

> 'jurisdiction' means actual authority, that is to say the possibility of imposing the will of the State on any person, whether exercised within the territory of the High Contracting Parties or outside that territory . . . The test should always be whether the person who claims to be within the 'jurisdiction' of a State, High Contracting Party to the Convention, in respect of a particular act can show that the act in question was the result of the exercise of authority by the State concerned.[56]

Moreover, the relevant test of 'actual authority' is not confined to situations where the state directly interferes with Convention rights, but also encompasses a state's 'failure to discharge its positive obligations in respect of any person if it was in a position to exercise its authority directly or even indirectly over that person or over the territory where such person is'.[57] A similar approach to extra-territorial human rights

---

[54] *Cyprus* v. *Turkey*, n. 45, para. 76.   [55] *Kovačič* v. *Slovenia*, n. 53.

[56] *Ilascu and Others* v. *Moldova and Russia*, Grand Chamber Judgment of 8 July 2004, ECtHR, Partly Dissenting Opinion of Judge Loucaides,139, citing *Assanidze* v. *Georgia*, Grand Chamber Judgment of 8 April 2004, ECtHR, Concurring Opinion of Judge Loucaides, 52.

[57] *Ibid.*

obligations is discernible in Judge Bonello's concurring opinion in *Al-Skeini*: 'the duties assumed through ratifying the Convention go hand in hand with the duty to perform and observe them',[58] on the state's own territory as well as beyond. Accordingly, '[j]urisdiction arises from the mere fact of having assumed those obligations *and from having the capability to fulfil them* (or not fulfil them).'[59] This resonates with a broader normative principle that has long informed the case law of the ECtHR: 'Article 1 of the Convention cannot be interpreted so as to allow a State party to perpetrate violations of the Convention on the territory of another State, which it could not perpetrate on its own territory.'[60]

The proposition that it is an act or omission of the state in relation to a corporate actor that brings the individual under the power of the state and triggers corresponding obligations to protect his or her human rights against corporate violations is also supported by a series of UN Treaty Body Comments and Concluding Observations issued over the past decade. In its General Comment No. 14 concerning the right to health, the Committee on Economic, Social and Cultural Rights noted:

> To comply with their international obligations in relation to article 12, States parties have to respect the enjoyment of the right to health in other countries, and to prevent third parties from violating the right in other countries, if they are able to influence these third parties by way of legal or political means, in accordance with the Charter of the United Nations and applicable international law.[61]

With regard to the right to water, the same Committee considered that '[i]nternational cooperation requires States parties to refrain from actions that interfere, directly or indirectly, with the enjoyment of the

---

[58] *Al-Skeini and Others* v. *United Kingdom*, Grand Chamber Judgment of 7 July 2011, ECtHR, Concurring Opinion of Judge Bonello, para. 13.

[59] *Ibid.* (emphasis in the original).

[60] *Isaak*, n. 47. In a similar vein, the Human Rights Committee has stressed that 'it would be unconscionable to so interpret the responsibility under article 2 [ICCPR] as to permit a State party to perpetrate violations of the Covenant on the territory of another State, which violations it could not perpetrate on its own territory'. *López Burgos*, n. 36, para. 12.3.

[61] CESCR, 'General Comment No. 14: The Right to the Highest Attainable Standard of Health', E/C.12/2000/4 (11 August 2000), para. 39.

right to water in other countries'.[62] Accordingly, states are called upon 'to prevent their own citizens and companies from violating the right to water of individuals and communities in other countries [w]here States parties can take steps to influence other third parties to respect the right, through legal or political means'.[63] The Committee's more recent General Comment on social security provides that 'State parties should extraterritorially protect the right to social security by preventing their own citizens and national entities from violating this right in other countries'.[64]

In a similar vein, the Committee on the Elimination of Racial Discrimination has recently called upon the United Kingdom 'to take appropriate legislative and administrative measures to ensure that acts of transnational corporations registered in the State party comply with the provisions of the Convention'.[65] With regard to Australia, the Committee noted 'with concern the absence of a legal framework regulating the obligation of Australian corporations at home and overseas whose activities, notably in the extractive sector, when carried out on the traditional territories of Indigenous peoples, have had a negative impact on Indigenous peoples' rights to land, health, living environment and livelihoods'.[66] Accordingly, the Committee encouraged the state party to 'regulate the extra-territorial activities of Australian corporations abroad'.[67]

The Committee on the Elimination of Racial Discrimination has made similar observations with regard to Canada and the USA, including recommendations that state parties should explore ways to hold business entities incorporated within their jurisdiction accountable for extra-territorial violations of the Convention.[68] Noting with concern reported participation and complicity of Australian mining companies in serious

---

[62] CESCR, 'General Comment No. 15: The Right to Water', E/C.12/2002/11 (20 January 2003), para. 31.

[63] *Ibid.*, para. 33.

[64] CESCR, 'General Comment No. 19: The Right to Social Security', E/C.12/GC/19 (4 February 2008), para. 54.

[65] CERD, 'Concluding Observations: United Kingdom of Great Britain and Northern Ireland', CERD/C/GBR/CO/18–20 (14 September 2011), para. 29.

[66] CERD, 'Concluding Observations: Australia', CERD/C/AUS/CO/15–17 (13 September 2010), para. 13.

[67] *Ibid.*

[68] CERD, 'Concluding Observations/Comments: Canada', CERD/C/CAN/CO/18 (25 May 2007), para. 17; CERD, 'Concluding Observations: United States', CERD/C/USA/CO/6 (8 May 2008), para. 30.

human rights violations in third countries, the Committee on the Rights of the Child called upon the State party to '[e]xamine and adapt its legislative framework (civil, criminal and administrative) . . . regarding abuses to human rights, especially child rights, committed in the territory of the State party or overseas and establish monitoring mechanisms, investigation, and redress of such abuses, with a view towards improved accountability, transparency and prevention of violations'.[69]

Conclusion

Whereas in the previous two sections we have tried to map extra-territorial human rights obligations onto the SRSG's distinction between 'direct extra-territorial jurisdiction' and 'domestic measures with extra-territorial implications', it is worth reiterating that this very distinction – driven by what we have called the 'permissive question' – is inadequate to capture the proper source and nature of extra-territorial state obligations to protect human rights against corporate violations. Whereas the SRSG focuses on states' *de jure* authority to exercise jurisdiction outside their territories as delimited by public international law, what is decisive for extra-territorial human rights obligations is states asserting *de facto* power over the individual rights-holder. Relatedly, whereas the SRSG's distinction between 'direct extra-territorial jurisdiction' and 'domestic measures with extra-territorial implications' primarily draws on the territorial location and/or nationality of the business entity as the perpetrator of human rights violations, what is decisive for extra-territorial human rights obligations is whether an act or omission of the state brings the individual victim of human rights violations within its jurisdiction. Whereas the primary concern of jurisdiction under public international law as associated with the 'permissive question' is to respect the sovereign territorial rights of other states, the primary concern of extra-territorial human rights obligations as associated with the 'prescriptive question' is to empower the individual against assertions of state power. From the latter perspective, a state's legal authority to exercise extra-territorial jurisdiction under public international law does not merely delimit the state's lawful competence to regulate and control business entities as perpetrators of extra-territorial human rights violations. The prospective *de jure* relationship between the state and the corporation further constitutes a *de facto* relationship of

---

[69] CRC, 'Concluding Observations: Australia', CRC/C/AUS/CO/4 (19 June 2012), para. 28(a).

power of the state over the individual that brings the individual within the state's human rights jurisdiction and triggers corresponding extra-territorial obligations.

It may be objected that such an approach to extra-territorial human rights obligations leads to virtually unlimited state responsibility for corporate human rights violations in third countries. However, it needs to be recalled that state obligations to protect individuals against violations by non-state actors constitute duties of conduct, and not of result. Accordingly, it needs to be shown that there is a sufficiently close nexus between the state and the private perpetrator, and that the state has failed to take all reasonable and appropriate measures to prevent, investigate and redress the human rights violation. International human rights courts have already fleshed out what is considered reasonable and appropriate within the state's territorial jurisdiction.[70] To clarify in what regard and to what extent the interpretation of these criteria will vary in the internal and external realms is an important task of international human rights jurisprudence. Our concern in this chapter has been a more principled one in that we enquired into the doctrinal foundations of extra-territorial human rights obligations upon which any further discussion of their specification and limitation should build.

From such a principled perspective, it would appear that in globalising economies the Westphalian allocation of human rights obligations within and between states that lay mutually exclusive claims to sovereign territorial rights is losing ground. State sovereignty is not what it used to be,[71] and the 'old' doctrinal preoccupation with human rights violations committed in the course of foreign military operations is insufficient to address effectively the 'new' challenges to extra-territorial human rights protection brought about by patterns of economic globalisation. The interdependencies of 'public' and 'territorial' states and 'private' and 'global' business entities increasingly undermine the Westphalian

---

[70] See, e.g., for a discussion of the ECtHR's interpretation of the state duty to protect in the context of 'environmental rights', D. Augenstein, 'The Human Rights Dimension of Environmental Protection in EU External Relations after Lisbon' in E. Morgera (ed.), *The External Environmental Policy of the European Union* (Cambridge University Press, 2012), 263.

[71] In fact, state sovereignty has not been what it used to be for quite a while. See P. Alston, 'The Myopia of Handmaidens: International Lawyers and Globalisation' (1997) 3 *European Journal of International Law* 435.

orthodoxy of the state as sole guarantor and violator of human rights. Examples abound: states authorising or insufficiently controlling the operations of dangerous facilities by private corporations that result in serious human rights violations 'at home' or 'abroad';[72] states employing private corporations to exercise public functions in human rights-sensitive areas, in some cases circumventing their own international human rights obligations;[73] states investing, through state-owned banks and public pension funds, in corporate undertakings that violate human rights in third countries;[74] states licensing or otherwise support-ing the export or import by business entities of goods that have been produced in violation of human rights standards, or that are used to commit human rights atrocities, in third countries;[75] and the increasing

---

[72] Various documented cases of cyanide spills in the course of corporate gold-mining operations in Europe and Latin America illustrate this. For example, the ECtHR's case of *Tatar* v. *Romania* arose out of a cyanide spill in a Romanian gold mine that contami-nated local fresh waters, but also the Tisza River in Hungary and the Danube River down to the Black Sea. Considering that the cyanide spill in Romania also affected Hungary and Serbia-Montenegro, the Court 'recalled that ... states have a general obligation to deter and prevent the transfer of substances to other countries that result in a serious deterioration of the environment'. *Tatar* v. *Romania*, Judgment of 27 January 2009, ECtHR, para. 109 (authors' translation).

[73] Such as the use of so-called 'shell companies' to execute extraordinary renditions for the purpose of illegal detention and coercive interrogation in third countries. See, e.g., European Parliament, Temporary Committee on the Alleged Use of European Countries by the CIA for the Transport and Illegal Detention of Prisoners, 'Working Document No. 7 on Extraordinary Renditions', PE 380.593v04–00 (16 November 2006) and 'Working Document No. 8 on the Companies Linked to the CIA, Aircraft Used by the CIA, and the European Countries in which CIA Aircraft have made Stopovers', PE 380.084v02-00 (16 November 2006).

[74] For example, in the UK, several NGOs applied for judicial review submitting that the UK Treasury was duty-bound to require nationalised banks not to support ventures or businesses that violate human rights and environmental standards in third countries. One allegation concerned bank investment in a US power-generating corporation whose activities are believed to have contributed to exacerbating the conflict between Uganda and the Democratic Republic of Congo. Another allegation concerned investment in corporate mining activities in India that violated international human rights and environmental law. For further details, see D. Augenstein *et al.*, 'Study of the Legal Framework on Human Rights and the Environment Applicable to European Enterprises Operating Outside the European Union', Study for the European Commission submit-ted by the University of Edinburgh, ENTR/09/45 (2010), http://ec.europa.eu/enterprise/policies/sustainable-business/files/csr/documents/stakeholder_forum/plenary-2010/101025_ec_study_final_report-exec_summary_en.pdf (last accessed 20 January 2013).

[75] Perhaps the most prominent example repeatedly addressed by the SRSG is the provision of export credits to corporate activities that negatively impact on human rights in third countries. SRSG, 'Engaging Export Credit Agencies in Respecting Human Rights: OECD

preference of states to outsource the delivery of military and security services to private corporations.[76]

In the light of these developments, it is unfortunate that the SRSG stopped short of taking a more robust and progressive stance on extra-territorial human rights obligations. In our view, the way forward lies in a critical reconstruction of the relationship between the first and second pillar of the Framework. The GPs make it clear that states have an important role in supporting business entities in complying with their corporate responsibility to respect human rights. However, for the state to comply fully with its human rights obligations under international law, it must ensure the protection of human rights for those who fall within its jurisdiction, whether inside or outside its territorial boundaries, and protect against threats to their rights, whether from states or non-state actors. The use of the term 'responsibility' in respect of the protection of human rights by corporations in the second pillar may be artfully distinct from the use of 'duty' in respect of states under the first pillar, but one must not thereby be lulled into supposing that corporations are *not* subject to legal duties to protect human rights. They are already under a host of domestic legislative regimes (including labour, occupational health and safety, non-discrimination, privacy and more) that encompass, in some cases, overseas corporate activities as well. We believe that such extra-territorial reach ought to be extended, not because states can do so under international law, but because under international human rights law they must.

Export Credit Group's "Common Approaches" Meeting' (23 June 2010). Another example would be states granting export licences to corporations for torture equipment. See the seminal article by M. Gibney, K. Tomaševski and J. Vested-Hansen, 'Transnational State Responsibility for Violations of Human Rights' (1999) 12 *Harvard Human Rights Journal* 267. In the European Union, this lacuna has now been addressed through Council Regulation (EC) No. 1236/2005 of June 2005 concerning trade in certain goods which could be used for capital punishment, torture or other cruel, inhuman or degrading treatment or punishment.

[76] For a discussion of the human rights implications of which, see D. Kinley and O. Murray, 'Corporations that Kill: Prosecuting Blackwater' in S. Bronitt, M. Gani and S. Hufnagel (eds.), *Shooting to Kill: Socio-Legal Perspectives on the Use of Lethal Force* (Oxford: Hart Publishing, 2012), 293.

12

Will transnational private regulation close the governance gap?

NICOLA JÄGERS

Introduction

The work of the Special Representative of the Secretary-General on the Issue of Human Rights and Transnational Corporations and Other Business Enterprises (SRSG) has made one thing abundantly clear. When it comes to addressing effectively the challenges posed by corporations to the enjoyment of human rights there is no easy solution, or to put it in the words of the SRSG: 'no silver bullet can resolve the business and human rights challenge'.[1]

When the Special Representative began his mission to clarify the relationship between corporations and human rights in 2005,[2] the discussion had become stuck in a rather counterproductive debate about the need for mandatory rules versus voluntary measures. The SRSG had to deal with the deadlock that had arisen following the top-down approach taken in the Draft UN Norms on the Responsibilities of Transnational Corporations and Other Business Enterprises with Regard to Human Rights' (UN Norms), which suggested that international law places direct obligations on multinational corporations.[3]

---

[1] Human Rights Council, 'Business and Human Rights: Mapping International Standards of Responsibility and Accountability for Corporate Acts: Report of the Special Representative of the Secretary-General on the Issue of Human Rights and Transnational Corporations and Other Business Enterprises', A/HRC/4/035 (9 February 2007), (SRSG, '2007 Report'), para. 88.

[2] For the mandate, see United Nations Human Rights Commission, 'Human Rights Resolution 2005/69' (20 April 2005), http://ap.ohchr.org/documents/E/CHR/resolutions/E-CN_4-RES-2005-69.doc (last accessed 9 November 2012).

[3] Commission on Human Rights, 'Economic, Social and Cultural Rights: Norms on the Responsibilities of Transnational Corporations and Other Business Enterprises with Regard to Human Rights', E/CN.4/Sub.2/2003/12/Rev.2 (26 August 2003) (CHR, '2003 Report'), para. 1. For a description by one of the main drafters of the UN Norms, see D. Weissbrodt, 'Norms on the Responsibilities of Transnational Corporations and Other

The SRSG steered a middle course focusing on a more bottom-up approach and giving a central role to the state. With this approach he succeeded in bringing all the parties back to the table, which led to the unanimous endorsement of the three-pillar framework 'Protect, Respect and Remedy' (Framework)[4] and the Guiding Principles (GPs)[5] in 2011.

In this chapter, the focus is upon the role given by the SRSG to transnational private regulation. The Framework and the GPs are the first instruments explicitly to acknowledge the existence and value of private governance. The fate of the above-mentioned UN Norms makes clear that inclusion of corporations is essential for the acceptance of any regulatory framework. In this chapter, an operational critique is presented. It is argued that, notwithstanding the importance of the Framework and GPs in stressing the contribution private regulation can make, they fall short in laying down *how* this is to be done. The effective operationalisation of the Framework, in my view, depends largely on the voluntary corporate uptake of social norms following from societal pressure. I shall argue that the availability of (independent) information for stakeholders[6] to monitor corporate behaviour is critical in this process. Without access to information about whether and how corporations are discharging their corporate duty to respect, stakeholders lack the necessary tools to press for the voluntary uptake of the corporate responsibility to respect.

The SRSG has made clear that even though the first and second pillars of his framework contain autonomous duties, they are interconnected. As will be made clear in this chapter, this connection between the pillars is essential when it comes to the issue of transparency. It is argued here that states have an important role to play in ensuring the transparency necessary for the effective operationalisation of the Framework.

Business Enterprises with Regard to Human Rights' (2003) 97 *American Journal of International Law* 901.

[4] Human Rights Council, 'Protect, Respect and Remedy: a Framework for Business and Human Rights: Report of the Special Representative of the Secretary-General on the Issue of Human Rights and Transnational Corporations and Other Business Enterprises', A/HRC/8/5 (7 April 2008) (SRSG, '2008 Framework').

[5] Human Rights Council, 'Guiding Principles on Business and Human Rights: Implementing the United Nations "Protect, Respect and Remedy" Framework: Report of the Special Representative of the Secretary-General on the Issue of Human Rights and Transnational Corporations and Other Business Enterprises', A/HRC/17/31 (21 March 2011) (SRSG, 'Guiding Principles').

[6] The term 'stakeholders' is defined here in a very broad manner encompassing all actors that can be affected by the behaviour of a company. It can include, *inter alia*, NGOs (representing affected communities or certain values), consumers, investors, states, employees and corporations.

Whether transnational private regulation, upon which the SRSG places so much reliance, can reach its full potential depends on the willingness of states to facilitate and support it. States can do this in various ways,[7] but in this chapter the focus is on transparency and, particularly, the disclosure of information. It is argued here that the SRSG's articulation of the state duty in this respect is underdeveloped, ultimately undermining the 'socialisation process' upon which the operationalisation of the Framework depends. I also argue that stronger state duties relating to access to information are mandated by international law. Looking more at international human rights law can and should be expected of the state when it comes to ensuring access to information, a precondition for the effectiveness of transnational private regulation and the operationalisation of the second pillar of the Framework in general.

This chapter will first discuss the contribution that the Framework and GPs have made to the business and human rights debate, specifically by pointing out the potential strengths of international private regulation aimed at improving corporate conduct. As will be explained, the voluntary character of private regulation does not diminish its importance given the fading voluntary/mandatory dichotomy. Subsequently, the crucial role of information in this socialisation process will be addressed. This will be illustrated by discussing the transnational private regulation that has been developed aimed at improving the human rights conduct of the private security industry.

The chapter then analyses the Framework and GPs on the issue of how access to information is to be assured. It is argued that more guidance is needed, and can be derived from international human rights law, on how the state is to assure access to independent information. Finally, recommendations are made to the UN Working Group on Business and Human Rights, established to work on the dissemination and implementation of the Framework and GPs after the finalisation of the mandate of the SRSG in June 2011.[8]

---

[7] See, for a discussion of the various ways in which states can – as they call it – orchestrate transnational private regulation in order for it to reach its full potential, K. W. Abbott and D. Snidal, 'Strengthening International Regulation through Transnational New Governance: Overcoming the Orchestration Deficit' (2009) 2 *Vanderbilt Journal of Transnational Law* 501.

[8] For the mandate of the Working Group on the Issue of Human Rights and Transnational Corporations and Other Business Enterprises see Human Rights Council, 'Human Rights and Transnational Corporations and Other Business Enterprises', A/HRC/17/L.17/Rev.1 (15 June 2011), (SRSG, '2011 Report'), paras. 2–4.

The corporate responsibility to respect
and transnational private regulation

To the dismay of many human rights advocates, the SRSG steered away from grounding the concept of corporate responsibility on any legal foundation, but rather based it on a 'societal expectation' for all corporations to respect human rights wherever they operate. Not constrained by a legal straightjacket, this notion of the corporate responsibility to respect is a very broad one: corporations have a responsibility towards all human rights[9] and, in principle, this responsibility applies to all corporations.[10]

The corporate duty to respect implies that corporations should 'avoid infringing on the human rights of others and should address adverse human rights impacts with which they are involved'.[11] In order to meet their responsibility to respect human rights, corporations should, according to Guiding Principle 15,

> have in place policies and processes appropriate to their size and circumstances, including:
>
> (a) A policy commitment to meet their responsibility to respect human rights;
> (b) A human rights due-diligence process to identify, prevent, mitigate and account for how they address their impacts on human rights;
> (c) Processes to enable the remediation of any adverse human rights impacts they cause or to which they contribute.

As stated above, this corporate responsibility to respect is of a non-legal character. Corporations are not mandated by law to take up their corporate responsibility to respect human rights. It may therefore be argued that the commitment of corporations to discharge this responsibility depends on the voluntary uptake by corporations. As the GPs

---

[9] SRSG, 'Guiding Principles', n. 5, para. 12 provides: 'The responsibility of business enterprises to respect human rights refers to internationally recognized human rights – understood, at a minimum, as those expressed in the International Bill of Human Rights and the principles concerning fundamental rights set out in the International Labour Organization's Declaration on Fundamental Principles and Rights at Work.'

[10] *Ibid.*, para. 14 provides: 'The responsibility of business enterprises to respect human rights applies to all enterprises regardless of their size, sector, operational context, ownership and structure. Nevertheless, the scale and complexity of the means through which enterprises meet that responsibility may vary according to these factors and with the severity of the enterprise's adverse human rights impacts.'

[11] *Ibid.*, para. 11.

make clear, a first step corporations should take is the adoption of a human rights policy. The critical stance taken by human rights advocates against this voluntary approach is understandable given the low number of corporations that have voluntarily adopted a human rights policy to date. According to the website of the Business and Human Rights Resource Centre, currently only 301 corporations have a human rights policy in place.[12] This is a negligible number when seen in light of the estimates made by the Special Representative, who calculated that there are currently approximately 80,000 transnational enterprises, ten times as many subsidiaries and countless millions of national firms.[13] Of course, compliance with substantive human rights norms is more important than adopting a human rights policy, but the fact that so few companies have even taken this first step of laying down a commitment in this direction is telling. However, by itself the non-legal nature of the corporate responsibility to respect is not a reason simply to dismiss this responsibility as merely an aspiration and consequently of little use in the quest for corporate accountability. Increasingly, it is understood that the mandatory/voluntary dichotomy is not very useful and is fading.[14] Voluntary commitments taken up by corporations are not without 'teeth'.[15] Whilst the adoption of measures to discharge the responsibility to respect might (initially) be of a voluntary nature,[16] compliance with these measures increasingly is not. Law is

---

[12] Business and Human Rights Resource Centre, 'Company Policy Statements on Human Rights' (date unavailable), www.business-humanrights.org/Documents/Policies (last accessed 29 November 2012). When looking at the topic of this chapter, transnational private regulation, the same discouraging picture emerges regarding corporate participation. Professor Ruggie acknowledges this by referring to the following examples: less than 200 firms out of a total of 1,500 participate in the US Chemical Industries Responsible Care Program, and the 800 companies participating in the Global Compact also is a very limited number in light of the estimated total number of multinational corporations. See J. G. Ruggie, 'The Global Compact and the Challenges of Global Governance' (11–13 December 2002), www.unglobalcompact.org/docs/news_events/9.6/ruggie_berlin.pdf (last accessed 2 November 2012).

[13] SRSG, '2011 Report', n. 8, para. 15 in Annex.

[14] For more on this see D. McBarnet, 'Corporate Social Responsibility beyond the Law, through the Law, for the Law: The New Corporate Accountability' in D. McBarnet, A. Voiculesco and T. Campbell (eds.), The New Corporate Accountability: Corporate Social Responsibility and the Law (Cambridge University Press, 2007), 9–56.

[15] See also Chapter 6.

[16] As argued below, adoption can become mandatory when adherence to voluntary regimes is a condition of market entrance and participation.

gradually encroaching upon voluntary CSR policies.[17] Stakeholders are turning to law to enforce voluntary commitments undertaken by corporations. As pointed out by McBarnet: 'This is not, on the whole, state regulation that we are discussing, nor indeed international law, though both come into the picture, but other facets of law, often private law being used by private parties, NGOs, business itself and indeed governments under a different hat.'[18] Besides using law to harden voluntary commitments, stakeholders can apply consumer pressure, and can cease to invest, purchase or lend. In other words a multifaceted form of accountability has started to emerge. Moreover, if and when the adoption of human rights policies becomes a condition for market entry, the taking up of such voluntary policies may become mandatory in practice.

The Framework relies on this societal pressure for the uptake of the corporate responsibility to respect. As the SRSG has pointed out, the failure of corporations to meet their responsibility to respect human rights

> can subject companies to the courts of public opinion – comprising employees, communities, consumers, civil society, as well as investors – and occasionally to charges in actual courts. Whereas governments define the scope of legal compliance, the broader scope of the responsibility to respect is defined by social expectations – as part of what is sometimes called a company's social license to operate.[19]

Corporations can discharge their corporate duty to respect by adopting human rights policies and conducting human rights due diligence investigations independently, or by joining existing private regulatory initiatives. The pressure coming from the 'courts of public opinion' has contributed to the proliferation of so-called transnational private regulation. Transnational private regulation is defined by Cafaggi as 'a new body of rules, practices, and processes, created primarily by private actors, firms, NGOs, independent experts like technical standard-setters and epistemic communities, either exercising autonomous regulatory power or implementing delegated power, conferred

---

[17] For the relationship between corporate social responsibility and the law, see R. Mares, 'Global Corporate Social Responsibility, Human Rights and Law: An Interactive Regulatory Perspective on the Voluntary-Mandatory Dichotomy' (2010) 1 *Transnational Legal Theory* 221–85.

[18] McBarnet, 'Corporate Social Responsibility beyond the Law' in McBarnet, Voiculesco and Campbell (eds.), *The New Corporate Accountability*, n. 14, 31.

[19] SRSG, '2008 Framework', n. 4, para. 54.

by international law or national legislation'.[20] The body of private regulation in the area of business and human rights defines standards for 'responsible' business behaviour and has to a certain and varying degree institutionalised the oversight regarding compliance with these standards. There are many terms used for such regulatory frameworks besides the already mentioned term transnational private regulation,[21] such as transnational new governance,[22] civil regulations,[23] or regimes.[24] All these refer to regulation coming from private actors, and not rooted (exclusively) in public authority. The last decades have witnessed a development towards such alternative regulatory techniques resulting from a complex interaction between various actors that does not always involve the regulatory state. There has been, it is argued, a 'blurring of the distinctions between normative forms, involving both the growth of soft law and the blurring of a simple public-private divide in the promulgation and enforcement of law'.[25] Such private regulation is taking place across all policy sectors, such as financial markets, food safety regulation, consumer protection, product safety, data protection, environmental protection and so on.

A growing number of corporations support the formation of or join transnational private regulatory regimes. There are several reasons why corporations choose to join such regimes instead of or in addition to

---

[20] F. Cafaggi, 'New Foundations of Transnational Private Regulation' (2011) 38:1 *Journal of Law and Society* 20. The term 'transnational' is used instead of 'international' as the effects of this regulation cross borders but it is not constituted in the form of a co-operation between states as reflected in treaties; see: C. Scott, F. Cafaggi and L. Senden, 'The Conceptual and Constitutional Challenge of Transnational Private Regulation' (2011) 38:1 *Journal of Law and Society* 3.

[21] F. Cafaggi, 'New Foundations of Transnational Private Regulation', *ibid.*, 21.

[22] T. J. Melish and E. Meidinger, 'Protect, Respect, Remedy and Participate: "New Governance" Lessons for the Ruggie Framework' in R. Mares (ed.), *The UN Guiding Principles on Business and Human Rights: Foundations and Implementation* (Leiden: Brill Publishing, 2011), 303; Abbot and Snidal, 'Strengthening International Regulation', n. 7, 501–79; D. Hess, 'Social Reporting and New Governance Regulation: The Prospects of Achieving Accountability through Transparency' (2007) 17:3 *Business Ethics Quarterly* 453.

[23] D. Vogel, 'The Private Regulation of Global Corporate Conduct' in W. Mattli and N. Woods (eds.), *The Politics of Global Regulation* (Princeton University Press, 2009), 151.

[24] As suggested by others, given the fragmented character of international regulation it is useful to speak of regimes instead of regulators. Regimes refer to a range of actors, institutions and policies who shape outcomes within a policy domain. See C. Scott, 'Regulating in Global Regimes' (30 April 2010), http://papers.ssrn.com/sol3/papers. cfm?abstract_id=1598262 (last accessed 9 November 2012).

[25] *Ibid.*, 7.

drawing up their own codes of conduct. First, unilaterally adopting standards raises the costs for individual corporations whereas regimes that include competitors create a level playing field.[26] Moreover, an incentive can be that certain industries feel the need to improve the image of the overall sector.[27] The SRSG has placed great confidence in private regulatory initiatives, especially those with a multi-stakeholder character.[28]

In light of the broad corporate support for the work of the SRSG, it may be expected that the Framework and the GPs will influence and further stimulate the development of transnational private regulation. This, for example, has already occurred in the case of transnational private regulation in the field of private security provision and human rights (which will be discussed in more detail below). The latest international code of conduct adopted in this area, the International Code of Conduct for Private Security Providers,[29] makes explicit reference to the Framework[30] and the notion that corporations have a responsibility to conduct human rights due diligence enquiries.[31]

Generally, it is expected that compliance with transnational private regulation will increase if that regulation mirrors public standards.[32] The Framework and GPs do not refer to human rights in a general abstract sense as a moral foundation, as is often the case in transnational private regulation,[33] but rather refer explicitly to the major legally binding human rights treaties and labour Conventions.[34] Therefore, if indeed the Framework and GPs find broad uptake in transnational private regulatory regimes, this possibly will increase the likelihood that those subject to such regulation will actually modify their behaviour in accordance with these standards.

---

[26] D. Vogel, 'The Private Regulation of Global Corporate Conduct', n. 23, 169.

[27] For example, this was mentioned as an important incentive for Private Security Companies (PSCs) to join the transnational private regulation that emerged and which was aimed at improving the human rights performance of these companies. This came clearly to the fore during the interviews conducted with representatives of PSCs in the context of the HiiL project mentioned below at n. 58.

[28] SRSG, '2007 Report', n. 1, paras. 52 and 53.

[29] Government of Switzerland, 'International Code of Conduct for Private Security Providers' (9 November 2010), www.icoc-psp.org (last accessed 2 November 2012).

[30] Ibid., para. 2.   [31] Ibid., paras. 2, 21 and 45.

[32] T.E. Lambooy, Corporate Social Responsibility: Legal and Semi-Legal Frameworks Supporting CSR Developments 2000–2010 and Case Studies (Deventer: Kluwer, 2010), 253.

[33] See, for example, United Nations Global Compact, www.unglobalcompact.org/AboutTheGC/TheTenPrinciples/principle1.html (last accessed 2 November 2012).

[34] SRSG, 'Guiding Principles', n. 5: see n. 9.

Strengths of transnational private regulation

In light of the fact that states in practice frequently do not live up to their human rights obligations, and the difficulty of holding corporations to account beyond the jurisdiction of a state, it should be viewed as a significant contribution that the SRSG has drawn attention to frameworks of governance beyond the state. It is clear that conventional international law-making has so far been unable to deliver a substantive answer to the challenges posed by corporations to the effective enjoyment of human rights. The relevance of alternative modes of regulation consequently increases. Scott has argued in general that the effectiveness of governmental and inter-governmental law-making when compared to private regulatory regimes is frequently played up and arguably overstated.[35]

This is not to ignore the capacity and role of states in global regulation. Important empirical studies have concluded that governments are central both to the initiation and implementation of much transnational regulatory activity but governmental activity is far from being the only show in town.[36]

Scott argues that multi-stakeholder regulation might be much better placed to ensure compliance as it may effectively invoke the gate-keeping capacity of others in the sector, such as clients and insurers, to require compliance.[37] A lot of the critique centres on the voluntary character of private regulatory regimes. However, as already mentioned, when participation is a *de facto* condition for market participation this fear might be 'more apparent than real'.[38]

There are some clear advantages to drawing in regulation emerging from private actors to face the corporate challenges to human rights. It is hoped that involving those most affected by the implementation of rules in the preparation and enforcement of the regulation will result in a sense of ownership of the policies and ultimately improved compliance. Arguably, the quality of a norm is better guaranteed in private regulation because of the involvement of professionals of a particular sector and the alleged greater flexibility and possibility to adjust to changing circumstances.[39] Private regulators possibly will have greater

[35] Scott, 'Regulating in Global Regimes', n. 24, 3.   [36] *Ibid.*   [37] *Ibid.*, 7.   [38] *Ibid.*
[39] Lambooy, *Corporate Social Responsibility*, n. 32, 252; The Hague Institute for the Internationalisation of Law (HiiL), 'The Added Value of Private Regulation in an International World? Towards a Model of the Legitimacy, Effectiveness, Enforcement

expertise, better appreciation of the challenges in practice and better access to information.

Effectiveness of transnational private regulation: the critical role of information

Two factors are distinguished here that are essential for the effectiveness of private transnational regulation.[40] First, for a transnational private regulatory regime to influence corporate behaviour, it is crucial that there is a significant degree of participation. Scaling up the regulatory regimes to include a significant number of corporations has proven problematic. Vogel argues that transnational private regulation has yet to prove to be an effective alternative to governmental regulation. He states that overall transnational private regulation 'remain[s] weaker than well-enforced command and control regulations in changing corporate behavior'.[41] An important reason for this, he concludes, is the limited participation of corporations.[42] Stakeholders such as NGOs can put pressure on corporations to join regulatory regimes by exposing possible human rights violations, which might damage the reputation of a corporation. Access to information about corporate activities is critical for this mechanism to be effective. If stakeholders are able to induce a critical mass to join a regulatory regime, other corporations are also likely to join. This 'herd effect' refers to the dynamic where one corporation joins a voluntary code and other corporations in the sector follow.[43] If a sufficient number of corporations take part this will

---

and Quality of Private Regulation' (May 2008), www.hiil.org (last accessed 5 November 2012).

[40] Besides the factors distinguished here, participation and enforcement, regulation theory also recognises other factors that can add to or diminish the effectiveness of transnational private regulation. For example, the quality and legitimacy of such regulation are also considered important factors. For more on this see the HiiL project, mentioned below at n. 58.

[41] It must be noted that Vogel is comparing the situation to governmental regulation in developed countries. In developing countries, he argues, civil regulations are undoubtedly more effective than many of the regulations drawn up by these countries. Vogel, 'The Private Regulation of Global Corporate Conduct', n. 23, 184.

[42] This conclusion, in particular, is drawn with regard to a number of transnational private regulations which he labels as 'moderately effective' (Fair Trade Labelling International and the Forest Certification Council) and 'relatively ineffective' (Publish What You Pay). Ibid., 176–79.

[43] Ibid., 170.

increase the legitimacy[44] of the regulatory regime and arguably its effectiveness.

Besides the degree of participation, the effectiveness of transnational private regulation depends on enforcement. Enforcement is understood as the activities through which compliance with regulatory norms is secured in relation to entities subject to such regulation. Compliance requires more than merely sanctions and mechanisms to enforce sanctions (*ex post*); it also requires *ex ante* mechanisms such as monitoring and supervision.[45] Moreover, it is necessary to look beyond the traditional notion of enforcement. As pointed out by Scott:

> Enforcement traditionally is associated with public institutions but scholars have also recognized the importance of private mechanisms for enforcement. Arbitration, mediation or private tribunals are well-known examples but also less formal, market-based mechanisms like the decision to contract, buy, invest, insure or certify have been identified as playing a significant role in enforcement, in particular in relation to transnational private standards.[46]

What transnational private regulation (and generally the corporate responsibility to conduct human rights due diligence enquiries) basically does is move the monitoring function beyond the state to a broader range of stakeholders. For these stakeholders to press for compliance with the corporate responsibility to respect, knowledge of compliance with standards is essential. Stakeholders should be able to make an informed decision whether or not to buy, lend, invest and so on. The necessary information about whether corporate activities are in conformity with private standard-setting can come to the fore in transnational private regulatory regimes that have reached a certain level of institutionalisation of oversight and monitoring. Regimes that involve other stakeholders (the multi-stakeholder initiatives) clearly have more potential for effectiveness. The participation of NGOs is considered critical to the emergence, legitimacy and effectiveness of many

---

[44] Legitimacy is defined as the acceptance that an organisation has a right to govern granted by those it seeks to govern and those on whose behalf it purports to govern. J. Black, 'Constructing and Contesting Legitimacy and Accountability in Polycentric Regulatory Regimes' (2008) 2 *Regulation and Governance* 137.

[45] *Ex ante* mechanisms refers to mechanisms that are put in place in order to prevent violations of the standards set, whereas *ex post* mechanisms are established to react to non-compliance.

[46] Scott, 'Regulating in Global Regimes', n. 24, 23.

transnational private regulatory regimes.[47] Whether stakeholders can actually access information on corporate compliance with the standards set by them depends on the degree of procedural transparency within the regulatory regime. However, the participation of stakeholders within a regulatory regime does not mean that compliance with standards is monitored externally. If there is no information made available by the regulatory regime regarding the decisions on compliance, the effectiveness of the regime will be undermined.[48]

In sum, a crucial element for the success of transnational private regulation as a regulatory tool that can influence corporate behaviour is the availability of information. Stakeholders need information on corporate activities, on the one hand, to put pressure on corporations to join private regulatory initiatives, and on the other, to expose non-compliance with private standards. Or, to use the words of Abbott and Snidal, '[a]udiences must be informed and "activated" to serve as demanders and sanctioners of [regulatory standard-setting]'.[49]

An illustration: transnational private regulation in the area of private security provision

The critical role of access to information will be illustrated here by discussing the emergent transnational private regulation aimed at improving the human rights performance of private security providers.[50]

Several high-profile incidents of human rights abuse involving Private Security Companies (PSCs) have highlighted the need for regulation.[51] The exceptional nature of the industry – it operates abroad, in complex environments and relies on the potential use of force – frequently makes it difficult to apply and enforce existing legal frameworks to it.[52] Recent

---

[47] Vogel, 'The Private Regulation of Global Corporate Conduct', n. 23, 165.

[48] See, for clear examples, the transnational private regulatory regimes that have been created by the trade associations in the field of private security provision and human rights, discussed below.

[49] Abbot and Snidal, 'Strengthening International Regulation', n. 7, 561–62.

[50] This section draws on N. Jägers, 'Regulating the Private Security Industry: Connecting the Public and the Private through Transnational Private Regulation' (2012) *Human Rights and International Legal Discourse* (Special Issue) 56.

[51] The follow-up to the shooting of civilians by contractors of the company then known as Blackwater has become emblematic of the impunity PSCs often enjoy.

[52] For more on the problems involved in regulating the private security market, see F. Francioni and N. Ronzitti (eds.), *War by Contract: Human Rights, Humanitarian Law and Private Contractors* (Oxford University Press, 2011); S. Chesterman and

years have seen a rapid development of standard-setting in this field. Transnational regulatory regimes have been established following the increased use of private security providers. States, but also non-state actors such as multinational corporations and NGOs, are more and more relying on the private provision of security to protect their assets and their employees, as we have seen in the wars in Iraq and Afghanistan.[53] However the hiring of PSCs is not limited to these situations of war. They are used in all parts of the world for a wide range of services including private policing, detention services, protection of employees and assets, training, and intelligence operations.

Transnational private regulatory regimes have been developed by trade associations such as the International Stability Operations Association (ISOA)[54] and the British Association for the Private Security Industry (BAPSC).[55] Moreover, regulatory regimes have been created in co-operation with states and other stakeholders, for example the Voluntary Principles on Security and Human Rights (VPs).[56] The

---

C. Lehnardt (eds.), *From Mercenaries to Market: The Rise and Regulation of Private Military Companies* (Oxford University Press, 2007).

[53] It is estimated that currently there are more than a million employees working as private soldiers or security officers for over 1,000 PSCs in over 100 countries. In 2006, the turnover in this new branch of the service industry was estimated at about US$200 billion: see Parliamentary Assembly of the Council of Europe, *Recommendation: Private Military and Security Firms and Erosion of the State Monopoly on the Use of Force*, Recommendation 1858 (2009). Figures on the number of private contractors employed in the wars in Iraq and Afghanistan differ. However, a recurring estimate is that at one point there were 180,000 people working for PSCs in Iraq: see the Dutch Advisory Council on International Affairs, *Employing Private Military Companies* (The Hague, December 2007) and Human Rights First, 'Private Security Contractors at War – Ending the Culture of Impunity' (2008), www.humanrightsfirst.info/pdf/08115-usls-psc-final. pdf (last accessed 4 November 2012). The number of private contractors working in Afghanistan is also difficult to ascertain given the many different armed groups. Over the last couple of years the number has surged. For estimates, see Human Rights Council, 'Report of the Working Group on the Use of Mercenaries as a Means of Violating Human Rights and Impeding the Exercise of the Right of Peoples to Self-Determination: Mission to Afghanistan', A/HRC/15/25/Add. 2 (14 June 2010) (RWG, '2010 Report'), para. 21.

[54] International Stability Operations Association, http://stability-operations.org (last accessed 23 December 2012).

[55] British Association for the Private Security Industry, http://www.bapsc.org.uk (last accessed 23 December 2012).

[56] This multi-stakeholder initiative indirectly addresses the private security industry with regulation dealing with how the energy and extractive industries (large clients of PSCs) deal with the provision of security. See Voluntary Principles on Security and Human Rights, www.voluntaryprinciples.org (last accessed 23 December 2012).

latest example of a multi-stakeholder initiative aimed at improving the human rights performance of PSCs is the International Code of Conduct for Private Security Providers (ICoC-PSP).[57]

When evaluating the effectiveness of this body of transnational private regulation,[58] it is clear that the lack of information severely hampers the effectiveness of transnational private regulation in this field. The activities of PSCs and those that contract with them are opaque.[59] This makes it extremely difficult, on the one hand, to put pressure on corporations to join the regulatory initiatives and, on the other, to evaluate whether companies and their clients are living up to the standards they have committed to. The transnational private regulatory regimes have to varying degrees institutionalised oversight and monitoring, but their effectiveness as vehicles for bringing information to the attention of stakeholders is limited. The secretive nature of the industry is reflected in the transnational regulatory regimes that are plagued by a lack of transparency.

The lack of transparency is especially problematic regarding the standards adopted by the trade associations ISOA and BAPSC. Corporations that are members of these trade associations are required to commit to certain human rights norms.[60] Both BAPSC and ISOA have criteria for participation; however, reasoned decisions on why a PSC can

---

[57] See Government of Switzerland, 'International Code of Conduct for Private Security Providers', n. 29.

[58] This builds on a case study conducted at Tilburg University into the effectiveness of transnational private regulation in the field of private security provision and human rights. For the case study, interviews were conducted with a range of stakeholders including NGOs and PSCs. Transcripts of the interviews are on file with the author. The case study is part of a larger project entitled 'Private Transnational Regulation: Constitutional Foundations and Governance Design'. This project aims to investigate the emergence, legitimacy and effectiveness of transnational private regulatory regimes and is funded by the Hague Institute for the Internationalisation of Law (HiiL). Further information can be found in Hague Institute for the Internationalisation of Law (HiiL), 'Private Transnational Regulation: Constitutional Foundations and Governance Design' (16–17 June 2010), www.privateregulation.eu/wp-content/uploads/2010/09/HiiL-Annual-Conference-on-Transnational-Private-Regulation-programme.pdf (last accessed 4 November 2012).

[59] This prompted the organisation of a conference addressing the problems posed by the lack of information; see: D. Avant and M. Berlin, 'Monitoring the Global Security Industry: What do we Know, What do we Need to Know and How can we Know It?' (date unavailable), http://igcc.ucsd.edu/publications/igcc-publications/publications_20110707.htm (last accessed 9 November 2012).

[60] See the BAPSC Charter, www.bapsc.org.uk/?keydocuments=charter (last accessed 30 January 2013), and the ISOA Code of Conduct, www.stability-operations.org/index.php (last accessed 30 January 2013).

or cannot become a member are not made public. The enforcement mechanisms developed by the trade associations have many flaws.[61] The associations do not provide for any *ex ante* compliance mechanisms. Both BAPSC and ISOA do not monitor compliance and can therefore not proactively address non-compliance. This is especially problematic as the associations are thus dependent on others to inform them about non-compliance. This is further complicated by the fact that security operations frequently take place in conflict areas where such information is difficult to come by.[62] Since 2006, ISOA has established a formal complaint mechanism. Any person can submit a complaint concerning non-compliance of a member company to the Standards Committee, which is made up of other member companies. Co-operation by the member company with the Standards Committee is, however, voluntary. When the Committee deems a complaint valid it can prescribe policy changes, place the company on probation or expel it from the ISOA.[63] There are no other stakeholders involved in the eventual handling of the complaint. It is difficult to ascertain the degree to which this enforcement mechanism is actually used,[64] and whether it enhances the effectiveness of the regime given the high level of secrecy surrounding the complaint procedure. There is no information made publicly available concerning the complaints to or the decisions taken by the Standards Committee. Compared to ISOA, the mechanisms within BAPSC to ensure compliance with its Charter are even more opaque. There is no formal grievance mechanism, but the Director General has suggested that the Association relies on fines, suspension and the withdrawal of membership.[65] There is, however, no evidence that this has ever

---

[61] See J. Cockayne *et al.*, 'Beyond Market Forces: Regulating the Global Security Industry' (2009), www.ipacademy.org/media/pdf/publications/beyond_market_forces_final.pdf (last accessed 9 November 2012), 134–44 (on IPOA, later renamed ISOA) and 158–64 (on BAPSC).

[62] R. De Nevers, 'The Effectiveness of Self-Regulation by the Private Military and Security Industry' (2010) 30:2 *Journal of Public Policy* 219, at 229.

[63] Information about the enforcement mechanism can be found on the website of ISOA: www.stability-operations.org.

[64] Referring to an interview held with the President of ISOA, Stephanie Brown states in her 2010 article that the ISOA had received less than twelve complaints against its members: S. Brown, 'Bottom-Up Law Making and the Regulation of Private Military and Security Companies' (2010) 2:1 *Cuadernos de Derecho Transnacional* 44, at 64.

[65] S. Ranganathan, 'Between Complicity and Irrelevance? Industry Associations and the Challenge of Regulating Private Security Contractors' (2010) 41 *Georgetown Journal of International Law* 303, at 324, quoting a policy paper written by BAPSC Director General Andrew Bearpark in 2007.

happened. In sum, the lack of *ex ante* compliance mechanisms and the lack of transparency surrounding the enforcement mechanisms seriously weaken the regulatory potential of the regimes set up by the trade associations.

Multi-stakeholder initiatives involving states and civil society in general carry more potential for creating an effective regulatory mechanism given that they have a greater claim to legitimacy and, possibly, more effective enforcement. The Voluntary Principles (VPs), involving not only corporations from the extractive and energy sectors but also NGOs and states, provide the possibility for these participating stakeholders actually to check compliance of the corporations with the standards set. According to a state representative in the VP process, these Principles have increasingly emerged as an important platform for standards implementation, due mainly to the active participation of the various stakeholders, not least those representing the intended beneficiaries of the regulation, NGOs.[66] Unlike the trade associations, the VPs do have *ex ante* mechanisms for checking compliance. According to the participation criteria, a reporting obligation has been agreed upon.[67] If participants do not live up to the reporting obligation, they can be labelled as inactive, meaning they can no longer exercise their rights as participants. A complaint can also be raised against a participant for not implementing the VPs.[68] The internal dispute resolution process can ultimately result in expulsion from the VPs.[69] However, this requires a unanimous decision. At the time of writing, no instance of expulsion has occurred within the VPs. The possibilities for stakeholders outside of the process to monitor compliance with the VPs are severely limited. For example, the VPs require that the Principles are included in the contracts of

[66] Interview with state representative, 21 September 2011, n. 58.

[67] According to Participant Criterion No. 5, participants are required to '[p]repare and submit to the Steering Committee, one month prior to the Annual Plenary Meeting, an Annual Report on efforts to implement or assist in the implementation of the Voluntary Principles according to criteria determined by the Participants; and section VIII of the VPs Governance Rules': The Plenary, 'The Initiative of the Voluntary Principles on Security and Human Rights: Governance Rules' (16 September 2011), www.voluntaryprinciples.org/files/VPs_Governance_Rules_Final.pdf (last accessed 9 November 2012).

[68] The VPs dispute resolution process was used for the first time by Oxfam in 2009, alleging that Newmont was violating the VPs. The company agreed to an independent review.

[69] Besides a failure to hand in the Annual Report, a categorical refusal to engage with other participants or the refusal to pay the fees can also lead to an inactive status and, ultimately, expulsion. See The Plenary, 'The Initiative of the Voluntary Principles', n. 67, s. XIII.

the participants. All interviewees claimed to have done so. However, verification of this is not possible given that these contracts are rarely made public. This severely hampers the above-mentioned process towards accountability. The lack of transparency following from confidentiality requirements and the limited number of participants in the VPs undermine the overall effectiveness of the regime. A number of large corporations in the extractive industry have joined, but small and medium-sized corporations are not represented at all. Moreover, corporate membership is confined mostly to North America and Western Europe. The number and geographical spread of the participating NGOs and governments is also limited. In 2007, the VPs' Plenary adopted formal participation criteria and removed the requirement that companies or NGOs can only participate in the Plenary if their home government is a participant, thus broadening the scope of possible participants. There is a continuing need to broaden the scope of participating countries – both home countries (important countries such as Germany and France are as of yet not part of the process) and host countries (those countries where the security problems actually occur) – and corporations.[70] Enlarging the number of participants has been explicitly included in the mission statement, as articulated by the 2011 governance rules of the VPs.[71] In sum, when compared to the single-actor industry initiatives discussed above, the VPs carry greater potential for effectiveness. However, the fact that information on compliance with the Principles is restricted to a relatively small number of participants undermines the effectiveness of this regulatory regime.

The latest regulatory regime, the International Code of Conduct for Private Security Providers (ICoC-PSP), adopted in Geneva in November 2010, holds some promise of effectiveness.[72] Since its adoption, a certain degree of convergence of transnational private regulation in this field seems to be taking place. A critical mass consisting of the USA, the UK and the trade associations have embraced the code and it is

---

[70] The views differ on whether the PSCs which currently are being regulated in an indirect manner – by means of their clients – in the VPs regime should be included in the process. Several of the participating companies expressed the view that there is no place for PSCs in the VPs, whereas state representatives felt that including them might be appropriate at some point. Private Military and Security Companies (PMSCs) have previously been invited to attend The Plenary.

[71] See The Plenary, 'The Initiative of the Voluntary Principles', n. 67, para. 2.

[72] For a detailed discussion see N. Jägers, 'Regulating the Private Security Industry', n. 50, 56.

already influencing national developments such as the standards being developed by the American National Standards Institute. This detailed code laying down human rights due diligence obligations on PSCs has enjoyed broad support (at the time of writing 659 signatory companies). However, at this point in time, the relative ease of becoming a signatory company must be taken into consideration, as this might give a rather distorted picture of the degree of actual support.[73] There are valid prudential considerations for bringing the ICoC-PSP to the attention of as many PSCs as possible, and in the future more stringent criteria for the signatory companies to become officially certified will apply.[74] From the interviews conducted, it is clear that there is a relatively small group of PSCs that can be considered to be frontrunners in efforts to regulate the industry for the sake of raising human rights performance. There seems to be a big gap between this group, actively involved in the development of the ICoC-PSP, and other PSCs.[75] During 2011 and 2012 an International Governance and Oversight Mechanism (IGOM) was developed which would seem to address many of the shortcomings identified in the other regulatory regimes. In February 2013 consensus was reached and, at the time of writing, efforts are being made formally to launch and set up an independent, external oversight mechanism.[76]

---

[73] At this stage, simply sending a letter with a description of the company is enough to be admitted as a signatory company. Some interviewed PMSCs mentioned the relative ease of becoming a member and did not seem to be aware of the future obligations this would entail. One interviewee even indicated that his company had no intention of including a reference to the ICoC-PSP in contracts as required by para. 18 of the ICoC-PSP. See ICoC-PSP. Interview with PMSC, n. 58, 8 September 2011.

[74] Articles 7 and 8 in Government of Switzerland, 'International Code of Conduct for Private Security Providers', n. 29. At the time of writing, consensus had been found that in order to participate, PMSCs will have to be certified, consent to and comply with the performance assessment process and reporting requirements: see International Code of Conduct Steering Committee, 'Minutes of Meeting 26–28 September 2011 in Washington DC' (September 2011), www.icoc-psp.org/uploads/2011.09_-_TSC_Activities_September.pdf (last accessed 7 November 2012).

[75] It will be interesting to see whether the code continues to enjoy broad support from PMSCs when more stringent criteria are introduced. If a large group of signatory companies fails to live up to the criteria and consequently (have to) leave the regime, this might negatively affect the legitimacy of the ICoC-PSP. From the perspective of legitimacy (and ultimately effectiveness), the approach taken in the VPs process – starting with a relatively small group and gradually increasing the number of participants – might prove more productive.

[76] Article 7(b) in Government of Switzerland, 'International Code of Conduct for Private Security Providers', n. 29. According to the draft Charter the future IGOM will have the following functions: verification and assessment through auditing, monitoring and

The intention is to also have strong *ex ante* mechanisms to monitor compliance. Monitoring will take place on a regular basis, including through field monitoring in high-risk areas.[77] Performance assessment will include reporting.[78] Relating to *ex post* mechanisms, agreement has been reached that certification or membership may be suspended or withdrawn according to the results of the performance assessment and the failure to implement corrective action. Moreover, the Charter provides for the possibility of third party complaints.[79] Including strong *ex ante* compliance mechanisms will add to the overall effectiveness of the ICoC-PSP.

Whether the code will be an effective regulatory tool for the sector is for now an open question. Its effectiveness will depend on the balance that is struck between the need to get a broad number of PSCs to participate and the degree of transparency that the mechanism will be able to achieve. In the draft Charter it is provided that the Board will implement necessary confidentiality and non-disclosure arrangements, and subject to these arrangements may issue a public statement on the status or outcome of a review of a member company.[80] A major challenge for the effectiveness of the mechanism will be how it deals with the requirements of confidentiality that have undermined the procedural transparency and, ultimately, the effectiveness of the other initiatives as regulatory tools under consideration here.[81]

This discussion of the (emergent) transnational private regulation in the field of private security provision and human rights illustrates the crucial role of information. The lack of transparency that plagues the industry severely undermines the effectiveness of the private regulatory regimes established by this sector. Effectiveness of the more transparent multi-stakeholder initiatives is hampered by the limited degree of

---

certification; report assessment and review; complaint verification and remediation; and code administration. The final draft of the Charter is available at www.icoc-psp.org/uploads/ICoC_Draft_Articles_of_Association_January_30_-_final.pdf (last accessed 4 June 2013).

[77] Signatory companies will be required to be open to in-field auditing as part of performance assessment. For more on the requirements of certification, see Art. 10 of the draft Charter, n.76.

[78] See Art. 11 of the final draft of the Charter, n. 76.

[79] See Art. 11.2.7 and Art. 12 of the draft Charter, n. 76.

[80] See Art. 11.2.9 of the draft Charter, n. 76.

[81] It was acknowledged during the meeting of the STC that this issue needed further elaboration; see International Code of Conduct Steering Committee, 'Minutes of Meeting 26–28 September 2011 in Washington DC', n. 74.

participation. The lack of information concerning the operations of many of the corporations in this industry has proven a major obstacle in monitoring them and, ultimately, in putting pressure on them to join transnational private regulatory regimes.

In sum, transnational private regulation basically moves the monitoring function beyond the state to other stakeholders. For this mechanism to be effective, the availability of information on corporate conduct is critical.

Transparency in the Guiding Principles

The need for transparency is reflected in the Framework and the GPs both in the first and second pillars.

The corporate responsibility to disclosure of information

Disclosure of information is considered part of the corporate responsibility to conduct a human rights due diligence enquiry. According to Principle 17, corporations should carry out a human rights due diligence investigation

> [i]n order to identify, prevent, mitigate and *account for* how they address their adverse human rights impacts ... The process should include assessing actual and potential human rights impacts, integrating and acting upon the findings, tracking responses, and *communicating* how impacts are addressed.[82]

In other words, monitoring (an inward-looking process) should be connected to disclosure (an outward-looking process). As stated in Guiding Principle 21, it is not only about knowing, it is also about showing.[83] This Guiding Principle further elaborates upon what the need to disclose information implies for corporations:

> [i]n order to account for how they address their human rights impacts, business enterprises should be prepared to communicate this externally, *particularly when concerns are raised by or on behalf of affected stakeholders.* Business enterprises whose operations or operating contexts *pose risks of severe human rights impacts should report formally* on how they address them.

---

[82] SRSG, 'Guiding Principles', n. 5, para. 17.   [83] *Ibid.*, para. 21.

In all instances, communications should:

(a) Be of a form and frequency that reflects an enterprise's human rights impacts and that are *accessible to its intended audiences*;
(b) Provide information that is sufficient to evaluate the adequacy of an enterprise's response to the particular human rights impact involved;
(c) In turn not pose risks to affected stakeholders, personnel or to *legitimate requirements of commercial confidentiality*.[84]

Even though this Principle recognises the need to communicate to stakeholders, several weaknesses plague this provision. Guiding Principle 21 places two responsibilities on corporations. First, it provides that the responsibility to communicate applies in particular in response to concerns 'raised by or on behalf of affected stakeholders'. In practice, it will not always be easy for vulnerable stakeholders to raise a complaint. The principle, however, also contains a proactive element: corporations should report formally if their operations or operating contexts 'pose risks of severe human rights impacts'. The question arises as to who is to determine what 'severe human rights impacts' actually means. The problem is that corporations are themselves left to evaluate whether or not their activities are high risk and thus whether they need to comply with this higher level of reporting. The GPs do not require corporations to communicate externally as to whether they consider their activities to be low risk. This provides corporations with a non-transparent alternative to formal reporting.

Moreover, Guiding Principle 21 (c) provides several grounds, including requirements of commercial confidentiality, which corporations can invoke as reasons not to disclose information. In practice, corporations tend not to disclose voluntarily but only when compelled. This can occur by means of market pressure, or, if this is absent, a corporation may be mandated by the state to disclose social and environmental information. Here the linkage between the pillars, between the state duty to protect and the corporate responsibility to respect, comes to the fore. The corporate responsibility to protect is an autonomous responsibility, independent from the state duty to protect, and it is intimately linked to the relationship a corporation has with its stakeholders. Stakeholders such as NGOs, however, do not have the possibility of demanding information that enables them to police corporate conduct.

Enforcing compliance with social norms is difficult to achieve without state backing. I contend that transnational private regulation can only

---

[84] *Ibid.*, emphasis added.

reach its full potential if a stronger role for the state is brought back into the equation. Stakeholders must have access to information to, on the one hand, put pressure on corporations to join transnational private regulatory regimes, and, on the other, check actual compliance with these standards. A public policy solution is necessary to secure the transparency that is needed to render transnational private regulation effective.

Disclosure of information according to Pillar 1

What do the GPs provide concerning the duty of the state to ensure transparency by disclosure of information? According to Guiding Principle 3:

> In meeting their duty to protect, States should:
>
> (a) Enforce laws that are aimed at, or have the effect of, requiring business enterprises to respect human rights, and periodically assess the adequacy of such laws and address any gaps;
> (b) Ensure that other laws and policies governing the creation and ongoing operation of business enterprises, such as corporate law, do not constrain but enable business respect for human rights;
> (c) Provide effective guidance to business enterprises on how to respect human rights throughout their operations;
> (d) *Encourage*, and *where appropriate require*, business enterprises to communicate how they address their human rights impacts.

This Guiding Principle bolsters the corporate responsibility to disclose information. However, given that information is a precondition for the effective operationalisation of the Framework by means of transnational private regulation or otherwise, it is argued that more guidance is needed as to what this duty to protect implies exactly. First, according to the GPs the main duty of states is to 'encourage' business enterprises to communicate how they are addressing their human rights impacts. According to the Commentary, 'incentives to communicate adequate information could include provisions to give weight to such self reporting in the event of any judicial or administrative proceeding'.[85] Here, a moral hazard problem arises.[86] The incentive to give weight to self-reporting in possible judicial

---

[85] SRSG, 'Guiding Principles', n. 5, para. 3.
[86] See Hess, 'Social Reporting and New Governance Regulation', n. 22, 457, pointing out the moral hazard that occurs when corporations are promised reduced sentences for criminal violations when they have compliance programmes in place.

proceedings may encourage corporations to adopt the appearance of a socially responsible programme, but if independent third-party verification is not assured the corporation might in fact not be addressing its actual impact. The adoption of a reporting procedure on paper nonetheless would grant a degree of impunity, making the corporation less accountable.

Notwithstanding the incentive, it is likely that many corporations will continue not to disclose information voluntarily. The SRSG has acknowledged this by adding that 'where appropriate' business enterprises 'should be required' to communicate such information. In the Commentary to Guiding Principle 3, some guidance is given on the rather vague 'where appropriate'. According to the Commentary 'a requirement to communicate can be particularly appropriate where the nature of business operations or operating contexts pose a significant risk to human rights'.[87] The Commentary qualifies this requirement on states with the following proviso: '[a]ny stipulation of what would constitute adequate communication should take into account risks that it may pose to the safety and security of individuals and facilities; legitimate requirements of commercial confidentiality; and variations in companies' size and structures'. It is argued that in light of the critical role of information and the fact that many corporations will not disclose it voluntarily, this state duty should have been more forcefully formulated. In Hess's words: 'To function as a bottom-up, participatory and experimental regulatory measure, social reporting must have top-down mandates for disclosure. This grants stakeholders negotiating power and allows true collaborative governance to develop around particular firms and issues.'[88]

Despite the rather weak formulation, the GPs might support the emerging trend towards mandatory due diligence and reporting. The best-known recent example is section 1502 of the US Dodd-Frank Act,[89] adopted in 2010, according to which companies will not only have to disclose (to the US Securities and Exchange Commission (SEC) and the public) whether conflict minerals (defined as gold, tin, tungsten and tantalum) in their products originate from the Democratic Republic of the Congo (DRC), but also report on the due diligence exercised down the supply chain. This regulation only applies to companies listed in the USA, but, in 2013, the European Union released a similar regulation on

---

[87] SRSG, 'Guiding Principles', n. 5, para. 3.
[88] Hess, 'Social Reporting and New Governance Regulation', n. 22, 471.
[89] Dodd-Frank Wall Street Reform and Consumer Protection Act of 2010 (Pub. L. No. 111–203, H.R. 4173).

the disclosure of non-financial information that will be applicable to EU-based corporations in the near future.[90] The California Transparency in Supply Chains Act[91] is another example of a regulatory initiative that requires companies (doing business in the state) to disclose their policies aimed at eradicating slavery and human trafficking. Companies must provide consumers with direct access to their disclosure from the home-page of their corporate websites. Since 1995, several European countries including Denmark,[92] France, the Netherlands, Norway, Sweden and the UK have adopted legislation mandating certain corporations to disclose social and environmental information annually.[93] An example of such mandatory reporting is a UK company law Act which lays down a legal requirement on corporations to produce a 'business review' that 'to the extent necessary' must inform members of the company and help them to assess the following issues: how directors have performed their duty to promote the success of the company; the main trends and factors that affect the future of the company; environmental matters; the situation of employees as well as social and community issues; and the use of con-tractors essential to the company. The business review must also give details on policies related to these matters and their effectiveness.[94] The UK's example is more limited in its reach when compared to the pre-viously mentioned examples, as the disclosure is only aimed at 'members of the company'. Another example can be found in the Netherlands, where listed corporations of a certain size are required to pay attention to environmental and social issues in their annual reports.[95] The law,

---

[90] On 16 April 2013, the European Commission proposed draft legislation on disclosure of non-financial and diversity information. See: http://europa.eu/rapid/press-release_AGENDA-13-13_en.htm?locale=en (last accessed on 4 June 2013). The European Parliament and the Council of the European Union, 'Directive 2003/51/EC of the European Parliament and of the Council' (18 June 2003), http://eur-lex.europa.eu/LexUriServ/LexUriServ.do?uri=OJ:L:2003:178:0016:0022:EN:PDF (last accessed 12 December 2012), already requires that large companies annually report on non-financial performance indicators, e.g. environmental and employee matters.

[91] The California Transparency in Supply Chains Act of 2010; s. 1714.43 of the California Civil Code; and s. 19547.5 of the California Revenue and Taxation Code.

[92] K. Buhmann, 'The Danish CSR Reporting Requirement: Migration of CSR-related International Norms into Companies' Self-Regulation through Company Law' (2 March 2011), http://papers.ssrn.com/sol3/papers.cfm?abstract_id=1774742 (last accessed 7 November 2012).

[93] For more, see Lambooy, *Corporate Social Responsibility*, n. 32, 235–37.

[94] Companies Act 2006 (UK), s. 417(5).

[95] See Art. 2:391, para. 1, Dutch Civil Code. This provision is in line with European Directive 2003/51/EC, n. 90.

however, does not stipulate *how* corporations are to report. The far-reaching Dodd-Frank Act mentioned above is, to date, an exception.

In general, it should be concluded that transparency requirements in most jurisdictions concern mainly financial information and are aimed primarily at shareholders and investors. Disclosure of information on the human rights impacts of corporate activities, relevant for other stakeholders, is overall not mandated.[96] Mandatory reporting will be a step in the right direction if it makes available information that empowers stakeholders to press for the voluntary uptake of and compliance with private standards. Not only is it essential that guidance is provided on how and what should be reported, but it is also imperative that reporting results are made accessible to all stakeholders.[97] For example, the California Transparency Act requires retailers and manufacturers doing business in California to provide easily accessible information on their website on how they are working to combat slavery and human trafficking in their supply chain. The recognition of the importance of transparency and the duty of the state in 'requiring disclosure where appropriate' in the GPs might prove to further accelerate this process towards mandatory reporting. The rather weak formulation, however, leaves a lot of discretion to states as to whether or not to mandate disclosure. The GPs fall short here in failing to provide a forceful connection between the first and second pillars. An essential part of the state duty to protect as laid down in the first pillar should be to mandate corporations to take up their responsibility to respect by disclosing certain information and making it accessible to stakeholders.

Towards a right to independent information?

The Framework and the GPs will, possibly, encourage corporate reporting, but fail to provide guidance on the mechanisms – such as third party verification – needed to prevent paper compliance. Reporting runs the

---

[96] Reporting that incorporates information in the field of corporate social responsibility is known as 'integrated reporting'. South Africa is the first country that requires integrated reporting from corporations listed on the Johannesburg Stock Exchange. See the Institute of Directors Southern Africa, 'King Code of Governance for South Africa 2009', www.ecgi.org/codes/documents/king3.pdf (last accessed 12 November 2012).

[97] This, for example, is the case in Sweden where the state has adopted legislation mandating state-owned companies to report externally in accordance with the Global Reporting Initiative Guidelines, www.globalreporting.org/reporting/latest-guidelines/Pages/default.aspx (last accessed 30 January 2013).

risk of focusing on showing formal uptake of procedures rather than on providing objective information on *whether* the company has been involved in, or runs a risk of being involved in, violations of international human rights standards. It has been argued that the evidence so far suggests that in the cases where corporations do voluntarily disclose social and environmental information, this reporting fails to provide significant organisational transparency and stakeholder engagement.[98] Hess has argued that corporations only disclose social and environmental information when they encounter a crisis that threatens their legitimacy. Consequently, the information disclosed 'voluntarily' is designed to repair lost legitimacy and therefore almost exclusively emphasises the positive aspects of a corporation's performance.[99] Taylor states that reporting

> offers companies the possibility to 'prove the negative', in other words to issue annual reports which show that they are in compliance and do not infringe on the rights of others ... These forms of CSR reporting are not well suited for reporting on where violations were encountered and how they were dealt with. In this sense, they are too superficial to secure real change in the business practices that result in violations.[100]

Hess concludes that, 'overall, current research suggests that the strategic disclosure of information that leads to incomplete and misleading social reports is the norm for corporations'.[101]

States mandating disclosure could address this problem if they provide clear standards on what and how to report and ensure that the information is verifiable. The GPs largely rely on corporations to determine how and what information should be gathered and disclosed. In order for stakeholders to verify corporate compliance with standards, it might be necessary for them to have access to independently acquired information for ensuring compliance with the corporate responsibility to respect.

---

[98] These are the two goals of social reporting mentioned by the leading standard on social reporting, Global Reporting Initiative's 'Sustainability Reporting Guidelines'. See Hess, 'Social Reporting and New Governance Regulation', n. 22, 455.

[99] See Hess, 'Social Reporting and New Governance Regulation', *ibid.*, 455–56 and the sources quoted there.

[100] M. B. Taylor, 'The Ruggie Framework: Polycentric Regulation and the Implications for Corporate Social Responsibility' (2011) 5:1 *Etikk i praksis – Nordic Journal of Applied Ethics*, 9 at 26.

[101] Hess, 'Social Reporting and New Governance Regulation', n. 22, 456.

Melish and Meidinger also point out the weakness of the GPs concerning the operationalisation of the second pillar, by stating that:

> [a]lthough the guiding principles do call for transparency and participation in the conduct of corporate due diligence responsibilities, such participation is not required under the framework; nor can it be asserted by civil society groups as a 'right' conferred under the framework.[102]

They conclude that the Framework is conceptually flawed by not explicitly recognising a right to participate for stakeholders. They argue:

> under the current conceptual framework, a business can legitimately claim that it need not allow for civil society participation in external monitoring of any of the aforementioned due diligence activities. This apparent corporate right of control over who has access to relevant information for human rights monitoring and impact assessment and who can speak on behalf of communities in voluntary consultation processes is a major operational gap in the Ruggie framework. Indeed, corporate actors are unlikely, at least in the short term, to see external monitoring of their operations on the human rights of affected communities as consistent with their economic interests.[103]

Consequently, Melish and Meidinger propose that the Framework needs to be adjusted to include a fourth pillar on the right to participate. They argue that '[a]dditional actors, with distinct ways of levering power over corporate and state conduct must be explicitly brought into the framework for it to be effective in closing the current governance gaps'.[104]

I agree with Melish and Meidinger that the exclusive dependence on corporations to gather and disclose information on the due diligence steps taken constitutes a weakness in the Framework. However, in contrast to their proposal to add a fourth pillar to the Framework, I contend that more guidance could and should have been given in the first pillar under the state duty to protect in order to ensure greater transparency for stakeholders, a necessary precondition for the voluntary uptake of social norms to take place. As will be argued below, this is not a revolutionary step: a foundation for such an obligation can be found in international law. It is understandable, from a strategic point of view, that in the thorny process leading up to the adoption of the Framework and the GPs, a more explicit inclusion of stakeholders such as NGOs was a bridge too far as this would most likely have alienated the

---

[102] Melish and Meidinger, 'Protect, Respect, Remedy and Participate' in Mares (ed.), *The UN Guiding Principles on Business and Human Rights*, n. 22, 29.
[103] Ibid., 29.   [104] *Ibid.*, 27.

corporate actors from the process. However, as will be elaborated upon below, ensuring transparency for the sake of stakeholders must be seen as part of the state duty to protect. This should be further elaborated upon in the process of operationalising the Framework and the GPs.

The best way to assure better corporate compliance with human rights standards is not by having certain policies in place but rather by providing stakeholders with actual power through information. In addition to mandating and guiding disclosure and ensuring that the information is accessible to stakeholders, states should therefore draw up legislation laying down a right for stakeholders to receive independent information so that they can monitor whether a business has been involved in certain human rights violations.[105] In the Netherlands, legislation to provide consumers with a right 'to know' has been proposed, but recently been rejected.[106]

Access to information in international law

It is argued here that a state duty can be discerned that goes beyond requiring the corporation to report on due diligence steps taken – a duty to include an independent right of stakeholders to access information on corporate conduct. This is not such a radical proposal as it might seem. The right to independent information and the corresponding positive duty on states to ensure the enjoyment of this right has a foundation in international human rights law.[107]

First, a right to information and a corresponding duty upon states to enable access to information has developed based on the freedom to 'seek, receive and impart information and ideas of all kinds'. This is a component of the freedom of opinion and expression as laid down in Article 19 of the Universal Declaration of Human Rights (UDHR) and

---

[105] See for a similar proposal Taylor, 'The Ruggie Framework', n. 100, 27. A parallel may be drawn with the 'right to know' as has been developed in EU consumer law, especially with regard to product safety. See for a comprehensive overview Lambooy, *Corporate Social Responsibility*, n. 32, 343–66.

[106] *Wet Openbaarheid Productie en Ketens* [Act on the Transparency of Supply Chains]. Following a study into the feasibility of such an Act, it was decided that such legislation would disturb competition and lead to disproportionate costs. For more on what the proposal entailed see Lambooy, *Corporate Social Responsibility*, n. 32, 371–74.

[107] For a more detailed analysis of developments concerning the right to information at the national and the international levels, see N. Jägers, 'The Missing Right to Know. A Critique of the UN Protect-Respect-Remedy Framework and the Guiding Principles' (2012) XXVIII:106 *Notizie de Politeia* 100.

legally enshrined in Article 19 of the International Covenant of Civil and Political Rights (ICCPR).[108] The right is also acknowledged in regional human rights documents.[109] The right to information is considered so important that, increasingly, it is being recognised as an independent right.[110] The core of the right to information concerns the entitlement to access official information, in other words information held by public bodies and the obligation of public bodies to disclose such information. However, the Special Rapporteur on the promotion and protection of the right to freedom of opinion and expression has held that 'public bodies' should be defined broadly and the obligation to disclose information focuses on the type of service provided rather than on formal designations. This implies that

> it should include all branches and levels of Government, including local government, elected bodies, bodies which operate under a statutory mandate, nationalized industries and public corporations, non-departmental bodies or 'quangos' (quasi non-governmental organizations), judicial bodies and private bodies which carry out public functions (such as maintaining roads or operating rail lines).[111]

In other words, in the case of public corporations or those carrying out public functions, a duty exists to adopt legislation providing stakeholders with a right to access information.

General Principle 5 addresses the situation in which states contract with business enterprises to provide services. According to this Principle, '[s]tates should exercise adequate oversight in order to meet their

---

[108] The Articles are practically identical. Art. 19 in the International Covenant on Civil and Political Rights (entered into force 23 March 1976) (ICCPR) reads: '[e]veryone shall have the right to freedom of expression; this right shall include freedom to seek, receive and impart information and ideas of all kinds, regardless of frontiers, either orally, in writing or in print, in the form of art, or through any other media of his choice'.

[109] See Art. 9(1) of the African Charter of Human and Peoples Rights (entered into force 21 October 1986); Art. 13(1) of the American Convention on Human Rights (entered into force 18 July 1978); Art. 10 in the European Convention on Human Rights (entered into force 21 September 1970) (ECHR); Art. 11 of the Charter of Fundamental Rights of the European Union (entered into force 7 December 2000).

[110] Commission on Human Rights, 'Civil and Political Rights including the Question of Freedom of Expression: Report of the Special Rapporteur on the Promotion and Protection of the Right of Freedom of Opinion and Expression', E/CN.4/2000/63 (18 January 2000), para. 42 (CHR, '2000 Report').

[111] CHR, '2000 Report', *ibid.*, Annex II: The Public's Right to Know: Principles of Freedom of Information Legislation, Principle 1.

international human rights obligations when they contract with, or legislate for, business enterprises to provide services that may impact upon the enjoyment of human rights'. According to the accompanying Commentary, '[s]tates should ensure that they can effectively oversee the enterprises' activities, including through the provision of adequate independent monitoring and accountability mechanisms'. It can be concluded that this means that a statutory right to access information should also cover enterprises carrying out public functions.

The right to information may, however, extend even further. According to the UN Principles on Freedom of Information Legislation, a duty exists to include private bodies in such legislation 'if they hold information whose disclosure is likely to diminish the risk of harm to key public interests, such as the environment and health'.[112] The 2002 non-legally binding Declaration of Principles on Freedom of Expression in Africa offers some further support for a right to access information held by private bodies. According to the Preamble, '[the] respect for freedom of expression, as well as the right of access to information held by public bodies and *companies*, will lead to greater public transparency and accountability, as well as to good governance and the strengthening of democracy'.[113] Principle IV goes on to provide that '[t]he right to information shall be guaranteed by law in accordance with the following principles: . . . everyone has the right to access information held by private bodies which is necessary for the exercise or protection of any right'.

Refusing to disclose information can only be justified under a limited number of circumstances. The following strict three-part test has been laid down in Principle 4 of the Principles on Freedom of Information Legislation: (1) the information relates to a legitimate aim listed in the law; (2) disclosure threatens to cause substantial harm to that aim; and (3) the harm outweighs any public interest benefit from releasing the information.[114]

Moreover, as noted above, it can be considered a flaw in the Framework that stakeholders are dependent exclusively on corporations to collect and disclose information. A foundational basis for a state duty

---

[112] *Ibid.*
[113] Art. 19, 'Declaration of Principles on Freedom of Expression in Africa' (22 October 2002), www.unhcr.org/refworld/docid/4753d3a40.html (last accessed 9 November 2012). (Emphasis added.)
[114] See Jägers, 'The Missing Right to Know', n. 107, 100.

to guide stakeholders to independent information may be found by drawing a parallel to the jurisprudence that has been developed concerning the right to information of indigenous peoples. In several landmark cases, regional courts have recognised the right to acquire independent information in the sense that indigenous peoples have the right to an independent environmental and social impact assessment preceding any issuing of a concession.[115] An early case where this duty of states regarding independent information was cautiously acknowledged was that against Nigeria brought before the African Commission on Human and Peoples Rights concerning, *inter alia*, destruction of the environment in Ogoniland. The Commission held that '[g]overnment compliance with the spirit of Articles 16 [right to health] and 24 [right to a general satisfactory environment] of the African Charter must also include ordering or at least permitting *independent* scientific monitoring of threatened environments'.[116] In the case of *Saramaka People* v. *Suriname*, the Inter-American Court held that by granting resource concessions to private companies within the territories of the Saramaka People without their consultation or consent, Suriname had violated the Saramaka People's rights, as tribal peoples, to judicial protection and property as defined in the American Convention.[117] According to the Inter-American Court, states must ensure that prior to granting any concession, *independent* and technically sound environmental and social impact assessments be undertaken to mitigate any negative effects. The Court held that the state had the duty to disseminate and receive information. The African Commission on Human and Peoples Rights has acknowledged a similar right to independent

---

[115] The right to independent information is part of the right to Free, Prior and Informed Consent (FPIC), which refers to the right of indigenous peoples to make free and informed choices about the development of their lands and their resources. The basic principles are to ensure that indigenous peoples are not coerced or intimidated, their consent is sought and freely given prior to the authorisation or start of any activities, that they have full information about the scope and impacts of any proposed developments, and that ultimately their choices to give or withhold consent are respected. The right to FPIC has been most clearly laid down in the United Nations General Assembly, 'Resolution 61/295 UN Declaration on the Rights of Indigenous Peoples', A/RES/66/295 (2 October 2007), para. 19 (GA, 'Resolution 61/295').

[116] *Communication 155/96, Social and Economic Rights Action Centre (SERAC) and Another* v. *Nigeria* (2001) AHRLR 60, African Commission on Human and Peoples Rights, para. 53 (emphasis added.).

[117] *Saramaka People* v. *Suriname* (28 November 2007), Inter-Am. Ct. HR (ser. C) No. 172, 131 and 136.

information in the *Endorois* v. *Kenya* case.[118] This case concerned the eviction of an indigenous community from their ancestral lands to make way for a wildlife reserve. Referring to the *Saramaka* case, the African Commission held that the state must 'ensure that no concession will be issued ... unless and until *independent* and technically capable entities, with the State's supervision, perform a prior environmental and social impact assessment'.[119] The Commission held that Kenya violated the right to property and the right to development, *inter alia*, by failing to provide the Endorois people with independent information.

This duty resting upon states to provide independent information has also been recognised by the Committee on the Elimination of Racial Discrimination, which, with respect to natural resource exploitation affecting indigenous peoples, has recommended that states 'set up an *independent* body to conduct environmental impact surveys before any operating licenses are issued and to conduct health and safety checks on small-scale and industrial gold mining'.[120]

In sum, regardless of whether a corporation discloses information, it may be argued that the above appears to indicate an emerging duty upon states to ensure access to independent information from corporations regarding activities that can adversely impact human rights.

Beyond the Framework and GPs: issues for the UN Working Group to consider

The work of the SRSG has drawn attention to the contribution private transnational regulation can make to improve corporate human rights performance. As pointed out by the SRSG, a general treaty directly regulating corporate human rights behaviour would most likely not prove to be a panacea to the problems posed in this area.[121] It is a fact that the effectiveness of international treaties leaves a lot to be desired.

---

[118] *Communication 276/03, Center for Minority Rights (Kenya) and Minority Rights Group International on Behalf of the Endorois Welfare Council* v. *Kenya* (2009) AHRLR 75, African Commission on Human and Peoples Rights.

[119] *Ibid.*, para. 227 (emphasis added).

[120] Committee on the Elimination of Racial Discrimination, 'Concluding Observations Suriname: Consideration of Reports Submitted by the State Parties under Article 9 of the Convention', CERD/C/64/CO/9 (27 March 2007), para. 15 (CERD, '2004 Report') (emphasis added).

[121] J. Ruggie, 'Business and Human Rights – Treaty Road Not Travelled' (6 May 2008), www.ethicalcorp.com/content/john-ruggie-business-and-human-rights-%E2%80%93-treaty-road-not-travelled (last accessed 9 November 2012).

Transnational private regulation is also not *the* answer. However, especially where it concerns highly visible corporations, i.e. in situations where there is sufficient information on their corporate activities, transnational private regulation can contribute in helping to change corporate behaviour. However, in cases where information on corporate activities is less transparent, the Framework provides insufficient guidance to ensure an effective bottom-up approach.

In this chapter, I have discussed what a state can and should do to achieve the transparency that is needed for transnational private regulation to be effective and for the successful operationalisation of the second pillar of the Framework. Firstly, states can actively support private transnational regulation by working towards more transparency in multi-stakeholder initiatives.[122]

Secondly, states must foster the trend toward mandatory reporting and ensure that the results of such reporting are properly designed and accessible to all stakeholders to enable third party monitoring of how corporations discharge their duty to respect.

Finally, states need to develop alternative means to ensure that stakeholders can acquire independent information necessary to ensure compliance with the commitments undertaken. International human rights law provides the foundation for this state duty to guide stakeholders to independent information concerning corporate involvement in (possible) human rights violations.

At the same time it should be acknowledged that it is unlikely that a sufficient degree of transparency for the effective operationalisation of the second pillar of the Framework will be feasible across all business sectors. At the end of the day transnational private regulation might simply not be the appropriate answer to the challenges posed by certain business sectors. The illustration of the private security industry used in this chapter is a case in point. Without prejudging the eventual effectiveness of the ICOC-PSP,[123] it remains questionable whether transnational

---

[122] The interviews conducted for the HiiL project mentioned in n. 58 above show that the potential of this regulatory mechanism increased significantly when states finally stepped up their commitment to and involvement in the process. This was, for instances mentioned during an interview with a state representative, 21 September 2011.

[123] For an analysis of the potential for this code of conduct to be effective in comparison to earlier transnational private regulatory regimes, see N. Jägers, 'Regulating the Private Security Industry', n. 50, 56.

private regulation will prove to be a sufficient answer.[124] This industry is still far removed from the 'tipping' point referred to by the SRSG where responsible behaviour becomes the new status quo.[125] The Framework will most likely not quell the call for a more top-down approach, especially where it concerns grave human rights violations such as those that PSCs have allegedly committed in weak governance zones.

The interplay between companies and their 'societal controllers' will decisively contribute to the effectiveness or otherwise of private regulatory mechanisms. Companies are allowed and encouraged to create their own regulatory systems, as long as they do so in a responsible way: the norms incorporated in these systems should be in line with international human rights standards, and corporate behaviour should not focus on the wish to escape public scrutiny, but to be more open. Such a 'nothing to hide' mentality will in the long run be in the interest of all players and make bottom-up private initiatives the right starting point. States should address the matter in a way that makes companies really live up to the promises made in their private regulatory schemes. And the best starting point for state and non-state actors alike would be to provide access to information.

---

[124] Hoppe and Quirico find strong indications that reliance on market mechanisms in this field is problematic, given several characteristics of the industry. They put forward the lack of reliable information as one of the main reasons. But they also point out the fact that the industry still contains a significant amount of non-repeat players (corporations reorganise, losing their tainted reputation, and thus the incentive to live up to human rights commitments). Moreover, other factors also undermine the incentive for PSCs to join regulatory initiatives, such as the lack of competition, and, as Hoppe and Quirico argue, clients simply may be indifferent to such values and therefore will not press for adherence to codes. C. Hoppe and O. Quirico, 'Codes of Conduct for Private Military and Security Companies' in F. Francioni and N. Ronzitti (eds.), *War by Contract*, n. 52, 362.

[125] Ruggie, 'The Global Compact and the Challenges of Global Governance', n. 12, 3.

13

An analysis and practical application of the Guiding Principles on providing remedies with special reference to case studies related to oil companies

TINEKE LAMBOOY, AIKATERINI ARGYROU
AND MARY VARNER*

Introduction

The third pillar of the Framework[1] developed by the UN Special Representative of the Secretary-General on the Issue of Human Rights and Transnational Corporations and Other Business Enterprises (SRSG) concerns the remedies that are available for victims of corporate human rights violations: 'Access to Remedy' (Remedy Pillar). According to the SRSG, companies and public authorities are required to provide effective courses of action and remedies to victims. In order to remediate adverse impacts of corporate misconduct, legal as well as non-legal remedies need to be available.

After consulting various stakeholders, the SRSG formulated and published the Guiding Principles (GPs), aimed at providing guidance to states and companies on how to put the Framework into practice.[2] The

---

* The research for this chapter closed on 30 May 2013.
[1] Human Rights Council, 'Protect, Respect and Remedy: a Framework for Business and Human Rights: Report of the Special Representative of the Secretary-General on the Issue of Human Rights and Transnational Corporations and Other Business Enterprises', A/HRC/8/5 (7 April 2008) (SRSG, '2008 Framework').
[2] Human Rights Council, 'Guiding Principles on Business and Human Rights: Implementing the United Nations "Protect, Respect and Remedy" Framework: Report of the Special Representative of the Secretary-General on the Issue of Human Rights and Transnational Corporations and Other Business Enterprises', A/HRC/17/31 (21 March 2011) (SRSG, 'Guiding Principles').

GPs were endorsed by the Human Rights Council on 16 June 2011.[3] GPs 25–31 include various principles on the Remedy Pillar, GPs 22–24 also focus on remediation by companies. In preparation of the GPs, the SRSG's team performed research on state-based and non-state-based remedies, and in-company grievance mechanisms such as complaints procedures.[4]

Many multinationals expressed support for the SRSG's process and the GPs. However, the question arises whether companies really understand what is expected from them under the Remedy Pillar. Worldwide, there are many serious and continuing conflicts between mining companies, workers and communities (about the safety situation, salaries and pollution respectively),[5] between energy-producing plants, dams and communities (about pollution and forced removal), and between oil companies and communities (about spills that have contaminated drinking and fishing water and agricultural land).[6] They exemplify the

---

[3] Human Rights Council, 'Human Rights and Transnational Corporations and Other Business Enterprises', A/HRC/RES/17/4 (6 July 2011) (HRC, '2011 Resolution').

[4] SRSG, '2008 Framework', n. 1. See both studies on in-company grievance mechanisms: C. Rees, 'Grievance Mechanisms for Business and Human Rights: Strengths, Weaknesses and Gaps' (January 2008), www.hks.harvard.edu/m-rcbg/CSRI/publications/workingpaper_40_Strengths_Weaknesses_Gaps.pdf and 'Access to Remedies for Corporate Human Rights Impacts: Improving Non-Judicial Mechanisms' (November 2008), www.hks.harvard.edu/m-rcbg/CSRI/publications/report_32_consultation_report_november_08.pdf (both websites last accessed 27 May 2013). See also BASESwiki, a database of non-judicial remedies set up by the Ruggie Project (date unavailable), www.baseswiki.org/en/Main_Page (last accessed 27 May 2013).

[5] For example, issues concerning Newmont Mining Company in Peru, Indonesia and Ghana; Anglo American in South Africa; BHP Billiton in Colombia and Pakistan; Freeport McMoran Copper and Gold in Papua New Guinea and Peru; Xstrata in Papua New Guinea; Shell in Nigeria and the Karoo (South Africa); Exxon in Alaska and Ecuador. The conflicts escalated when mining companies were accused of poor occupational health and safety standards, toxic emissions, water pollution and serious and fatal accidents. See e.g. RepRisk, 'Most Controversial Mining Companies of 2011' (March 2012), www.reprisk.com/downloads/mccreports/23/150312%20Top%2010%20Most%20Controversial%20Mining%20Companies_RepRisk.pdf (last accessed 27 May 2013).

[6] P. Verma, 'Linking Policy Process to Environmental Impacts in the United States Environmental Protection Agency's National Estuary Program: A Comparative Case Study Analysis of the Science Policy Interface' (September 2011), Ph.D. dissertation, University of California, p. 6, http://gradworks.umi.com/3489136.pdf. See also three documentaries produced by CSRI and Harvard Kennedy School, i.e. 'Corporate Community Dialogue: An Introduction' (8 June 2012), www.baseswiki.org/en/Compilation; 'Putting Ourselves in their Shoes: The Dialogue Table of Tintaya' (19 October 2011), www.baseswiki.org/en/Video/Tintaya_Dialogue; 'Making Monkey Business: Building Company/Community Dialogue in the Philippines' (15 June 2011), www.baseswiki.org/en/Video/Philippines_Dialogue (all websites last accessed 27 May 2013).

fact that companies are struggling to provide remedies when facing Corporate Social Responsibility (CSR) conflicts. The question arises as to how the GPs can provide guidance to companies on what would constitute effective action in situations where they have to remediate adverse impacts, including infringements on human rights, stemming from their business operations.

The object of the study in this chapter is (i) to summarise what the GPs state about remedies; (ii) to make the concept more perspicuous by assessing the non-judicial and judicial remedies that were employed in three oil spill cases (Chevron, Shell and BP); (iii) to discuss and compare, against the background of the GPs on remedies, the applicable corporate policies, the available non-judicial corporate remedies and the approaches taken by the oil companies regarding the adverse impacts of their operations; and (iv) to analyse how these companies could have dealt more effectively with the complaints of the victims had they followed the GPs. The focus of this chapter is thus on the corporate approach towards providing remedies rather than the state's actions.

The Guiding Principles and the concept of effective remedies

As the Remedy Pillar applies to both states and business enterprises, the GPs indicate that each is required to provide remediation and organise effective remedies in order to address human rights violations. In this section, we will discuss the roles of companies and states in respect of providing effective remedies.

GP 22 directs that 'where business enterprises identify that they have caused or contributed to adverse impacts, they should provide for or cooperate in their remediation through legitimate processes'. The Commentary to GP 25 adds that states must take 'appropriate steps to investigate, punish and redress business-related human rights abuses'.

It is important to note that providing remedies entails more than responding to legal claims or offering financial compensation. The Commentary to GP 25 explains that a 'remedy may include apologies, restitution, rehabilitation, financial or non-financial compensation and punitive sanctions (whether criminal or administrative, such as fines), as well as the prevention of harm through, for example, injunctions or guarantees of non-repetition'.

One could consider that a company that intends to remediate misconduct starts with making an apology and, where possible, undoing the misconduct and restoring the situation as if it had never happened, e.g. by remediation in kind. When this is impossible, it is important that access should be provided to judicial and non-judicial means. Judicial means include the courts (for both criminal and civil actions), labour tribunals and national human rights institutions. Examples of non-judicial means are National Contact Points (NCPs) under the Guidelines for Multinational Enterprises of the Organisation for Economic Co-operation and Development (OECD Guidelines), ombudsperson offices and government-run complaints offices (Commentary to GP 25). Within some mechanisms, victims can seek remedies directly; in others, an intermediary can do so on their behalf.

Besides state-based remedy mechanisms, there are also mechanisms established by non-state actors, such as companies, to address grievances. A 'grievance' is understood to be 'a perceived injustice evoking an individual's or a group's sense of entitlement, which may be based on law, contract, explicit or implicit promises, customary practice, or general notions of fairness of aggrieved communities' (Commentary to GP 25). By 'grievance mechanism' reference is made to 'any routinized, State-based or non-State-based, judicial or non-judicial process through which grievances concerning business-related human rights abuse can be raised and remedy can be sought' (Commentary to GP 25). Rees and Kovick (from the Ruggie team) published a 'grievance-centric' guidance paper for companies.[7] The paper contains an overview of various regional, international and domestic non-state grievance mechanisms which could be employed in the operationalisation of the Framework. Additionally, it is worth mentioning 'ACCESS', a new institute in The Hague,[8] which puts emphasis on a new way of resolving company–community conflicts by using alternative dispute resolution mechanisms such as information facilitation and mediation. ACCESS hosts the database BASESwiki (Business and Society Exploring Solutions) set up by Ruggie's team, and develops this further.[9]

Remedies are included in the last pillar, the third pillar, because when states and companies have not succeeded in preventing human rights

---

[7] C. Rees, 'Grievance Mechanisms for Business and Human Rights' and 'Access to Remedies', n. 4.

[8] 'ACCESS' was initiated by the 'HUGO Programme' based in The Hague, the Netherlands. ACCESS collects and provides information and advice to assist in solving company–community conflicts. Ruggie, Rees and Kovick are involved. See World Legal Forum, 'About the HUGO Programme' (2010), www.worldlegalforum.org/index.php?option=com_content&view=article&id=2&Itemid=110 (last accessed 27 May 2013).

[9] BASESwiki, 'Business and Society Exploring Solutions: A Dispute Resolution Community' (date unavailable), www.baseswiki.org/en/Main_Page (last accessed 27 May 2013).

violations in relation to corporate activities, the only next step is to remedy such violation. As Ruggie explains in the Commentary to GP 22:

> Even with the best policies and practices, a business enterprise may cause or contribute to an adverse human rights impact that it has not foreseen or been able to prevent. Where a business enterprise identifies such a situation, whether through its human rights due diligence process or other means, its responsibility to respect human rights requires active engagement in remediation, by itself or in cooperation with other actors.

Against this background, it is important to consider the effectiveness of remedies offered, as non-effective remedies lack any significance. GP 31 offers a number of criteria to assess the effectiveness of state-based and non-state-based non-judicial grievance mechanisms.[10] These effectiveness criteria can also assist in considering whether a certain corporate remediation policy or approach can be considered meaningful from the perspective of the GPs. The following criteria are specified:

(a) Legitimate: enabling trust from the stakeholder groups for whose use they are intended, and being accountable for the fair conduct of grievance processes;

(b) Accessible: being known to all stakeholder groups for whose use they are intended, and providing adequate assistance for those who may face particular barriers to access;

(c) Predictable: providing a clear and known procedure with an indicative timeframe for each stage, and clarity on the types of processes and outcome available and the means of monitoring implementation;

(d) Equitable: seeking to ensure that aggrieved parties have reasonable access to sources of information, advice and expertise necessary to engage in a grievance process on fair, informed and respectful terms;

(e) Transparent: keeping parties to a grievance informed about its progress, and providing sufficient information about the mechanism's performance to build confidence in its effectiveness and to meet any public interest at stake;

(f) Rights-compatible: ensuring that outcomes and remedies are in accordance with internationally recognised human rights; and

(g) A source of continuous learning: drawing on relevant measures to identify lessons for improving the mechanism and preventing future grievances and harms.

---

[10] The Commentary to GP 31 explains that the term 'grievance mechanism' is used here as a term of art. The term itself may not always be appropriate or helpful when applied to a specific mechanism, but the criteria for effectiveness remain the same.

Operational-level mechanisms should also be:

(h) Based on engagement and dialogue: consulting the stakeholder groups for whose use they are intended on their design and performance, and focusing on dialogue as the means to address and resolve grievances.

To make the theoretical information about the GPs more understandable, the third section of this chapter will outline three case studies in which companies were accused of human rights violations. In each case, we will discuss the responses of the oil companies towards the grievances of the people that claimed to have suffered from the oil operations and pollution in their area. Hence, no chart will be made of the available state-centred remedial mechanisms.

In order to test whether the oil companies have provided for or co-operated in remediation through legitimate processes as suggested by GP 22, we have examined the following matters on the basis of publicly available information: (i) what type of adverse impacts were caused by the oil operations (where possible by referring to reports prepared by independent institutions); (ii) which types of remedies (see the categories mentioned in GP 25 and Commentary) were provided; (iii) whether the state has interfered, contributed or set up any remediation mechanism (see the discussion in GPs 26–27); (iv) the manner in which the companies responded to victims' requests, protests and legal claims (i.e. adequately and swiftly? Taking into account the guidance of GPs 20–22, and 24); (v) what legal strategies the companies pursued; and whether they complied with GP 23 (i.e. business enterprises should ensure that they do not exacerbate the situation);[11] and (vi) which time periods were involved in the remedies (GP 29: early and direct remediation?). The presentation of the three case studies in the third section will be limited to describing such elements that the GPs indicate as important matters in relation to the Respect and Remedy pillars.

An analysis of these issues can assist the reader in acquiring an insight into the effectiveness of the remedial approaches of the three oil companies. Therefore, the fourth section of the chapter contains a

---

[11] Commentary to GP 23: 'In complex contexts such as these, business enterprises should ensure that they do not exacerbate the situation. In assessing how best to respond, they will often be well advised to draw on not only expertise and cross-functional consultation within the enterprise, but also to consult externally with credible, independent experts, including from governments, civil society, national human rights institutions and relevant multi-stakeholder initiatives.'

breakdown of the case studies, testing the matters described in the third section against the relevant GPs mentioned in this section. The goal is to study to what extent the remedy principles of the GPs have or have not yet been implemented by each of the three oil companies. Additionally, we want to explore how their remedies could have been provided in a more effective way had the oil companies followed the GPs.

Furthermore, in order to analyse and compare the 'house policies' of the three companies with respect to misconduct and grievances, we have studied the oil companies' websites and Annual Reports to find out if they: (i) have indicated that they support the Ruggie Framework and the GPs; (ii) provide for non-judicial company grievance mechanisms (as suggested in GP 31); (iii) participate in any industry, multi-stakeholder or other collaborative initiatives that are based on respect for human rights-related standards which should ensure that effective grievance mechanisms are available in multi-stakeholder initiatives (as advised in GP 30); and (iv) actively engage with the communities where the oil operations were or are being undertaken (see GP 31(h)). These elements have also been extracted from the GPs. The results will be presented in the fourth section.

In the final discussion, the fifth section, an attempt will be made to evaluate whether the victims of the oil pollution in the three cases have been provided with a remedy in a meaningful and effective way, and how guidance from the GPs could contribute to better corporate practices when providing access to remedies.

Case studies on remedies and human rights

The three case studies that will be presented in this section concern conflicts between companies and communities because of major oil spillages: (i) *Chevron* has been held accountable by Ecuadorian communities for the oil pollution in their water basins and soil caused by the operations of Texaco (presently part of the Chevron group) in the period from the 1960s to the beginning of the 1990s; (ii) *Shell* defended itself against tort claims from three local communities in the Ogoni Delta in Nigeria; and (iii) *BP*,[12] whose platform in the Gulf of Mexico exploded in 2010, was blamed for the subsequent oil pollution of fishing grounds and recreation areas on the southern shore of the USA. In these cases, human rights and environmental problems with local communities were escalated, ultimately resulting in protests and litigation.

---

[12] Previously 'BP-Amoco' (1990s), presently 'BP'.

Chevron *v.* Ecuador

The oil operations and the pollution

Local communities have submitted that during twenty years of operations in rural Ecuador, Texaco Inc. (Texaco) and its wholly owned subsidiary *Compania Texaco de Petroleos del Ecuador CA* (Texpet) released millions of gallons of toxic waste whilst generating oil from local resources.[13] Most of this waste was deposited in open natural pits, from where the waste directly leaked into the environment.[14] Cheap facilities and pipeline network infrastructure caused permanent contamination of the water, farmlands and forests, while the burning of the debris and waste products in the open pits resulted in air contamination.

Texaco commenced operations in Ecuador in 1964, after a concession agreement had been concluded between the government of Ecuador and Texpet. From the outset, Texpet operated through a consortium with *Gulf Ecuatoriana de Petroleo SA* (Gulf).[15] In response to the oil boom, the State of Ecuador attempted to gain dominion over its natural resources via a state-owned company, *Corporacion Estatal Petrolera Ecuatoriana* (CEPE). From 1974 onwards,[16] CEPE gradually acquired ownership of the consortium, eventually assuming full ownership in 1992.

The 1992–98 settlement and remediation programme

Chevron argues that, in 1992, Texpet, CEPE (later *Petroecuador*) and the government undertook negotiations concerning the environmental impact of Texpet's operations. Texpet agreed to assume responsibility for specified environmental remediation projects, corresponding to its

---

[13] *Maria Aguinda et al.* v. *Texaco Inc.* [1993] SDNY, 93 Civ. 7527, 'Aguinda Complaint', 23–25.

[14] Center for Economic and Social Rights, 'Rights Violations in the Ecuadorian Amazon: The Human Consequences of Oil Development' (March 1994), 5–6, www.cesr.org/downloads/ Rights%20Violation%20in%20the%20Ecuadorian%20Amazon%20The%20Human%20Con sequences%20of%20Oil%20Development%201.pdf (last accessed 27 May 2013).

[15] Texpet and Gulf had formed a consortium in 1965 with 50 per cent participation each and acquired the right to exploit the area (the 'consortium'). A Joint Operating Agreement (JOA) was executed. This was replaced in 1973 by a new JOA including the government's company CEPE as a party. Under this contract, Texpet was still the operator of the oil infrastructure in the Oriente region (i.e. east Ecuador).

[16] In 1974, CEPE acquired a 24 per cent participating interest from the Texaco-Gulf Consortium. By 1976, CEPE had bought more shares resulting in 62.5 per cent participation. Upon the expiration of the contract in 1992, CEPE (renamed Petroecuador) assumed full ownership of the consortium.

minority ownership interest in the consortium (from 1976–92, 37.5 per cent). In exchange, it would be released from all future liability.[17] A Memorandum of Understanding in 1995 (MoU) stated that Texpet would be forgiven 'for environmental impacts arising from the operations of the consortium',[18] and that the company would be released from any responsibility for environmental impacts included or not included in the specified repair projects that would be undertaken by it. Contractors implemented the remediation programme and Texpet provided $1 million in funding to certain social community programmes. Texpet settled its disputes with four Ecuadorian municipalities by entering into written agreements and releases. In 1998, the government certified that Texpet had successfully conducted its remediation programme.

Chevron and Texaco

In October 2001, Texaco merged with the US-based multinational Chevron,[19] establishing ChevronTexaco.[20] From 2001 to 2005, Texaco maintained its legal capacity as an independent company, without Chevron assuming its liabilities and obligations relating to its operations in Ecuador.[21] In this period, Chevron used 'ChevronTexaco' as its brand name.[22] In 2005, ChevronTexaco became 'Chevron'.[23]

---

[17] Permanent Court of Arbitration (PCA), *Chevron Corporation and Texaco Petroleum Company* v. *The Republic of Ecuador*, 'Claimant's Notice of Arbitration' (23 September 2009), 3–6; for all the court documents of the case see (date unavailable) www.italaw. com/cases/257 (last accessed 27 May 2013).

[18] *Ibid.*

[19] Chevron is currently the second largest oil company in the USA. Chevron, 'Company Profile' (April 2013), www.chevron.com/about/leadership/ (last accessed 27 May 2013).

[20] Federal Trade Commission (FTC), 'FTC Consent Agreement Allows the Merger of Chevron Corp. and Texaco Inc., Preserves Market Competition' (7 September 2001), www.ftc.gov/opa/2001/09/chevtex.shtm (last accessed 27 May 2013).

[21] *Maria Aguinda et al.* v. *Chevron Texaco Corp.* [2003] Superior Court of Nueva Loja, 19, 'Lago Agrio Complaint', www.chevrontoxico.com/assets/docs/2003-ecuador-legal-complaint.pdf (last accessed 27 May 2013). See also Chevron's answer on the lawsuit (21 October 2003), 3–7, www.texaco.com/sitelets/ecuador/docs/2003oct21_dismiss.pdf (last accessed 27 May 2013).

[22] Chevron, 'History' (date unavailable), www.chevron.com/about/history/1980/ (last accessed 27 May 2013).

[23] Chevron, 'ChevronTexaco Corporation Changes Name to Chevron Corporation, Unveils a New Visual Image' (9 May 2005), www.chevron.com/chevron/pressreleases/article/05092005_chevrontexacocorporationchangesnametochevroncorporationunveilsanewvisualimage.news (last accessed 27 May 2013).

US and Ecuador class action litigation (1993–2010)

Despite the Texpet remediation programme, the local inhabitants of Oriente were not satisfied with the clean-up by Texaco.[24] They stated that the polluting elements still existed and continued to cause ecological and personal injuries.[25] In 1993, 30,000 indigenous Ecuadorian citizens commenced a class action (the *Aguinda*[26] action) under the US Alien Tort Claims Act (ATCA).[27] It is important to note that, until 1999, when the new Environmental Management Act (EMA) was enacted in Ecuador, citizens were procedurally unable to file a class action before the Ecuadorian courts.[28] In the ATCA case, the claimants sought compensatory and punitive damages as well as equitable relief[29] for human rights violations and environmental damages to the Ecuadorian Amazon rainforest. After several appeals, the US court finally dismissed the case in August 2002 on grounds of *forum non conveniens*,[30] and requested Texaco's consent to be bound by any ruling of the Ecuadorean courts.

Taking advantage of the new EMA, the claimants[31] filed a (new) suit in 2003 against ChevronTexaco, seeking removal of the contaminating elements and the cleaning of all the contaminated areas (*Lago Agrio* case).[32] Chevron denied the court's jurisdiction and the retroactive application of the EMA, stating that ChevronTexaco is not the successor

---

[24] As shown by protests, public campaigns and legal action in the US and Ecuadorean courts. Ecuadorian people even travelled to attend the annual shareholders' meeting of Chevron in California. See D. R. Baker, 'Chevron CEO John Watson Addresses Protesters' (25 May 2011), www.sfgate.com/business/article/Chevron-CEO-John-Watson-addresses-protesters-2369886.php (last accessed 27 May 2013).

[25] Aguinda Complaint (1993), n. 13, 23–25, 6–17.

[26] Maria Aguinda and Carlos Crefa were the guardians of the class.

[27] Aguinda Complaint (1993), n. 13, 3, 35.

[28] Despite the recognition of an '*actio popularis*', there was no legal basis in the Ecuadorean legal system to support the claimants' claims for remediation and compensation for environmental damages. As of 1999, pursuant to EMA, claimants have been allowed to bring an action for the cost of the remediation of environmental harm. See the Ecuadorean Civil Code, in Spanish, § 2236 for '*actio popularis*', www.wipo.int/wipolex/en/text.jsp?file_id=251955; see also EMA, in Spanish, Arts. 41 and 42, www.revenue-watch.org/sites/default/files/Ley%20de%20Gestion%20Ambiental_0.pdf (both websites last accessed 27 May 2013).

[29] Aguinda Complaint (1993), n. 13, 7 and 28–35. Claimants alleged that Texaco had failed to comply with safety and protection standards. They sought redress for injuries and extensive damages to their livelihoods and living environment.

[30] *Maria Aguinda et al.* v. *Texaco Inc.* [1996] SDNY, 945 F.Supp 625, *Maria Aguinda et al.* v. *Texaco Inc.* [2001] SDNY, No. 93 Civ. 7527, 'Aguinda Order', paras. 4, 7, 8, 18, 19.

[31] The majority of the claimants overlap with those of the Aguinda Class.

[32] Lago Agrio Complaint, n. 21, 22–25.

of Texaco and thus has never acted in Ecuador nor has it been a party to a concession contract with the Ecuadorean government.[33]

Before the Ecuadorean court had issued a judgment, Chevron had commenced parallel arbitration proceedings under the US-Ecuador Bilateral Investment Treaty (BIT) before the international Permanent Court of Arbitration in The Hague.[34] Chevron claimed that any Ecuadorean judgment would violate Chevron's due process rights because the *Lago Agrio* litigation was in violation of the settlement agreement of 1995.[35]

The Ecuadorean court in *Lago Agrio*, after eight years of litigation, delivered its judgment in February 2011, finding Chevron liable for a total of $18.2 billion in damages and punitive penalties.[36] It ruled that the MoU of 1995 released Texaco only from governmental claims, not from claims brought by third parties or civilians.[37] The *Lago Agrio* judgment confirmed that the majority of the sites mentioned in the 'Remediation Agreement' were as polluted as those which had not been cleaned up by Texpet. The court also ordered Chevron to issue a public apology within fifteen days of the judgment.[38] Chevron refused to issue the apology and appealed the case in March 2011.[39]

On 9 February 2011, the BIT tribunal ordered the State of Ecuador to suspend the enforcement of the *Lago Agrio* judgment within and outside Ecuador (in fact, the latter judgment was actually rendered later, that is, on 14 February 2011).[40] It should be noted that Chevron at the time had

---

[33] Chevron's answer on the lawsuit (21 October 2003), n. 21, 3–7.

[34] PCA, *Chevron Corporation and Texaco Petroleum Company* v. *The Republic of Ecuador*, 'Claimants' Memorial on the Merits' (6 September 2010), www.italaw.com/sites/default/files/case-documents/ita0164.pdf (last accessed 27 May 2013).

[35] *Ibid.*, para. 69.

[36] *Maria Aguinda et al.* v. *Chevron Texaco Corp.* [2011] Superior Court of Nueva Loja, No. 2003–0002, 'Judgment' (14 February 2011), www.earthrights.org/sites/default/files/documents/Lago-Agrio-judgment_0.pdf (last accessed 27 May 2013). The court imposed $8.6 billion in damages for reparations measures, $8.6 billion as a punitive penalty, and decided that almost one billion should be paid directly to the NGO Amazon Defence Front.

[37] *Ibid.*, 31–32, 176.   [38] *Ibid.*, 185–86.

[39] *Maria Aguinda et al.* v. *Chevron Texaco Corp.* [2011] Sucumbíos Court of Justice, No. 002–2003, 'Chevron's Appeal', www.chevron.com/documents/pdf/ecuador/LagoAgrio Appeal_030911.pdf (last accessed 21 January 2013).

[40] PCA, 'Chevron's Notice for Arbitration', n. 17 and also 'Claimants' Memorial on the Merits', n. 34.

no assets in Ecuador. Therefore, the claimants could only seek enforcement in jurisdictions in which Chevron held assets.[41]

On 3 January 2012, the Ecuadorean Court of Appeals affirmed the lower court's ruling of 14 February 2011 against Chevron.[42] On 20 January 2012, Chevron announced its decision to file an appeal at the highest National Court of Justice in Ecuador asking for a review of the adverse Ecuadorean Court of Appeals judgment of 3 January 2012.[43] On 26 January 2012, the US District Court for the Southern District of New York denied Chevron's pre-trial motion for a pre-emptive order of attachment on Chevron's assets that the Ecuadorean plaintiffs might possibly want to collect in order to enforce the judgment.[44]

---

[41] The Ecuadorean plaintiffs attempted to enforce the *Lago Agrio* judgment in Canada, Brazil and Argentina (information as per 30 May 2013). The Canadian Superior Court of Ontario dismissed the plaintiffs' claims, ruling that there is no connection between the parent company of Chevron and its subsidiary in Canada. A lawsuit was also filed by the plaintiffs before the Court of Brasilia targeting Chevron's subsidiary in Brazil. The Commercial Court of Justice in Buenos Aires accepted the claims of the Ecuadorean plaintiffs, freezing some of Chevron's assets in Argentina. An appeal was filed by Chevron Argentina which failed in the Argentinian Court. The Court ruled that although the company could maintain its operations in the country, its stock, dividends and 40 per cent of its oil revenues had to sit in an escrow account until the Court had determined whether the Ecuadorean judgment could be enforced in Argentina or not. In parallel to the proceedings, the Permanent Court of Arbitration in The Hague delivered its Fourth Interim Award affirming that the Republic of Ecuador had violated the tribunal's previous interim awards by not preventing the enforcement of the Ecuadorean judgment in other countries. See *Yaiguaje et al.* v. *Chevron Corporation* [2013] ONSC 2527, CV-12-9808-00CL; Fair Pensions, 'Chevron: Argentine Assets Frozen' (date unavailable), www.shareaction.org/sites/default/files/uploaded_files/ investorresources/ArgentineFreeze.pdf; PCA, *Chevron Corporation and Texaco Petroleum Company* v. *The Republic of Ecuador*, 'Fourth Interim Award of Interim Measures (7 February 2013), www.theamazonpost.com/wp-content/uploads/Fourth-Interim-Award-on-Interim-Measures.pdf; Fair Pensions, 'Chevron Corporation: Time to Change Course (date unavailable), www.fairpensions.org.uk/sites/default/files/uploaded_files/investorresources/ChangeCourseChevron.pdf (all websites last accessed 30 May 2013).

[42] *Maria Aguinda et al.* v. *Chevron Texaco Corp.* [2012] Superior Court of Nueva Loja, No. 2011–0106, 'Appeals Court Decision', www.chevrontoxico.com/assets/docs/2012-01-03-appeal-decision-english.pdf (last accessed 27 May 2013).

[43] *Ibid.* Chevron, 'Chevron Appeals Illegitimate Ruling in Ecuador' (20 January 2012), www.chevron.com/chevron/pressreleases/article/01202012_chevronappealsillegitimat erulinginecuador.news (last accessed 27 May 2013).

[44] *Chevron Corp.* v. *Naranjo et al.* [2012] SDNY, No. 11–1150-cv (L), 'Court of Appeals Decision', www.chevrontoxico.com/assets/docs/2012-01-26-2nd-circuit-final-ruling.pdf (last accessed 27 May 2013). On 19 January 2012, the US Court of Appeals for the Second Circuit rejected Chevron's motion to reargue the pre-trial motion.

In summary, what we found in this case study is that the oil company had concluded an agreement with the government of Ecuador in the 1990s on cleaning up the oil pollution. However, the local communities were dissatisfied with the results and have tried since 1993 to draw attention to their perspective in various court cases, first in the USA, while class actions were not possible under domestic law, and later in Ecuador, when after a change of the law, a class action was possible. Meanwhile, Texaco and later Chevron have always taken the position that remediation has taken place and that the Ecuadorean government had released them from any further liability for cleaning up the pollution. Besides substantive defences, Chevron put forward formal defences, including that when it took over Texaco it had not taken over these liabilities. The Ecuadorian court, in 2011, decided that Chevron was indeed liable for the pollution. Chevron, however, has publicly communicated that it did not intend to respect this court's judgment, and it had even started other lawsuits to prevent enforcement of the Ecuadorean judgment (the international arbitration and the pre-emptive order in the USA). In 2013, twenty years have passed and a new generation of Ecuadorean community members has been born.

Shell *v.* Nigeria

Pollution impacting human rights: the UNEP Report

On 4 August 2011, UNEP presented to the Nigerian President its report 'Environmental Assessment of Ogoniland' (the Report).[45] Based on ample scientific evidence,[46] the Report confirmed that Nigeria's Niger Delta was heavily polluted due to over fifty years of oil operations. UNEP

---

[45] See the Report at United Nations Environment Programme (UNEP), 'Environmental Assessment of Ogoniland' (4 August 2011), www.unep.org/nigeria/ (last accessed 27 May 2013) (UNEP Report). See also an abstract at UNEP news items, 'UNEP Ogoniland Oil Assessment Reveals Extent of Environmental Contamination and Threats to Human Health' (4 August 2011), www.unep.org/Documents.Multilingual/Default.asp? DocumentID=2649&ArticleID=8827&l=en&t=long (last accessed 27 May 2013).

[46] UNEP Report, n. 45, 94–200. UNEP has been working with the Rivers State University of Science and Technology, Nigerian government officials at the national and Rivers State levels, traditional rulers, local landholders, laboratories and other stakeholders. During 14 months, the UNEP team had examined in detail soil and groundwater contamination at more than 200 locations in Ogoniland, assessed approximately 1,000 square km, surveyed 122 km of pipeline rights of way, reviewed more than 5,000 medical records and engaged over 23,000 people at local community meetings.

recommended immediate and full remediation.[47] The Ogoni had claimed for decades that Shell had devastated their area, that they were suffering from health problems and that oil pollution had destroyed farmlands and fish ponds, their very means of existence. They had tried to stop the pollution and gas flaring by protesting and filing court cases against Shell and the Nigerian State.[48] They partly succeeded in stopping new operations in the area,[49] but the existing exploitation continued.

The Report supports the Ogoni people's claims[50] of violations of their rights to water, food, health and the environment, and that they should be allowed to maintain a traditional way of living.[51] Additionally, 'control and maintenance of oilfield infrastructure in Ogoniland has been and remains inadequate: the Shell Petroleum Development Company's own procedures have not been applied'. The Report estimates that cleaning up the pollution could take twenty-five to thirty years. UNEP recommends establishing an Ogoniland Environmental Restoration Authority, an Environmental Restoration Fund for Ogoniland and a Centre of Excellence for Environmental Restoration.[52] The cost will exceed

[47] See the map of the area concerned in UNEP Report, *ibid.*, 21. UNEP recommendations in UNEP Report, *ibid.*, 207.

[48] See: T. E. Lambooy and M. E. Rancourt, 'Shell in Nigeria: From Human Rights Abuse to Corporate Social Responsibility' (2010) 2 *Human Rights and International Legal Discourse* 255–59. See also Amnesty International, 'Nigeria: Petroleum, Pollution and Poverty in the Niger Delta' (June 2009), www.amnesty.nl/sites/default/files/public/nigerdelta_rapport.pdf; Amnesty International, Friends of the Earth (FoE) and FoE Netherlands, 'Complaint to the UK and Dutch National Contact Points under the Specific Instance Procedure of the OECD Guidelines for Multinational Enterprises' (25 January 2011), www.foei.org/en/resources/publications/pdfs/2011/oecd-submission; Milieudefensie and FoE, the (spoof) 'Erratum to Shell's 2010 Annual Report' (17 May 2011), www.milieudefensie.nl/publicaties/rapporten/erratum-to-annual-report (all websites last accessed 27 May 2013).

[49] Lambooy and Rancourt, 'Shell in Nigeria', n. 48, 237; see also the 'Shell 2010 Annual Report and Form 20F, Nigeria Onshore Operations in the Niger Delta' (31 December 2010), www.annualreportandform20f.shell.com/2010/servicepages/search.php?q=nigeria&pageID=37843&cat=m (last accessed 27 May 2013).

[50] Amnesty International, 'Nigeria: Petroleum, Pollution and Poverty in the Niger Delta', n. 48, 57.

[51] Evidence presented in the UNEP Report, n. 45, 169–75. It is shown that in many Ogoni communities, drinking water is contaminated with high levels of hydrocarbons, which seriously threatens public health. In one community (Nisisioken Ogale), the water wells are contaminated with benzene – a known carcinogen – at levels over 900 times above World Health Organization guidelines. UNEP calls for emergency action before all other remediation efforts.

[52] UNEP Report, *ibid.*, 227–28.

$1 billion.[53] Following the release of the Report, the value of Shell's shares dropped around 15 per cent.[54]

Shell's oil operations in Nigeria

In Nigeria, the oil operations are performed by the Shell Petroleum Development Company of Nigeria Limited (SPDC, or Shell Nigeria).[55]

Since the early 1990s, local communities have lodged many complaints about the oil polluting soil and waterways, especially regarding the operations in the Ogoni river delta in south-eastern Nigeria. Yet, according to Shell, more than 80 per cent of the spills from SPDC facilities in the Niger Delta in 2010 resulted from sabotage or theft. Shell argues that communities delay SPDC teams from accessing sites: 'they are angry or worried about the impact on their land and lives'.[56] In this context, it is noted that Amnesty has lodged a complaint with the Dutch National Contact Point (NCP) (a non-judicial state-based grievance mechanism) alleging that Shell violates the OECD Guidelines because it does not provide transparency about the methodology employed to calculate the percentage indicated in regard to the spills caused by sabotage or theft.

Litigation in the Netherlands

In 2009, three tort cases concerning the oil pollution in the Ogoni Delta were initiated before the District Court of The Hague in the Netherlands, the home of Shell's headquarters. The cases were filed against Shell Nigeria and the leading parent company Royal Dutch Shell plc (RDS)

---

[53] *Ibid.*, 227.

[54] 'Information on the Share Price of Shell in the Week from 1–8 August 2011', http://uk. finance.yahoo.com/echarts?s=RDSB.L#symbol=rdsb.l;range=20110801,20110808;com pare=;indicator=volume;charttype=area;crosshair=on;ohlcvalues=0;logscale=off;source= (last accessed 27 May 2013).

[55] SPDC is the operator of a joint venture between the government-owned Nigerian National Petroleum (55 per cent), SPDC (30 per cent), a subsidiary of Total (10 per cent) and the Nigerian Agip Oil Company (5 per cent). Shell, The Shell Petroleum Development Company of Nigeria Limited (SPDC), 'Shell in Nigeria: Shell Interests in Nigeria' (April 2012), www-static.shell.com/static/nga/downloads/pdfs/briefing_notes/ shell_interests.pdf (last accessed 27 May 2013).

[56] Shell uses different figures when referring to spills caused by sabotage: sometimes 80 per cent, at other places 75, 70 or even 95 per cent. See Shell, 'Oil Leaks in Nigeria' (date unavailable), www.shell.com/global/environment-society/society/nigeria/spills.html (last accessed 27 May 2013). See also the UNEP Report, n. 45, on this issue and Amnesty International, FoE and FoE Netherlands, 'Complaint to the UK and Dutch National Contact Points', n. 48.

(see diagram of corporate structure below). Claimants are farmers from the villages of Oruma, Goi and Ikot Ada Udo, who assert that they have suffered as a result of oil pollution from Shell installations. NGOs Milieudefensie and Friends of the Earth Nigeria support the cases.

Claimants argue that they have ineffectively protested for decades regarding systematic pollution,[57] and in May 2008 they filed a formal liability claim. Shell denied any wrongdoing or responsibility, asserting that RDS is a publicly listed holding company with 'no direct involvement in the operations of its subsidiaries'.[58]

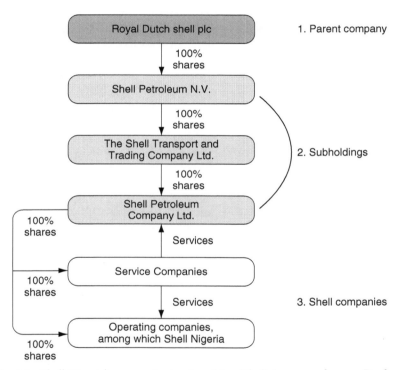

Chart 1   Shell Nigeria's corporate structure (simplified) (source: subpoena Dooh, inhabitant of Goi, p. 7)

[57] *Dooh et al.* v. *RDS and SPDC* [2009] District Court of The Hague, 'Dagvaarding' [subpoena] Dooh, 14–17. See also Milieudefensie, 'Factsheet: The Legal Case: Step by Step' (5 June 2009), www.milieudefensie.nl/publicaties/factsheets/timeline-courtcase-shell (last accessed 27 May 2013).
[58] Shell letter of 20 June 2008, cited by claimants in the Dooh subpoena on p. 36.

Shell contested the jurisdiction of the court in The Hague over Shell Nigeria[59] on formal grounds, stating that Shell Nigeria is a Nigerian company and is thus not required to appear before a Dutch court.[60] Shell stated that a Dutch court is not competent because there is no connection between (i) the claims based on oil pollution in Nigeria with only local impact and (ii) the UK company Shell, and that there is no connection with the Dutch legal sphere. This defence is comparable with the *forum non conveniens* defences before a UK or US court. Shell also asserted that Nigerian law is applicable.[61] Furthermore, it brought up that the NGO Milieudefensie had no standing.

Shell also argued that RDS came into existence only in 2005 and cannot be held accountable. Because of this formal defence, the claimants have decided also to sue the former two parent companies and to draw them into this litigation. Shell reiterated that the parent company (RDS) is not responsible because it is only a shareholder without any direct involvement in the operations of its subsidiaries.

The Nigerian claimants and Milieudefensie argued that the multinational company Shell operates as a single economic unit and that it is therefore lawful jointly to try both Shell Nigeria and the parent company.

The Dutch court ruled in an intermediate judgment that (i) it is competent to decide on claims against Shell Nigeria; (ii) there is no abuse of Dutch procedural law; and (iii) Milieudefensie may be a claimant.[62]

---

[59] *Oguru et al.* v. *RDS and SPDC* [2009] District Court of the Hague, 'The Shell Oruma case defence' (13 May 2009); *Akpan et al.* v. *RDS and SPDC* [2009] District Court of the Hague, 'Subpoena', 'the Goi and Ikot Ada Udo case defences' (28 October 2009).

[60] *Ibid.*; see the Shell Oruma case defence, p. 64, www.shellcourtcase.org and www.milieu defensie.nl/oliewinning/shell/olielekkages/documenten-shellrechtszaak#juridischedocu menten (last accessed 27 May 2013).

[61] L. F. H. Enneking, T. E. Lambooy *et al.*, 'Privaatrechtelijke handhaving in reactie op mensenrechtenschendingen door internationaal opererende ondernemingen. De (on) mogelijkheden van het aansprakelijk stellen van Nederlandse multinationals voor extraterritoriale mensenrechten-en milieuschendingen naar Nederlands' (2011) 36:5 *Nederlands Tijdschrift voor de Mensenrechten* [Dutch Journal for Human Rights] 541–60 (original article in Dutch). Generally, regarding a tort claim which encompasses international elements, the Dutch conflict of law rules determine whether: (i) the Dutch court is competent to decide on the matter; and (ii) Dutch law will be applied in the case. Dutch conflicts of law rules are predominantly governed by EU law, i.e. the EEX and Rome II Regulations. Generally, a Dutch court will consider itself competent to judge a tort claim against a parent company of a multinational company to the extent that this company is registered, domiciled or has its headquarters in the Netherlands.

[62] *Oguru et al.* v. *RDS and SPDC* [2009] District Court of The Hague, 'Judgment in the Oruma Case in a Motion Contesting Jurisdiction of 30 December 2009' (30 December 2009), www.milieudefensie.nl/publicaties/bezwaren-uitspraken/judgment-courtcase-

After these formal defences, Shell's next line of defence was that oil bandits and saboteurs had caused (most of) the oil spills.[63]

The claimants asserted that even if third parties had played a role in causing the spills, it was Shell's duty to protect its installations.[64] Claimants also alleged that the parent company itself has a duty of care to avoid oil pollution. They argued that Shell owns, directly or indirectly, 100 per cent of the subsidiaries' shares, including SPDC, and can direct their practices.

In fact, under Dutch law, a holding company can be held liable for its own acts, omissions and conduct, together with one or more of its group companies. There is, however, no substantial Dutch case law about the duty of care of a parent company to prevent infringements of human rights by a subsidiary company. The duty of care – that is, what may be expected from a parent company such as the MNC Shell – changes from time to time. The standard of expectation will be influenced by international legal and semi-legal standards such as the OECD Guidelines and the GPs.[65]

Oral proceedings took place on 11 October 2012.[66] The District Court of The Hague delivered its judgments in the three cases on 30 January 2013.

The Court applied Nigerian Law in deciding on the substantive matters, i.e. including on the parent companies' duty of care question. In the judgment, the Dutch court referred to the common law notions of

---

shell-in-jurisdiction-motion-oruma (last accessed 21 January 2013); *Akpan et al.* v. *RDS and SPDC* [2010] District Court of The Hague, 'Judgment'.

[63] *Ibid.*, 3–4 and 24–32.   [64] Subpoena Dooh, n. 57, 22–34 and 58–72.

[65] See for an overview of evolving norms in this field T. E. Lambooy, 'Corporate Due Diligence as a Tool to Respect Human Rights' (2010) 3 *Netherlands Quarterly on Human Rights* 404, at 417. See also Enneking, Lambooy *et al.*, n. 61. Dutch law provides for a limited number of situations in which a tort claim does not need to be based on culpability but can instead be based on a certain quality or situation, the so-called 'strict liability', e.g. the liability of the owner of a building or land for damage caused thereby. The question has emerged whether a multinational's parent company should acquire a certain form of strict liability for human rights violations by any one or more of its group companies. See also C. van Dam, *European Tort Law* (Oxford University Press, 2006), 256 and 260–64.

[66] See Milieudefensie website for details on the court documents: Milieudefensie, 'Dutch Legal Case against Shell' (11 October 2012), www.milieudefensie.nl/english/shell/news/11-october-dutch-legal-case-against-shell-legal (last accessed 27 May 2013); see also Shell background information: Milieudefensie, 'Cases *Milieudefensie et al.* v. *SPDC, RDS and Other Shell Companies*: District Court of the Hague, Oral Pleading 11 October 2012' (11 October 2012), www.shell.nl/content/dam/shell/static/nld/downloads/nigeria/background-information111012.pdf (last accessed 27 May 2013).

'proximity' and 'incremental approach',[67] thereby using UK doctrines and case law such as the *Chandler* v. *Cape* case.[68]

The judgment stated that the proximity between the parent companies and the plaintiffs was insufficient and rejected those claims.

Also, the claims-based torts of negligence by the operating company, i.e. SPDC, were not very successful. In two of the three cases these claims were rejected.[69] All parties have filed an appeal.[70]

Settlement negotiations: Bodo oil spills

Another tort case had been filed against Shell in the UK. Nigerian farmers alleged damages resulting from two massive oil leaks in 2008–09 from Shell operations.[71] Shell disputed responsibility, and asserted that it had been informed of the first leak in early October 2008. The Bodo community argued that the leak by then had already been pumping oil for some six weeks and that it took Shell over a month to repair the pipeline. A further spill occurred in December 2008, also as a result of equipment failure. It was not stopped until February 2009. According to oil spill assessment experts, more than 280,000 barrels may have been spilled. According to the Centre for Environment, Human Rights and Development in Port Harcourt, these spills impacted an exceptionally sensitive ecosystem for a long period.[72]

---

[67] *Dooh et al.* v. *RDS and SPDC* [2013] District Court of The Hague, 'Judgment', 20, paras. 4.27–4.29; *Akpan and Milieudefensie* v. *Shell* [2013] District Court of The Hague, 'Judgment', 16, paras. 4.23–4.25; *Oguru et al.* v. *Shell* [2013] District Court of The Hague, 'Judgment', 21, paras. 4.20, 4.31.

[68] *Dooh et al.* v. *RDS and SPDC*, *ibid.*, 22, para. 4.32; *Akpan and Milieudefensie* v. *Shell*, *ibid.*, 17 para. 4.27; *Oguru et al.* v. *Shell*, *ibid.*, 23, para. 4.34.

[69] See for a detailed analysis L. Enneking, 'The Future of Foreign Direct Liability? Exploring the International Relevance of the Dutch Shell Nigeria Case', *Netherlands International Law Review* (forthcoming, 2013).

[70] Information as per May 2013.

[71] J. Vidal, 'Shell Accepts Liability for Two Oil Spills in Nigeria', *The Guardian* (3 August 2011), www.guardian.co.uk/environment/2011/aug/03/shell-liability-oil-spills-nigeria; E. Dooh, 'Local Farmer about the Oil Pollution in his Village' (19 May 2011), http://nos.nl/video/241642-nigeriaanse-boer-wij-zijn-altijd-ziek.html. See J. Vidal, 'Shell Oil Spills in the Niger Delta: Nowhere and No One has Escaped' (3 August 2011), www.guardian.co.uk/environment/2011/aug/03/shell-oil-spills-niger-delta-bodo/print (all websites last accessed 27 May 2013).

[72] Vidal, 'Shell Oil Spills in the Niger Delta', *ibid.*; in this article, the statement of Nenibarini Zabby, head of conservation at the Centre for Environment, Human Rights and Development in Port Harcourt.

Apparently, 80 per cent of the Bodo people are fishermen or depend on the water resources.[73]

In an agreement between the parties, SPDC agreed to concede to UK jurisdiction; the claimants agreed to exclude RDS from the original action. RDS confirmed that settlement talks had started between Shell Nigeria (SPDC) and the affected community[74] in the autumn of 2011. An SPDC spokesman confirmed that Shell expected to pay compensation: 'SPDC has always acknowledged that the two spills which affected the Bodo community and which are the subject of this legal action were operational. As such, SPDC will pay compensation in accordance with Nigerian law.'[75] The shares in Shell stock went down in the week of the announcement of the settlement negotiations.[76]

In summary, the oil pollution has caused unrest in the Ogoni Delta for more than two decades. Relatively recently, court cases have been commenced by members of affected communities against SPDC and the Shell parent company in the Netherlands and the UK. The parent company responded by bringing up many formal defences. The appeal cases before the Dutch court are still ongoing; the case in the UK has reached a settlement.

---

[73] *Ibid.* According to Chief James, assistant secretary to the Bodo Council of Chiefs and Elders, and Groobadi Petta, president of the Bodo City Youth Federation, youths from the area started to steal oil and refine it in illegal camps after the two spills occurred. Sylvester Vikpee, a barrister and legal adviser to the Council of Chiefs, said Shell had not responded humanely to the disaster; see statements by Nimmo Bassey, chair of Friends of the Earth International, from Lagos.

[74] A. Flynn, 'Shell in Nigeria Settlement Talks Ahead of UN Delta Study' (3 August 2011), http://english.capital.gr/News.asp?id=1254242 (last accessed 27 May 2013); see the information posted by Leigh Day & Co., representing the victims, in Leigh Day & Co., 'Shell Accepts Responsibility for Oil Spill in Nigeria' (3 August 2011), www.leighday.co.uk/News/2011/August-2011/Shell-accepts-responsibility-for-oil-spill-in-Nige (last accessed 27 May 2013). The Shell websites did not contain any information on this litigation and settlement as of 4 August 2011.

[75] S. Pfeifer and J. Croft, 'Shell's Nigeria Pay-Out Could Top £250m' (3 August 2011), www.ft.com/intl/cms/s/0/4209f536-bde8-11e0-ab9f-00144feabdc0.html#axzz2IiFQS7da (last accessed 27 May 2013).

[76] Shell share price in the week of 2–8 August 2011. See J. Donovan, 'Royal Dutch Shell has 14.40% Drop in Stock Price' (11 August 2011), www.royaldutchshellplc.com/2011/08/11/royal-dutch-shell-has-14-40-drop-in-stock-price/ (last accessed 27 May 2013).

BP *v.* The Gulf of Mexico

Failures in safety culture

The Final Report of the US Commission on the Deepwater Horizon Oil Spill and Offshore Drilling states: 'The immediate causes of the Deepwater Horizon well blowout can be traced to a series of identifiable mistakes made by BP, Halliburton, and Transocean that reveal such systematic failures in risk management that they place in doubt the safety culture of the entire industry.'[77]

On 20 April 2010, the oil rig Deepwater Horizon exploded in the Gulf of Mexico.[78] It leaked for 87 days, discharging 205.8 million gallons of oil into the Gulf of Mexico.[79] BP leased the rig from Transocean, a company that had committed multiple safety violations prior to the incident,[80] and is responsible for 'three of every four incidents that triggered federal investigations into safety on deep-water drilling rigs in the Gulf of Mexico since 2008'.[81] BP's own report finds a 'lack of a robust Transocean maintenance management system for Deepwater Horizon'.[82] It will be the courts' competence to allocate responsibility for the incident.[83] While legal responsibility for the oil spill has yet to be determined, it is clear that safety measures on the rig were inadequate.

---

[77] National Commission on the BP Deepwater Horizon Oil Spill and Offshore Drilling, 'Final Report' (11 January 2011), 7, www.oilspillcommission.gov/sites/default/files/documents/FinalReportIntro.pdf (last accessed 27 May 2013).

[78] Testimony of Professor R. Bea, 'Failures of the Deepwater Horizon Semi-Submersible Drilling Unit' – Statement for the Deepwater Horizon Study Group (20 May 2010), http://operating experience.doe-hss.wikispaces.net/file/view/Bob+Bea_s+Preliminary+Analyses-rev3.pdf (last accessed 27 May 2013).

[79] Internal BP Incident Investigation Team, 'Deepwater Horizon Accident Investigation Report' (8 September 2010), 3, www.bp.com/liveassets/bp_internet/globalbp/globalbp_uk_english/incident_response/STAGING/local_assets/downloads_pdfs/Deepwater_Horizon_Accident_Investigation_Report_Executive_summary.pdf (last accessed 27 May 2013).

[80] B. Meier, 'Owner of Exploded Rig Known for Testing Rules' (7 July 2010), www.nytimes.com/2010/07/08/business/global/08ocean.html?hp (last accessed 27 May 2013); the company's own safety statistics state that, through 2009 only, four (out of at least sixty-seven) rigs achieved a zero incident record in that period. The statistics have been removed from the company's website.

[81] B. Casselman, 'Gulf Rig Owner had Rising Tally of Accidents' (10 May 2010), online.wsj.com/article/SB10001424052748704307804575234471807539054.html (last accessed 27 May 2013).

[82] Internal BP Incident Investigation Team, 'Deepwater Horizon Accident Investigation Report', n. 79.

[83] J. Stempel and P. Bansal, 'BP also Sues Transocean for 40 billion over Oil Spill' (21 April 2011), www.reuters.com/article/2011/04/21/us-bp-cameron-lawsuit-idUSTRE73J7NR2011 0421 (last accessed 27 May 2013).

Besides safety management issues on the rig, drilling in US territory (Deepwater Horizon was located in US waters) is supported by guidelines for pre-spill behaviour: a 'plan to prevent spills',[84] as well as a 'detailed containment and clean-up plan'.[85] Prior to beginning the project, BP filed an 'Exploration and Environmental Impact' plan which did not include the required detailed impact analysis.[86] A post-spill review of the plan suggests that it was merely an adaptation of a previous plan for spills in Alaska, as it referenced the need to protect 'sea lions, seals, sea otters (and) walruses', which indeed concerns wildlife which is not found in the Gulf.[87] Following the lengthy clean-up process, many have expressed the view that the plan was insufficient.

Reponses to the incident

In this section, we will examine how BP responded to the oil spill. BP suffered reputational damage, demonstrated by a decrease in stock prices and removal from the Dow Jones Sustainability Index.[88] Clearly, the investment community had concerns about BP's ability to remedy the problem. BP worked to generate positive PR and to improve its image, as shown by its publications on its contributions to the clean-up. BP published advertisements in *The Economist* and various newspapers on the progress made in cleaning up the Gulf.[89] Its website, on the one-year

---

[84] M. A. Cherry and J. F. Sneirson, 'Beyond Profit: Rethinking Corporate Social Responsibility and Greenwashing after the BP Oil Disaster' (2011) 85:4 *Tulane Law Review* 983–1038.

[85] *Ibid.*

[86] J. Eilperin, 'US Exempted Gulf of Mexico's Drilling from an Environmental Impact Study' (5 May 2010), www.washingtonpost.com/wp-dyn/content/article/2010/05/04/AR2010050404118.html (last accessed 27 May 2013).

[87] D. Zabarenko, 'Walruses in Louisiana? Eyebrow-Raising Details of BP's Spill Response Plan' (27 May 2010), http://blogs.reuters.com/environment/2010/05/27/walruses-in-louisiana-eyebrow-raising-details-of-bps-spill-response-plan/ (last accessed 27 May 2013).

[88] BP was removed from the Dow Jones Sustainability Index and the FTSE4Good Index. 'BP among Companies Removed from Global Sustainability Index' (11 June 2010), www.social-funds.com/news/article.cgi?sfArticleId=2964; BP does not link bonus pay to CSR ratings, though after the Gulf oil spill it now links bonuses to safety. See BP, 'BP Directors' Remuneration Report 2011' (March 2012), 142–45, www.bp.com/assets/bp_internet/globalbp/globalbp_uk_english/set_branch/STAGING/common_assets/downloads/pdf/IC_DRR11_directors_remuneration_report_2011.pdf; Milieudefensie, 'Shell Excluded from Dow Jones Sustainability Index because of Oil Pollution in Nigeria' (September 2010), www.milieudefensie.nl/english/shell/news/shell-excluded-from-dow-jones-sustainability-index-because-of-oil-pollution-in-nigeria (all websites last accessed 27 May 2013).

[89] J. Quinn, 'BP to Admit $1m a Week Advertising Spree' (28 August 2010), www.telegraph.co.uk/finance/newsbysector/energy/oilandgas/7969586/BP-to-admit-1m-a-week-advertising-spree.html (last accessed 27 May 2013).

anniversary of the incident, featured beautiful images of local wildlife and discussed the company's involvement in 'restoring the environment' and 'restoring the economy'.[90]

US domestic law: tort and collective action

American jurisprudence does not recognise a right to a clean and healthy environment, to make a living, or to clean water.[91] Hence, tort theory proves the most practical means of achieving recompense in the US domestic courts for damages incurred due to the Deepwater Horizon oil spill.

Special measures for recovering for environmental damages are provided by the Oil Pollution Act of 1990 (OPA),[92] though not at the individual level. In the next paragraph, this will be further explained. For individuals with injuries or damages that are not recognised or are denied under the OPA measures,[93] a class action suit alleging tort is perhaps the most likely means of receiving compensation. While class action suits allow for the recompense of claims that are impractical to pursue on an individual basis, individuals in the Gulf region will have some difficulties in pursuing this litigation. The reason is that the US Class Action Fairness Act of 2005 requires such class action suits to be moved to the federal district courts whenever certain conditions are met, including the situation in which a contested amount exceeds $5 million or when parties come from different states.[94] This precludes forum shopping and allows for greater federal scrutiny.

The US Department of Justice has filed criminal charges.[95]

---

[90] F. Lemond, 'Gulf of Mexico Restoration' (date unavailable), www.bp.com/sectionbody-copy.do?categoryId=41&contentId=7067505 (last accessed 27 May 2013).

[91] Note that the Clean Water Act, 33 U.S.C. § 1251 *et seq.* does set out water quality standards and allows for citizens to bring suits concerning violations. However, such suits are not brought under a rights-based framework, as in a right to clean water, but regarding violations of a statute which prohibits, for example, the discharge of pollutants into a water supply.

[92] The Oil Pollution Act, 33 U.S.C. § 2701 *et seq.*; S. A. Millan, 'Escaping the "Black Hole" in the Gulf' (2010) 24 *Tulane Environmental Law Journal* 41, at 43, citing the Oil Pollution Act, 33 U.S.C. § 2702(b)–(f).

[93] E.g., if a subsistence fisherman cannot produce sufficient documentation for recovery from the Fund. A class action suit that focuses upon the damage to the community might be a more effective vehicle for litigation.

[94] Class Action Fairness Act, Federal district court jurisdiction for interstate class actions, § 4, provision (2).

[95] *United States of America* v. *BP Exploration & Production Inc. et al.* [2010] USDC of Luisiana, Civ. Action No. 2:10-cv-04536, 'Complaint', www.justice.gov/enrd/ConsentDecrees/DWH_Transocean_COMPLAINT.PDF. See also Transocean, which

Settlements: a commitment to 'all' legitimate claims?

The OPA[96] was created in the aftermath of the Exxon Valdez oil spill.[97] The OPA provides an overarching framework for evaluating fault and rapidly distributing compensation, thereby simplifying the recovery process for victims.[98] While the US government oversees clean-up plans, the responsible company is required to be involved in the process. The OPA requires a company to establish a fund for the payment of compensation for such damages.[99] The OPA also includes limitations on the liability for damages resulting from oil pollution. However there are exceptions to this limitation on liability in the case of gross negligence, wilful misconduct or a violation of an applicable federal safety, construction or operating regulation.[100]

The OPA places a $75 million cap upon damages which are applicable to the Deepwater Horizon incident.[101] The cap is not absolute; as stated, oil companies are also responsible for 'clean-up costs' and there is the possibility of additional damages in the case of 'gross negligence' or criminal actions. However, if BP 'can establish that the removal costs and damages resulting from an incident were caused solely by an act or omission by a third party, the third party will be held liable for such costs and damages'.[102] As discussed previously, BP has filed a suit against Transocean and Halliburton (responsible for pouring the concrete that may have buckled and contributed to the disaster).[103]

At the time of the incident there was discussion in Congress over raising the cap.[104] This was ultimately unsuccessful for reasons best

---

agreed to pay $1.4 billion in criminal fines and penalties for the oil spill: 'Partial Consent Decree with Transocean Defendants' (28 December 2012), MDL No. 2179; No 2:10-cv-04536, 39–43, www.epa.gov/enforcement/water/documents/decrees/transocean-cd.pdf (last accessed 27 May 2013).

[96] Oil Pollution Act of 1990, § 1002 and § 100 Elements and Limits of Liability.

[97] R. Perry, 'The Deepwater Horizon Oil Spill and the Limits of Civil Liability', (2011) 86:1 *Washington Law Review* 50.

[98] OPA, n. 92.   [99] *Ibid.*, § 1005(a)(b).   [100] *Ibid.*   [101] *Ibid.*, § 1004(a)(3).

[102] *Ibid.*, § 1002(d). See also S. A. Millan, 'Escaping the "Black Hole" in the Gulf', n. 92, 47–66.

[103] H. R. Weber, 'BP Sues Transocean, Gulf Oil Spill Rig Owner for Disaster' (20 April 2011), www.huffingtonpost.com/2011/04/20/bp-sues-cameron-international-blowout-preventer_n_851770.html (last accessed 27 May 2013).

[104] House of Representatives, 'Report: Securing Protection for the Injured from Limitations on Liability Act', No. 111–521 (2010), 5–9, www.gpo.gov/fdsys/pkg/CRPT-111hrpt521/pdf/CRPT-111hrpt521-pt1.pdf (last accessed 27 May 2013).

summed up by Louisiana Senator Landrieu: 'we want to be careful . . . that we don't jeopardise the operations of an on-going industry, because there are 4,000 other wells in the Gulf that have to go on'.[105]

The Fund

Fishermen along the Gulf Coast have lost their livelihoods due to the immense volume of oil on and in the sea. BP anticipated many tort claims. Strongly 'encouraged' by President Obama, BP set up a fund, The Gulf Coast Claims Facility (the Fund), with the objective to settle the claims of victims in the most efficient way.[106] The Fund was jointly created by BP and the US Department of Justice, and contained $20 billion. It was managed by an administrator, Kenneth Feingold,[107] and appointed trustees.[108] There has been debate over Feingold's neutrality, as BP was involved in the creation of the Fund and compensates Feingold for his role as administrator.[109] Ethics experts have debated this,[110] but the US District Judge Carl Barbier ruled that Feingold was '"independent" in the sense that BP did not control Feinberg's evaluation of individual claims . . . but [he] cannot be considered "neutral" or totally "independent" of BP'.[111] The Court criticised Feingold's misleading behaviour, including 'publicly advising potential claimants that they do not need to hire a lawyer and will be much better off accepting what he offers rather than going to court'.[112] After the case, the claims website

---

[105] L. Lerer, 'Effort to Raise Oil-Spill Liability Fails in Senate' (14 May 2010), www.bloomberg.com/news/2010-05-14/effort-to-increase-oil-spill-liability-after-gulf-disaster-fails-in-senate.html (last accessed 27 May 2013).

[106] The Fund was introduced on 23 August 2010. RestoreTheGulf.gov, 'Claims Process for Individuals and Business' (17 September 2010), www.restorethegulf.gov/release/2010/09/17/claims-process-individuals-and-businesses (last accessed 27 May 2013).

[107] Mr. Feingold, an attorney at law, is responsible for determining the eligibility of the claims on the basis of supporting documentation submitted by the claimants.

[108] N. F. Larson, 'Wust Law Dean to Oversee 20 billion BP Gulf Fund' (9 August 2010), http://news.wustl.edu/news/Pages/21000.aspx (last accessed 27 May 2013).

[109] Center for Justice and Democracy, 'Letter of Stephen Gillers to Feinberg' (5 January 2011), www.google.com/url?sa=t&rct=j&q=&esrc=s&source=web&cd=1&ved=0CDYQFjAA&url=http%3A%2F%2Fcenterjd.org%2Fsystem%2Ffiles%2FCJDBPGillersF.pdf&ei=SVO2UNP0E4nW0QXs1oCQDg&usg=AFQjCNGYawKg3GZShU9ti_MQnX_6CY17Ww&sig2=O_8Nhub8EBEUIPRYKx981A&cad=rja (last accessed 27 May 2013).

[110] Ibid.

[111] B. Skoloff and H. R. Weber, 'US Judge: Spill Claims Czar not Independent from BP' (2 February 2011), www.aolnews.com/2011/02/02/us-judge-spill-claims-czar-not-independent-of-bp/ (last accessed 27 May 2013).

[112] In re: Oil Spill by the Oil Rig 'Deepwater Horizon' in the Gulf of Mexico (20 April 2010) – see the Court's order, 8–10, www.laed.uscourts.gov/OilSpill/Orders/222011Orderon

was modified to state the following: 'You have the right to consult with an attorney of your choosing before accepting any settlement or signing a release of legal rights.'[113]

Filing process

The filing process itself was simple. An injured party had to file a claims form and supporting documentation by email, fax or postal service.[114] The administrator reviewed the claim and the trustees distributed the funds. The process allowed injured parties to recover without the cost of a lawyer and litigation fees. It was also much quicker as it bypassed a busy agenda of the court. BP also benefited from the Fund, as individuals choosing to settle were prohibited from bringing suits later in time when the long-term damage of the oil spill to the ecosystem and sea life would have become apparent.[115]

Criticism

The Fund has faced further criticism. Claimants have criticised the claims process for its lack of transparency.[116] Debate still rages over whether affected parties have received adequate compensation, while some parties have claimed that their losses have not been fully compensated.[117] Cases of fraud also existed.[118] As a result, the Department of Justice called for an audit of the facility,[119] and the State of Mississippi

---

RecDoc912.pdf; see BP court documents, www.laed.uscourts.gov/OilSpill/OilSpill.htm (both websites last accessed 27 May 2013).

[113] The Gulf Coast Claims Facility, 'Protocol for Emergency Advance Payments' (23 August 2010), www.restorethegulf.gov/sites/default/files/imported_pdfs/library/assets/gccf-emergency-advance-payments.pdf (last accessed 27 May 2013).

[114] *Ibid.*, filing for an emergency advance payment, 5–6.

[115] *Ibid.*, period for application for Emergency Advance Payments, 7–8.

[116] K. O. Spear, 'BP Oil Spill Hit Florida Hard, but Claimants Remain Frustrated' (26 December 2010), articles.orlandosentinel.com/2010-12-26/news/os-bp-spill-claims-florida-20101226_1_bp-oil-spill-bp-plc-gulf-coast-claims-facility (last accessed 27 May 2013).

[117] D. Hammer, 'Oil Spill Claims of $357 million have been Paid to 12,300 Louisiana Residents' (11 September 2011), www.nola.com/news/gulf-oil-spill/index.ssf/2011/09/oil_spill_claims_of_357_millio.html (last accessed 27 May 2013).

[118] The US Department of Justice, Office of Public Affairs, 'Justice Department Charges Seventh Individual for Allegedly Filing Fraudulent Claims for Oil Spill Compensation' (10 December 2010), www.justice.gov/opa/pr/2010/December/10-crm-1423.html (last accessed 27 May 2013).

[119] Department of Justice, 'Audit of Gulf Coast Claims Facility Results in $64 million in Additional Payments' (19 April 2012), www.justice.gov/opa/pr/2012/April/12-asg-500.html (last accessed 27 May 2013).

filed a suit, alleging that a lack of transparency in the process constituted a failure to comply with state consumer protection laws.[120]

In August 2010, the claimants started submitting their claims to the Fund. From 2010–12 the Fund accepted and processed more than a million claims providing more than $6.2 billion to various individuals and business claimants in emergency advance payments. More than 550,000 claimants were involved. During its maximum operational performance, the Fund managed to pay an average of more than $27 million per day to the claimants.[121] While remediation was quick for some small settlements with individuals, in the evaluation it was found that people with substantial business claims were unable to be properly remediated as the OPA requires.[122] Uncertainty and a lack of transparency brought governmental criticism concerning how the process relating to the Fund was taking place, and resulted in the intervention by the Department of Justice asking for more transparent, predictable and fair processes for the victims.

Parallel litigation against BP leading to a 'Settlement Program'

In parallel to the establishment of the Fund (August 2010), litigation started against BP. All of the lawsuits were gathered before one court under the name *In re Oil Spill by the Oil Rig 'Deepwater Horizon' in the Gulf of Mexico on April 20, 2010* (MDL 2179). Prior to the trial and before litigation started, a settlement process began between BP and the Claimants Steering Committee. The parties reached an agreement a year later by drafting the Economic and Property Damages Settlement.[123] The new Settlement Program opened in June 2012 after the Court's preliminary approval.[124]

---

[120] See *State of Missississipi* v. *Gulf Coast Claims Facility and Kenneth Feinberg* [2011] US District Court of Mississipi,'Order of Demand', docs.justia.com/cases/federal/district-courts/mississippi/mssdce/3:2011cv00509/76201/20/0.pdf?1321454188 (last accessed 27 May 2013).

[121] BDO Consulting, 'Independent Evaluation of the GCCF: Report of Findings and Observations to the US Department of Justice' (5 June 2012), 58–64, www.justice. gov/iso/opa/resources/66520126611210351178.pdf (last accessed 27 May 2013).

[122] *Ibid.*, 39–40 and 62–63. Under the OPA, when an oil spill occurs, the 'responsible party' should make an offer to a person with a substantial damage because of the spill within ninety days of receiving a final demand (OPA, § 1005).

[123] Deepwater Horizon Claims Center, 'Frequently Asked Questions' (2012), http://cert. gardencitygroup.com/dwh/fs/faq?.delloginType=faqs#Q1 (last accessed 27 May 2013).

[124] US District Court for the Eastern District of Louisiana, 'Preliminary Approval of the Settlement Project' (2 May 2012), www.deepwaterhorizoneconomicsettlement.com/docs/Preliminary_Approval_Order_5.2.12.pdf (last accessed 27 May 2013).

Final approval took place on 21 December 2012,[125] after the Fairness Hearing in which the Court was to contemplate whether the new Settlement Program could be regarded as fair, reasonable and adequate.[126]

As the Fund had stopped accepting claims by the end of 2011 and became inactive, claimants who could not attain remediation, or claimants who were denied remediation or accepted advanced payment or an interim payment but not remediation in full, could join the Settlement Program seeking full remediation.

The Settlement Program represents and handles all the private claims against BP which are considered part of the Economic Class. The Economic and Property Damages Settlement is a class action settlement. The class representatives are the individuals and businesses named as plaintiffs in the Class Action Complaint against BP. These class representatives represent a larger group of individuals and businesses with similar claims (the Economic Class). Those who meet the class definition are called the Economic Class Members.[127] Only these claimants are included in the Settlement Program and only their claims will be considered and remediated in full. Simultaneously, together with the Settlement Program, BP introduced an 'OPA grievance mechanism', the 'BP Claims Program', where individuals can submit their claims for economic and property damages related directly to the BP oil incident. Substantial claims can be filed by individuals and businesses who do not constitute members of the Economic Class and by parties, members of the class, but who have decided in a proper time to exercise their legal right separately from the class.[128] If claims are not promptly considered or are denied by BP, the claimants have the ability to exercise their rights

---

[125] The Court gave final approval of the Economic and Property Settlement. See, for the judgment and its amendment, *In re Oil Spill by the Oil Rig 'Deepwater Horizon' in the Gulf of Mexico on 20 April 2010* [2012] ED La., 'Order and Judgment'. See the court documents at the court's website (date unavailable), www.laed.uscourts.gov/OilSpill/OilSpill.htm (last accessed 30 May 2013).

[126] *In re Oil Spill by the Oil Rig 'Deepwater Horizon' in the Gulf of Mexico on 20 April 2010* [2012] ED La., 'Final Fairness Hearing' (8 November 2012), www.laed.uscourts.gov/OilSpill/Orders%5C11082012MinuteEntry.pdf (last accessed 30 May 2013). The content of the hearing has been transcribed by the Official Court Rapporteur and is not available online.

[127] Deepwater Horizon Court-Supervised Settlement Program, 'Economic Notices' (22 December 2012), www.deepwaterhorizonsettlements.com/Economic/SummaryNotice.aspx (last accessed 27 May 2013).

[128] BP, 'Claims Information' (31 October 2012), www.bp.com/sectiongenericarticle800.do?categoryId=9048911&contentId=7082592&nicam=vanity&redirect=www.bp.com/claims. See also the report published by BP illustrating the overall amount paid for civil

in court by filing a lawsuit, or to present their case to the National Pollution Funds Center (NPFC).[129]

In conclusion, the Deepwater Horizon incident represents a failure of safety standards, a fact recognised both by BP itself and the preliminary investigation team. BP suffered great reputational damage, and therefore agreed to support the establishment of the Gulf Coast Claims Facility (the Fund), with the objective to settle the claims of the oil spill victims. The Fund was jointly created by BP and the US Department of Justice. For two operational years (2010–12), the Fund accepted and processed more than a million claims. However, it faced wide criticism for its lack of transparency. Parallel to the Fund process, in 2010, litigation commenced against BP. Before going to trial, this developed into a settlement process between BP and the class of the claimants. The settlement process ended up in the Settlement Program, which handles all the private claims against BP.

Comparisons

All three companies featuring in the case studies have stated on their websites that they have engaged with the SRSG's Framework. Against the background of these three studies, in this section we will analyse to what extent the remedy principles of the GPs have or have not yet been implemented by each of the three oil companies, and how their remedies could have been provided in a more effective manner. In this way, we seek to take into consideration the effectiveness indicators stated in GP 31.

In the first part of the comparison we will provide information on the attitude of the three companies towards the SRSG's process. Thereafter, we will make an attempt to find out whether such attitudes have been put into practice, looking particularly at the ongoing litigation commenced by victims, and comparing these with the relevant GPs.

In the second part of the comparison we will discuss, for each of the companies, which non-judicial remedies, grievance mechanisms and local engagement methods they employ in line with the GPs. An overview thereof is provided in Table 1 below.

claims: BP, Gulf of Mexico Oil Spill: Claims and Other Payments: Public Report (30 April 2013), www.bp.com/liveassets/bp_internet/globalbp/globalbp_uk_english/gom_2012/STAGING/local_assets/downloads_pdfs/Public_Report_April_2013.pdf (both websites last accessed 30 May 2013).

[129] United States Coast Guard, 'National Pollution Funds Center' (22 October 2012), www.uscg.mil/npfc/ (last accessed 27 May 2013).

In the third part of the comparison, we will summarise to what extent the corporate structure of each of the three multinational companies poses an additional complication for victims in relation to having access to remedies.

Implementing the Ruggie Framework: corporate legal and policy strategies

Chevron

Since 2007, Chevron has actively participated in the public consultation process with the SRSG. Between 2010 and 2012, Chevron publicly declared its commitment to the GPs by stating: 'Along with our engagement with key international human rights institutions, our participation with the UN Framework continues to complement the implementation of Chevron's Human Rights Policy. The business responsibility to respect human rights, as outlined by Ruggie, suggests an operational framework to manage potential human rights issues related to business operations. Chevron's Human Rights Policy is consistent with the UN Framework.' By 2013, this statement had been removed from the Chevron website and replaced by an expression of support for the Voluntary Principles on Security and Human Rights (VPSHR).[130]

This removal poses the question whether Chevron actually wants to ensure that the GPs are put into practice within Chevron's operations.

The Chevron case study above demonstrates that judicial remedies have so far not brought any physical remediation or financial compensation for the Ecuadorean victims. GP 26 presupposes that judicial remedies are one way of providing access to remedies. The Chevron litigation process with the Ecuadorean people cannot be considered an example of providing adequate remediation as GP 22 requires. The facts show that the judicial proceedings are lengthy. The first Ecuadorean claims were filed in 1993 (*Aguinda* litigation in the USA) and claims were again filed in 2003 (*Lago Agrio* litigation in Ecuador). A first instance judgment was rendered only after eight years of litigation, in 2011. Moreover, this judgment was challenged by Chevron and appealed in 2012. By the time of writing in May 2013, the victims had not yet been compensated at all. None of the decisions can be enforced in Ecuador against Chevron assets as there are none. The process of seeking

---

[130] Chevron, 'Human Rights' (date unavailable), www.chevron.com/globalissues/human-rights/ (last accessed 27 May 2013).

remediation has also proved to be quite unpredictable. Chevron started the BIT arbitration and the claim to block enforcement in the USA even before the Ecuadorean court had rendered its judgment. Furthermore, legal remedies, generally, are inaccessible for the majority of the victims because of the costs and the lack of education. As a final observation, transparency is also lacking, due to the emphasis on the adversarial legal process rather than proceeding with more equitable and joint means of fact-finding and providing reparation in kind.

The SRSG's Framework requires Chevron to respect the *Lago Agrio* judgment and provide physical compensation, remediation and reparation of the environment to the state it was in prior to the harm being done (GP 15c). The *Lago Agrio* judgment, and finally also the most recent appeal court decision of the superior Ecuadorean court, affirmed Chevron's liability in this respect. The Ecuadorean court further affirmed Chevron's obligation to provide a remedy for the victims. However, Chevron's response to the *Lago Agrio* judgment was both to challenge the Ecuadorean court by appealing the decision and to negate the SRSG's recommendations for a cooperative and dialogue-based process of remediation (GPs 28, 29). Subsequent to the first-instance decision, the company refused to provide any apology as was demanded by the people and ordered by the court, replying: 'Chevron does not believe that today's judgment is enforceable in any court that observes the rule of law. Chevron intends to see that the perpetrators of this fraud are held accountable for their misconduct.'[131] A public apology could have been regarded as a demonstration of Chevron's intention to implement effectively the Framework and to engage with the community in a dialogue (GP 18b). However, Chevron decided to escalate the litigation by starting a BIT arbitration and commencing litigation in the USA to block the enforcement of the Ecuadorian judgment instead of collaborating with the Ecuadorian plaintiffs for an early stage recourse and resolution of the dispute (GPs 23, 25). Recently, Chevron has disclosed that it has employed more than 40 law firms and 500 US lawyers to assess and counter the Ecuadorean claims.[132] One could speculate whether the lawyers' fees exceed the costs of any cleaning-up.

---

[131] Chevron, 'Illegitimate Judgment against Chevron in Ecuador Lawsuit' (14 February 2011), www.chevron.com/chevron/pressreleases/article/02142011_illegitimatejudgmentagainstchevroninecuadorlawsuit.news (last accessed 27 May 2013).

[132] *Chevron Corp.* v. *Naranjo et al.* [2011] SDNY, Case 1:11-cv-03718-LAK-JCF, 'Ecuadoreans Discovery Request', www.chevrontoxico.com/assets/docs/2011-08-31-declaration-chevron-lawyers.pdf (last accessed 27 May 2013).

Shell

The Shell Sustainability Report declares that Shell contributed to the work of the SRSG, and the Shell website has a heading which refers to the 'UN Special Representative', stating: 'We have worked closely with Professor John Ruggie ... as he developed the Protect, Respect and Remedy Framework'.[133]

Shell also formulated its own General Business Principles and Code of Conduct.

Shell expressly declares that a failure to follow the General Business Principles could harm its reputation. A company is mainly judged by the way it acts, and 'failure – real or perceived – to follow these principles, or other real or perceived failures of governance or regulatory compliance, could harm our reputation. This could impact our licence to operate, damage our brand, harm our ability to secure new resources, limit our ability to access the capital market and affect our operational performance and financial condition.'[134]

Although Shell declares that it adheres to the Framework, there is still ample room for improvement in the area of judicial and non-judicial remedies. In the Shell cases, due to the involvement of NGOs in organising legal action, one sees more direct participation on the part of the affected individuals in litigation (GP 26). Particularly, there are issues about access to information that make it difficult for the claimants to find evidence for their claims. According to GP 26, limited access to information is considered a barrier to effective remediation which is caused by the dominant position of companies in the legal process. GP 26 states that these barriers, frequently involving imbalances between the parties in terms of financial resources, access to information and expertise, should be diminished.

Furthermore, Shell brings up many formal defences which add to the cost of litigation on the side of the claimants and generate further practical and procedural barriers that disable access to remedies (GPs 26, 22). While Shell continues to argue in court in the Netherlands that it is not responsible for remedying pollution incidents in Nigeria, it has

---

[133] Shell, 'Shell Sustainability Report 2010' in the 'Introduction from the CEO' (date unavailable), reports.shell.com/sustainability-report/2010/servicepages/previous/files/all_shell_sr10.pdf (last accessed 27 May 2013).

[134] Shell, 'Shell Annual Report 2011: Risk Factors', www.ceaa.gc.ca/050/documents/p59540/83261E.pdf; Shell, 'Shell General Business Principles' (2010), www-static.shell.com/static/aboutshell/downloads/who_we_are/sgbps/sgbp_english.pdf (both websites last accessed 27 May 2013).

assumed some responsibility in a case filed in the UK for the pollution concerning the Bodo village. Since the release of the UNEP Report in 2011, however, Shell has not indicated that it will engage in any concrete course of action that has been suggested in the Report (information as of May 2013).

In view of the effectiveness criteria stated in the GPs, of particular concern here is the lack of transparency about the procedures of remediation, the status of remediation projects, the causes of oil spills, the risks of the lack of pipeline maintenance in the Delta, and the costs of remediation. The UNEP report also remarked that Shell has not followed its own procedures in a diligent way.

Despite Shell's policies, many stakeholders are still dissatisfied with the company's practices, as can be witnessed by the many loud protests against the company about polluting the soil, water and air in the Niger Delta; about collaborating with the Nigerian authorities even when public corruption is apparent; and about the unfair distribution of the oil wealth in Nigeria.[135]

Shell claims that the Nigerian context is extremely complex and difficult to work in, that most oil spills are caused by sabotage, that Shell has difficulties in maintaining its installations and pipelines in the Niger Delta, and that it depends on others such as the Nigerian government as a shareholder in their Nigerian joint venture, of which Shell Nigeria is the operator, to stop gas flaring.[136]

Shell could create much more transparency about each of these issues (GP 26). As to the public complaints that Shell collaborates too much and in a non-transparent way with the Nigerian government, Shell states that this is necessary to protect its commercial interests.[137] Regarding public complaints that Shell is not prepared to share the results of oil spill investigations and findings in Environmental Impact Assessments (EIAs) and Human Rights Impact Assessments (HRIAs), the company generally states that it cannot do so in order to maintain a solid legal position.[138]

---

[135] See Milieudefensie, 'Milieudefensie to Speak about Shell in Nigeria at Parliamentary Hearing' (26 January 2011), www.milieudefensie.nl/english/shell/news/milieudefensie-to-speak-about-shell-in-nigeria-at-parliamentary-hearing (last accessed 27 May 2013); Youtube, 'Dutch Parliamentary Hearing: Parts 1, 2 and 3' (26 January 2011), www.youtube.com/watch?v=z3tPPaYV8oU, www.youtube.com/watch?v=-Dhuemp-LxY, www.youtube.com/watch?v=QVgduC6UXyg&feature=related (last accessed 27 May 2013).

[136] Ibid.   [137] Ibid.   [138] Ibid.

These responses, however, do not produce a healthy ground for collaboration with stakeholders and for providing remedies in a quick and smooth way in the manner the GPs suggest (GPs 18b, 22).

As regards the claims instituted in the Dutch court, the company defended itself first by bringing forward many formal defences that delayed the cases from leading to a substantive evaluation by the court on the question of the duty of care that can be expected from Shell. The company defends itself by stating that it is entitled to use all legal means that are available to defend its position. However, as has also been confirmed by John Ruggie more recently, this 'legal paradise' attitude does not align itself with providing effective remedies.[139]

In the same court cases, the Nigerian claimants felt the need to present certain factual information regarding the oil spills and cleaning-up operations. As it was apparently difficult to obtain this information from Shell, the claimants asked the court to order Shell to provide such information. The UK and US doctrines of 'pre-trial discovery' or 'document disclosure' are not part of Dutch law. In practice, it appears difficult and sometimes impossible to obtain documents in the possession of opponents who are unwilling to submit them. The requesting party must (i) have a legitimate interest; (ii) specify the desired documents in sufficient detail; and (iii) the documents must 'relate' to a legal relationship (based on contract or tort) to which it is a party. In the Shell cases, the defendants only partly succeeded in their document request since, in particular, the second requirement was hard to fulfil.[140]

Consequently, taking into account the GPs, there is room for improvement for Shell in supporting effective judicial remedies and providing access to effective non-judicial remedies for its activities in causing environmental damage and gas flaring (GP 20). In particular, providing an immediate response to incidents is important. Shell could enhance accessibility and predictability of judicial remedies by co-operating in fact-finding and by

---

[139] Issues Brief in J. Ruggie, 'Kiobel and Corporate Social Responsibility' (4 September 2012), 6, shiftproject.org/sites/default/files/KIOBEL%20AND%20CORPORATE%20SOCIAL%20RESPONSIBILITY.pdf (last accessed 27 May 2013); Brief *Amici Curiae* of John Ruggie, official court document (12 June 2012), www.americanbar.org/content/dam/aba/publications/supreme_court_preview/briefs/10-1491_neutralamcufm runspecialrepetal.authcheckdam.pdf (last accessed 27 May 2013).

[140] *Akpan and Milieudefensie* v. *Shell* [2011] District Court of The Hague, the Netherlands; *Oguru et al.* v. *Shell* [2011] District Court of The Hague; *Dooh et al.* v. *Shell* [2011] District Court of The Hague, the Netherlands.

sharing data about pipeline maintenance, company policies, oil spills, sabotage, incidents and remediation efforts (GP 21). Another issue is the present lack of transparency on contact with authorities (GP 31). In order to provide equitable remedies, Shell could participate in jointly governed (re-) mediation projects and set up settlement funds for remediation as suggested in the UNEP Report (GPs 28, 31). The funds and programmes initiated by BP in the aftermath of the Gulf of Mexico accident could serve as useful precedents for Shell. A future plan for Shell could be to start and participate in jointly governed oil exploitation and exploration projects together with the local inhabitants of the affected areas (GP 18). In this respect, by gradually building community engagement and community–company dialogue, mediation is preferred in resolving disputes rather than escalated litigation. A sample of community engagement and participation is suggested in the UNEP Report,[141] but Shell has not yet given any public consideration to this.

BP

BP 'participated in discussions about the development of a new human rights Framework led by Professor John Ruggie'.[142] While one cannot find any reference to the Framework in its current dealings,[143] the company has announced its intention to carry out some detailed analysis of its current practices regarding human rights and consider whether it needs to make any changes to them in light of the SRSG's Framework.[144] The Deepwater Horizon accident represents a failure in safety standards, a fact recognised both by BP itself and the preliminary investigation team. BP has provided remedies to victims through its financial contribution to the Fund (GP 22). The Fund has, however, garnered criticism due to its lack of transparency and finality (for the fishermen's damages may be much higher than compensated from the Fund if it turns out that sea life does not recover soon enough; see the elements stated in GP 31). Thus while the Fund is a step towards providing remedies as discussed in the Framework, it is not sufficient. This demonstrates the need for

---

[141] The UNEP Report, n. 45.
[142] BP, 'Human Rights and Sustainability' (date unavailable), www.bp.com/sectiongener icarticle800.do?categoryId=9040217&contentId=7073401 (last accessed 27 May 2013).
[143] Compare to the concrete discussion of Chevron's use of the Framework at that company's website.
[144] BP, 'BP and the UN Guiding Principles' (2011), www.bp.com/extendedsectiongener icarticle.do?categoryId=9048970&contentId=7085280 (last accessed 27 May 2013).

community interaction for the creation of effective remedies (GP 18b). By using community interaction and community engagement, the Fund could provide extensive assistance to those who face accessibility barriers, while ensuring that the parties will participate in the process in fair and equitable terms. The Fund would, in this way, help clarify which claimants really need compensation and which ones are fraudulent. This company–community dialogue would lead to the effective usage of non-judicial grievance mechanisms which would facilitate resolving all types of conflicts and disputes between the parties.

The Fund was set up in collaboration with the US government. The Framework indeed suggests that states and companies should co-operate to protect human rights, in particular under the Remedy Pillar. The Fund, although it does not explicitly discuss the influence of the Framework, takes this a step further. The Fund is a mix of company and state efforts to offer a remedy to victims. This legal and practical scheme allows for the reparation of individual damages in a timely fashion, rather than through lengthy litigation.

The SRSG's Framework provides for the interaction of state and company forms of remediation (GPs 22, 25). One sees an example of this in the case of BP, where BP created the Fund at the behest of the US government. As discussed above in the third section, this Fund is not without problems, but represents an attempt to assist victims without requiring lengthy unpredictable and inaccessible litigation (GP 31). Interestingly, the Fund is available to victims even without a direct finding of fault on the part of BP. BP may recover these costs if it successfully brings a suit against a subcontractor and is found not to be liable. In the meantime, however, fishermen can use the funds to receive compensation for a lost season so as to help improve their boats and attempt to return to normality. Again, the Fund does raise concerns which often relate to a lack of transparency (GP 31), but it represents the most successful melding of state and corporate remedy procedures developed thus far. It is interesting that the UNEP Report provides recommendations along the same lines, i.e. to set up a fund, paid into by the oil companies and the Nigerian government, under joint governance of the communities, companies and the government, in order to restore the environment and compensate the people who have been harmed by the oil pollution.[145]

---

[145] The UNEP Report, n. 45, 205–29.

Non-judicial remedies: grievance mechanisms, settlement, local engagement

Following the GPs in parallel with the three cases, the authors understand the necessity for the introduction of a wider and more efficient system of remedy by Chevron, Shell and BP. As the SRSG recommends in GP 29, grievances could be addressed earlier and remediated directly by business enterprises. The following section elaborates on this effort that could result in the establishment or participation of Chevron, Shell and BP in effective operational-level grievance mechanisms for individuals and communities who may be adversely impacted. Furthermore, considering that many international companies have linked their performance to existing industry, multi-stakeholder and collaborative initiatives which address the protection of human rights, the SRSG has in GP 30 encouraged these initiatives to ensure that effective grievance mechanisms are available. Table 1 at the end of this section provides a recommended list of non-judicial grievance mechanisms that Chevron, Shell and BP could be engaged with.

Chevron

The case study demonstrates that Chevron has failed to develop adequate non-judicial or company grievance mechanisms according to GP 29. It also does not promote the existing international or regional ones. It has established a system of company hotlines,[146] but they are only accessible to Chevron's employees. And only Chevron's employees, not third parties, can report misconduct during work.

As regards communicating human rights issues and local engagement, Chevron reports that it has introduced the content of the Voluntary Principles on Security and Human Rights (VPSHR) into private security contracts with its employees and contractors.[147] It states that it wishes to promote engagement with the local communities where it operates by contributing to the socio-economic development of the operating areas.[148] It aims to achieve an ongoing, proactive and two-way

---

[146] Chevron, 'Business Ethics' (June 2012), www.chevron.com/globalissues/busines sethics/ (last accessed 27 May 2013).

[147] UN Global Compact, 'Human Rights and Business Dilemmas Forum, Chevron Guidelines on the Voluntary Principles and Inclusion in Contracts' (date unavailable), human-rights.unglobalcompact.org/case_studies/security-forces-and-human-rights/ (last accessed 27 May 2013).

[148] Chevron, 'Social Investment' (April 2012), www.chevron.com/globalissues/economic communitydevelopment/ (last accessed 27 May 2013).

communication with all the potential stakeholders while performing Environmental, Health and Security Impact Assessments prior to any action (GP 19).[149] In 2011/12, after the Deepwater Horizon accident, Chevron ran a campaign entitled 'We agree'. Herein, Chevron admits that: 'For decades, oil companies have worked in disadvantaged areas, influencing policy in order to do there what we can't do at home. It's time this changed. People in Ecuador, Nigeria, the Gulf of Mexico, Richmond, and elsewhere have a right to a clean and healthy environment.'[150]

Arguably, in order to implement the Remedy Pillar, engagement with the existing international and regional non-judicial grievance mechanisms would be imperative for Chevron (GPs 29, 30). Furthermore, the establishment of local access points as community engagement spots for the victims of human rights violations in all the operating areas of the company would be required in view of implementing the Framework (GP 31b). Their introduction would provide not only access to non-judicial grievance mechanisms but also to dispute resolution and remedy mechanisms. These local access points would enhance accessibility and will support community–company engagement. In collaboration with some regional non-judicial mechanisms, complaints could be filed therein showcasing an example of active co-operation with the public sector and the existing state-based non-judicial mechanisms such as ombudsmen and NCPs. The local access points for community–company engagement could contribute to the development of mediation and arbitration facilities for non-judicial access to remedies.

Shell

Concerning grievance mechanisms, stakeholder involvement and community engagement, all Shell companies, joint venture partners and (sub)-contractors are expected by Shell to comply with the General Business Principles. This is in line with GP 30.[151] Principle 6 testifies to the ambition to perform well in respect of 'Local Communities': 'Shell companies aim to be good neighbours by continuously improving the ways in which we contribute directly or indirectly to the general

---

[149] Chevron, 'Stakeholders' Engagement is Considered a Part of the Assessment' (April 2012), www.chevron.com/globalissues/environment/ (last accessed 27 May 2013).

[150] Chevron, 'We Agree' campaign, 'Oil Companies Should Clean up their Messes' (27 October 2010), www.chevron-weagree.com/#mainad-2. See also E. Bast, 'Change Chevron' (27 October 2010), www.priceofoil.org/2010/10/27/change-chevron/ (both websites last accessed 27 May 2013).

[151] Shell General Business Principles, n. 134.

wellbeing of the communities within which we work. We manage the social impacts of our business activities carefully and work with others to enhance the benefits to local communities, and to mitigate any negative impacts from our activities ... Shell companies recognise that regular dialogue and engagement with our stakeholders is essential.'

The establishment of local access points is also recommended for Shell. Shell already communicates that SPDC and its joint venture partners invest in social projects and programmes in Niger Delta communities. As of 2006, several 'Global Memoranda of Understanding' were concluded, emphasising transparent and accountable processes, regular communication, sustainability and conflict prevention according to GP 30.[152] The existence of local access points in all Shell's operating areas would achieve smoother implementation of the Global Memoranda by providing places where mediation and arbitration on the existing terms of the Memoranda could be addressed.

BP

BP addresses human rights concerns via its corporate policy. It publishes an internal 'Guide to Human Rights',[153] with instructions on what to do upon the discovery of human rights abuses. This is in accordance with GP 29.[154] BP clarifies the limits of its responsibility in the following statement: 'according to current legal convention, only governments or individuals acting on behalf of government can commit human rights abuses. (Companies can [only] directly breach national civil and criminal laws.)'[155] The authors of this chapter find this statement to be an inaccurate statement of the law; for example, companies are certainly capable of hiring children, despite multiple conventions prohibiting child labour.[156]

BP utilises an internal grievance process for its employees through its confidential OpenTalk hotline.[157] BP's reporting procedure also

---

[152] Shell, 'Shell in Nigeria: Global Memorandum of Understanding – A New Way of Working with Communities' (April 2012), www-static.shell.com/static/nga/down loads/pdfs/briefing_notes/gmou.pdf (last accessed 27 May 2013).

[153] BP, 'Human Rights' (2006), www.bp.com/liveassets/bp_internet/globalbp/STAGING/global_assets/downloads/BP_Human_Rights_2005.pdf (last accessed 27 May 2013).

[154] *Ibid.* [155] *Ibid.*

[156] United Nations Convention on the Rights of the Child (entered into force 2 September 1990), UNTS (CRC). Indeed, see Chapter 5, where David Bilchitz argues that corporations are directly bound by international human rights.

[157] BP, 'Speaking Up' (date unavailable), www.bp.com/sectiongenericarticle800.do?categoryId=9048986&contentId=7082831 (last accessed 27 May 2013).

introduced the BP America Ombudsman Program (GP 29).[158] However, this programme is geographically limited to the territory of the USA and applies only to BP's contractors and employees.[159] Therefore, the establishment of local access points in the operating areas of BP, and especially in collaboration with the existing internal grievances mechanisms, is suggested for BP. In this way, BP will provide access internationally to affected parties who are not presently covered by the existing internal grievance mechanisms.

Complicated corporate structure of multinational oil companies leads to employing formal legal defences

In the third section, the authors elaborated on the remedial responses of Chevron, Shell and BP, especially on their overall responsibility to provide or co-operate in remediation processes after causing or contributing to adverse human rights impacts (GP 22). In this regard, it became clear that Chevron and Shell use their complicated corporate structure as a formal defence in legal proceedings, while BP follows a different legal strategy.

Chevron

Chevron, in its legal defence, rejects the company's responsibility to remedy human rights violations suffered by the Ecuadorean victims, declaring that Texaco maintained its legal capacity as an independent company until 2005. Thus, in this case, determining the responsibility to remedy was further complicated by questions of succession. While the Ecuadorean plaintiffs claim that Chevron is the successor of Texaco after their merger in 2001, Chevron insists that it is a totally different company which never acted in Ecuador or signed any agreement with the Republic of Ecuador. Therefore, any judgment against Chevron in Ecuador lacks jurisdiction and competency. Interestingly, in October 2010, Chevron announced the 'We Agree' campaign, a global advertising campaign[160] in which the company admits

---

[158] T. Webb, 'BP Plans to Close its US Safety Watchdog' (10 October 2010), www.guardian.co.uk/business/2010/oct/10/bp-us-safety-ombudsman-closure (last accessed 27 May 2013); see BP America Office of the Ombudsman, 'BP America Ombudsman Program' (2007), www.ombudsmanecp.com/ (last accessed 27 May 2013).

[159] BP America Ombudsman Program, *ibid.*

[160] The amount spent on the "We Agree" campaign by Chevron is confidential. But it is estimated that Chevron spends $90 million per year on marketing in the territory of the USA alone; Rainforest Action Network, 'Amazon Watch and Rainforest Action Network Activists Punk Chevron in DC' (date unavailable), ran.org/ran-yes-men-punkd-chevron# (last accessed 27 May 2013).

Table 1 *Non-judicial grievance mechanisms, including applicable codes of conduct, multi-stakeholder initiatives, international initiatives, national and multilateral initiatives*

Chevron	Shell	BP
• Voluntary Principles for Security and Human Rights (VPSHR)	• Voluntary Principles for Security and Human Rights (VPSHR)	• Voluntary Principles for Security and Human Rights (VPSHR)
• Social Accountability International (SAI)	• Social Accountability International (SAI)	• Social Accountability International (SAI)
• Compliance/Advisor Ombudsman (CAO)	• Compliance/Advisor Ombudsman (CAO)	• Compliance/Advisor Ombudsman (CAO)
• Ecuadorean Human Rights Institutions – Defensoria del Pueblo del Ecuador	• Nigerian Human Rights Institutions – National Human Rights Commission Nigeria	• US Human Rights Institutions – US Commission on Civil Rights
• OECD – NCP Ecuador	• OECD – NCP Nigeria	• OECD – NCP US
• UN Global Compact	• UN Global Compact	• UN Global Compact
• BASESwiki	• BASESwiki	• BASESwiki
• Inter-American Development Bank – Independent Consultation and Investigation Mechanism		
• The Inspection Panel – International Bank for Reconstruction and Development	• The Inspection Panel – International Bank for Reconstruction and Development	• The Inspection Panel – International Bank for Reconstruction and Development
• Equator Principles	• Equator Principles	• Equator Principles
	• African Development Bank – Independent Review Mechanism	
• Global Union Federation – International Framework Agreements	• Global Union Federation – International Framework Agreements	• Global Union Federation – International Framework Agreements

the social responsibility of the oil industry for environmental damages and human rights abuses in operating areas.

Shell

RDS is the parent company of the Shell group. In the Dutch court cases, as a defence, Shell emphasised that RDS was only incorporated in 2005 and could not bear responsibility for the oil spills in Nigeria. Hence, an internal reorganisation was used as a formal defence. Additionally, Shell pointed out that its parent companies have insufficient control over the Nigerian operations and thus cannot prevent pollution nor ensure the implementation of remedies. However, as the plaintiffs argue, the economic reality shows that Shell presents itself as one corporate group that manages one business organisation, one brand name for all of its products and operations ('Shell'), one corporate communications strategy, one set of group business principles, one set of financial statements and one 'Sustainability Report'.[161] Moreover, it has one board of directors. Shell's shares are listed on the stock exchanges in Amsterdam, London and New York, and its shareholders are entitled to dividends based on the operations of the whole group.[162]

BP

BP America Inc.[163] is the US operation of BP;[164] the corporation 'does not distinguish between the activities and operations of the parent company and those of its subsidiaries'.[165] BP has not attempted to limit liability to the US subsidiary, though due to the lack of separation between operations, such a strategy would likely be unsuccessful.[166]

---

[161] Shell, 'Sustainability Report' (2010), reports.shell.com/sustainability-report/2010/serv icepages/previous/files/all_shell_sr10.pdf (last accessed 27 May 2013).

[162] €0.07 is the nominal value of the ordinary shares.

[163] Note, though, that there are rumours regarding a split between BP's US and foreign operations so as to contain the fallout from the Deepwater Horizon incident. BP has not commented upon these rumours; see The Economist, 'Should BP Split? The Pros and Cons of Slicing Oil Giants Apart' (30 July 2011), www.economist.com/node/21524921 (last accessed 27 May 2013).

[164] United States Securities and Exchange Commission, 'SEC Filings' (14 March 2012), www.sec.gov/cgi-bin/browse-edgar?action=getcompany&CIK=0000790303&owner= exclude&count=40 (last accessed 27 May 2013).

[165] BP, 'Refining and Marketing: Information for Shareholders' (date unavailable), www.bp. com/sectiongenericarticle800.do?categoryId=9039496&contentId=7072390 (last accessed 27 May 2013).

[166] BP, 'BP Releases Report on Causes of Gulf of Mexico Tragedy' (8 September 2010), www. bp.com/genericarticle.do?categoryId=2012968&contentId=7064893 (last accessed 27 May 2013).

Concluding comparative analysis of corporate remedial responses to oil pollution incidents

In the following section, a concluding comparative analysis of the corporate remedial responses will be conducted. The conclusions will assist Chevron, Shell and BP to assess the effectiveness of their remedial responses in order to verify whether adverse human rights impacts have been properly addressed and tracked as recommended by GP 30. They will also provide guidance on how these three companies could use external resources and the feedback of the affected stakeholders in moving towards more effective remedies.

In the third section, three case studies were presented, with a focus on the remedies provided. In the fourth, an attempt has been made to analyse the actions taken by the companies and to compare these with the guidance of the GPs. The key question has been whether the companies effectively remedied any wrongdoings (i.e. the oil spills and the impact on the human rights of health, food, water, to make a living, and a clean and healthy environment). As stated, the GPs discuss standards for determining the effectiveness of remedies, such as legitimacy, accessibility, predictability, equitability, transparency, rights compatibility and the application of lessons learned. Table 2 illustrates the findings of the analysis concerning to what extent the companies have provided effective judicial and non-judicial remedies. The table also illustrates whether these companies collaborated with the state-based mechanisms towards providing effective judicial mechanisms. With this table, the authors aim to draw a roadmap that pinpoints weaknesses and includes suggestions for the examined companies, distilled from the GPs, for the improvement of effectiveness in the existing judicial and non-judicial remedies provided in the case studies.

After analysing the facts of the case studies, the authors found that the judicial and non-judicial remedies provided suffer mostly in 'accessibility' and 'transparency'. They decided to draft a table which showcases the existing weaknesses of effectiveness of the offered remedies tested against the standards of GP 31. The focus of the analysis is thus concentrated mostly on transparency and accessibility. The names in bold indicate, per effectiveness criterion, which of the three companies undertook the recommended action according to the GPs (satisfactory), could have done so in a better way (insufficient), or did not comply at all with the effectiveness criterion tested (non-compliant).

Table 2 *Overview of elements of effective remediation and performance of the three companies*

Accessibility	Transparency	Other criteria: predictability, equity, legitimacy, human rights compatibility and application of lessons learned
1. Co-operation and engagement with established and recognised effective grievance mechanisms such as: NCPs, Ombudsman – **Shell, BP and Chevron insufficient.** 2. Development of the established corporate grievance mechanisms such as OpenTalk lines and employee hotlines – **all three companies insufficient.** 3. Establishment of local access points for companies, victims and third parties to develop and provide non-judicial remedies to the victims or to commence negotiation processes – **all three companies insufficient.** 4. Participation and active co-operation with the public sector in developing	9. Active participation of the parties in the available remedy processes – **all three insufficient.** 10. Promoting awareness of the benefits and the advantages of the remedy process – **all three insufficient.** 11. Development of process standards and principles towards remedy – **BP and Chevron especially, insufficient.** 12. Avoidance of corruption and the establishment of clear processes by advanced public disclosure – **all three companies insufficient.** 13. Promotion of adequate and effective information and risk assessment mechanisms for the victims towards remedy; sharing	17. Apology, recognition of the harm – **all three insufficient for enhanced predictability, legitimacy and rights compatibility. Especially Chevron when it was asked to do so by the Ecuadorean Court.** 18. Building trust with the harmed and society – **all three insufficient to achieve legitimacy.** 19. Physical compensation – remediation and reparation of the environment. Reparation of the natural landscape as it was before the harm – **Shell and BP, especially, insufficient and Chevron did it inadequately. The UNEP Report also emphasised the importance of a full**

Table 2 *(cont.)*

Accessibility	Transparency	Other criteria: predictability, equity, legitimacy, human rights compatibility and application of lessons learned
mediation and arbitration institutes that provide non-judicial access to remedies – **all three companies insufficient.** 5. Avoidance of any accessibility barriers for remedy, such as local illiteracy, physical or natural barriers, lack of financial means, voluntary legal aid – **all three companies insufficient.** 6. Access points that are adjusted to the victim's cultural and educational background – **Chevron and Shell especially insufficient.** 7. Helping victims to assess, and understand, their options for accessing remedies and relate the existing remedies to the necessary and available resources –	information about environmental assessments, both before and after spills – **Shell, Chevron and especially BP insufficient.** 14. Avoidance of the disadvantages of the adversarial legal system by providing information-sharing processes and disclosure between the parties – **Shell especially insufficient under Dutch Law.** 15. Dialogue-based approach, alleviation of the conflicts of interest between the parties to achieve a final consensus – **all three companies insufficient.** 16. Specific determination of the role of third parties in the remediation processes, such as government and	**restoration of the environment.** 20. Financial compensation to the victims: the introduction and the establishment of remediation funds. **BP satisfactory and the UNEP Report proposed such measures for the Ogoni victims.** 21. Participation of the companies in collaborative initiatives providing reasonable information to the victims – **all three companies insufficient for the enhancement of equity.** 22. Alternative and community dispute resolution mechanisms, mediation/arbitration initiatives. Governance by a diverse multi-stakeholder advisory

Table 2 *(cont.)*

Accessibility	Transparency	Other criteria: predictability, equity, legitimacy, human rights compatibility and application of lessons learned
all three companies insufficient. 8. Community education programmes on the access to remedies – **all three companies insufficient.**	NGOs –**Chevron especially insufficient regarding the Ecuadorean government, and Shell insufficient by not accepting the role of Milieudefensie in the Dutch tort litigation.**	body or governing board to enhance credibility and confidence – institutional co-operation and affiliation. **Chevron satisfactory and BP and Shell insufficient for enhancement of equity, legitimacy and predictability.** 23. Avoidance of costly litigation and emphasis on the physical remediation of victims – **all three companies insufficient for enhancement of equity.**

Interestingly, in all three cases, the companies rely heavily upon existing judicial remedies as has been demonstrated in the previous sections and in Table 2. Remedies in kind, company or sector grievance mechanisms and alternative dispute resolution mechanisms are almost completely ignored except in respect of the BP Fund. Such initiatives should be explored further in our view, but must be of a complementary character without undermining the existing legal and judicial possibilities for victims. The form of these remedial mechanisms is of a hybrid character that stands between public consultation, mediation and formal litigation.

Looking at the solutions offered by the three companies, one sees a common thread, namely, the lack of transparency and accessibility either in judicial or non-judicial remedies.[167] There exists a lack of coherent information provided to citizens about oil operations and potential health risks, as the right to a healthy environment requires. Those affected by the disasters are both uncertain about their options for recompense and whether the actions taken by the companies are sufficient (consider the cases of BP and Chevron and contradictory evidence regarding the presence of toxic chemicals). Further transparency regarding both the relief procedure and the facts of the incident (e.g. Shell was not willing to share information about oil spills and the internal analyses thereof) would go a long way towards assisting victims in rebuilding their lives. Unfortunately, the current litigation system does not encourage such transparency; due to the adversarial process, companies have every incentive to keep disclosure limited to the minimum required by law (for example, Shell in the document disclosure incident). The adversarial process also negatively affects community relations: an apology and recognition of the harm caused by oil spills would be beneficial in building the necessary trust for working together to rebuild affected communities. For liability reasons, however, companies are reluctant to apologise or otherwise admit fault. While judicial remedies are a necessary part of the remedy process, one must be aware that their existence and the process of trial preparation may impede other efforts to provide effective non-judicial remedies. The GPs do not offer a way out of this dilemma. Hence, it will depend on a company's attitude as to whether it will apply a co-operative or confrontational approach when addressing its adverse impacts and stakeholders who complain about this.

The lack of accessibility is also obvious in all the examined case studies, especially in the Chevron and Shell cases. For Chevron's victims, the lack of a legal basis to address their claims in the Ecuadorean courts forced them to file claims before the US courts without any success. The Ecuadorean people even travelled to the company's headquarters to notify Chevron's executive members of their grievances. Even though both Chevron and Shell managed to develop corporate grievance mechanisms such as OpenTalk lines and employee hotlines, these mechanisms are not accessible to independent third-party claimants such as victims of human rights violations or NGOs. Considering that the

---

[167] On the importance of access to information, see Chapter 12, in which Nicola Jägers considers the issue in light of transnational private regulation.

majority of the claimants are village people both in the *Chevron* and *Shell* cases, none of the companies assisted the victims to assess, and understand their options for accessing, judicial or non-judicial remedies. The existing financial constraints in litigating with Chevron were tremendous considering that the company itself hired more than 500 lawyers to handle the cases. In contrast, the BP Fund proved to be an accessible tool towards the effective remediation of the victims. BP's support of the Fund ensured accessibility to all individuals and business enterprises with substantive claims.

From the cases, one also sees an evolution from minimal public involvement in the Texaco settlement, to NGO co-operation in the *Shell* case, and finally to BP's Fund. These steps toward a fully effective remedy show the vital importance of involvement by the company, the community and the government. It is only by learning from these and the partial successes of the past that a fully effective remedy procedure can be created and implemented. Notably, the UNEP Report also suggested the establishment of a remedy fund to restore the Ogoni Delta, governed by neutral fund managers, and paid into by the oil companies *and* the Nigerian government.

It is interesting to note that parliamentary hearings were organised (i) in the Netherlands to question Shell's practices in Nigeria and (ii) in the USA to question BP executives about the Gulf accident and oil spill. These companies were publicly requested to explain their corporate policies concerning the avoidance of environmental pollution and respecting human rights. Also, in 2009, banks were invited by parliaments in various countries to explain their role in the financial crisis of 2008. One could consider this as a way to hold multinational companies publicly accountable for their policies and the ways in which they provide remedies when things go wrong. In the Netherlands, MPs explicitly alluded to the SRSG's Framework and raised the question of the extent to which Shell is remedying the problems connected with the oil exploitation. One could see these new types of hearings as public stakeholder meetings in which companies are questioned about their CSR strategy and policies and, in particular, which remedies they employ to solve problems.

Retroactively cleaning up and being a responsible company would include allocating part of the company's profits so as to start anew in the area of human rights. Obviously, the shareholders would have fewer dividends that year, but these incidents concern human rights problems which, while they are a result of past actions, still have significant consequences. This is clear from the continuing protests and litigation. Consequently, effective remedies involve both recompense for the past and safer plans for future operations by BP, Shell and Chevron.

Overall, one sees in these cases a positive but reluctant development of companies in embracing non-judicial remedies: the cases are presented in chronological order but also show how the remedy process has developed over time. Corporations are now considering taking into account the importance of proactive stakeholder involvement in remedies. These cases also highlight the importance of effective government oversight: one cannot expect a corporation effectively to balance the interests of people, planet and profits and be fully cognisant of all aspects of human rights protection. Co-operation and communication are, therefore, a vital part of the remedy process.

14

Access to remedy: the United Kingdom experience of MNC tort litigation for human rights violations

RICHARD MEERAN[*]

Introduction

Holding a multinational corporation (MNC) to account, legally, for harm arising from its developing-country operations has been generally regarded an almost impenetrable challenge. Over the past two decades, human rights litigation against MNCs has been of two main types: (i) claims under the Alien Tort Statute 1789 (ATS),[1] a domestic legislation which gives the district courts of the United States of America (USA) jurisdiction in cases alleging international human rights violations; and (ii) conventional tort litigation alleging harm caused by a breach of a duty of care to take reasonable steps to avoid the harm.

ATS claims have generally been viewed as providing the most promising potential, perhaps most notably resulting in settlements in *Doe* v. *Unocal*[2] and *Wiwa* v. *Royal Dutch Shell*.[3] However, this avenue has now been significantly curtailed as a means of holding corporations to

---

[*] This chapter utilises some material from a previously published article written by the author: R. Meeran, 'Tort Litigation against Multinational Corporations for Violation of Human Rights: An Overview of the Position Outside the United States' (2011) 3 *City University of Hong Kong Law Review* 1.

[1] 28 U.S.C. 1350.

[2] In this case, Burmese villagers sued the California-based energy giant for its alleged direct complicity in abuses committed by the Burmese military, being Unocal's partner in a natural gas pipeline joint venture. EarthRights International, 'Final Settlement Reached in Doe v Unocal' (21 March 2005), www.earthrights.org/legal/final-settlement-reached-doe-v-unocal (last accessed 13 December 2011).

[3] In this case, it was alleged that Shell was complicit in supporting military operations against the Ogoni and that Shell actively pursued the convictions and execution of the Ogoni Nine, including by bribing witnesses against them. EarthRights International, 'Wiwa v Royal Dutch/Shell', www.earthrights.org/legal/wiwa-v-royal-dutchshell (last accessed 13 June 2011).

account legally for their overseas conduct as a result of a decision of the US Supreme Court in *Kiobel* v. *Royal Dutch Petroleum Co.*[4] An important *amicus curiae* brief in support of Shell's motion to dismiss the claim was filed by the United Kingdom (UK) government in conjunction with the government of the Netherlands.[5] This brief argued essentially that ATS claims against corporations were based on violations of international law to which corporations were not subject.[6]

However, during the same period, claims by alleged victims of harm caused by the operations of the UK-headquartered MNCs have enjoyed an increasingly successful track record in the English courts. This contrasts with the position generally: in developing countries where the harm occurs; in relation to MNCs based in other European countries; and in other common law countries such as Australia, Canada and the USA.

In general, apart from potentially using the ATS, it is not possible to obtain civil legal redress for human rights violations *per se* directly against corporations – whether as direct perpetrators or on the grounds of complicity with state perpetrators. Cases against MNCs have been pursued on the basis of the tort of negligence.[7] Tort cases against corporations allege harm caused by 'negligence' arising from a breach of a 'duty of care' (rather than, for example, torture or violation of the right to life). Since they involve claims for compensation and are invariably costly, these cases may serve to achieve critical elements of MNCs' accountability, namely, monetary redress for victims and deterrence against future human rights violations.

An approach entailing allegations of negligence could be criticised as diminishing the significance of the alleged misconduct and harm. Conversely, the use of allegations of fundamental international human rights violations in ATS claims against MNCs might be considered by

---

[4] *Esther Kiobel* v. *Royal Dutch Petroleum Co.*, 133 S. Ct. 1659 (2013).

[5] 'Brief of the Governments of the United Kingdom of Great Britain and Northern Ireland and the Kingdom of the Netherlands as *Amici Curiae* in Support of the Respondents', www.americanbar.org/content/dam/aba/publications/supreme_court_preview/briefs/10-1491_respondentamcuthegovernments.authcheckdam.pdf (last accessed 6 June 2013).

[6] *Ibid.* See, by contrast, 'Brief of *Amici Curiae* English Law Practitioners Martyn Day, Richard Hermer QC, Richard Meeran, and Blinne Ní Ghrálaigh in Support of Petitioners', www.americanbar.org/content/dam/aba/publications/supreme_court_preview/briefs/10-1491_petitioneramcu4englawpractitioners.authcheckdam.pdf (last accessed 6 June 2013).

[7] Prior to the use of the ATS, cases against US MNCs had also been pursued on this basis. See, for example, *In re Union Carbide Corporation Gas Plant Disaster at Bhopal, India in December 1984*, 634 F. Supp. 842 (1986).

the commercial world to be inappropriate and excessive. Nevertheless, the approach of relying on tort law has the advantage of relatively less complexity and more favourable law on jurisdiction, at least in the European Union (EU). The advantages arise because *forum non conveniens* (FNC) – a key barrier in most common law states, including the USA – is no longer an obstacle in the EU with regard to EU-domiciled defendants. Furthermore, under English law, the notion of MNC parent company 'duty of care' has increasingly gained recognition, notwithstanding the 'corporate veil' obstacle.

In the UK this area has developed over the past eighteen years and has included the following cases:[8] *Connelly* v. *RTZ Corporation plc*[9] (Namibian uranium mine and throat cancer); *Ngcobo* v. *Thor Chemicals Holdings Ltd and Desmond Cowley*[10] (mercury poisoning of South African workers); *Sithole* v. *Thor Chemicals Holdings and Desmond Cowley*[11] (mercury poisoning of South African workers); *Lubbe* v. *Cape plc*[12] (7,500 South African asbestos miners); *The OCENSA Pipeline Group Litigation*[13] (claim by 73 Colombian peasents for damage to land); *Motto* v. *Trafigura Limited*[14] (claims by 30,000 residents of Côte d'Ivoire for injuries allegedly caused by toxic waste); *Guerrero* v. *Monterrico Metals plc*[15] (torture/mistreatment of 33 Peruvian environmental protesters); *Bodo Community* v. *Shell Petroleum Development Company (Nigeria) Ltd*[16] (claim by a Nigerian fishing community in Ogoniland for environmental damage caused by oil leaks);[17] and *Vava and Ors* v. *Anglo American South Africa Ltd*[18] (South African gold miners' silicosis mass tort claim in England).

In addition to a favourable legal position regarding FNC and MNC parent direct duty of care, various procedural and practical factors are critical to victims' access to a legal remedy against an MNC. These

---

[8] The author conducted the litigation against RTZ (Connelly), Thor Chemicals, Cape plc, Monterrico Metals and Anglo American.

[9] [1998] AC 854.   [10] Times L Rep., 10 November 1995.   [11] 2000 WL 1421183.

[12] [1998] CLC 1559 (CA); [2000] 1 WLR 1545 (HL).

[13] *Arroyo* v. *Equion Energia Ltd* (formerly known as BP Exploration Company (Colombia) Ltd), Claim No. HQ08X00328.

[14] *Yao Essaie Motto* v. *Trafigura Ltd and Trafigura Beheer BV*, HQ06X03370.

[15] [2009] EWHC 2475; [2010] EWHC 3228.

[16] *Bodo Community* v. *Shell Petroleum Development Company of Nigeria*, Case No. HQ11X01280.

[17] J. Vidal, 'Shell Accepts Liability for Two Oil Spills in Nigeria', *The Guardian* (3 August 2011), www.guardian.co.uk/environment/2011/aug/03/shell-liability-oil-spills-nigeria (last accessed 13 December 2011).

[18] Claim No. HQ11X03245.

include access to relevant corporate documents and ensuring that MNC assets are not placed beyond the reach of claimants. The availability of funding and lawyers who are willing and able to represent victims in this complex, hugely expensive and risky type of litigation are also of fundamental importance. Assessment of the financial viability of cases by victims' lawyers is influenced by various factors, in particular the existence of legal procedural mechanisms such as class actions, financial costs incentives for victims' lawyers and damages levels.

The progressive approach of the English courts contrasts with that of the UK government, which over the same period has, among others, proposed legislation to reverse the effect of an FNC ruling in favour of MNC claimants and sought (unsuccessfully) to reintroduce FNC into European law with regard to EU-domiciled defendants.[19] The government also recently proceeded to pass civil costs legislation,[20] which adversely impacts on access to justice for MNC human rights victims, especially in claims relating to environmental damage. This state of affairs has been exacerbated – probably inadvertently – by European law provisions stipulating that damages by courts be set at local rather than MNC home-state levels.[21] In addition, as indicated above, the UK government actively sought to close a potential avenue of redress for MNC victims in the US court by filing an *amicus* brief in *Kiobel*.

The above approach of the UK government seems to call into question its stated commitment[22] to the third pillar of the Guiding Principles on Business and Human Rights (GPs): access to remedy.[23] Drawing on insights gained from MNC litigation conducted by the author over the past eighteen years, this chapter reflects on how these issues – identified by the GPs as 'legal barriers' and 'practical and procedural barriers'[24] – operate as

---

[19] UK Ministry of Justice Response to the 'European Commission Green Paper Relating to the Operation of the Brussels I Regulation in the International Legal Order', paras. 12–15 (UK Ministry of Justice Response).

[20] Legal Aid, Sentencing and Punishment of Offenders Act 2012 (LASPO).

[21] Rome II Regulation on the Law Applicable to Non-contractual Obligations, No. 864/2007, Arts. 4 and 15 (Rome II Regulation).

[22] 'Securing adoption by consensus of the resolution which endorsed his draft Guiding Principles on Business and Human Rights was a UK priority at the June session of the Human Rights Council.' Response of the Secretary of State for Foreign and Commonwealth Affairs to the Eighth Report from the Foreign Affairs Committee of Session 2010–12, para. 86.

[23] Human Rights Council, 'Guiding Principles on Business and Human Rights: Implementing the United Nations "Protect, Respect and Remedy" Framework', A/HRC/17/31 (21 March 2011) (SRSG, 'Guiding Principles').

[24] *Ibid.*, Commentary on Principle 26.

obstacles to access to remedy, and how these obstacles could be overcome by developing appropriate legal principles and/or enacting suitable legislation.

The two key legal obstacles: jurisdiction and the 'corporate veil'

Access to justice in victims' local courts – in the host states of MNCs – may be impeded by intimidation, corruption, or victims' invariable inability to fund lawyers and to muster the legal resources and expertise necessary to litigate against a well-resourced MNC.[25] Access to adequate legal resources (namely, lawyers who are in a position and willing to take on complex, protracted and expensive litigation) has resulted in victims filing claims in courts of an MNC's home state where the parent MNC is based and over which its home courts can exercise jurisdiction. In the past this approach has usually been confronted by two key obstacles: firstly, whether the court has, or will exercise, jurisdiction; and secondly, whether the court will lift the 'corporate veil' to hold a parent company liable in respect of operations ostensibly conducted by foreign subsidiaries.

Jurisdiction

Under Article 2 of the Brussels I Regulation,[26] the EU courts have jurisdiction over claims against defendants that are domiciled in their jurisdiction. In the case of a corporation, 'domicile' is defined by Article 60 as the location of its 'statutory seat', 'central administration' or 'principal place of business'. All of the above-mentioned UK cases – except for those against Anglo American South Africa Ltd (AASA) and Shell Petroleum Development Company (Nigeria) Ltd (SPDC) – were against UK-registered MNC entities.

The FNC principle, however, applied in common law countries, serves as a procedural means of ensuring that cases are heard where they have their closest connection, thereby providing a means of limiting the exercise of extra-territorial jurisdiction. In the present context, the issue is essentially whether there is a 'more appropriate forum' for

---

[25] See Human Rights Council, 'Business and Human Rights: Towards Operationalizing the "Protect, Respect and Remedy" Framework', A/HRC/11/13 (22 April 2009), para. 94.

[26] Brussels Regulation on Jurisdiction and the Recognition and Enforcement of Judgments in Civil and Commercial Matters, Council Regulation (EC) No. 44/2001 of 22 December 2000 (Brussels I Regulation).

the trial than the MNC's home court in which the ends of justice can be served. Under English law, answering the above question involves the application of a two-stage test: whether there is a forum that has a more real and substantial connection with the case; if yes, whether there are nevertheless reasons why justice requires that the MNC home court should retain jurisdiction.[27]

The *Connelly, Thor Chemicals* and *Lubbe* cases were subject to protracted FNC applications by the MNC defendants. It was contended that notwithstanding the fact that the English court had jurisdiction, it should decline to exercise it essentially because the claimants, the activities that caused the harm, the evidence and the witnesses were almost exclusively in the location of the subsidiaries' operations, thus making the claimants' local courts the natural or 'most appropriate' venue for the litigation.

In commercial cases, forum disputes will usually reflect the parties' thinking on the anticipated differences in the outcome of the litigation in the two competing venues in question with regard to the amount of damages payable if the case succeeds. However, in MNC cases, the difference is usually starker: the claimant has a prospect of obtaining justice in the MNC's home courts but no real prospect of doing so in his or her local courts. Thus the FNC principle was invoked by Rio Tinto in the *Connelly* case even though the MNC conceded that legal aid was not available in Namibia to pay lawyers to represent Mr Connelly, and that lawyers in Namibia were prohibited from acting on a contingency or 'no win no fee' (NWNF) basis. Against this background, arguments in MNC cases about the relative strengths of the connections between the dispute and the competing venues, and the location of evidence and witnesses etc. become mostly academic. An absurd example of the artificiality was an argument advanced by Cape plc that the case should be heard in South Africa because, for the purposes of trial, the company supposedly intended to recreate the conditions around an asbestos mine. *Ex post facto* evidence of the artificiality is that these cases never seem to reach anywhere near trial, and that the issues that it is argued during the forum dispute will be central to the litigation rarely see the light of day. In short, unlike the position generally in commercial cases, FNC in tort or human rights cases provides an opportunity for an MNC to avoid justice altogether. This explains why in MNC cases, FNC applications (which are supposed to be dealt with speedily) took on a 'life of their own'.

---

[27] *Connelly*, n. 9, 871–72.

In a triumph for justice, the House of Lords (now the Supreme Court) in *Connelly* laid down the principle that a claimant who would be denied substantial justice in his or her local courts, due to the inability to pay for lawyers and experts to pursue a case, but who was able to obtain such representation in the courts where she had instigated her claim, would be allowed to proceed with her claim, even though the local courts were otherwise the more appropriate venue:

> [T]he availability of financial assistance in this country coupled with its non-availability in the appropriate forum, may exceptionally be a relevant factor in this context. The question, however, remains whether the plaintiff can establish that substantial justice will not in the particular circumstances of the case be done if the plaintiff has to proceed in the appropriate forum where no financial assistance is available.[28]

The *Connelly* ruling was widely criticised by the commercial world,[29] which echoed the sentiment expressed in the dissenting judgment of Lord Hoffmann: 'If the presence of the defendants, as parent company and local subsidiary of a multinational, can enable them to be sued here, any multinational with its parent company in England will be liable to be sued here in respect of its activities anywhere in the world.'[30] Subsequently, the Lord Chancellor (the UK Minister of Justice) proposed legislation to reverse the effect of the House of Lords' ruling,[31] without which he suggested there could well be an exodus of MNCs from the UK, but the proposal did not appear to find favour and was not implemented.

In July 2000, in a landmark decision in favour of the Cape plc claimants, all five Law Lords held that the case should be allowed to continue in the English High Court.[32] Applying the principle it had developed exactly three years earlier in *Connelly*,[33] the House of Lords held that a case of such magnitude required expert legal representation and experts on technical and medical issues, none of which could be funded in South Africa.

Although the funding issue also arose in the *Thor* case, the court refused the application of FNC on the basis that South Africa was not a 'clearly more appropriate forum' (stage one of the FNC test).[34]

---

[28] *Ibid.*, 873.
[29] 'RTZ Ruling Threatens Other Multinationals', *Financial Times* (25 July 1997).
[30] *Connelly*, n. 9, 876.
[31] 'Mining Firm Tries to Change Law to Block £100m Claims', *The Guardian* (19 March 1999).
[32] *Lubbe* (HL), n. 12.   [33] *Connelly*, n. 9.
[34] *Ngcobo v. Thor Chemicals Holdings and Desmond John Cowley*, judgment of Deputy High Court judge James Stewart QC (11 April 1995, unreported).

It is only if and when the FNC issue is resolved in a claimant's favour that a case can proceed to a hearing on its merits. During the course of the FNC dispute in *Lubbe*, about 1,000 of the 7,500 claimants died. FNC, therefore, constituted a serious impediment to justice.

It might have been impossible for the claimants to see the FNC application through, with the number of appeals and interlocutory hearings that were entailed, had it not been for the assistance of UK legal aid in funding the litigation, the Legal Services Commission (which administers the legal aid system) having classified the case as being of 'high public importance'. Subsequently, UK legal aid was progressively curtailed and the MNC cases were funded by lawyers representing claimants on a NWNF basis. It is doubtful whether claimants' lawyers acting on a NWNF basis would have been willing to embark on such cases if, in addition to the intrinsic complexity and hard-fought nature of the substantive issues, they had first had to overcome a costly and protracted FNC application.

Until 2005, the English courts had interpreted Article 2 of the Brussels I Regulation as allowing dismissal of a case against a UK-domiciled defendant in circumstances where there was a more appropriate forum located in a non-EU state.[35] It was on this basis that the English courts entertained FNC applications in the *Connelly*, *Thor Chemicals* and *Lubbe* cases.[36]

In 2005, a decision of the European Court of Justice – the highest court across the EU, the decisions of which are binding on the courts of all EU states – clarified that the national courts of the EU (including those of the UK) did not have the power to halt proceedings on FNC grounds in cases brought against EU-domiciled defendants, where the alternative venue was outside the EU.[37] Consequently, FNC is no longer an issue in the UK in these MNC cases and that is the reason why the litigation in the *Trafigura*, *Ocensa Pipeline* and *Monterrico* cases was not plagued by this obstacle. By contrast with the *Lubbe* litigation, which had been ongoing for eight years at the time of settlement and was nowhere close to trial, the *Monterrico* case was settled two years after commencement of proceedings (and three months before trial), and the *Trafigura* case was

---

[35] *In re Harrods (Buenos Aires) Ltd* [1992] Ch 72.

[36] In *Lubbe*, however, it was contended on behalf of the claimants that the UK courts had no power to apply the FNC principle to a case involving a UK defendant. In its ruling, the House of Lords concluded that the position was not 'acte clair' and that had the Court found in Cape's favour, it would have referred the issue to the European Court of Justice for resolution.

[37] *Owusu v. Jackson* [2005] ECR 1383.

settled approximately three years after commencement of proceedings. It is noteworthy that FNC is not an issue in the silicosis litigation against AASA,[38] or in the Bodo oil pollution claims against Shell.[39]

Notwithstanding the above, the submission by the UK government in 2011, in response to the consultation on the review of the Brussels I Regulation, that FNC should be introduced into European law[40] – albeit almost certainly futile due to the lack of recognition of FNC in other EU jurisdictions – indicates that access to justice for MNC victims is of little concern to the UK government. This impression is reinforced by recent civil costs legislation, as discussed below.

Corporate veil: development of English law on MNC parent company liability

Apart from the cases against Trafigura, Shell and BP Exploration, the UK claims have been against MNC parent companies, rather than against locally operating subsidiaries. Victims' difficulties in obtaining access to justice locally have led to a search for remedies in the home courts of MNCs. This depends on securing jurisdiction in the home courts by pursuing the head office parent company, rather than the local operating subsidiary.[41] This gives rise to the 'corporate veil' legal complications:

---

[38] Litigation against AASA was commenced by South African silicosis victims in the English High Court in September 2011. AASA is a wholly owned subsidiary of London-based mining giant, Anglo American plc. Unlike the corporate defendants in the *Connelly*, *Cape plc* and *Thor Chemicals* cases, AASA is not a UK-registered company. The claimants contend that the 'central administration' or 'principal place of business' of the defendant is in London and that accordingly, by virtue of Art. 60 of the Brussels I Regulation, AASA is domiciled in the UK. Anglo is challenging UK jurisdiction, though not on FNC grounds. The Court upheld the jurisdictional challenge but granted permission to appeal: *Vaua v. Anglo American South Africa Ltd.* [2013] EWHC 2326 (WB).

[39] In the Bodo Shell Nigeria litigation, the Nigerian-registered defendant, SPDC, would at first blush seem to be in the same position, with regard to jurisdiction, as AASA. However, the UK-registered Royal Dutch Shell (RDS) was originally a co-defendant with its subsidiary SPDC. By virtue of Art. 2 of the Brussels I Regulation, an FNC application was not possible against RDS and under English law the court had jurisdiction over the claim against SPDC as a 'necessary and proper party' to the claim against RDS. In return for SPDC agreeing to submit to the jurisdiction, the claimants agreed not to pursue a claim against RDS.

[40] UK Ministry of Justice Response, n. 19.

[41] Note that the *Trafigura* case for victims of toxic waste dumping in Côte d'Ivoire was atypical in this respect as it involved the UK head office company itself as the defendant rather than a subsidiary. *Yao Essaie Motto v. Trafigura Ltd and Trafigura Beheer BV*, HQ06X03370.

under the principle of separate corporate personality, a parent company is not generally liable, simply by virtue of being a shareholder, for the conduct of its subsidiaries in which it invests.[42] Were it otherwise, the effect would be to undermine the distinct legal personality which separates a company from its shareholders and to treat 'the rights or liabilities or activities of a company as the rights or liabilities or activities of its shareholders'.[43]

The corporate veil has been used to protect the head office parent company at the centre of the organisation, and MNC group structures have been devised accordingly. Of course, the degree to which an MNC parent company controls or influences its worldwide activities varies from one MNC group to another, but an MNC parent is rarely a mere 'hands-off' shareholder.

The corporate veil can be 'pierced', for instance on the ground of fraud. In such a case, the subsidiary is treated as the creature of the parent acting on its behalf, and the parent company becomes liable on the basis that the subsidiary's conduct should be treated as its conduct. This is obviously an extreme situation and courts have not pierced the corporate veil on the ground of fraud in many cases.

In an attempt to circumvent the corporate veil, allegations in MNC cases in the UK have centred on the 'direct negligence' of the parent company for harm caused by its own wrongdoing (in relation to the functions for which it was responsible or over which it had control) instead of, or in addition to, its responsibility for the negligence of its subsidiaries. The principal allegation is that the parent company breached a 'duty of care' – itself and/or through the conduct of individuals for whom it is vicariously liable – which it owed to individuals affected by its overseas operations (e.g. workers employed by subsidiaries and local communities), and that this breach resulted in harm.

Under English law, whether or not a duty arises is dependent on a three-stage test: (i) was the harm foreseeable; (ii) was there sufficient proximity between the parties; and (iii) is it fair, just and reasonable to impose a duty of care?[44] The issue of a duty of care of an MNC parent company was formulated by the English Court of Appeal in *Lubbe*, as follows:

---

[42] See *Salomon* v. *Salomon and Co. Ltd* [1897] AC 22; *Adams* v. *Cape Industries plc* [1991] 1 All ER 929.

[43] *Atlas Maritime Co. SA* v. *Avalon Maritime Ltd* (No. 1) [1991] 4 All ER 769.

[44] *Caparo* v. *Dickman* [1990] 1 All ER 568 (HL).

Whether a parent company which is proved to exercise *de facto* control over the operations of a (foreign) subsidiary and which knows, through its directors, that those operations involve risks to the health of workers employed by the subsidiary and/or persons in the vicinity of its factory or other business premises, owes a duty of care to those workers and/or other persons in relation to the control which it exercises over and the advice which it gives to the subsidiary company?[45]

Key negligence allegations against the parent MNC in some of the MNC cases litigated in the UK were as follows:[46]

- *Thor Chemicals Holdings Ltd:* Negligent design and transfer of hazardous chemical technology to South Africa and negligent monitoring and supervision of the health of South African workers by the parent company as well as by directors and employees for whose conduct it was vicariously liable.
- *Connelly:* 'It was alleged that RTZ had devised RUL's [the Namibian subsidiary] policy on health, safety and the environment, or alternatively had advised RUL as to the contents of the policy. It was further alleged that an employee or employees of RTZ, referred to as RTZ supervisors, implemented the policy and supervised health, safety and/or environmental protection at the mine.'[47]
- *Lubbe v. Cape plc:* Negligent exercise of its 'effective control' of health and safety at its South African subsidiaries' asbestos mining operations.
- *Peruvian torture victims' litigation against Monterrico Metals:* Negligent management and control – primarily on account of the alleged violations of the Peruvian Civil Code – of the response to an environmental protest and the treatment of detained protesters.
- *Gold Miners' Silicosis Litigation against Anglo American South Africa:* Whether the UK litigation proceeds will depend on the outcome of the appeal on juridiction (see footnote 38). If it does proceed, as in the ongoing South African litigation against AASA, the allegations are likely to be based on negligent control over mining operations and/or negligent advice given to mining subsidiaries pursuant to technical service contracts between the parent and the mining subsidiaries, in particular relating to medical and dust-prevention systems.

---

[45] *Lubbe* (CA), n. 12, 1568.
[46] For details of these cases, see R. Meeran, 'Tort Litigation against Multinational Corporations for Violation of Human Rights: An Overview of the Position Outside the United States' (2011) 3 *City University of Hong Kong Law Review* 1, 25–41.
[47] *Connelly*, n. 9, 864.

The issue of parent company liability has not, however, been subject to a final determination in any of these MNC cases, which were either settled before trial (e.g. *Thor Chemicals*) or struck out for other reasons (e.g. *Connelly*). A positive decision (though not a determination) in respect of parent company liability was the dismissal of an attempted strike-out application by Thor Chemicals in 1996, where the court held that it was 'clear on the face of it that the statement of claim without consideration of evidence discloses a reasonable cause or causes of action' against the parent company, and that the evidence went 'well beyond establishing a clear evidential basis' for liability against the parent company.[48]

Although the *Connelly* action was ultimately struck out on the grounds of limitation, Rio Tinto failed in its attempt to strike the case out for lack of a cause of action. Justice Wright ruled that:

> On a fair reading of this pleading, it seems to me that . . . [RTZ] had taken into its own hands the responsibility for devising and operating the policy for health and safety at the Rossing mine, and that either . . . [RTZ] or one or other of its English subsidiaries implemented that policy and super-vised the precautions necessary to ensure so far as was reasonably possible, the health and safety of Rossing employees through the RTZ supervisors. Such an allegation, if true, seems to me to impose a duty of care upon those defendants who undertook those responsibilities, what-ever contribution Rossing itself may have made towards safety proce-dures in the mine. The situation would be an unusual one; but if the pleading represents the actuality then, as it seems to me, the situation is likely to give rise to a duty of care.[49]

Consistent with the notion that parent company liability may stem from the functions over which it has assumed responsibility, the judgment contained the following analysis:

> Mr Spencer asserts that no other person other than the plaintiff's actual employer can owe the duty owed by a master to his servant to the plaintiff. As a matter of strict language this may well be true; but that is not to say that in appropriate circumstances there may not be some other person or persons who owe a duty of care to an individual plaintiff which may be very close to the duty owed by a master to his servant. For example, the consultant who advises the employer upon the safety of his work processes may owe a duty to the individual employee who he can foresee may be affected by the contents of that advice – see, for example, *Clay* v. *Crumb and Sons Limited* [1964] 1 QB 533. Even more

---

[48] *Ngcobo*, n. 10 (Maurice Kay J).
[49] *Connelly* v. *RTZ Corporation plc*, unreported, QBD 4/12/98, para. 538.

clearly, if the situation is that an employer has entirely handed over
responsibility for devising, installing and operating the various safety
precautions required of an employer to an independent contractor, then
that contractor may owe a duty to the individual employee which is
virtually coterminous with that of the employer himself. That is not to
say that the employer, by so handing over such responsibility, will
necessarily escape his own liability to his employee.[50]

Winding the clock forward a decade, the landmark decision of the
English Court of Appeal in *Chandler* v. *Cape plc*[51] significantly clarified
and advanced English law on parent company liability. The claimant
sued for asbestosis contracted as a result of exposure to dust during his
employment by Cape Products, a subsidiary of Cape plc. He alleged that
Cape plc owed him a duty of care, *inter alia*, because it employed a
medical and a scientific officer responsible for overseeing health and
safety across the group, including at Cape Products. An essential issue at
trial was '[w]hether Cape was proved to have assumed responsibility for
the safety of the employees of its subsidiary, Cape Products, so as to give
rise to a relevant duty of care owed by Cape to Mr Chandler to prevent
the exposure of which he complained'.[52]

The Court held that the conventional three-part *Caparo*[53] test of
foreseeability of harm, proximity and reasonableness applied to a parent
company just as it did to an individual. The Court of Appeal specifically
noted that it had been held in *Connelly* v. *Rio Tinto* and *Ngcobo* v. *Thor
Chemicals* that it was arguable that a parent company may owe a duty of
care to employees of subsidiaries.[54] The Court held that 'if a parent
company has responsibility towards the employees of a subsidiary
there may not be an exact correlation between the responsibilities of
the two companies. The parent company is not likely to accept responsibility towards its subsidiary's employees in all respects but only for
example in relation to what might be called high level advice or
strategy.'[55]

Regarding the defendant's contention that imposing liability would
require a lifting of the corporate veil, the Court in *Chandler*

> emphatically reject[ed] any suggestion that [it had been] in any way
> concerned with what is usually referred to as piercing the corporate
> veil. A subsidiary and its company are separate entities. There is no
> imposition or assumption of responsibility by reason only that a

---

[50] *Ibid.*   [51] [2012] EWCA (Civ) 525.   [52] *Ibid.*, para. 33.   [53] *Caparo*, n. 44.
[54] *Chandler*, n. 51, para. 66.   [55] *Ibid.*

company is the parent company of another company. The question is simply whether what the parent company did amounted to taking on a direct duty to the subsidiary's employees.[56]

The Court of Appeal further held that in view of Cape's 'superior knowledge about the nature and management of asbestos risks', it was 'appropriate to find that Cape plc assumed a duty of care either to advise Cape Products on the steps it had to take in the light of knowledge then available to provide those employees with a safe system of work or to ensure that those steps were taken'.[57]

The Court in *Chandler* concluded that

> in appropriate circumstances the law may impose on a parent company responsibility for the health and safety of its subsidiary's employees. Those circumstances include a situation where, as in the present case, (1) the businesses of the parent and subsidiary are in a relevant respect the same; (2) the parent has, or ought to have, superior knowledge on some relevant aspect of health and safety in the particular industry; (3) the subsidiary's system of work is unsafe as the parent company knew, or ought to have known; and (4) the parent knew or ought to have foreseen that the subsidiary or its employees would rely on its using that superior knowledge for the employees' protection. For the purposes of (4) it is not necessary to show that the parent is in the practice of intervening in the health and safety policies of the subsidiary. The court will look at the relationship between the companies more widely. The court may find that element (4) is established where the evidence shows that the parent has a practice of intervening in the trading operations of the subsidiary, for example production and funding issues.[58]

The Court of Appeal acknowledged that 'this is one of the first cases in which an employee has established at trial liability to him on the part of his employer's parent company, and thus this appeal is of some importance not only to the parties but to other cases'.[59]

It is argued there is no reason in principle why, like any other legal entity or person, a parent company which is responsible for, or in control of, specific functions at overseas subsidiary operations should not be liable for damage arising from those functions or deficiencies in them. After all, an outside contractor which was engaged by an MNC's subsidiary to undertake, or supervise, a hazardous task would be considered to owe a duty of care to those who could foreseeably be damaged by the task. It would seem illogical that an MNC parent company, which undertakes or controls such a task, should be able to avoid liability by virtue of the fact of its shareholding

[56] *Ibid.*, paras. 69–70.   [57] *Ibid.*, para. 78.   [58] *Ibid.*, para. 80.   [59] *Ibid.*, para. 2.

in the subsidiary. Where, for example as in the *Thor Chemicals* case, a parent company designs a hazardous process, the legal position of the parent towards workers at the operation would seem to be analogous to that of manufacturers of products, who are universally regarded as owing a duty of care to consumers, notwithstanding the absence of any contractual relationship.[60]

As a result of *Chandler*, there can be no principled legal objection, under English law, to the imposition of a legal duty of care on a parent company. But whether or not such a duty should be imposed will depend on the facts, and consequently there will be instances when the degree of involvement and control by the parent warrant its imposition and other instances where it does not.

In the *Lubbe*, *Thor Chemicals* and *Connelly* cases, the claimants contended that English law should be applied on the grounds that the key actions of the parent company defendant (decisions of the parent company board etc.) occurred in England. This contention was quite plausible at that time, but is far less so now in light of the provisions of European law (the Rome II Regulation) effective since January 2009, under which the applicable law in tort claims will usually be the law of the country 'where *the damage occurs irrespective of the country in which the event giving rise to the damage occurred* unless the tort is *manifestly more closely connected* with another country'.[61] In claims for 'environmental damage', the claimant may elect to have the claim governed by the law of the country where the 'event giving rise to the damage' occurred.[62]

Thus, in the MNC cases the law of the host state will usually apply and the *Chandler* decision will not be directly applicable to claims arising from overseas harm. Nevertheless, where the local law in question is based on, or strongly infused with, English law principles, decisions of the higher courts of England and Wales will be influential. A recent example is a decision of the South African Constitutional Court in *Lee* v. *Minister of Correctional Services*.[63] The Constitutional Court cited with approval a series of English authorities that have replaced the conventional 'but for' test of causation in certain cases where, essentially due to

---

[60] R. Meeran, 'Process Liability of Multinationals: Overcoming the Forum Hurdle' (November 1995) *Journal of Personal Injury Litigation* 170.

[61] Rome II Regulation, n. 21, Art. 4 (emphasis added). This provision superseded s. 11(2)(a) of the Private International Law (Miscellaneous Provisions) Act 1995.

[62] Rome II Regulation, n. 21, Art. 7.   [63] [2012] ZACC 30.

limitations in scientific and medical understanding, this standard is impossible to meet with the 'material contribution' or 'material increase in risk' principles.[64] Referring to the obligations of the Bill of Rights, the Court noted that there was a 'powerful case' for developing South African common law of causation along similar lines.[65] It will be interesting to see whether the arbitrators' decision in gold miners' silicosis litigation brought against AASA in South Africa follows the *Chandler* decision.

Other procedural issues

Experience of MNC litigation indicates that procedural issues, which may only be peripherally related to the merits of cases, frequently have a decisive effect on access to justice. Detailed reference has already been made to FNC, which prior to 2005 was a 'make or break' issue in MNC cases in the UK (and still is in the USA, Canada and Australia).

Proper access to documents and information, especially relating to relevant decisions and functions of an MNC and which precise MNC corporate entities were responsible for them, is critical, as this type of information is usually uniquely available to the MNC concerned. English procedural rules provide for general and specific disclosure of relevant documents by parties to litigation,[66] and also for answers to be given on oath to a request for information.[67] In the silicosis litigation against AASA,[68] the claimants sought specific disclosure of documents relating to the location of AASA's 'central administration', an issue in AASA's jurisdictional challenge. In ordering disclosure, the English High Court concluded that without disclosure of documents there was a 'very great risk that the claimants will be contesting jurisdiction at an unfair disadvantage'.[69]

Another issue of fundamental importance to access to justice is that the defendant's assets are not dissipated beyond the reach of claimants. This was graphically illustrated in the *Thor Chemicals* and *Monterrico* cases. In mid-2000, in the lead-up to the trial of the second *Thor Chemicals* case (*Sithole*), it emerged from company documents filed in

---

[64] *Fairchild* v. *Glenhaven Funeral Services Ltd* [2002] 3 All ER 305; *McGhee* v. *National Coal Board* [1973] 1 WLR 1; *Barker* v. *Corus UK Ltd* [2006] 2 WLR 1027.

[65] *Lee*, n. 63, para. 101.   [66] Civil Procedure Rules 1998 (UK) (CPR), r. 31(12).

[67] *Ibid.*, r. 18. Note however that disclosure need only be 'proportionate', in particular to the value, complexity and importance of the case.

[68] *Vava* v. *Anglo American South Africa Ltd* [2012] EWHC 1969 (QB).   [69] *Ibid.*, para. 69.

December 1999 that Thor's parent company, Thor Chemicals Holdings Ltd (the defendant), had undertaken a demerger which involved transfer of subsidiaries valued at £19.55 million to a newly formed company, Tato Holdings Ltd (Tato). At the same time, Thor Chemicals Holdings Ltd had been renamed 'Guernica Holdings Ltd'.[70] Thor wrote to the UK Legal Services Commission, which was funding the claimants' representation, arguing that continued public funding of the case was futile in light of the restructuring. Two weeks before the start of the three-month trial, an application to the Court was then made, on behalf of the claimants, for a declaration under section 423 of the (English) Companies Act 1986 that the 'predominant purpose' of the demerger was to defraud creditors, such as the claimants, and it was thus void. Thor and its chairman disputed that this was the purpose, but the Court of Appeal held that in the absence of information to the contrary, the inference that the demerger of Thor was connected with the present claims was 'irresistible'.[71] The Court ordered Thor to pay £400,000 into court within seven days and to disclose documents concerning the demerger. The case was settled on the first day of trial in October 2000.[72]

Prior to notification of the Peruvian torture victims' claims, Monterrico had decided to relocate its corporate headquarters to Hong Kong and accordingly announced an intention to de-list from the AIM London Stock Exchange.[73] Since the relocation was for commercial reasons unconnected with the claims, there was no possibility of a section 423 application as in the *Thor* case. Nevertheless, action to prevent dissipation of assets below the potential value of the claims (and accompanying legal costs and expenses) was fundamental to the viability of the case, because otherwise the claimants might later find themselves in a position of winning at trial but without any assets over which to enforce the judgment – a prospect which would have rendered legal action unviable at the outset. Therefore, the *Monterrico* claimants applied for and succeeded in obtaining from the English High Court a worldwide freezing injunction over £5 million of the company's assets.[74] An ancillary freezing injunction in aid of the UK injunction was also obtained in the High Court of Hong Kong.[75]

---

[70] According to Cowley, this was to symbolise the 'fascist attacks' made against Thor Chemicals. See 'Thor Point', *Private Eye* (October 2000), 27.

[71] *Sithole*, n. 11.   [72] *Ibid.*

[73] *Mario Alberto Tabra Guerrero v. Monterrico Metals plc, Rio Blanco Copper SA* [2009] EWHC 2475 (QB), para. 28.

[74] *Guerrero*, n. 15.   [75] *Guerrero v. Monterrico Metals plc*, HCMP 1736/2009.

The importance of costs, resources and financial incentives for claimants' lawyers

Context

In considering the potential for legal action in the home courts of MNCs, the relevance of financial resources and incentives for claimants' lawyers cannot be overstated. The fact of the matter is that, barring a few exceptions such as cases in the USA, claimants' lawyers in MNCs' home states have shown a distinct lack of enthusiasm for undertaking such cases. The reasons are clear: these cases are complex, risky, hard-fought by MNCs and resource-intensive. Therefore they are expensive to fund, are of uncertain duration and outcome, and have significant cash-flow implications for the claimants' lawyers (the MNC lawyers, by contrast, are paid on an ongoing basis, irrespective of the outcome). Furthermore, the magnitude of the financial risk is that only lawyers who are experienced in this field are likely to feel sufficiently confident to take the risk – in other words, the perceived risk for lawyers who are new to this field is even greater. Having said this, if these cases succeed, they may potentially be very profitable, thereby increasing the financial incentive for claimants' lawyers with experience and sufficient resources to take on such cases.[76]

The *Connelly*, *Lubbe* and *Thor Chemicals* cases were publicly funded by the UK Legal Services Commission. This meant that the claimants' lawyers received a regular stream of funding for expenses and legal fees, albeit not at very high rates.[77] With progressive curtailment of UK legal aid over the past decade, cases are now run on a NWNF basis, a system authorised by legislation in the UK.[78] This means that lawyers are paid only if they win, but if they do win, they may charge an uplift fee on their costs. The US-style contingency fee agreements, by which lawyers are entitled to a share of a claimant's damages, are expressly prohibited in the UK. Prior to 1 April 2013, another benefit to claimants suing in the UK was that the costs uplift (or the 'success fee') was payable

---

[76] In Europe, Australia and South Africa, claimants' lawyers tend to form the less wealthy end of the legal profession. Commercial law firms – which undertake a variety of impressive pro bono work in the UK, Australia and South Africa – would be ideally placed, in terms of resources and expertise, to undertake these MNC cases, but as they represent MNCs they would invariably be reluctant to act or might have a conflict of interest.

[77] Obtaining such public funding in the UK is no longer realistic.

[78] Courts and Legal Services Act 1990 (UK), ss. 58 and 58A.

by the unsuccessful defendant, rather than from the claimant's compensation.[79]

In terms of victims' access to lawyers with expertise in the field, a regular feature of the settlement of litigation is that the claimants' lawyers are precluded from acting in future cases against the MNC in question. Whilst the benefit to the MNC of binding claimants' lawyers in this way can be viewed as aid to settlement of litigation, it is also contrary to public interest to neutralise potential victims' legal representation in this manner.[80]

The adverse effects of the Legal Aid, Sentencing and Punishment of Offenders Act 2012 and the Rome II Regulation on access to a remedy[81]

The Legal Aid, Sentencing and Punishment of Offenders Act 2012 (LASPO), effective from 1 April 2013, fundamentally reformed the civil costs system, in particular abolishing the right of successful claimants to recover success fees from the defendant.[82] Success fees, if they are to be paid, are now to be deducted from claimants' damages, and cannot in any event exceed a specific percentage of the damages[83] (which will be fixed, by regulations, at 25 per cent). The impetus underlying this reform was the view that the 'current regime, with recoverable success fees ... allows claims to be pursued with no real financial risk to claimants and with the threat of excessive costs to the defendant'.[84] Clearly, if the level of damages is high in comparison with costs – as it might well be in a case involving a large number of claimants – then a pro rata success fee deduction might have only a small impact on the compensation received by individual claimants. However, in cases involving fewer claimants, deducting a success fee will be impossible to countenance. This will deter claimants' lawyers from undertaking such cases and act as a barrier to access to a remedy.

---

[79] CPR, n. 66, Practice Direction to Part 44, s. 9.1.

[80] Human Rights Council, 'Business and Human Rights: Further Steps toward the Operationalization of the "Protect, Respect and Remedy" Framework', A/HRC/14/27 (9 April 2010), para. 112.

[81] This section builds on R. Meeran, 'Multinationals will Profit from the Government's Civil Litigation Shake-up', *The Guardian* (24 May 2011).

[82] LASPO, n. 20, s. 44.   [83] *Ibid.*

[84] Ministry of Justice, 'Civil Justice Reforms' (20 November 2012), 5, www.justice.gov.uk/ downloads/publications/policy/moj/civil-justice-reforms-full-package.pdf (last accessed 20 January 2013).

Equally significant for these MNC cases is the stricter application of the 'proportionality principle'.[85] Changes introduced into the Civil Procedure Rules stipulate that costs should not generally exceed damages.[86] Due to the complex and protracted nature of this litigation, legal costs are often substantially higher than compensation. If a successful claimant's legal costs can only be recovered from an MNC to the extent that they correspond to the level of compensation, and the actual costs exceed this level, it means that claimants' lawyers will receive only a proportion of their fees. This provision is thus a further barrier to access to a remedy.

A yet further development which interacts negatively with the LASPO is caused by provisions of the Rome II Regulation.[87] These provisions, which took effect from January 2009, require damages to be assessed in accordance with the law and procedure of the country where the harm occurred.[88] Previously, the position under English law was that damages would be assessed in accordance with the law and procedure of the country in which the case was proceeding (even where the claim was governed by foreign law).[89] The combined effect of the LASPO and the Rome II Regulation can be illustrated as follows.

Take a case where, under the old system, the total damages are £2 million and the costs were also £2 million; the claimants' lawyer could previously have charged a 100 per cent success fee payable by the defendant, with the result that the claimants received their £2 million damages in full and the claimants' lawyer received £4 million costs. Under the new Rome II/LASPO system, the damages might (optimistically) be £1 million and the costs would still be £ 2million. The maximum success fee would be £250,000 (that is, 25 per cent of the awarded damages) – equivalent to a 12.5 per cent success fee (that is, 12.5 per

---

[85] The overriding objective includes 'dealing with the case in ways which are proportionate (i) to the amount of money involved; (ii) to the importance of the case; (iii) to the complexity of the issues; and (iv) to the financial position of each party'. CPR, n. 66, r. 1.1.

[86] 'Costs which are disproportionate in amount may be disallowed or reduced even if they were reasonably or necessarily incurred.' CPR, n. 66, r. 44.3(2). Rule 44.3(5) provides that costs incurred are proportionate if they bear a reasonable relationship to the sums in issue, the value of any non-monetary relief, the complexity of the litigation, additional work generated by the paying party, and wider factors such as reputation or public importance.

[87] Rome II Regulation, n. 21.   [88] *Ibid.*, Arts. 4 and 15.

[89] *Harding* v. *Wealands* [2006] UKHL 32.

cent of the base costs of £2 million). Since the recoverable costs would need to be 'proportionate', they could not exceed £1 million in any event. Therefore, the claimants' lawyer would receive at best a total of £1.25 million compared with £4 million under the old system (in which a 100 per cent success fee could be charged and recovered from the defendant).

Taken together, the LASPO and the Rome II Regulation constitute a deterrent to claimants' lawyers, who have already shown a lack of enthusiasm for taking on financial risk of the magnitude that this type of litigation entails. It seems certain that smaller cases, of the *Monterrico* variety, will be harder to contemplate in the future. It is ironical that the UK government specifically cited the *Monterrico* case as an illustration of a legal approach to achieving MNC liability without the ATS; this is precisely the type of case – having involved only thirty-one claimants – the financial viability of which has been undermined by the LASPO. The point here is not that anyone should have sympathy for the commercial interests of claimants' lawyers, but to highlight the effect that these significant changes will have on the financial viability of claims and thus on access to justice.

A further LASPO revision that has, in relation to MNC cases, impacted specifically on environmental claims, is that 'after the event insurance premiums' (ATE) will no longer be payable by an unsuccessful defendant.[90] The UK courts generally apply the 'loser pays' costs rule. A system of insurance has, therefore, developed to cover this adverse costs risk. Due to magnitude of the risk of losing and the potential costs – which are based on the defendant's anticipated costs to trial – the insurance premiums can be extremely high, as much as 80–90 per cent of the cover. This particular change in the law is understandable. However, the result is to place a claimant in the position of being personally liable to pay the defendant's costs, which will in many cases deter legal action. To address this problem, a 'qualified one-way costs-shifting' principle is to be introduced in personal injury cases,[91] which will mean that an unsuccessful defendant will be liable to pay a claimant's costs but an unsuccessful claimant will not be liable to pay the defendant's costs and consequently, ATE will be unnecessary. This 'qualified one-way costs-shifting' principle has *not*, however, been extended to environmental cases.

---

[90] LASPO, n. 20, s. 46. [91] Ministry of Justice, 'Civil Justice Reforms', n. 84, at 2.

Class or group actions

For claimants and their lawyers, Australian, Canadian and American legal systems have a potential advantage of providing for class actions,[92] that is, a representative claimant may sue for the benefit of a group of individuals falling within a given class. Once instituted, a class action suspends the limitation period for all class members. Such a mechanism is potentially speedier and far less costly, and thus presents less of a financial disincentive for claimants' lawyers. These class action systems are of the 'opt-out' variety, meaning that members of the class are included in, and bound by, the outcome of the action unless they opt out.[93] This also enables key legal issues to be resolved without instructions having to be taken from a large number of individual claimants. Provision is made for payment of class action lawyers' fees by the court managing the class action.

A recent decision of the Supreme Court of Appeal of South Africa in the 'Bread Price-fixing case' also endorsed the principle of 'opt-out' class actions in damages claims.[94]

Save to a limited extent, the UK does not yet have opt-out class actions.[95] Instead, 'group action' procedures in the UK enable multiple claims involving common legal or factual issues to be made the subject of a 'group litigation order'.[96] 'Lead cases' are then selected as the vehicle through which to resolve common issues.[97] This assists in ensuring that cases are managed in a cost-effective manner. These group actions are 'opt-in' class actions which require commencement or registration of legal action or claims by all members of the class. The result is that instructions must be taken from all members of the group, thereby increasing the costs and decreasing the financial viability (in comparison with opt-out class actions). Only those who 'opt in' are bound by decisions made in respect of the

---

[92] See R. Mulheron, *The Class Action in Common Law Legal Systems: A Comparative Perspective* (Oxford: Hart Publishing, 2004).

[93] *Ibid.*, 29–37.

[94] *Trustees for the Time Being for the Children's Resource Centre Trust and Others* v. *Pioneer Food (Pty) Ltd and Others* [2012] ZASCA 182 (29 November 2012).

[95] The UK government recently proposed 'opt-out' class action for competition law-related litigation. Lexology, 'UK to Reform Competition Litigation Regime and Introduce Opt-out Class Actions' (31 January 2013), www.lexology.com/library/detail.aspx?g=b6b93231&0e79&47de&9166&20f44e09dfbe (last accessed 1 February 2013).

[96] CPR, n. 66, r. 19.11.

[97] See, for example, the Ocensa Pipeline Litigation. Ministry of Justice, 'Group Litigation Orders', www.justice.gov.uk/courts/rcj-rolls-building/queens-bench/group-litigation-orders (last accessed 31 January 2013).

group. Those who do not opt in may file separate claims and will not be protected against limitation unless they do so.

Access to a remedy under the GPs

The UN Secretary-General's Special Representative on the Issue of Human Rights and Transnational Corporations and Other Business Enterprises (SRSG) had alluded to many of the obstacles to access to justice discussed above. His final report to the Human Rights Council specifically referred to 'practical and procedural barriers' arising from difficulties in attributing responsibility among members of a corporate group, excessive legal cost, difficulty in claimants accessing adequate legal representation due to lack of resources or other incentives for lawyers, inadequate class action procedures, and imbalances between the parties in relation to financial resources, access to information and expertise.[98]

Although the GPs do not stipulate specific measures to overcome these barriers, with regard to 'state-based judicial mechanisms', Principle 26 recommends that 'States should take appropriate steps to ensure the effectiveness of domestic judicial mechanisms when addressing business-related human rights abuses, including considering ways to reduce legal, practical and other relevant barriers that could lead to denial of access to remedy.'[99]

As noted above, the UK government has confirmed its endorsement of the GPs.[100] Moreover, the potential ramifications of the LASPO on MNC human rights cases were specifically drawn to the attention of the UK government by the SRSG in advance, as is evident from the following question and answer in the House of Commons:

> **Mr Slaughter:** To ask the Secretary of State for Foreign and Commonwealth Affairs pursuant to the answer of 5 December 2011, Official Report, column 56W, on Legal Aid, Sentencing and Punishment of Offenders Bill 2010–12, and with reference to his confirmation of the UK's commitment to the Ruggie principles, what assessment he has made of the letter sent by Professor Ruggie to the Parliamentary Under-Secretary of State, Ministry of Justice, the Hon. Member for Huntingdon (Mr Djanogly), on effects of his proposed reforms in the Legal Aid, Sentencing and Punishment of Offenders Bill on the ability of

---

[98] SRSG, 'Guiding Principles', n. 23, Commentary on Principle 26.
[99] *Ibid.*, Principle 26.   [100] UK Ministry of Justice Response, n. 19.

impecunious people to secure representation and justice in cases (*a*) against businesses and (*b*) of human rights abuse.

Mr Jeremy Browne: Following the UN Human Rights Council's endorsement in June of the UN Guiding Principles on Business and Human Rights, in which the UK played an important role, the Government are fully committed to implementing those principles as part of a wider strategy on business and human rights. We do not believe that the reform of the Legal Aid, Sentencing and Punishment of Offenders Bill is incompatible with this commitment. We believe that it will still be possible to bring claims against (*a*) multinational companies or (*b*) those allegedly guilty of human rights abuses once these reforms are implemented. However, reforms will help ensure that meritorious claims will be resolved at a more proportional cost; while unnecessary and avoidable claims will be deterred from progressing to court.[101]

Contrary to the above assertion by the Minister, as I have tried to show in this chapter, the LASPO will have a significant detrimental impact with regard to access to justice and on victims' ability to hold MNCs accountable for the violation of human rights.

Conclusion

Considerable strides forward have been made in the courts in holding MNCs accountable under UK law and in providing victims from developing countries with a viable and practical means of access to a remedy through tort litigation. The notion of a parent company's 'duty of care' has gained increasing recognition, notwithstanding the 'corporate veil' obstacle and the absence of any final legal determination on the point. Cases can now proceed against home-domiciled MNC parent companies across the EU, without the obstruction of expensive and protracted FNC disputes. Opt-in group action procedures assist in enabling claims to be run by victims' lawyers in a reasonably cost-effective manner. However, an opt-out class action mechanism would enable claimants' precious legal resources to be focused on generic issues.

The progressive approach of the UK courts is, however, in stark contrast with that of the UK government, which has shown no inclination to assist MNC claimants in accessing a remedy but much commitment in protecting

---

[101] Hansard: House of Commons Debates (15 December 2011), vol. 537, col. 862W.

the interests of MNCs. The proposals to legislate against the *Connelly* ruling and more recently to reintroduce FNC into European law are direct evidence of this. The civil costs reforms under the LASPO will have a significant impact on access to a remedy for MNC victims, in particular by reducing the financial viability of cases and thereby the incentive for claimants' lawyers to act. Whilst the reforms may not have been motivated by any intention to undermine the MNC cases, the UK government was in no doubt – following a concerted campaign by non-governmental organisations, trade unions and politicians, and the submission by the SRSG himself – that these consequences would result. Yet, the government decided to proceed full steam ahead with the legislation. Nevertheless, despite the lack of government commitment to protect MNC victims' access to a remedy, this area of litigation should continue to progress and hopefully in the process further increase the pressure on MNCs to behave responsibly wherever their operations are located.

INDEX

Abbott, K. W., 306
ACCESS, 332
accountability and transparency. *See*
    transparency and accountability
active complicity, 247
actus reus analysis of complicity
    liability, 228, 239
Addo, M. K., 161
Advisory Opinion on the Legality of the
    Wall in the Occupied Palestinian
    Territory (ICJ), 282
Afghanistan, use of private security
    providers in, 307
African Charter on Human and
    Peoples' Rights, 102, 325
African Commission on Human and
    Peoples Rights, 325
African Union Convention on
    Preventing and Combating
    Corruption (2006), 176
after the event (ATE)
    insurance premiums in UK
    tort litigation, 398
Aguinda case (*Maria Aguinda et al.* v.
    Texaco Inc., US SDNY), 338, 358
Alien Tort Claims Act of 1789 (ATCA;
    USA), litigation of corporate
    responsibility under, 73–77,
    94–95, 179, 227–28, 232, 234, 238,
    338, 378–79
alignment, regulatory, SRSG push for,
    11, 67
American National Standards Institute
    (ANSI), 312
Amnesty International, 34, 36, 37, 80,
    171–72, 343
Annan, Kofi, xvi, 6, 169

ANSI (American National Standards
    Institute), 312
anti-corruption movement and treaty
    approach to corporate regulation,
    163, 172–83
apartheid regime in South Africa,
    corporate complicity in, 226,
    229–30
apology and recognition of harm done,
    corporate reluctance to supply,
    375
Argyron, Aikaterini, vii, 24, 329
Arnold, Denis, 263
assets of corporation, dissipation of,
    393–94
ATCA (Alien Tort Claims Act of 1789;
    USA), litigation of corporate
    responsibility under, 73–77,
    94–95, 179, 227–28, 232, 234, 238,
    338, 378–79
ATE (after the event) insurance
    premiums in UK tort litigation,
    398
Augenstein, Daniel, vii, xx, 14, 271
Aust, A., 82
Australia: class or group actions in,
    399; Committee on the
    Elimination of Racial
    Discrimination to, 290; illegal
    logging laws, 186; tort law in, 379
autopoiesis, 31

Ban Ki Moon, 173
Bandung Conference (1955), 165
BAPSC (British Association for the
    Private Security Industry), 307, 308
Barbier, Carl, 353

403